A THEORY
OF SEMIOTICS

ADVANCES IN SEMIOTICS

General Editor, Thomas A. Sebeok

A THEORY
OF SEMIOTICS

UMBERTO ECO

INDIANA UNIVERSITY PRESS
Bloomington

FIRST MIDLAND BOOK EDITION, 1979

Published by arrangement with Bompiani, Milan
Copyright © 1976 by Indiana University Press

Manufactured in the United States of America

Library of Congress Cataloging in Publication Data
Eco, Umberto.
A theory of semiotics.
(Advances in semiotics)
Includes index.
1. Semiotics. I. Title. II. Series.
P99.E3   301.2'1   74-22833
ISBN 0-253-35955-4   8   9   10   89   88   87

CONTENTS

v

FOREWORD

A preliminary and tentative version of this text (dealing with a semiotics of visual and architectural signs) was written and published in 1967 as *Appunti per una semiologia delle comunicazioni visive*. A more theoretically oriented version – offering an overall view of semiotics and containing a long epistemological discussion on structuralism – was published in 1968 as *La struttura assente*. I worked for two years on the French, German, Spanish and Swedish translations (only the Yugoslavian, Polish and Brazilian ones appeared with sufficient speed to reproduce the original Italian edition without any addition) re-arranging and enlarging the book – and correcting many parts of it to take into account reviews of the first Italian edition. The result was a book half way between· *La struttura assente* and something else. This 'something else' appeared in Italian as a collection of essays, *Le forme del contenuto*, 1971.

As for the English version, after two unsatisfactory attempts at translation and many unsuccessful revisions, I decided (in 1973) to give up and to re-write the book directly in English – with the help of David Osmond-Smith, who has put more work into adapting my semiotic pidgin than he would have done if translating a new book, though he should not be held responsible for the results of this symbiotic adventure. To re-write in another language means to *re-think*: and the result of this truly semiotic experience (which would have strongly interested Benjamin Lee Whorf) is that this book no longer has anything to do with *La struttura assente* — so that I have now retranslated it into Italian as a brand-new work (*Trattato di semiotica generale*).

Apart from the different (but by no means irrelevant) organization of the material, four new elements characterize the present text as a partial critique of my own preceding researches: (i) an attempt to introduce into the semiotic framework a theory of referents; (ii) an attempt to relate pragmatics to semantics; (iii) a critique of the notion of 'sign' and of the classical typologies of signs; (iv) a different approach to the notion of icon-ism — whose critique, developed in my preceding works, I still maintain, but without substituting for the naive assumption that icons are non-coded analogical devices, the equally naive one that icons are arbitrary and fully analyzable devices. The replacement of a typology of signs by a typology of modes of sign production has helped me, I hope, to dissolve the umbrella-notion of iconism into a more complex network of semiotic operations. In doing so, the book has acquired a sort of 'chiasmatic' structure. In its first part, devoted to a *theory of codes*, I have tried to propose a restricted and unified set of categories able to explain verbal and non-verbal devices and to extend the notion of sign-function to various types of significant units, so-called signs, strings of signs, texts and macro-texts — the whole attempt being governed by the principle of Ockham's razor, *non sunt multiplicanda entia praeter necessitatem* — which would seem to be a rather scientific procedure.

In the second part, devoted to a *theory of sign production*, I felt obliged to proceed in an inverse direction: the categories under consideration (such as symbol, icon and index) were unable to explain a lot of different phenomena that I believed to fall within the domain of semiotics. I was therefore forced to adopt an anti-Ockhamistic principle: *entia sunt multipli-canda propter necessitatem*. I believe that, under given circumstances, this procedure is also a scientific one.

I would not have arrived at the results outlined in this book without the help of many friends, without the discussions that have appeared in the first six issues of the review *VS-Quaderni di studi semiotici*, and without confrontations with my students at Florence, Bologna, New York University, Northwestern University, La Plata and many other places around the world. Since the list of references allows me to pay my debts, I shall limit myself to warmly thanking my friends Ugo Volli and Paolo Fabbri, who have helped me throughout the various stages of the research — mainly by merciless criticism — and whose ideas I have freely used in various circumstances.

Milan, 1967-1974.

NOTE ON GRAPHIC CONVENTIONS

Single slashes indicate something intended as an expression or a sign-vehicle, while guillemets indicate something intended as content. Therefore /xxxx/ means, expresses or refers to «xxxx». When there is no question of phonology, verbal expressions will be written in their alphabetic form. However, since this book is concerned not only with verbal signs but also with objects, images or behavior intended as signs, these phenomena must be expressed through verbal expressions: in order to distinguish, for instance, the object automobile from the word automobile, the former is written between double slashes and in italic. Therefore //*automobile*// is the object corresponding to the verbal expression /automobile/, and both refer to the content unit «automobile». Single quotation marks serve to emphasize a certain word; double marks are used for quotations. *Italic* denotes terms used in a technical sense.

A THEORY
OF SEMIOTICS

INTRODUCTION:
TOWARD A LOGIC OF CULTURE

0.1. Design for a semiotic theory

0.1.1. Aims of the research

The aim of this book is to explore the theoretical possibility and the social function of a unified approach to every phenomenon of signification and/or communication. Such an approach should take the form of a *general semiotic theory*, able to explain every case of sign-function in terms of underlying systems of elements mutually correlated by one or more codes.

A design for a general semiotics[1] should consider: (a) a *theory of codes* and (b) a *theory of sign production* — the latter taking into account a large range of phenomena such as the common use of languages, the evolution of codes, aesthetic communication, different types of interactional communicative behavior, the use of signs in order to mention things or states of the world and so on.

Since this book represents only a preliminary exploration of such a theoretical possibility, its first chapters are necessarily conditioned by the present state of the art, and cannot evade some questions that — in a further perspective — will definitely be left aside. In particular one must first take

3

into account the all-purpose notion of 'sign' and the problem of a typology of signs (along with the apparently irreducible forms of semiotic enquiry they presuppose) in order to arrive at a more rigorous definition of sign-function and at a typology of modes of sign-production.

Therefore a first chapter will be devoted to the analysis of the notion of 'sign' in order to distinguish signs from non-signs and to translate the notion of 'sign' into the more flexible one of *sign-function* (which can be explained within the framework of a theory of codes). This discussion will allow me to posit a distinction between 'signification' and 'communication': in principle, a semiotics of signification entails a theory of codes, while a semiotics of communication entails a theory of sign production.

The distinction between a theory of codes and a theory of sign-production does not correspond to the ones between *'langue'* and *'parole'*, competence and performance, syntactics (and semantics) and pragmatics. One of the claims of the present book is to overcome these distinctions and to outline a theory of codes which takes into account even rules of discoursive competence, text formation, contextual and circumstantial (or situational) disambiguation, therefore proposing a semantics which solves within its own framework many problems of the so-called pragmatics.

It is not by chance that the discriminating categories are the ones of signification and communication. As will be seen in chapters 1 and 2, there is a signification system (and therefore a code) when there is the socially conventionalized possibility of generating sign-functions, whether the functives of such functions are discrete units called signs or vast portions of discourse, provided that the correlation has been previously posited by a social convention. There is on the contrary a communication process when the possibilities provided by a signification system are exploited in order to physically produce expressions for many practical purposes. Thus the difference between the two theoretical approaches outlined in chapters 2 and 3 concerns the difference between rules and processes (or, in Aristotelian terms, metaphorically used, power and act). But when the requirements for performing a process are socially recognized and precede the process itself, then these requirements are to be listed among the rules (they become rules of discoursive competence, or rules of *'parole'* foreseen by the *'langue'*) and can be taken into account by a theory of physical production of signs only insofar as they have been already coded. Even if the theory of codes and the theory of sign production succeed in eliminating the naive and non-relational notion of 'sign', this notion appears to be so suitable in ordinary language and in colloquial semiotic discussions that it should not be completely aban-

Lewis called,
— for Sun.
Mike — choric reading
for 3 people

(Lewis made up and will run
off and bring by
tomorrow)

doned. It would be uselessly oversophisticated to get rid of it. An atomic scientist knows very well that so-called 'things' are the results of a complex interplay of microphysical correlations, and nevertheless he can quite happily continue to speak about 'things' when it is convenient to do so. In the same way I shall continue to use the word /sign/ every time the correlational nature of the sign-function may be presupposed. Nevertheless the fourth chapter of the book will be devoted to a discussion of the very notion of the 'typology of signs': starting from Peirce's trichotomy (symbols, indices and icons), I shall show to what degree these categories cover both a more segmentable field of sign-functions and an articulated range of 'sign producing' operations, giving rise to a more comprehensive *n*-chotomy of various modes of sign production.

A general semiotic theory will be considered powerful according to its capacity for offering an appropriate formal definition for every sort of sign-function, whether it has already been described and coded or not. So the typology of modes of sign-production aims at proposing categories able to describe even those as yet uncoded sign-functions conventionally posited in the very moment in which they appear for the first time.

0.1.2. Boundaries of the research

Dealing as it does with all these subjects, a project for a general semiotics will encounter some boundaries or thresholds. Some of these must be posited by a purely transitory agreement, others are determined by the very object of the discipline. The former will be called 'political boundaries', the latter 'natural boundaries'; (it will be shown in 0.9 that there also exists a third form of threshold, of an epistemological nature).

A general introduction to semiotics has either to recognize or to posit, to respect or to trespass on all these thresholds. The *political boundaries* are of three types:

(i) There are 'academic' limits in the·sense that many disciplines other than semiotics have already undertaken or are at present undertaking research on subjects that a semiotician cannot but recognize as his own concern; for instance formal logic, philosophical semantics and the logic of natural languages deal with the problem of the truth value of a sentence and with the various sorts of so-called 'speech acts', while many currents in cultural anthropology (for instance 'ethnomethodology') are concerned with the same problems seen from a different angle; the semiotician may express the wish that one of these days there will be a general semiotic discipline of which all these researches and sciences can be recognized as particular branches; in the meantime a tentative semiotic approach may try to incorporate the results of these disciplines and to redefine them within its own theoretical framework.

(ii) There are 'co-operative' limits in the sense that various disciplines have elaborated theories or descriptions that everybody recognizes as having semiotic relevance (for instance both linguistics and information theory have done important work on the notion of code; kinesics and proxemics are richly exploring non-verbal modes of communication, and so on): in this case a general semiotic approach should only propose a unified set of categories in order to make this collaboration more and more fruitful; at the same time it can eliminate the naive habit of translating (by dangerous metaphorical substitutions) the categories of linguistics into different frameworks.

(iii) There are 'empirical' limits beyond which stand a whole group of phenomena which unquestionably have a semiotic relevance even though the various semiotic approaches have not yet completely succeeded in giving them a satisfactory theoretical definition: such as paintings and many types of complex architectural and urban objects; these empirical boundaries are rather imprecise and are shifting step by step as new researches come into being (for instance the problem of a semiotics of architecture from 1964 to 1974, see Eco 1973 *e*).

By *natural boundaries* I mean principally those beyond which a semiotic approach cannot go; for there is non-semiotic territory since there are phenomena that cannot be taken as sign-functions. But by the same term I also mean a vast range of phenomena prematurely assumed not to have a semiotic relevance. These are the cultural territories in which people do not recognize the underlying existence of codes or, if they do, do not recognize the semiotic nature of those codes, i.e., their ability to generate a continuous production of signs. Since I shall be proposing a very broad and comprehensive definition of sign-function — therefore challenging the above refusals — this book is also concerned with such phenomena. These will be directly dealt with in this Introduction: they happen to be co-extensive with the whole range of cultural phenomena, however pretentious that approach may at first seem.

0.1.3. A theory of the lie

This project for semiotics, to study the whole of culture, and thus to view an immense range of objects and events as signs, may give the impression of an arrogant 'imperialism' on the part of semioticians. When a discipline defines 'everything' as its proper object, and therefore declares itself as concerned with the entire universe (and nothing else) it's playing a risky game. The common objection to the 'imperialist' semiotician is: well, if you define a peanut as a sign, obviously semiotics is then concerned with peanut butter as well — but isn't this procedure a little unfair? What I shall try to demonstrate in this book, basing myself on a highly reliable philosophical and semiotical tradition, is that — semiotically speaking — there is not a substantial difference between peanuts and peanut butter, on the one hand, and the words /peanuts/ and /peanut butter/ on the other. Semiotics is concerned with everything that can be *taken* as a sign. A sign is everything which can be taken as significantly substituting for something else. This something else does not necessarily have to exist or to actually be somewhere at the moment in which a sign stands in for it. Thus *semiotics is in principle the discipline studying everything which can be used in order to lie*. If something cannot be used to tell a lie, conversely it cannot be used to tell the truth: it cannot in fact be used 'to tell' at all. I think that the definition of a 'theory of the lie' should be taken as a pretty comprehensive program for a general semiotics.

0.2. 'Semiotics': field or discipline?

Any study of the limits and laws of semiotics must begin by determining whether (a) one means by the term 'semiotics' a *specific discipline* with its own method and a precise object; or whether (b) semiotics is a *field of studies* and thus a repertoire of interests that is not as yet completely unified. If semiotics is a field then the various semiotic studies would be justified by their very existence: it should be possible to define semiotics inductively by extrapolating from the field of studies a series of constant tendencies and therefore a unified model. If semiotics is a discipline, then the researcher ought to propose a semiotic model deductively which would serve as a parameter on which to base the inclusion or exclusion of the various studies from the field of semiotics.

One cannot do theoretical research without having the courage to put forward a theory, and, therefore, an elementary model as a guide for subsequent discourse; all theoretical research must however have the courage to specify its own contradictions, and should make them obvious where they are not apparent.

As a result, we must, above all, keep in mind the *semiotic field* as it appears today, in all its many and varied forms and in all its disorder. We must then propose an apparently simplified *research model*. Finally we must constantly contradict this model, isolating all the phenomena which do not fit in with it and which force it to restructure itself and to broaden its range. In this way we shall perhaps succeed in tracing (however provisionally) the limits of future semiotic research and of suggesting a unified method of approach to phenomena which apparently are very different from each other, and as yet irreducible.

0.3. Communication and/or signification

At first glance this survey will appear as a list of *communicative* behaviors, thus suggesting *one* of the hypotheses governing my research: semiotics studies all cultural processes as *processes of communication*. Therefore each of these processes would seem to be permitted by an underlying *system of significations*. It is very important to make this distinction clear in order to avoid either dangerous misunderstandings or a sort of compulsory choice imposed by some contemporary semioticians: it is absolutely true that there are some important differences between a semiotics of communication and a semiotics of signification; this distinction does not, however, set two mutually exclusive approaches in opposition.

So let us define a communicative process as the passage of a signal (not necessarily a sign) from a source (through a transmitter, along a channel) to a destination. In a machine-to-machine process the signal has no power to signify in so far as it may determine the destination *sub specie stimuli*. In this case we have no signification, but we do have the passage of some information.

When the destination is a human being, or 'addressee' (it is not necessary that the source or the transmitter be human, provided that they emit the signal following a system of rules known by the human addressee), we are on the contrary witnessing a process of signification — provided that the signal is not merely a stimulus but arouses an interpretive response in the addressee. This process is made possible by the existence of a code.

A code is a system of signification, insofar as it couples present entities with absent units. When — on the basis of an underlying rule — something actually presented to the perception of the addressee *stands for* something else, there is *signification*. In this sense the addressee's actual perception and interpretive behavior are not necessary for the definition of a significant relationship as such: it is enough that the code should foresee an established correspondence between that which '*stands for*' and its correlate, valid for every possible addressee even if no addressee exists or ever will exist.

A signification system is an autonomous semiotic construct that has an abstract mode of existence independent of any possible communicative act it makes possible. On the contrary (except for stimulation processes) *every act of communication to or between human beings* — or any other intelligent biological or mechanical apparatus — *presupposes a signification system as its necessary condition*.

It is possible, if not perhaps particularly desirable, to establish a semiotics of signification independently of a semiotics of communication: but it is impossible to establish a semiotics of communication without a semiotics of signification.

Once we admit that the two approaches must follow different methodological paths and require different sets of categories, it is methodologically necessary to recognize that, in cultural processes, they are strictly intertwined. This is the reason why the following directory of problems and research techniques mixes together both aspects of the semiotic phenomenon.

0.4. Political boundaries: the field

Granted this much, the following areas of contemporary research — starting from the apparently more 'natural' and 'spontaneous' communicative processes and going on to more complex 'cultural' systems — may be considered to belong to the semiotic field.

Zoosemiotics: it represents the lower limit of semiotics because it concerns itself with the communicative behavior of non-human (and therefore non-cultural) communities. But through the study of animal communication we can achieve a definition of what the biological components of human communication are: or else a recognition that even on the animal level there exist patterns of signification which can, to a certain degree, be defined as cultural and social. Therefore the semantic area of these terms is broadened and, consequently, also our notion of culture and society (Sebeok, 1967, 1968, 1969, 1973).

Olfactory signs: Romantic poetry (Baudelaire) has already singled out the existence of a 'code of scents'. If there are scents with a connotative value in an emotive sense, then there are also odors with precise referential values. These can be studied as indices (Peirce, 1931) as proxemic indicators (Hall, 1966) as chemical qualifiers, etc.

Tactile communication: studied by psychology, present and recognized in communication among the blind and in proxemic behavior (Hall, 1966), it is amplified to include clearly codified social behavior such as the kiss, the embrace, the smack, the slap on the shoulder, etc. (Frank, 1957; Efron, 1941).

Codes of taste: present in culinary practice, studied by cultural anthropology, they have found a clearly 'semiotic' systematization in Lévi-Strauss (1964).

Paralinguistics: studies the so-called suprasegmental features and the free variants which corroborate linguistic communication and which increasingly appear as institutionalized and systematized. See the studies of Fonagy (1964), Stankiewicz (1964), Mahl and Schulze (1964, with a bibliography of 274 titles). Trager (1964) subdivides all the sounds without linguistic structure into (a) "voice sets", connected with sex, age, state of health, etc.; (b) paralanguage, divided into (i) "voice qualities" (pitch range, vocal lip control, glottis control, articulatory control, etc.); (ii) "vocalizations", in turn divided into (ii-1) "vocal characterizers" (laughing, crying, whimpering, sobbing, whining, whispering, yawning, belching, etc.), (ii-2) "vocal qualifiers" (intensity, pitch height, extent), (ii-3) "vocal segregates" (noises of the tongue and lips which accompany interjections, nasalizations, breathing, interlocutory grunts, etc.). Another object of paralinguistics is the study of the language of drums and whistles (La Barre, 1964).

Medical semiotics: until a short time ago this was the only type of research which might be termed 'semiotics' or 'semiology' (so that even today there is still some misunderstanding). In any case it belongs to general semiotics (as treated in this book), and in two senses. As a study of the connection between certain signs or symptoms and the illness that they indicate, this is a study and a classification of indices in Peirce's sense (Ostwald, 1964). As a study of the way in which the patient verbalizes his own internal symptoms, this extends on its most complex level to psychoanalysis, which, apart from being a general theory of neuroses and a therapy, is a systematic codification of the meaning of certain symbols furnished by the patient (Morris, 1946; Lacan, 1966; Piro, 1967; Maccagnani, 1967; Szasz, 1961; Barison, 1961).

Kinesics and proxemics: the idea that gesturing depends on cultural codes is now an acquired notion of cultural anthropology. As to pioneer studies in this field see De Jorio (1832), Mallery (1881), Kleinpaul (1888), Efron (1941), Mauss (1950); as to contemporary developments see Birdwhistell (1952, 1960, 1963, 1965, 1966, 1970), Guilhot (1962), LaBarre (1964), Hall (1959, 1966), Greimas (1968), Ekman and Friesen (1969), Argyle (1972) and others. Ritualized gesture, from etiquette to liturgy and pantomime, is studied by Civ'ian (1962, 1965).

Musical codes: the whole of musical science since the Pythagoreans has been an attempt to describe the field of musical communication as a rigorously structured system. We note that until a few years ago contemporary musicology had scarcely been influenced by the current structuralist studies, which are concerned with methods and themes that it had absorbed centuries ago. Nevertheless in the last two or three years musical semiotics has been definitely established as a discipline aiming to find its 'pedigree' and developing new perspectives. Among the pioneer works let us quote the bibliography elaborated by J.J. Nattiez in *Musique en jeu*, 5, 1971. As for the relationship between music and linguistics, and between music and cultural anthropology, see Jakobson (1964, 1967), Ruwet (1959, 1973) and Lévi-Strauss (1965, in the preface to *The Raw and the Cooked*). Outlines of new trends are to be found in Nattiez (1971, 1972, 1973), Osmond-Smith (1972, 1973), Stefani (1973), Pousseur (1972) and others. As a matter of fact music presents, on the one hand, the problem of a semiotic system without a semantic level (or a content plane): on the other hand, however, there are musical 'signs' (or syntagms) with an explicit denotative value (trumpet signals in the army) and there are syntagms or entire 'texts' possessing pre-culturalized connotative value ('pastoral' or 'thrilling' music, etc.). In some historical eras music was conceived as conveying precise emotional and conceptual meanings, established by codes, or, at least, 'repertoires' (see, for the Baroque era, Stefani, 1973, and Pagnini, 1974).

Formalized languages: from algebra to chemistry there can be no doubt that the study of these languages lies within the scope of semiotics. Of relevance to these researches are the studies of mathematical structures (Vailati, 1909; Barhut, 1966; Prieto, 1966; Gross and Lentin, 1967; Bertin, 1967), not to forget the ancient studies of *'ars combinatoria'* from Raimundo Lullo to Leibniz (see Mäll, 1968; Kristeva, 1968 as well as Rossi, 1960). Also included under this heading are the attempts to find a cosmic and interplanetary language (Freudentahl, 1960 [2]), the structures of systems such as Morse code or Boole's algebra as well as the formalized languages for electronic computers (see *Linguaggi nella società e nella tecnica*, 1970). Here there appears the problem of a "meta-semiology". [3]

Written languages, unknown alphabets, secret codes: whereas the study of ancient alphabets and secret codes has famous precedents in archeology and cryptography, the attention paid to writing, as distinct from the laws of language which writing transcribes, is relatively new (for a survey on classical bibliography see Gelb, 1952 and Trager, 1972). We call to mind either studies such as that of McLuhan (1962) on the *Weltanschauung* determined by printing techniques, and the anthropological revolution of the "Gutenberg Galaxy" or the "grammatology" of Derrida (1967b). Bridging the gap between classic semantics and cryptography are studies such as that of Greimas (1970) on *"écriture cruciverbiste"* and all the studies on the topic of riddles and puzzles (e.g. Krzyzanowski, 1960).

Natural languages: every bibliographical reference in this area should refer back to the general bibliography of linguistics, logic, philosophy of language, cultural anthropology, psychology etc. We should only add that semiotic interests, though arising on the one hand from studies in logic and the philosophy of language (Locke, Peirce, and so on), on the other hand assume their most complete form in studies on *structural* linguistics (Saussure, Jakobson, Hjelmslev).

Visual communication: there is no need for bibliographical reference because this item is dealt with explicitly in this book (in ch. 3). But we must remember that studies of this kind cover an area extending from systems possessing the highest degree of formalization (Prieto, 1966), through graphic systems (Bertin, 1967), color systems (Itten, 1961), to the study of iconic signs (Peirce, 1931; Morris, 1946, etc).

This last notion has been particularly questioned in the recent years by

Eco (1968, 1971, 1973), Metz (1970, 1971), Verón (1971, 1973), Krampen (1973), Volli (1973) and others. The latest developments begin to recognize beneath the rather vague category of 'iconism' a more complex series of signs, thus moving beyond Peirce's tripartition of signs into *Symbols, Icons* and *Indices*. Finally at the highest levels we have the study of large iconographic units (Panofsky and Schapiro in general), visual phenomena in mass communication, from advertisements to comic strips, from paper money system to playing-cards and fortune-telling cards (Lekomceva, 1962; Egorov, 1965), rebuses, clothes (Barthes, 1967) until finally we come to the visual study of architecture (see Eco, 1973 *e*), choreographical notation, geographic and topographic maps (Bertin, 1967), and film (Metz, 1970c, 1974; Bettetini, 1968, 1971, 1973; and others).

Systems of objects: objects as communicative devices come within the realm of semiotics, ranging from architecture to objects in general (see Baudrillard, 1968, and the issue of "Communications" 13, 1969 *Les Objets*). On architecture see Eco, 1968; Koenig, 1970; Garroni, 1973; De Fusco, 1973.

Plot structure: ranging from the studies of Propp (1928) to more recent European contributions (Bremond, 1964, 1966, 1973; Greimas, 1966, 1970; Metz, 1968; Barthes, 1966; Todorov, 1966, 1967, 1968, 1970; Genette, 1966; V. Morin, 1966; Gritti, 1966, 1968). Worthy of emphasis are the studies of the Soviets (Ščeglov, 1962; Žolkovskij, 1962, 1967; Karpinskaja-Revzin, 1966; as well as the classic Russian formalists). The study of plot has found its most important development in the study of primitive mythology (Lévi-Strauss, 1958a, 1958c, 1964; Greimas, 1966; Maranda, 1968) and of games and tales belonging to folklore (Dundes, 1964; Beaujour, 1968; Greimas-Rastier, 1968; Maranda, E.K. & P., 1962). But it also reaches to studies on mass communication, from comic strips (Eco, 1964) to the detective story (Ščeglov, 1962 a) and the popular nineteenth-century romance (Eco, 1965, 1967).

Text theory: the exigencies of a 'transphrastic' linguistic and developments in plot analysis (as well as the poetic language analysis) have led semiotics to recognize the notion of *text* as a macro-unit, ruled by particular generative rules, in which sometimes the very notion of 'sign' — as an elementary semiotic unit — is practically annihilated (Barthes, 1971, 1973; Kristeva, 1969). As for a generative text grammar see van Dijk (1970) and Petöfi (1972).

Cultural codes: semiotic research finally shifts its attention to phenomena which it would be difficult to term sign systems in a strict sense, nor even communicative systems, but which are rather behavior and value systems. I refer to systems of etiquette, hierarchies and the so-called 'modelling secondary systems' — under which heading the Soviets bring in myths, legends, primitive theologies which present in an organized way the world vision of a certain society (see Ivanov and Toporov, 1962; Todorov, 1966) and finally the typology of cultures (Lotman, 1964, 1967 a), which study the codes which define a given cultural model (for example the code of the mentality of medieval chivalry); finally models of social organization such as family systems (Lévi-Strauss, 1947) or the organized communicative network of more advanced groups and societies (Moles, 1967).

Aesthetic texts: the semiotic field also spills over into the area traditionally belonging to aesthetics. Certainly aesthetics is also concerned with non-semiotic aspects of art (such as the psychology of artistic creation, the relations between artistic form and natural form, the physical-psychological definition of aesthetic enjoyment, the analysis of the relations between art and society, etc.). But clearly all these problems could be dealt with from a semiotic point of view as soon as it is recognized (see 3.7) that every code allows for an *aesthetic use* of its elements.

Mass communication: as with aesthetics, this is a field which concerns many disciplines, from psychology to sociology and pedagogy (see Eco, 1964). But in most recent years the tendency has been to see the problem of mass communication in a semiotic perspective, while semiotic methods have been found useful in the explanation of numerous phenomena of mass communication.

The study of mass communication exists as a discipline not when it examines the technique or effects of a particular genre (detective story or comic strip, song or film) by means of a particular method of study, but when it establishes that all these genres, within an industrial society, have a characteristic in common.

The theories and analyses of mass communication are in fact applied to various genres, granted: 1) an industrial society which seems to be comparatively homogeneous but is in reality full of differences and contrasts; 2) channels of communication which make it possible to reach not determined groups but an indefinite circle of receivers in various sociological situations; 3) productive groups which work out and send out given messages by industrial means.

When these three conditions exist the differences in nature and effect between the various means of communication (movie, newspaper, television or comic strips) fade into the background compared with the emergence of common structures and effects.

The study of mass communication proposes a unitary object inasmuch as it claims that the industrialization of communications changes not only the conditions for receiving and sending out messages but (and it is with this apparent paradox that the methodology of these studies is concerned) the very meaning of the message (which is to say that block of meanings which was thought to be an unchangeable part of the message as devised by the author irrespective of its means of diffusion). In order to study mass communication one can and should resort to disparate methods ranging from psychology to sociology and stylistics; but one can plan a unitary study of such phenomena only if the theories and analyses of mass communication are considered as one sector of a general semiotics (see Fabbri, 1973).

Rhetoric: the revival in studies of rhetoric is currently converging on the study of mass communication (and therefore of communication with the

intention of persuasion). A rereading of traditional studies in the light of semiotics produces a great many new suggestions. From Aristotle to Quintilian,
through the medieval and Renaissance theoreticians up to Perelman, rhetoric
appears as a second chapter in the general study of semiotics (following
linguistics) elaborated centuries ago, and now providing tools for a discipline
which encompasses it. Therefore a bibliography of the semiotic aspects of
rhetoric seems identical with a bibliography of rhetoric (for a preliminary
orientation see Lausberg, 1960; Groupe μ, 1970; Chatman, 1974).

0.5. Natural boundaries: two definitions of semiotics

0.5.1. Saussure

Now that we have surveyed the whole semiotic field in a somewhat
approximate and disordered fashion, one question emerges: can these diverse
problems and diverse approaches be unified? To answer such a question we
must abandon mere description and hazard a provisional theoretical
definition of semiotics.

We could start by using the definitions put forward by two scholars
who foretold the official birth and scientific organization of the discipline:
Saussure and Peirce. According to Saussure (1916) "la langue est un système
de signes exprimant des idées et par là comparable à l'écriture, à l'alphabet
des sourds-muets, aux rites symboliques, aux formes de politesse, aux signaux
militaires, etc. etc. Elle est seulement le plus important de ces systèmes. On
peut donc concevoir une science qui étudie la vie des signes au sein de la vie
sociale; elle formerait une partie de la psychologie sociale, et par conséquent
de la psychologie générale; nous la nommerons sémiologie (du grec sēmeion,
'signe'). Elle nous apprendrait en quoi consistent les signes, quelles lois les
régissent. Puisqu'elle n'existe pas encore, on ne peut pas dire ce qu'elle sera;
mais elle a droit à l'existence, sa place est determinée d'avance".

Saussure's definition is rather important and has done much to increase
semiotic awareness. As will be shown in chapter 1 the notion of a sign as a
twofold entity (signifier and signified or *sign-vehicle* and *meaning*) has
anticipated and promoted all correlational definitions of sign-function.
Insofar as the relationship between signifier and signified is established on the
basis of a system of rules which is '*la langue*', Saussurean semiology would
seem to be a rigorous semiotics of signification. But it is not by chance that
those who see semiotics as a theory of communication rely basically on
Saussure's linguistics. Saussure did not define the signified any too clearly,
leaving it half way between a mental image, a concept and a psychological

reality; but he did clearly stress the fact that the signified is something which has to do with the mental activity of anybody receiving a signifier: according to Saussure signs 'express' ideas and provided that he did not share a Platonic interpretation of the term 'idea', such ideas must be mental events that concern a human mind. Thus the sign is implicitly regarded as a communicative device taking place between two human beings intentionally aiming to communicate or to express something. It is not by chance that all the examples of semiological systems given by Saussure are without any shade of doubt strictly conventionalized systems of artificial signs, such as military signals, rules of etiquette and visual alphabets. Those who share Saussure's notion of *sémiologie* distinguish sharply between intentional, artificial devices (which they call 'signs') and other natural or unintentional manifestations which do not, strictly speaking, deserve such a name.

0.5.2. Peirce

In this sense the definition given by Peirce seems to me more comprehensive and semiotically more fruitful: "I am, as far as I know, a pioneer, or rather a backwoodsman, in the work of clearing and opening up what I call *semiotic*, that is the doctrine of the essential nature and fundamental varieties of possible semiosis" (1931, 5.488). "By semiosis I mean an action, an influence, which is, or involves, a cooperation of *three* subjects, such as a sign, its object and its interpretant, this tri-relative influence not being in anyway resolvable into actions between pairs" (5.484). I shall define the 'interpretant' better later (chapter 2), but it is clear that the 'subjects' of Peirce's 'semiosis' are not human subjects but rather three abstract semiotic entities, the dialectic between which is not affected by concrete communicative behavior. According to Peirce a sign is "something which stands to somebody for something in some respects or capacity" (2.228). As will be seen, a sign can *stand for* something else to somebody only because this 'standing-for' relation is mediated by an interpretant. I do not deny that Peirce also thought of the interpretant (which was another sign translating and explaining the first one, and so on *ad infinitum*) as a psychological event in the mind of a possible interpreter; I only maintain that it is possible to interpret Peirce's definition in a non-anthropomorphic way (as is proposed in chapters 1 and 2). It is true that the same interpretation could also fit Saussure's proposal; but Peirce's definition offers us something more. It does not demand, as part of a sign's definition, the qualities of being intentionally emitted and artificially produced.

The Peircean triad can be also applied to phenomena that do not have a human emitter, provided that they do have a human receiver, such being the case with meteorological symptoms or any other sort of index.

Those who reduce semiotics to a theory of communicational acts cannot consider symptoms as signs, nor can they accept as signs any other human behavioral feature from which a receiver infers something about the situation of the sender even though this sender is unaware of sending something to somebody (see for instance Buyssens, 1943; Segre, 1969 etc.). Since such authors maintain that they are solely concerned with communication, they have the right to exclude a lot of phenomena from the set of signs. Instead of denying that right I would like to defend the right to establish a semiotic theory able to take into account a broader range of sign-phenomena.

I propose to define as a sign *everything* that, on the grounds of a previously established social convention, can be taken as *something standing for something else*. In other terms I would like to accept the definition proposed by Morris (1938) according to which "something is a sign only because it is interpreted as a sign of something by some interpreter . . . . Semiotics, then, is not concerned with the study of a particular kind of objects, but with ordinary objects insofar (and only insofar) as they participate in semiosis". I suppose it is in this sense that one must take Peirce's definition of the 'standing-for' power of the sign "in some respect or capacity". The only modification that I would introduce into Morris's definition is that the interpretation by an interpreter, which would seem to characterize a sign, must be understood as the *possible* interpretation by a *possible* interpreter. But this point will be made clearer in chapter 2. Here it suffices to say that the human addressee is the methodological (and not the empirical) guarantee of the existence of a signification, that is of a sign-function established by a code. But on the other hand the supposed presence of a human sender is not the guarantee of the sign-nature of a supposed sign. Only under this condition is it possible to understand symptom and indices as signs (as Peirce does).

0.6. Natural boundaries: inference and signification

0.6.1. Natural signs

The semiotic nature of indices and symptoms will be examined and reformulated in ch. 3. Here we only need to consider two types of so-called 'signs' that seem to escape a communicational definition: they are (a) physical events coming from a natural source and (b) human behavior not intentionally emitted by its senders. Let us look more closely at these two instances.

We are able to infer from smoke the presence of fire, from a wet spot the fall of a raindrop, from a track on the sand the passage of a given animal, and so on. All these are cases of *inference* and our everyday life is filled with a lot of these inferential acts. It is incorrect to say that every act of inference is a 'semiosic' act — even though Peirce did so — and it is probably too rash a statement to assert that every semiosic process implies an act of inference, but it can be maintained that *there exist acts of inference which must be recognized as semiosic acts*. It is not by chance that ancient philosophy has so frequently associated signification and inference. A sign was defined as the evident antecedent of a consequent or the consequent of an antecedent when similar consequences have been previously observed (Hobbes, *Leviathan*, 1,3); as an entity from which the present or the future or past existence of another being is inferred (Wolff, *Ontology*, 1952); as a proposition constituted by a valid and revealing connection to its consequent (Sextus Empiricus, *Adv. math.*, VIII, 245). Probably this straightforward identification of inference and signification leaves many shades of difference unexplained: it only needs to be corrected by adding the expression 'when this association is culturally recognized and systematically coded'.

The first doctor who discovered a sort of constant relationship between an array of red spots on the patient's face and a given disease (measles) made an inference: but insofar as this relationship has been made conventional and has been registered as such in medical treatises a semiotic convention [4] has been established. There is a sign every time a human group decides to use and to recognize something as the vehicle of something else.

In this sense events coming from a *natural source* must also be listed as signs: for there is a convention positing a coded correlation between an expression (the perceived event) and a content (its cause or its possible effect). An event can be a sign-vehicle of its cause or its effect provided that both the cause and the effect are not actually detectable. Smoke is only a sign of fire to the extent that fire is not actually perceived along with the smoke: but smoke can be a sign-vehicle standing for a non-visible fire, provided that a social rule has necessarily and usually associated smoke with fire.

0.6.2. Non-intentional signs

The second case is one in which a human being performs acts that are perceived by someone as signalling devices,revealing something else,even if the sender is unaware of the revelative property of his behavior. A typical example is gestural behavior. Under some conditions it is perfectly possible to detect the cultural origin of a gesturer because his gestures have a clear connotative capacity. Even if we do not know the socialized meanings of those gestures we can at any rate recognize the gesturer as Italian, Jew, Anglo-Saxon and so on (see Efron, 1941) just as almost everybody is able to recognize a Chinese or German speaker as such even if he does not know Chinese or German. These behaviors are able to signify even though the sender does not attribute such a capacity to them.

One might assume that this case is similar to that of medical symptoms: provided there is a rule assigning a cultural origin to certain gestural styles, those gestures will be understood as signs, independently of the will of the sender. But no one can escape the suspicion that, as long as the gesture is performed by a human being, there is an underlying significative intention. So in this case our example is complicated by the fact that we are dealing with something which has strong links with communicational practice. If in the case of symptoms it was easy to recognize a signification relationship without any suspicion of actual communication, in this second case there is always the suspicion that the subject is *pretending* to act unconsciously with a specially communicative intention; he may, on the other hand, want to show his communicative intention, while the addressee interprets his behavior as unconscious. Moreover, the subject can act unconsciously while the addressee attributes a misleading intention to him. And so on. This interplay of acts of awareness and unawareness, and of the attribution of voluntarity and involuntarity to the sender, generates many communicative exchanges that can give rise to an entire repertoire of mistakes, *arrière pensées*, double thinks and so on.

Table 1 should generate all possible understandings and misunderstandings. S stands for Sender, A for Addressee, IS for 'the intention attributed to the Sender by the Addressee', while + and - mean either intentional/unintentional emission (for the Sender) or conscious/unconscious reception (for the Addressee): In case number 1, for instance, a liar intentionally shows the signs of a given sickness in order to deceive the addressee, while the addressee is quite well aware that the sender is lying. In case number 2 the deception is successful. In cases number 3 and 4 the sender intentionally emits a significant behavior which the addressee receives as a simple stimulus devoid of any intentionality: as when, in order to get rid of a boring visitor, I drum on the desk with my fingers, thus expressing nervous tension. The addressee may only

Table 1

	S	A	IS
1	+	+	+
2	+	+	-
3	+	-	(+)
4	+	-	(-)
5	-	+	+
6	-	+	-
7	-	-	(+)
8	-	-	(-)

perceive it as a subliminal stimulus which irritates him; in such a case he cannot attribute either intentionality or unintentionality to me (which is why + and - are put into brackets), although later he might (or might not) realize that my behavior was intentional.

Cases 1 and 2 also express the opposite of the last situation: I drum intentionally and the addressee perceives my behavior as significant, though he may or may not attribute to me a specifically significative intention. In all these cases (which could constitute a suitable combinatorial explanation of many interpersonal relations, of the type studied by Goffman (1963, 1967, 1969)), behaviors become signs because of a decision on the part of the addressee (trained by cultural convention) or of a decision on the part of the sender to stimulate in the addressee the decision to take these behaviors as signs.

0.7. Natural boundaries: the lower threshold

0.7.1. Stimuli

If both non-human and human but unintentional events can become signs, then semiotics has extended its domain beyond a frequently fetishized threshold: that which separates signs from things and artificial signs from natural ones. But while gaining this territory, general semiotics inevitably loses its grip on another strategical position to which it had unduly laid claim. For since everything can be understood as a sign if and only if there exists a convention which allows it to stand for something else, and since some behavioral responses are not elicited by convention, stimuli *cannot* be regarded as signs.

According to the well-known Pavlov experiment, a dog salivates when stimulated by the ring of a bell because of a conditioned stimulus. The ring of the bell provokes salivation without any other mediation. However, from the point of view of the scientist, who knows that to every ring must correspond a salivation, the ring stands for salivation (even if the dog is not there): there is a coded correspondence between two events so that one can stand for the other. There is an old joke according to which two dogs meet in Moscow, one of them very fat and wealthy, the other pathetically emaciated. The latter asks the former: "How can you find food?". The former zoosemiotically replies: "That's easy. Every day, at noon, I enter the Pavlov Institute and I begin to salivate: immediately afterward a conditioned scientist arrives, rings a bell and gives me food". In this case the scientist reacts to a stimulus but the dog establishes a sort of reversible relationship between salivation and food: it knows that to a given stimulus a given reaction must correspond and therefore the dog possesses a code. Salivation is for it the sign of the possible reaction on the part of the scientist. Unfortunately for dogs, this is not the way things are — at least within the framework of classical experiment: the sound of the bell is a stimulus for the dog, which salivates independently of any social code, while the psychologist regards the dog's salivation as a sign (or symptom) that the stimulus has been received and has elicited the appropriate response.

To my mind, the difference between the attitude of the dog and that of the psychologist is an enlightening one: to assert that stimuli are not signs does not necessarily mean that a semiotic approach ought not to be concerned with them. Semiotics is dealing with sign-function, but a sign-function represents the correlation of two functives which (outside that correlation) are not by nature semiotic. However, insofar as — once correlated — they can acquire such a nature, they deserve some attention on the part of semioticians. There are some phenomena that could be imprudently listed among supposedly non-signifying stimuli without realizing that 'in some respect or capacity' they can act as signs 'to somebody'.

0.7.2. Signals

For instance, the proper objects of a theory of information are not signs but rather units of transmission which can be computed quantitatively irrespective of their possible meaning, and which therefore must properly be called 'signals' and not 'signs'. To assert that these *signals* are of no importance for a semiotic approach would be rather hasty. One would then be unable to take into account the various features of the linguistic '*significant*' face of a sign, which, although strictly organized and computatively detectable, can be independent of its meaning and only possesses an oppositional value. Semiotics here comes face to face with its lower threshold. Yet the decision as to whether or not to respect this threshold seems to me a very difficult one to make.

0.7.3. Physical information

One must undoubtedly exclude from semiotic consideration neurophysiological and genetic phenomena, as well as the circulation of the blood or the activity of the lungs. But what about the informational theories that view sensory phenomena as the passage of signals from peripherical nerve ends to the cerebral cortex, or genetic heredity as a coded transmission of information? Probably it would be prudent to say that neurophysiological and genetic phenomena are not a matter for semioticians, but that neurophysiological and genetic informational theories are so.

All these problems seem to suggest that one should consider this lower threshold more carefully and with greater attention, as will be done in chapter 1.

Granted that semiotics takes many of its own tools (for example the notions of information and binary choice) from disciplines dealing with this lower threshold, one can hardly exclude it from consideration without embarrassing results. The phenomena on the lower threshold should rather be isolated as indicating the point where semiotic phenomena arise from something non-semiotic, as a sort of 'missing link' between the universe of signals and the universe of signs.

0.8. Natural boundaries: the upper threshold

0.8.1. Two hypotheses on culture

If the term 'culture' is accepted in its correct anthropological sense, then we are immediately confronted with three elementary cultural phenomena which can apparently be denied the characteristic of being communicative phenomena: (a) the production and employment of objects used for transforming the relationship between man and nature; (b) kinship relations as the primary nucleus of institutionalized social relations; (c) the economic exchange of goods.

We did not choose these three phenomena by accident: not only are they the constituent phenomena of every culture (along with the birth of articulated language) but they have been singled out as the objects of various semio-anthropological studies in order to show that the whole of culture is signification and communication and that humanity and society exist only when communicative and significative relationships are established.

One must be careful to note that this type of research can be articulated through two hypotheses, of which one is comparatively 'radical' — a kind of 'unnegotiable demand on the part of semiotics' — and the other appears to be comparatively 'moderate'.

The two hypotheses are: (i) the whole of culture *must* be studied as a semiotic phenomenon; (ii) all aspects of a culture *can* be studied as the contents of a semiotic activity. The radical hypothesis usually circulated in two extreme forms: "culture is *only* communication" and "culture is *no more* than a system of structured significations". These formulas hint dangerously at idealism and should be changed to: "the whole of culture *should* be studied as a communicative phenomenon based on signification systems". This means that not only *can* culture be studied in this way but — as will be seen — only by studying it in this way can certain of its fundamental mechanisms be clarified.

The difference between saying culture 'should be studied as' and 'culture is', is immediately apparent. In fact it is one thing to say that an object is *essentialiter* something and another to say that it can be seen *sub ratione* of that something.

0.8.2. Tools

I shall try and give a few examples. When Australopithecines used a stone to split the skull of a baboon, there was as yet no culture, even if an Australopithecine had in fact transformed an element of nature into a tool. We would say that culture is born when: (i) a thinking being establishes the new function of the stone (irrespective of whether he works on it, transforming it into a flint-stone); (ii) he calls it "a stone that serves for something" (irrespective of whether he calls it so to others, or out loud); (iii) he recognizes it as "the stone that responds to the function F and that has the name Y" (irrespective of whether he uses it as such a second time: it is sufficient that he recognizes it). [5]

These three conditions result in a semiotic process of the following kind: In Table 2, S_1 is the first stone used for the first time as a tool and S_2 is another stone, different in size, color and weight from the first one. Now suppose that our Australopithecine, after having used the first stone by

Table 2

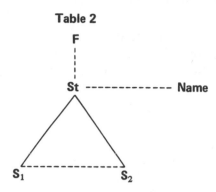

chance and after having discovered its possible function, comes upon a second stone (S_2) some days later and recognizes it as a *token*, an individual occurrence of a more general model (St), which is the abstract *type* to which S_1 also refers. Encountering S_2 and being able to subsume it (along with S_1) under type St, our Australopithecine regards it as the *sign-vehicle* of a possible function F. S_1 and S_2, as tokens of the type St, are significant forms *referring back to* and *standing for* F. According to a typical characteristic of every sign, S_1 and S_2 have not only to be considered as the sign-vehicle of a possible meaning (the function F): insofar as both stand for F (and vice versa) both are simultaneously (and from different points of view) the sign-vehicle and meaning of F, following a *law of total reversibility*.

The possibility of giving a *name* to the type-stone (and to everyone of its occurrence) adds a new semiotic dimension to our diagram. As we will see in the pages devoted to the relationship between *denotation* and *connotation* (2.3) the name denotes the type-stone as its meaning but immediately connotes the function of which the object-stone (or the type-stone) is the signifier.

In principle this represents no more than a *signification system* and does not imply an actual *process of communication* (except that it is impossible to conceive of the institution of such significant relationships if not for communicative purposes).

However, these conditions do not even imply that two human beings actually exist: the situation is equally possible in the case of a solitary, shipwrecked Robinson Crusoe. It is necessary, however, that whoever uses the stone for the first time should consider the possibility of passing on the information he has acquired to himself the next day, and in order to do this should elaborate a mnemonic device, a significant relationship between object and function. A single use of the stone is not culture. To establish how the function can be repeated and to transmit this information from today's solitary shipwrecked man to the same man tomorrow, is culture. The solitary man becomes both transmitter and receiver of a communication (on the basis of a very elementary code). It is clear that a definition such as this (in its totally simple terms) can imply an identification of thought and language: it is a question of saying, as Peirce does (5.470-480) that *even ideas are signs*. But the problem appears in its extreme form only if one considers the extreme example of a shipwrecked individual communicating with himself. As soon as there are two individuals, one can translate the problem into terms not of ideas but of *observable sign-vehicles*.

The moment that communication occurs between two men, one might well imagine that what can be observed is the verbal or pictographic sign with which the sender communicates to the addressee the object-stone and its possible function by means of a name (for example: /headsplitter/ or /weapon/). But with this we only arrive at our second hypothesis: the cultural object has become the content of a possible verbal communication. The *primary hypothesis* instead presupposes that the sender could communicate the function of the object even without necessarily involving the verbal name, by merely showing the object. It thus supposes that once the possible use of the stone has been conceptualized, the stone itself becomes the concrete sign of its virtual use. Thus it is a question of stating (Barthes, 1964 a) that once society exists every function is automatically transformed into a *sign of that function*. This is possible once culture exists. But culture exists only because this is possible.

0.8.3. Commodities

We will move on now to phenomena such as economic exchange. We must above all eliminate the ambiguity whereby every 'exchange' would be 'communication' (just as some think that every communication is a 'transfer'). True, as every communication implies an exchange of signals (just as the exchange of signals implies the transfer of energy); but there are exchanges such as those of goods (or of women) which are exchanges not only of signals but also of consumable physical bodies. It is possible to consider the exchange of commodities as a semiotic phenomenon (Rossi-Landi, 1968) not because the exchange of goods implies a physical exchange, but because in the exchange the *use value* of the goods is transformed into their *exchange value* — and therefore a process of signification or *symboliza-*

tion takes place, this later being perfected by the appearance of money, which *stands for something else*.

The economic relationships ruling the exchange of commodities (as described in the first book of *Das Kapital* by Karl Marx) may be represented in the same way as was the sign-function performed by the tool-stone (Table 3).

Table 3

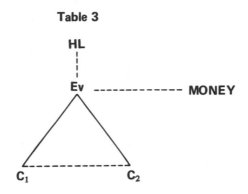

In Table 3, C_1 and C_2 are two commodities devoid of any use value (this having been semiotically represented in Table 2). In the first book of *Das Kapital* Marx not only shows how all commodities, in a general exchange system, can become signs standing for other commodities: he also suggests that this relation of mutual significance is made possible because the commodities system is structured by means of *oppositions* (similar to those which linguistics has elaborated in order to describe — for example — the structure of phonological systems). Within this system *//Commodity number 1//* becomes the Commodity *in which* the exchange value of «Commodity number 2» is expressed («Commodity number 2» being the item *of which* the exchange value is expressed by *//Commodity number 1//*). [6] This significant relationship is made possible by the cultural existence of an exchange parameter that we can record as Ev (exchange value). If in a use value system all the items referred back to a function F (corresponding to the use value) in an exchange value system Ev refers back to the quantity of human labor necessary to the production of both C_1 and C_2 (this parameter being recorded as HL). All these items can be correlated, in a more sophisticated cultural system, with the universal equivalent, money (which corresponds in some respects to the cultural name standing for both commodities and their abstract and 'type' equivalents, HL and Ev). The only difference between a coin (as sign-vehicle) and a word is that the word can be reproduced without economic effort while a coin is an irreproducible item (which shares some of the characters of its commodity-object). This simply means that there are different kinds of signs which must also be differentiated according to the economic value of their *expression-matter*. The Marxist analysis also shows that the semiotic diagram ruling a capitalistic economy differentiates both HL and Ev (which are mutually equivalent) from a third element, the *salary* received by the worker who performs HL. This gap between HL, Ev and Salary constitutes the *plus value*. But this fact, highly significant from the point of view of an economic enquiry, does not contradict our semiotic model; on the contrary it shows how semiotics can clarify certain aspects of cultural life; and how, from a certain point of view, a scientific approach to economics consists in discovering the one-sidedness of some surface semiotic codes, that is their *ideological* quality (see 3.9.).

If one turns back to Table 2 one realizes that even that was a one-sided representation of more complex relationships. As a matter of fact a stone has not only *that* particular function F (head-splitting), but many others too; and a possible global semiotic system (that is, a representation of a culture in its totality) must take into account every possible use value (that is, every possible semantic content or meaning) or a given object — thus recording every kind of functional *synonymy* and *homonymy*.

0.8.4. Women

Let us now consider the exchange of women. In what sense can this be considered a symbolic process? In this context women would appear to be *physical objects* to be used through physiological operations (to be *consumed* as in the case of food and other goods). However, if the woman were merely the physical body with which the husband enters into sexual relations in order to produce sons, it could not then be explained why *every* man does not copulate with *every* woman. Why is man obliged by certain conventions to choose one (or more, according to the custom) following very precise and inflexible rules of choice? Because it is only a woman's symbolic value which puts her *in opposition*, within the system, to other women. The woman, the moment she becomes 'wife', is no longer merely a physical body: she is a *sign* which connotes a system of social obligations (Lévi-Strauss, 1947).

0.8.5. Culture as a semiotic phenomenon

So it is clear how my first hypothesis makes a general theory of culture out of semiotics and in the final analysis makes semiotics a substitute for cultural anthropology. But to reduce the whole of culture to semiotics does not mean that one has to reduce the whole of material life to pure mental events. To look at the whole of culture *sub specie semiotica* is not to say that culture is only communication and signification but that it can be understood more thoroughly if it is seen from the semiotic point of view. And that objects, behavior and relationships of production and value function as such socially precisely because they obey semiotic laws. As for the *moderate hypothesis*, it simply means that every aspect of culture becomes a semantic unit.

To say that a class of objects (for example «automobile») becomes a semantic entity insofar as it is signified by means of the sign=vehicle /automobile/ will not get us very far. It is obvious that semiotics is also concerned with sodium chloride (which is not a cultural but a natural entity) the moment it is seen as the meaning of the sign-vehicle /salt/ (and vice versa).

But our second hypothesis implicitly suggests something more, i.e., that the systems of meanings (understood as systems of cultural units) are organized as structures (semantic fields and axes) which follow the same semiotic rules as were set out for the structures of the sign-vehicle. In other words, «automobile» is not only a semantic entity once it is correlated with the sign-vehicle /automobile/. It is a semantic unit as soon as it is arranged in an axis of oppositions and relationships with other semantic units such as «carriage», «bicycle» or «feet» (in the opposition "by car" vs. "on foot"). In this sense there is *at least one way* of considering all cultural phenomena on the semiotic level: everything which cannot be studied any other way in semiotics is studied at the level of structural semantics. But the problem is not that simple. An automobile can be considered on different levels (from different points of view): (a) the *physical level* (it has a weight, is made of a certain metal and other materials); (b) the *mechanical level* (it functions and fulfills a certain function on the basis of certain laws); (c) the *economic level* (it has an exchange value, a set price); (d) the *social level* (it indicates a certain social status); (e) the *semantic level* (it is not only an object as such but a cultural unit inserted into a system of cultural units with which it enters into certain relationships which are studied by structural semantics, relationships which remain the same even if the sign-vehicles with which we indicate them are changed; even − that is − if instead of /automobile/ we were to say /car/ or /coche/).

Let us now return to level (d), i.e. to the social level. If an automobile (as an individual concrete object) indicates a certain social status, it has then acquired a symbolic value, not only when it is an abstract class signified as the content of a verbal or iconic communication (that is when the semantic unit «automobile» is indicated by means of the sign-vehicle /car/ or /voiture/ or /bagnole/). It also has symbolic value when it is used an *object*. In other words, the object //automobile// becomes the sign-vehicle of a semantic unit which is not only «automobile» but, for example, «speed» or «convenience» or «wealth». The object //automobile// also becomes the sign-vehicle for its possible use. On the social level the object, *as object*, already has its own sign function, and therefore a semiotic nature. Thus the second hypothesis, according to which cultural phenomena are the contents of a possible signification, already refers back to the first hypothesis, according to which cultural phenomena must be seen as significant devices.

Now let us examine level (c) — the economic level. We have seen that an object, on the basis of its exchange value, can become the sign-vehicle of other objects. It is only because all goods acquire a position in the system, by means of which they are in opposition to other goods, that it is possible to establish a *code of goods* in which one semantic axis is made to correspond to another semantic axis, and the goods of the first axis become the sign-vehicles for the goods of the second axis, which in turn become their meaning. Similarly even in verbal language a sign-vehicle (/automobile/) can become the meaning of another sign-vehicle (/car/) within a metalinguistic discussion such as we have been pursuing in the preceding pages. The second hypothesis refers therefore to the first hypothesis. In culture every entity can become a semiotic phenomenon. The laws of signification are the laws of culture. For this reason culture allows a continuous process of communicative exchanges, in so far as it subsists as a system of systems of signification. *Culture can be studied completely under a semiotic profile.*

0.9. Epistemological boundaries

But there is a third sort of threshold, an epistemological one, which does not depend on the definition of the semiotic object but rather on the definition of the theoretical 'purity' of the discipline itself. In other words the semiotician should always question both his object and his categories in order to decide whether he is dealing with the abstract theory of the pure competence of an ideal sign-producer (a competence which can be posited in an axiomatic and highly formalized way) or whether he is concerned with a social phenomenon subject to changes and restructuring, resembling a network of intertwined partial and transitory competences rather than a crystal-like and unchanging model. I would put the matter this way: the object of semiotics may somewhat resemble (i) either the surface of the sea, where, independently of the continuous movement of water molecules and the interplay of submarine streams, there is a sort of average resulting form which is called the Sea, (ii) or a carefully ordered landscape, where human intervention continuously changes the form of settlements, dwellings, plantations, canals and so on. If one accepts the second hypothesis, which constitutes the epistemological assumption underlying this book, one must also accept another condition of the semiotic approach which will not be like exploring the sea, where a ship's wake disappears as soon as it has passed, but more like exploring a forest where cart-trails or footprints do modify the explored landscape, so that the description the explorer gives of it must also take into account the ecological variations that he has produced.

According to the theory of codes and sign production that I intend to propose, it will be clear that the semiotic approach is ruled by a sort of *indeterminacy principle*: in so far as signifying and communicating are social functions that determine both social organization and social evolution, to 'speak' about 'speaking', to signify signification or to communicate about communication cannot but influence the universe of speaking, signifying and communicating.

The semiotic approach to the phenomenon of 'semiosis' must be characterized by this kind of awareness of its own limits. Frequently to be really 'scientific' means not pretending to be more 'scientific' than the situation allows. In the 'human' sciences one often finds an 'ideological fallacy' common to many scientific approaches, which consists in believing that one's own approach is not ideological because it succeeds in being 'objective' and 'neutral'. For my own part, I share the same skeptical opinion that all enquiry is 'motivated'. Theoretical research is a form of social practice. Everybody who wants to know something wants to know it in order to do something. If he claims that he wants to know it only in order 'to know' and not in order 'to do' it means that he wants to know it in order to do nothing, which is in fact a surreptitious way of doing something, i.e. leaving the world just as it is (or as his approach assumes that it ought to be).

Ceteris paribus, I think that it is more 'scientific' not to conceal my own motivations, so as to spare my readers any 'scientific' delusions. If semiotics is a theory, then it should be a theory that permits a continuous critical intervention in semiotic phenomena. Since people speak, to explain why and how they speak cannot help but determine their future way of speaking. At any rate, I can hardly deny that it determines my own way of speaking.

NOTES

1. There is some discussion as to whether the discipline should be called *Semiotics* or *Semiology*. 'Semiology' with reference to Saussure's definition; 'Semiotics' or 'semiotic' with reference to those of Peirce's and Morris'. Furthermore one could presumably speak of semiology with reference to a general discipline which studies signs, and regards linguistic signs as no more than a special area; but Barthes (1964 a) has turned Saussure's definition upside down by viewing semiology as a *translinguistics* which examines all sign systems with reference to linguistic laws.

So it would seem that anyone inclining toward a study of sign systems that has no necessary dependence on linguistics must speak of semiotics. On the other hand the fact that Barthes has interpreted Saussure's suggestion in the way he has does not prevent us from going back to the original meaning. However, here I have decided to adopt the formula 'semiotics' once and for all, without paying attention to arguments about the philosophical and methodological implications of the two terms, thus complying with the decision taken in January 1969 in Paris by an international committee which brought into existence the International Association for Semiotic Studies. Sticking to Ockham's razor, some other important distinctions are not taken into account in this book. Hjelmslev (1943), for instance, proposes to divide semiotics into (a) scientific semiotic and (b) non-scientific semiotic, both studied by (c) metasemiotic. A metasemiotic studying a non-scientific semiotic is a semiology, whose terminology is studied by a metasemiology.Insofar as there also exists a connotative semiotic, there will likewise be a meta-(connotative) semiotic. This division, however, does not take into account (for historical reasons) many new approaches to significant and communicative phenomena. For instance, Hjelmslev called 'connotators' such phenomena as tones, registers, gestures which, not being at that time the object of a scientific semiotics, should have been studied by a metasemiology, while today the same phenomena fall within the domain of paralinguistics, which would seem to be a 'scientific semiotic'. Hjelmslev's great credit was that of having emphasized that there is no object which is not illuminated by linguistic (and semiotic) theory. Even if his semiotic hierarchy could be reformulated, his proposals must be constantly kept in mind. Following Hjelmslev, Metz (1966 b) had proposed calling all the formalizations of the natural sciences 'semiotics' and those of the human sciences 'semiology'. Greimas (1970) suggests applying the term 'semiotics' to the sciences of expression and the term 'semiology' to the sciences of content. Various other classifications have been proposed, such as those of Peirce and Morris, or the distinction proposed by the Soviet school of Tartu between 'primary modelling systems' (the proper object of linguistics) and 'secondary modelling systems'. Some other classifications can be found in the discussion published in *Approaches to Semiotics* (Sebeok, Bateson, Hayes, 1964) such as the one by Goffman: (a) detective models (indices); (b) semantic codes; (c) communicative systems in the strict sense; (d) social relations; (e) phenomena of interaction between speakers. See also Sebeok (1973) and Garroni (1973).

2. But see the objections raised to this book by Robert M.W. Dixon in his review in *Linguistics*, 5, where he observes that even mathematical formulae, considered 'universal' by the author, are abstractions from Indo-European syntactical models, and that they can therefore be understood only by someone who already knows the codes of certain natural languages.

3. This concerns the need for a hyperformalized language, formed by *empty signs*, and adapted to the description of all semiotic possibilities. As for this project, proposed by modern semiologists, see Julia Kristeva, "L'expansion de la sémiotique" (1967). She refers to the research of the Russian Linzbach and predicts an axiomatics through which "semiotics will be built up on the corpse of linguistics, a death already predicted by Linzbach, and one to which linguistics will become resigned after having prepared the ground for semiotics, demonstrating the isomorphism of semiotic practices with the other complexes of our universe." Semiotics will therefore be presented as the axiomatic meeting-place of all possible knowledge, including arts and sciences. This proposal is developed by Kristeva in "Pour une sémiologie des paragrammes" (1967) and in "Distance et anti-representation" (1968), where she introduces Linnart Mall, "Une approche possible du Sunyayada", whose study of the 'zero-logical subject' and of the notion of 'emptiness' in ancient Buddhist texts is curiously reminiscent of Lacan's *'vide'*. But it must be pointed out that the whole of this axiomatic program refers semiotics back to the *characteristica universalis* of Leibniz, and from Leibniz back to the late medieval *artes combinatoriae*, and to Lullo.

4. One should establish from this point on what a *convention* is. It is not so difficult to explain how someone can posit the conventional relationship between a red spot and measles: one can use verbal language as a metalinguistic device. But what about those conventions that cannot rely upon a previous metalanguage? Paragraphs 3.6.7. to 3.6.9. (about the mode of sign production called 'invention') will be devoted to this subject. For a preliminary and satisfactory notion of 'convention' let us assume for the time being the one proposed by Lewis, 1969.

5. Whether or not all this applies to the Australopithecines we do not know. It is sufficient to maintain that all this must apply to the first being which performed a semiotic behavior. This could mean — as Piaget (1968, p. 79) suggests — that intelligence precedes 'language'. But this does not mean that intelligence precedes semiosis. If the equation 'semiosis=verbal language' is eliminated, one can view intelligence and signification as a single process.

6. Since this is a book on *semiotics* and not only on linguistics, I will be obliged at times to quote a non-verbal device as the sign-vehicle of a given cultural content (see chapter 2). Having adopted the decision of representing the sign-vehicles between slashes (/xxx/), and since in a book even the quotation of an object needs to be realized through a word, let me assume that when something which is not a word is taken as a sign-vehicle and is therefore represented by a word, this corresponding word will be written *in italics* between double slashes (//xxx//). Double slashes thus mean «the object usually corresponding to this word». Thus /automobile/ represents the word 'automobile', while //*automobile*// represents the object usually called /automobile/.

1: SIGNIFICATION
AND COMMUNICATION

1.1. An elementary communicational model

If every communication process must be explained as relating to a system of significations, it is necessary to single out *the elementary structure of communication* at the point where communication may be seen in its most elementary terms. Although every pattern of signification is a cultural convention, there is one communicative process in which there seems to be no cultural convention at all, but only — as was proposed in 0.7 — the passage of stimuli. This occurs when so-called physical 'information' is transmitted between two mechanical devices.

When a floating buoy signals to the control panel of an automobile the level reached by the gasoline, this process occurs entirely by means of a mechanical chain of causes and effects. Nevertheless, according to the principles of information theory, there is an 'informational' process that is in some way considered a communicational process too. Our example does not consider what happens once the signal (from the buoy) reaches the control panel and is converted into a visible measuring device (a red moving line or an oscillating arm): this is an undoubted case of sign-process in which the position of the arm *stands for* the level of the gasoline, in accordance with a conventionalized *code*.

But what is puzzling for a semiotic theory is the process which takes place before a human being looks at the pointer: although at the moment when he does so the pointer is the starting point of a signification process, before that moment it is only the *final result* of a preceding communicational process. During this process we cannot say that the position of the buoy stands for the movement of the pointer: instead of 'standing-for', the buoy *stimulates, provokes, causes, gives rise to* the movement of the pointer.

It is then necessary to gain a deeper knowledge of this type of process, which constitutes the lower threshold of semiotics. Let us outline a very simple communicative situation[1]. An engineer — downstream — needs to know when a watershed located in a basin between two mountains, and closed by a watergate, reaches a certain level of saturation, which he defines as 'danger level'.

Whether there is water or not; whether it is above or below the danger level; how much above or below; at what rate it is rising: all this constitutes pieces of information which can be transmitted from the watershed, which will therefore be considered as a *source* of information.

So the engineer puts in the watershed a sort of buoy which, when it reaches danger level, activates a *transmitter* capable of emitting an electric *signal* which travels through a *channel* (an electric wire) and is picked up downstream by a *receiver*; this device converts the signal into a given string of elements (i.e. releases a series of mechanical commands) that constitute a *message* for a *destination* apparatus. The destination, at this point, can release a mechanical response in order to correct the situation at the source (for instance opening the watergate so that the water can be slowly evacuated). Such a situation is usually represented as follows:

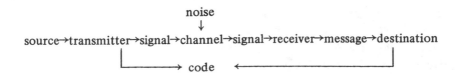

In this model the code is the device which assures that a given electric signal produces a given mechanical message, and that this elicits a given response. The engineer can establish the following code: presence of signal (+ A) *versus* absence of signal (- A). The signal + A is released when the buoy sensitizes the transmitter.

But this 'Watergate Model' also foresees the presence of potential *noise* on the channel, which is to say any disturbance that could alter the nature of the signals, making them difficult to detect, or producing + A when - A is intended and vice versa. Therefore the engineer has to complicate his code. For instance, if he establishes two different levels of signal, namely + A and +B, he then disposes of three signals [2] and the destination may accordingly be instructed in order to release three kinds of response.

+ A produces 'state of rest'
+ B produces 'feedback'
- AB (and + AB) produces an emergency signal (meaning that something does not work)

This complication of the code increases the cost of the entire apparatus but makes the transmission of information more secure. Nevertheless there can be so much noise as to produce + A instead of + B. In order to avoid this risk, the code must be considerably complicated. Suppose that the engineer now disposes of four positive signals and establishes that every message must be composed of two signals. The four positive signals can be represented by four different levels but in order to better control the entire process the engineer decides to represent them by four electric bulbs as well. They can be set out in a positional series, so that A is recognizable inasmuch as it precedes B and so on; they can also be designed as four bulbs of differing colors, following a wave-length progression (green, yellow, orange, red). It must be made absolutely clear that the destination apparatus does not need to 'see' bulbs (for it has no sensory organs): but the bulbs are useful for the engineer so that he can follow what is happening.

I should add that the correspondence between electric signals (received by the transmitter and translated into mechanical messages) and the lighting of the bulbs (obviously activated by another receiver) undoubtedly constitutes a new coding phenomenon that would need to receive separate attention; but for the sake of convenience I shall consider both the message to the destination and the bulbs as two aspects of the same phenomenon. At this point the engineer has — at least from a theoretical point of view — 16 possible messages at his disposal:

AA	BA	CA	DA
AB	BB	CB	DB
AC	BC	CC	DC
AD	BD	CD	DD

Since AA, BB, CC, DD are simply repetitions of a single signal, and therefore cannot be instantaneously emitted, and since six messages are simply the reverse of six others (for instance, BA is the reverse of AB, and the temporal succession of two signals is not being considered in this case), the engineer actually disposes of six messages: AB, BC, CD, AD, AC and BD. Suppose that he assigns to the message AB the task of signalling "danger level". He has at his disposal 5 'empty' messages.

Thus the engineer has achieved two interesting results: (i) it is highly improbable that a noise will activate two wrong bulbs and it is probable that any wrong activation will give rise to a 'senseless' message, such as ABC or ABCD: therefore it is easier to detect a misfunctioning; (ii) since the code has been complicated and the cost of the transmission has been increased, the engineer may take advantage of this investment to amortize it through a more informative exploitation of the code.

In fact with such a code he can get a more comprehensive range of information about what happens at the source and he can better instruct the destination, selecting more events to be informed about and more mechanical responses to be released by the apparatus in order to control the entire process more tightly. He therefore establishes a new code, able to signal more states of the water in the watershed and to elicit more articulated responses (Table 4).

Table 4

(a) bulbs	(b) states of water or notions about the states of water	(c) responses of the destination
AB =	danger level	= water dumping
BC =	alarm level	= state of alarm
CD =	security level	= state of rest
AD =	insufficency level	= water make-up

The fact of having complicated the code has introduced *redundancy* into it: *two* signals are used in order to give *one* piece of information. But the redundancy has also provided a supply of messages, thus enabling the engineer to recognize a larger array of situations at the source and to establish a larger array of responses at the destination. As a matter of fact redundancy has also provided two more messages (AC and BD) that the engineer does not want to use and by means of which he could signal other states within the watershed (combined with appropriate additional responses): they could also be used in order to introduce synonymies (danger level being signalled both by AB and by AC). Anyway the code which has been adopted would seem to be an optimal one for an engineer's purposes and it would be unwise to complicate it too much. [3]

1.2. Systems and codes

Once the Watergate Model is established and the engineer has finished his project, a semiotician could ask him a few questions, such as: (i) what do you call a 'code'? the device by which you know that a given state in the watershed corresponds to a given set of illuminated bulbs? (ii) if so, does the mechanical apparatus possess a code, that is, does the destination recognize the 'meaning' of the received message or does it simply respond to mechanical stimuli? (iii) and is the fact that the destination responds to a given array of stimuli by means of a given sequence of responses based on a code? (iv) who is that code for? you or the apparatus? (v) and anyway, is it not true that many people would call the internal organization of the system of bulbs a code, irrespective of the state of things that can be signalled through its combinational articultation? (vi) finally, is not the fact that the water's infinite number of potential positions within the watershed have been segmented into four, and only four 'pertinent' states, sometimes called a 'code'?

One could carry on like this for a long time. But it seems unnecessary, since it will already be quite clear that under the name of /code/ the engineer is considering at least four different phenomena:

(a) A set of *signals* ruled by internal combinatory laws These signals are not necessarily connected or connectable with the state of the water that they conveyed in the Watergate Model, nor with the destination responses that the engineer decided they should be allowed to elicit. They could convey different notions about things and they could elicit a different set of responses: for instance they could be used to communicate the engineer's love for the next-watershed girl, or to persuade the girl to return his passion. Moreover these signals can travel through the channel without conveying or eliciting anything, simply in order to test the mechanical efficiency of the transmitting and receiving apparatuses. Finally they can be considered as a pure combinational structure that only takes the form of electric signals by chance, an interplay of empty positions and mutual oppositions, as will be seen in 1.3. They could be called a *syntactic system*.

(b) A set of states of the water which are taken into account as a set of *notions* about the state of the water and which can become (as happened in the Watergate Model) a set of possible communicative contents. As such, they can be conveyed by signals (bulbs), but are independent of them: in fact they could be conveyed by any other type of signal, such as flags, smoke, words, whistles, drums and so on. Let me call this set of 'contents' a *semantic system*.

(c) A set of possible *behavioral responses* on the part of the destination. These responses are independent of the (b) system: they could be released in order to make a washing-machine work or (supposing that the engineer was a 'mad scientist') to admit more water into the watershed just when danger level was reached, thereby provoking a flood. They can also be elicited by another (a) system: for example the destination can be instructed to evacuate the water only when, by means of a photoelectric cell, it detects an image of Fred Astaire kissing Ginger Rogers. Communicationally speaking the responses are the proofs that the message has been correctly received (and many philosophers maintain that 'meaning' is nothing more than this detectable disposition to respond to a given stimulus (see Morris, 1946)): but this side of the problem can be disregarded, for at present the responses are being considered independently of any conveying element.

(d) A *rule* coupling some items from the (a) system with some from the (b) or the (c) system. This rule establishes that a given array of syntactic signals refers back to a given state of the water, or to a given 'pertinent' segmentation of the semantic system; that both the syntactic and the semantic units, once coupled, may correspond to a given response; or that a given array of signals corresponds to a given response even though no semantic unit is supposed to be signalled; and so on.

Only this complex form of rule may properly be called a '*code*'. Nevertheless in many contexts the term /code/ covers not only the phenomenon (d) — as in the case of the Morse code — but also the notion of purely combinational systems such as (a), (b) and (c). For instance, the so-called 'phonological code' is a system like (a); the so-called 'genetic code' seems to be a system like (c); the so-called 'code of kinship' is either an underlying combinational system like (a) or a system of pertinent parenthood units very similar to (b).

Since this homonymy has empirical roots and can in some circumstances prove itself very useful, I do not want to challenge it. But in order to avoid the considerable theoretical damage that its presence can produce, one must clearly distinguish the two kinds of so-called 'codes' that it confuses: I shall therefore call a system of elements such as the syntactic, semantic and behavioral ones outlined in (a), (b) and (c) an *s-code* (or code as system); whereas a rule coupling the items of one s-code with the items of another or several other s-codes, as outlined in (d), will simply be called a *code*.

S-codes are systems or 'structures' that can also subsist independently of any sort of significant or communicative purpose, and as such may be studied by information theory or by various types of generative grammar. They are made up of finite sets of elements oppositionally structured and governed by combinational rules that can generate both finite and infinite strings or chains of these elements. However, in the social sciences (as well as in some mathematical disciplines), such systems are almost always recognized or posited in order to show how one such system can convey all or some of the elements of another such system, the latter being to some extent correlated with the former (and vice versa). In other words these systems are usually taken into account only insofar as they constitute one of the planes of a correlational function called a 'code'.

Since an s-code deserves theoretical attention only when it is inserted within a significant or communicational framework (the code), the theoretical attention is focused on its intended purpose: therefore a non-significant system is called a 'code' by a sort of *metonymical* transference, being understood as part of a semiotic whole with which it shares some properties.

Thus an s-code is usually called a 'code' but this habit relies on a rhetorical convention that it would be wise to eliminate. On the contrary the term /s-code/ can be legitimately applied to the semiotic phenomena (a), (b) and (c) without any danger of rhetorical abuse since all of these are, technically speaking, 'systems', submitted to the same formal rules even though composed of very different elements; i.e. (a) electric signals; (b) notions about states of the world, (c) behavioral responses.

1.3. The s-code as structure

Taken independently of the other systems with which it can be correlated, an s-code is a *structure*; that is, a system (i) in which every value is established by positions and differences and (ii) which appears only when different phenomena are mutually compared with reference to the same system of relations. "That arrangement alone is structured which meets two conditions: that it be a system, ruled by an internal cohesiveness; and this cohesiveness, inaccessible to observation in an isolated system, be revealed in the study of transformations, through which the similar properties in apparently different systems are brought to light" (Lévi-Strauss, 1960).

In the Watergate Model systems (a), (b) and (c) are homologously structured. Let us consider system (a): there are four elements (A; B; C; D) which can be either present or absent:

$$A = 1000$$
$$B = 0100$$
$$C = 0010$$
$$D = 0001$$

The message they generate can be detected in the same way:

$$AB = 1100$$
$$CD = 0011$$
$$BC = 0110$$
$$AD = 1001$$

AB is recognizable because the order of its features is oppositionally different from that of BC, CD and AD and so on. Each element of the system can be submitted to substitution and commutation tests, and can be generated by the transformation of another element; furthermore the whole system could work equally well even if it organized four fruits, four animals or the four musketeers instead of four bulbs.

The (b) system relies upon the same structural mechanism. Taking 1 as the minimal pertinent unit of water, the increase of water from insufficiency to danger might follow a sort of 'iconic' progression whose opposite would be the regression represented by the (c) system, in which 0 represents the minimal pertinent unit of evacuated water:

(b)		(c)
(danger)	1111	0000 (evacuation)
(alarm)	1110	0001 (alarm)
(security)	1100	0011 (rest)
(insuff.)	1000	0111 (admission)

By the way, if an inverse symmetry appears between (b) and (c), this is because the two systems are in fact considered as balancing each other out; whereas the representation of the structural properties of the system (a) does not look homologous to the other two because the correspondence between the strings in (a) and the units of (b) and (c) was *arbitrarily* chosen. One could have chosen the message ABCD (IIII), in order to signal "danger" and to elicit "evacuation". But, as was noted in 1.1.3, this choice would have submitted the informational process to greater risk of noise. Since the three systems are not here considered according to their possible correlation, I am only concerned to show how each can, independently of the others, rely on the *same structural matrix*, this being able to generate different combinations following diverse combinational rules. When the formats of the three systems are compared, their differences and their potential for mutual transformation become clear, precisely because they have the same underlying structure.

The structural arrangement of a system has an important practical function and shows certain properties[4]. It makes a situation comprehensible and comparable to other situations, therefore preparing the way for a possible coding correlation. It arranges a repertoire of items as a structured whole in which each unit is differentiated from the others by means of a series of *binary exclusions*. Thus a system (or an s-code) has an *internal grammar* that is properly studied by the mathematics of information. The mathematics of information, in principle, has nothing to do with engineering the transmission of information, insofar as it only studies the statistical properties of an s-code. These statistical properties permit a correct and economic calculation as to the best transmission of information within a given informational situation, but the two aspects can be considered independently.

What is important, on the other hand, is that the elements of an informational 'grammar' explain the functioning not only of a syntactic system, but of every kind of structured system, such as for example a semantic or a behavioral one. What information theory does not explain is the functioning of a code as a correlating rule. In this sense information theory is neither a theory of signification nor a theory of communication but only a theory of the abstract combinational possibilities of an s-code.

1.4. Information, communication, signification

1.4.1. Some methodological distinctions

Let us summarize the state of the present methodological situation:

The term /information/ has two basic senses: (a) it means a statistical property of the source, in other words it designates the amount of information that *can be transmitted*; (b) it means a precise amount of selected information which *has actually been transmitted and received*. Information in sense (a) can be view as either (a, i) the information at one's disposal at a given natural source or (a, ii) the information at one's disposal once an s-code has reduced the equi-probability of that source. Information in sense (b) can be computationally studied either: as (b, i) the passage through a channel of signals which do not have any communicative function and are thus simply stimuli, or as (b, ii) the passage through a channel of signals which do have a communicational function, which — in other words — been coded as the vehicles of some content units.

Therefore we must take into account *four* different approaches to four different formal objects, namely:

(a, i) the results of a mathematical theory of information as a *structural theory of the statistical properties of a source* (see 1.4.2); this theory does not directly concern a semiotic approach except insofar as it leads to approach (a, ii);

(a, ii) the results of a mathematical theory of information as a *structural theory of the generative properties of an s-code* (see 1.4.3); such an approach is useful for semiotic purposes insofar as it provides the elements for a grammar of functives (see 2.1.);

(b, i) the results of studies in informational engineering concerning the *process whereby non-significant pieces of information are transmitted* as mere signals or stimuli (see 1.4.4); these studies do not directly concern a semiotic approach except insofar as they lead to approach (b, ii);

(b, ii) the result of studies in informational engineering concerning the *processes whereby significant pieces of information used for communicational purposes are transmitted* (see 1.4.5); such an approach is useful from a semiotic point of view insofar as it provides the elements for a theory of sign production (see chapter 3).

Thus a semiotic approach is principally interested in (a, ii) and (b, ii); it is also interested in (a, i) and (b, i) — these constituting the lower threshold of semiotics — inasmuch as the theory and the engineering of information offer it useful and more effective categories.

As will be shown in chapter 2, a theory of codes, which studies the way in which a system of type (a, ii) becomes the content plane of another system of the same type, will use categories such as 'meaning' or 'content'. These have nothing to do with the category of 'information', since information theory is not concerned with the contents that the units it deals with can convey but, at best, with the internal combinational properties of the system of conveyed units, insofar as this too is an s-code.[5]

1.4.2. Information at the source

According to sense (a, i) information is only the measure of the probability of an event within an equi-probable system. The probability is the ratio between the number of cases that turn out to be realized and the total number of possible cases. The relationship between a series of events and the series of probabilities connected to it is the relationship between an arithmetical progression and a geometrical one, the latter representing the binary logarithm of the former. Thus, given an event to be realized among n different probabilities of realization, the amount of information represented by the occurrence of that event, once it has been selected, is given by

$$\log n = x$$

In order to isolate that event, x binary choices are necessary and the realization of the event is worth x bits of information. In this sense the value 'information' cannot be identified with the possible content of that event when used as a communicational device. What counts is the number of alternatives necessary to define the event without ambiguity.

Nevertheless the event, inasmuch as it is selected, is already a detected piece of information, ready to be eventually transmitted, and in this sense it concerns theory (b, i) more specifically.

On the contrary, information in the sense (a, i) is not so much what is 'said' as what can be 'said'. Information represents the freedom of choice available in the possible selection of an event and therefore it is first of all *a statistical property of the source*. Information is the value of equi-probability among several combinational possibilities, a value which increases along with the number of possible choices: a system where not two or sixteen but millions of equi-probable events are involved is a highly informative system. Whoever selected an event from a source of this kind would receive many bits of information. Obviously the received information would represent a reduction, an impoverishment of that endless wealth of possible choices which existed at the source before the event was chosen.

Insofar as it measures the equi-probability of a uniform statistical distribution at the source, information — according to its theorists — is directly proportional to the 'entropy' of a system (Shannon and Weaver, 1949), since the entropy of a system is the state of equi-probability to which its elements tend. If information is sometimes defined as entropy and sometimes as 'neg-entropy' (and is therefore considered inversely proportional to the entropy) this is because in the former case information is understood in sense (a, i), while in the latter information is understood in sense (b, i), that is, information as a selected, transmitted and received piece of information.

1.4.3. Information of the s-code

Nevertheless in the preceding pages information has instead appeared to be the measure of freedom of choice provided by the organized structure known as an s-code. And in the Watergate Model the s-code appeared as a reductive network, superimposed on the infinite array of events that could have taken place within the watershed in order to isolate a few pertinent events.

I shall now try to demonstrate how such a reduction is usually due to a project for transmitting information (sense b, i), and how this project gives rise to an s-code that can in itself be considered *a new type of source* endowed with particular informational properties — which are the object of a theory of s-codes in the sense (a, ii).

Examples of this kind of theory are represented by structural phonology and many types of distributional linguistics, as well as by some structural theories of semantic space (for instance Greimas, 1966, 1970), by theories of generative grammar (Chomsky & Miller, 1968; etc.) and by many theories of plot structure (Bremond, 1973) and of text-grammar (Van Dijk, 1970; Petöfi, 1972).

If all the letters of the alphabet available on a typewriter keyboard were to constitute a system of very high entropy, we would have a situation of maximum information. According to an example of Guilbaud's, we would say that, since in a typewriter page I can predict the existence of 25 lines, each with 60 spaces, and since the typewriter keyboard has (in this case) 42 keys — each of which can produce 2 characters — and since, with the addition of spacing (which has the value of a sign), the keyboard can thus produce 85 different signs, the result is the following problem: given that 25 lines of 60 spaces make 1,500 spaces available, how many different sequences of 1,500 spaces can be produced by choosing each of the 85 signs provided on the keyboard?

We can obtain the total number of messages of length L provided by a keyboard of C signs, by raising C to the power of L. In our case we know that we would be able to produce $85^{1,500}$ possible messages. This is the situation of equi-probability which exists at the source; the possible messages are expressed by a number of 2,895 digits.

But how many binary choices are necessary to single out one of the possible messages? An extremely large number, the transmission of which would require an impressive expense of time and energy.

The information as freedom of choice at the source would be noteworthy, but the possibility of transmitting this potential information so as to realize finished messages is very limited (Guilbaud, 1954). Here is where an s-code's regulative function comes into play.

The number of elements (the repertoire) is reduced, as are their possible combinations. Into the original situation of equi-probability is introduced a system of constraints: certain combinations are possible and others less so. The original information diminishes, the possibility of transmitting messages increases.

Shannon (1949) defines the information of a message, which implies N choices among h symbols, as:

$$I = N \log_2 h$$

(a formula which is reminiscent of that of entropy). A message selected from a very large number of symbols (among which an astronomical number of combinations may be possible) would consequently be very informative, but would be impossible to transmit because it would require too many binary choices.

Therefore, in order to make it possible to form and transmit messages, one must reduce the values of N and h. It is easier to transmit a message which is to provide information about a system of elements whose combinations are governed by a system of established rules. The fewer the alternatives, the easier the communication.

The s-code, with its criteria of order, introduces these communicative possibilities: the s-code represents a system of discrete states superimposed on the equi-probability of the original system, in order to make it more manageable.

However, it is not the statistical value 'information' which requires this element of order, but ease of transmission.

When the s-code is superimposed upon a source of extreme entropy like the typewriter keyboard, the possibilities that the latter offers for choice are reduced; as soon as I, possessing such an s-code as the English grammar, begin to write, the source possesses a lesser entropy. In other words the keyboard cannot produce all of the $85^{1,500}$ messages that are possible on one page, but a much smaller number, taken from rules of probability, which correspond to a system of expectations, and are therefore much more predictable. Even though, of course, the number of possible messages on a typed page is still very high, nevertheless the system of rules introduced by the s-code prevents my message from containing a sequence of letters such as /Wxwxscxwxscxwxx/ (except in the case of metalinguistic formulations such as the present one).

1.4.4. Physical transmission of information

Given, for instance, the syntactic system of signals in the Watergate Model, the engineer had a set of distinctive features (A, B, C, D) to combine in order to produce as many pertinent larger units (messages like AB) as possible[6].

Since the probability of the occurrence of a given feature among four is 1/4 and since the probability of the co-occurrence of two features is 1/16, the engineer had at his disposal (as shown in 1.1) sixteen possible messages, each of them amounting to 4 bits of information. This system constitutes a convenient reduction of the information possible at the source (so that the engineer no longer has to control and to predict an infinite set of states of the water), and is at the same time a rich (although reduced) source of equi-probabilities. Nevertheless we have already seen that the acceptance of all of the 16 possible messages would have led to many ambiguous situations. The engineer has therefore thoroughly reduced his field of probabilities, selecting as pertinent only four states of the water (as well as four mechanical responses and four conveying signals). By reducing the number of probabilities in his syntactic system, the engineer has also reduced the number of events he can detect at the source. The s-code of signals, entailing two other structurally homologous s-codes (semantic and behavioral system), has superimposed a restricted system of possible states on that larger one which an information theory in the sense (a, I) might have considered as a property of an indeterminate source. Now every message transmitted and received according to the rules of the syntactic system, even though it is always theoretically worth 4 bits, can, technically speaking, be selected by means of two alternative choices, granted that these are limited to four pre-selected combinations (AB, BC, CD, AD) and therefore 'costs' only 2 bits.

1.4.5. Communication

By means of the same structural simplification, the engineer has brought under semiotic control three different systems; and it is because of this that he has been able to correlate the elements of one system to the elements of the others, thus instituting a code. Certain technical communicative intentions (b, ii), relying on certain technical principles of the type(b, i), have led him, basing himself on the principles of (a, i), to establish systems of the type (a, ii) in order to set out a system of sign-functions called a 'code'[7].

This chapter may justifiably leave unexplained, regarding it as a pseudo-problem, the question of whether the engineer first produced three organized s-codes in order to correlate them within the framework of a code, or whether, step by step, he correlated scattered and unorganized units from different planes of reality, and then structured them into homologous systems. The option between these two hypotheses demands, in the case of the Watergate Model, a psychological study of the engineer or a biographical sketch; but for more complicated cases such as the natural languages, it demands a theory of the origins of language, a matter which has up to now been avoided by linguists. In the final analysis, what is needed is a theory of intelligence, which is not my particular concern in this context, even though a semiotic enquiry must continuously emphasize the entire range of its possible correlations with it.

What remains undisputed is that *pour cause* a code is continuously confused with the s-codes: whether the code has determined the format of the s-codes or vice versa, a code exists because the s-codes exist, and the s-codes exist because a code exists, has existed or has to exist. Signification encompasses the whole of cultural life, even at the lower threshold of semiotics.

                                    NOTES

    1. The following model is borrowed from De Mauro, 1966 (now in De Mauro, 1971). It is one of the clearest and most useful introductions to the problems of coding in semiotics.
    2. The absence of one of the signals is no longer a signal, as it was in the preceding case   (+A vs. -A),   for now the absence of one signal is the condition for the detected presence of the other. On the other hand, both their concurrent absence and their concurrent presence can be taken as synonymous devices, both of which reveal something wrong with the apparatus.
    3. Clearly from now on the code is valid even if the machine (whether by mistake or under the influence of a *malin genie*) *lies*: the signals are supposed to refer to *actual* states of the water but what they convey are not actual states, but *notions* about actual states.
    4. A problem appears at this point: is structure, thus defined, an *objective reality* or an *operational hypothesis*? In the following pages the term 'structure' will be used in accordance with the following epistemological presupposition: a structure is a model built and *posited* in order to standardize diverse phenomena from a unified point of view. One is entitled to suspect that, as long as these simplifying models succeed in explaining

many phenomena, they may well reproduce some 'natural' order or reflect some 'universal' functioning of the human mind. The methodological fault it seems to me important to avoid is the *ultimate* assumption that, when succeeding in explaining some phenomena by unified structural models, one has grasped the format of the world (or of the human mind, or of social mechanisms) as an ontological *datum*. For arguments against this kind of *ontological* structuralism see Eco, 1968.

5. Thus it is correct to say that in the Watergate Model the destination apparatus does not rely on a code, that is, does not receive any communication, and therefore does not 'understand' any sign-function. For the destination apparatus is the formal object of a theory (b, i) which studies the amount of stimuli which pass through a channel and arrive at a destination. On the contrary the engineer who has established the model is also concerned with a theory (b, ii) according to which — as far as he is concerned — signals convey contents and are therefore signs. The same happens for the so-called 'genetic code'. It is the object of a theory of both types (a, i) and (b, i); it only could be the object of a theory of type (b, ii) for God or for any other being able to design a system of transmission of genetic information. As a matter of fact the description the geneticists give of genetic phenomena, superimposing an explanatory structure on an imprecise array of biological processes, is an s-code: therefore the 'genetic code' can be the object of a theory of the type (a, ii) thus allowing metaphorical and didactic explanation of the type (b, ii). See note 4 and the discussion in 0.7. As to a semiotic 'reading' of the genetic code see also Grassi, 1972.

6. In linguistics, features such as A, B, C, D are elements of *second articulation*, devoid of meaning (like the phonemes in verbal language), that combine in order to form elements of *first articulation* (such as AB), endowed with meaning (like the morphemes — or *monèmes* in Martinet's sense). According to Hjelmslev, when pertinent and non-significant features such as A, B, C, D are elements of a non-verbal system, they can be called *'figurae'*.

7. The ambiguous relation between source, s-code, and code arises because an s-code is posited in order to enable some syntactic units to convey semantic units that are supposed to coincide with events happening at a given source. In this sense a syntactic code is so strongly conditioned by its final purpose (and a semantic system so heavily marked by its supposed capacity to reflect what actually happens in the world), that it is easy to understand (though less so to justify) why all three formal objects of the three diverse theories are naively called 'code' *tout court*.

2: THEORY OF CODES

2.1. The sign-function

When a code apportions the elements of a conveying system to the elements of a conveyed system, the former becomes the expression of the latter and the latter becomes the content of the former. A sign-function arises when an expression is correlated to a content, both the correlated elements being the functives of such a correlation.

We are now in a position to recognize the difference between a signal and a sign. A signal is a pertinent unit of a system that may be an expression system ordered to a content, but could also be a physical system without any semiotic purpose; as such it is studied by information theory in the stricter sense of the term. A signal can be a stimulus that does not mean anything but causes or elicits something; however, when used as the recognized *antecedent* of a foreseen *consequent* it may be viewed as a sign, inasmuch as it stands for its consequent (as far as the sender is concerned). On the other hand a sign is always an element of an *expression plane* conventionally correlated to one (or several) elements of a *content plane*.

Every time there is a correlation of this kind, recognized by a human society, there is a sign. Only in this sense is it possible to accept Saussure's definition according to which a sign is the correspondence between a signifier and a signified. This assumption entails some consequences: a) *a sign is not a physical entity*, the physical entity being at most the concrete occurrence of the expressive pertinent element; b) *a sign is not a fixed semiotic entity* but rather the meeting ground for independent elements (coming from two different systems of two different planes and meeting on the basis of a coding correlation).

Properly speaking there are not signs, but only *sign-functions*. Hjelmslev remarked that "it appears more appropriate to use the word sign as the name for the unit consisting of content form and the expression-form and established by the solidarity that we have called the sign-function" (1943:58). A sign-function is realized when two *functives* (expression and content) enter into a mutual correlation; the same functive can also enter into another correlation, thus becoming a different functive and therefore giving rise to a new sign-function. Thus signs are the provisional result of coding rules which establish *transitory* correlations of elements, each of these elements being entitled to enter — under given coded circumstances — into another correlation and thus form a new sign.

Take for instance the expression item /plane/: the English language provides many content items for it, i.e. «carpentry tool» or «level» or «aircraft». In this sense we are faced with three sign-functions: (plane=X), (plane=Y) and (plane=K).

Moreover, if one accepts a somewhat widespread semiotic theory which maintains that the expressive function is not undertaken by the 'morpheme' or the 'word' but by a more complex expression (see Buyssens, 1943; Prieto, 1964; De Mauro, 1970), one might say that the expression /give me it/ — which acquires many different contents depending on the presuppositions that it involves — gives rise to an impressive number of signs (except that in this case the correlation between expression and content is not established by the code alone but by a complex interpretative contextual 'reading').

One can then maintain that it is not true that a code organizes signs; it is more correct to say that codes provide the rules which *generate* signs as concrete occurrences in communicative intercourse. Therefore the classical notion of 'sign' *dissolves* itself into a highly complex network of changing relationships. Semiotics suggests a sort of molecular landscape in which what we are accustomed to recognize as everyday forms turn out to be the result of transitory chemical aggregations and so-called 'things' are only the surface appearance assumed by an underlying network of more elementary units. Or rather, semiotics gives us a sort of photomechanical explanation of semiosis, revealing that where we thought we saw images there were only strategically arranged aggregations of black and white points, alternations of presence and absence, the insignificant basic features of a raster, sometimes differentiated in shape, position and chromatic intensity. Semiotics, like musical theory, states that where we recognize familiar melodies there is only a sophisticated intertwining of intervals and notes, and where we perceive notes there are only a bunch of formants.

2.2. Expression and content

Let us return to the Watergate Model (chapter 1) and imagine that the destination is no longer a mechanical apparatus but the engineer himself, who receives information about the situation within the watershed and who knows that he must respond to a given communication about the state of the water by activating certain levers or switching certain knobs. The code outlined in 1.1 remains unchanged.

If one examines the internal articulation of the signs provided by the code, one can analyze them in this way: (i) a continuum of physical possibilities that is used as the unformed material from which the engineer obtains discrete elements to be used as expressive devices; (ii) token expressive devices such as A, B, C, D plus their combinations (AB, BC, CD, AD) which represent elements selected from the original material; (iii) a system of empty positions, a structure, by virtue of which the token expressive devices assume a positional and oppositional nature; (iv) both (ii) and (iii) chosen as the expression planes of a content plane represented by both (v) and (vi); (v) a system of empty positions, a structure, by virtue of which some token content units will assume a positional and oppositional nature; (vi) token content units such as «danger level», «security level» and so on, which represent selected elements 'cut' from an imprecise continuum of facts or notions; (vii) a continuum of physical possibilities, psychic events, behaviors and thoughts to which the system (v) has given an order, selecting a structured set of recognizable semantic units (see Table 5).

Thus (a) a code establishes the correlation of an expression plane (in its purely formal and systematic aspect) with a content plane (in its purely formal and systematic aspect); (b) a sign-function establishes the correlation of an abstract element of the expression system with an abstract element of the content system; (c) in this way a code establishes general *types*, therefore producing the rule which generates concrete *tokens*, i.e., signs such as usually

Table 5

	Expression Plane		Content Plane		
Continuum	Units	System	System	Units	Continuum
Light, electric phenomena	AB	1100	1111	danger level	the unshaped continuum of the position of the water along with everything one can think about it
	BC	0110	1110	alarm level	
	CD	0011	1100	security level	
	AD	1001	1000	insufficiency	
Non-semiotic matter	↑ sign-function ↑ token sign ↑			↑	Non-semiotic matter

occur in communicative processes; (d) both the continua represent elements which precede the semiotic correlation and with which semiotics is not concerned (they are respectively beyond the lower and the upper thresholds of semiotics). In the Watergate Model semiotics is not concerned with electrical laws, nor with the electronic 'stuff' which allows us to 'make' electric signals; it is only interested in the selected signals insofar as they convey some content. In the same way semiotics is not concerned with the physics of the differing states of water, but only with the fact that a semantic system has organized notions about a possible state of water. Obviously a science like physics, being interested in defining and studying water and its states, needs a specific semiotic treatment of its own object: in this sense, when defining such entities as 'atoms', 'molecules', 'H_2O' and so on, physics segments its own continuum into a specific semantic field to be expressed by vehicular units which constitute the syntactic system of physics. It means, as Hjelmslev said, that, if we consider the sign-function in the following way:

$$\text{Content} \quad \frac{\text{(purport)}}{\dfrac{\text{substance}}{\text{form}}}$$

$$\text{Expression} \quad \dfrac{\dfrac{\text{form}}{\text{substance}}}{\text{(purport)}}$$

the 'purport' "remains, each time, substance for a new form". This is the case, for instance, when a physicist considers the wave-lengths of each bulb in the Watergate Model in terms of the substantial units of a wave-length system that semiotics had not taken into account, because it was only directly concerned with perceptible differences of color, or indeed with the respective positions of the bulbs.

If by 'purport' one means 'continuum', 'matter' or 'stuff', then one may agree with Hjelmslev when he says that "the description of purport, in respect of both the linguistic expression and the linguistic content, may in all essentials be thought of as belonging partly to the sphere of physics and partly to that of (social) anthropology . . . . Consequently for both planes both a physical and a phenomenological description of the purport should be required" (1943:77-78).

In the Watergate Model the signals AB, BC etc. are expression-substance, organized by an expression-form and conveying notions such as «danger level» which are content-substance organized by a content-form. The electric stuff with which the signals are made is an expression-purport studied by physics, while the states of water to which the units of the semantic system refer are content-purport studied by hydrography or some other discipline; the possible responses, organized as a semantic system on the content plane of another code, are the object of psychology or some other behavioral science.

The model that I am proposing here represents, however, an *interpretation* of Hjelmslev's. For example, in Hjelmslev the word /purport/ (which translates the Danish word /mening/) is pretty misleading. While the Hjelmslevian context suggests that its proper sense is that of «matter»[1] (he frequently calls it "stuff" or "continuum"), the word used has shades of decidedly different concepts. The notion of substance is equally ambiguous: while in the case of the expression substances are undoubtedly material occurrences (tokens) of the type provided by the form (sounds, lights, lines on a paper, and so on), in the case of the content Hjelmslev repeatedly suggests the idea that substances are the *things* isolated by linguistic form. For the sake of theoretical purity I shall rather consider them as token semantic units generated by the semantic system (see 2.6).

While the Hjelmslevian model in spite of its apparently Byzantine complexity is perfectly suitable for the purposes of a theory of the codes, it has to be simplified within the framework of that part of the theory of sign production which constitutes communication theory. In this perspective the sign-function is nothing more than the correspondence between a signifier

Table 6

Formal Model	Theory of Codes	Theory of Communication	Theory of Mentions	Theory of Communicational Acts
Continuum	Experience	Source	World	Addressee
posited units	interpreted units (tokens) — Content	Meaning — Message	Proposition — Mentioning	Message — Pragmatic Processes
system of empty positions	semantic system (types) — Content	Meaning — Message	Proposition — Mentioning	Message — Pragmatic Processes
system of empty positions	syntactic system (types) — Expression	Sign-vehicle — Message	Sentence	Message
posited units	produced units (tokens) — Expression	Sign-vehicle — Message	Sentence	Message
Continuum	Stuff	Channel	Utterance	Sender

Correlation between functives

and a signified, or between a *sign-vehicle* and a *meaning*; a message is nothing more than such a correspondence as realized during a transmission process. When on the other hand a theory of sign production concerns itself with the elaboration of sign-functions as complex as aesthetic texts, the six-fold division of Hjelmslev's model will come into its own (see 3.7).

There is, finally, another aspect of the theory of sign production represented by the emission of sentences aiming to indicate something true or false, in other words an actual state of the world; this aspect of sign production (and interpretation) is studied by a theory of mentions or referring acts. In this perspective the content-purport (or the content-continuum) comes into play, because the task of such a theory is to secure the correspondence between a given content conveyed by an expression and a real and actual state of the world (see 3.1.2). Therefore the proposed Hjelmslev-like model of a sign-function, and of its underlying code, should be differently applied within different disciplinary contexts (see Table 6).

This comparative model allows a rewriting of 'informational' categories in stricter semiotic terms; the source is nothing more than the content-continuum, while the channel is the expression-continuum; the signal becomes a token-functive (expression); the message is a twofold entity, that is, a token-sign-function. Both source and channel lie beyond the reach of a theory of codes but, as will be shown in ch. 3, they can be taken into account within the framework of a theory of sign production. The aesthetic text is a system of messages in which the particular treatment of the channel (that is of the stuff of which sign-vehicles are made) becomes pertinent.

In a sentence mentioning something, that is, referring to an actual state of the world, what happens at the source is the so-called 'referent' (see 2.5).

As for the sender and the addressee, they are of no concern to a theory of codes though they do turn out to be relevant within the framework of that chapter of a theory of sign production which deals with these communicational acts that the philosophy of verbal language has called "speech acts" (see 3.1.).

2.3. Denotation and connotation

When speaking about the destination apparatus of the Watergate Model I said that a given signal could instantaneously convey both information on the state of the water and an instruction for the destination. Since the engineer as a human being has been substituted for the destination apparatus, one has now to put the question in another way: the engineer receives information about a given state of the water and therefore, according to previous conventions, knows (or decides) that he must respond in a given way.

In this sense the behavioral response is not elicited by a signal-stimulus: it is *signified* (or imperatively communicated) by the fact that a given state of water has been signified. There arises a signification conveyed by a previous signification, which gives rise to a superelevation of codes of the following type:

Table 7

Expression		Content
Expression	Content	
AB = danger level		= evacuation of water
BC = alarm level		= state of alarm
CD = security level		= state of rest
AD = insufficiency		= admission of water

Such a superelevation of codes is what Hjelmslev defined as a *connotative semiotics*, whose form is:

Expression		Content
Expression	Content	

There is a connotative semiotics when there is a semiotics whose expression plane is another semiotics. In the above example the content of the former signification (along with the units that conveyed it) becomes the expression of a further content. Thus the expression AB *denotes* «danger level» and *connotes* «evacuation».

The difference between denotation and connotation is not (as many authors maintain) the difference between 'univocal' and 'vague' signification, or between 'referential' and 'emotional' communication, and so on. What constitutes a connotation as such is the connotative code which establishes it; the characteristic of a connotative code is the fact that the further signification conventionally relies on a primary one (the engineer knows that he must evacuate the water because he knows that the water has reached the danger level). Obviously one could have instructed an addressee in such a way that the message AB would convey to him the meaning «evacuation», without his knowing anything about a system subdividing the water into four levels. In this case the code would have been a denotative one and the relation between AB and «evacuation» would have been a straightforward denotation. So the difference between denotation and connotation is only due to a coding convention, irrespective of the fact that connotations are frequently less stable than denotations: the stability concerns the force and the duration of the coding convention, but once the convention has been established, the connotation is the stable functive of a sign-function of which the underlying functive is another sign-function.

A connotative code, insofar as it relies on a more basic one, can be called a *subcode*.

One may also suppose that stable social convention, a scholarly training, a system of expectations deeply rooted in the patrimony of common opinions that the engineer shares, make the first denotative code correlated with a third connoted system. Suppose that, for instance, the engineer knows that danger level means «actual flood», alarm level means «flood menace» and so on, down to the connotation of «drought» conveyed by the signification of insufficiency. Another connoted system is added to the first one, and the first denotative code allows its sign-functions to entertain a double connotative sign-function. Thus AB denotes «danger level» and connotes both «evacuation» and «flood» — 'both' rather than 'either'. As a matter of fact the two connotations are not mutually exclusive and the format of the double connotative coding is as follows:

content	expression	expression	content
	content	expression	content	
		expression	content		

Whether the engineer chooses to detect or grasp one or the other of the connotations; whether he grasps both; whether, grasping only the connotation of «flood», he forgets to evacuate the water and shifts to other more or less emotional kinds of connotation or of free association; these and many other problems do not concern a theory of codes. They are commonly considered a matter of pragmatics[2] and will be dealt with at most within the framework of a theory of sign production. What is important here is that codes provide the conditions for a complex interplay of sign-functions.

A theory of codes should rather be concerned to state to what degree the superelevation of connotation can be made possible; how much its overlapping of senses may produce a maze-like network of intertwined sign-functions; and either this maze-like situation can constitute the object of a semiotic structural description, or it produces a sort of topological knot that a theory of codes can define but cannot structurally reproduce by means of a finite model. All this will be discussed in 2.12 and 2.13.

2.4. Message and text

In any case there is a distinction regarding a theory of sign production that must be anticipated when speaking about a theory of codes, for it helps one to better establish what is meant by 'code'. When the engineer received the sign-vehicle AB, did he get one or more messages?

Since there are at least three codes, a denotative one and two connotative ones, if all three are referred to when interpreting the sign-vehicle, then the engineer has got three messages, namely: (i) «the water has reached danger level»; (ii) «you must activate the evacuation lever»; (iii) «there is a flood». Thus a single sign-vehicle, insofar as several codes make it become the functive of several sign-functions (although connotatively linked), can become the expression of several contents, and produce a complex discourse such as: «Since water has reached the danger level, you must evacuate it, otherwise there will be a flood». I am not saying that a single code can produce many messages, one after the other, for this is a mere truism; I am not saying that the contents of many messages can be conveyed by the same kind of sign-vehicle, according to diverse codes, for this too is a truism; I am saying that usually a single sign-vehicle conveys many intertwined contents and therefore what is commonly called a 'message' is in fact a *text* whose content is a multilevelled *discourse*.

Metz (1970) has advanced the hypothesis that in every case of communication (except maybe some rare cases of a very elementary and univocal type) we are not dealing with a message but with a *text*. A text represents the result of the coexistence of many codes (or, at least, or many subcodes). Metz gives the example of the expression /*voulez vous tenir ceci, s'il vous plaît?*/ and recognizes that in this simple phrase there are at least two codes at work: the first being the plain denotative code of the French language and the other a French *courtoisie* code. Without the latter we are unable to understand the real meaning of /*s'il vous plaît*/: a purely denotative interpretation of the expression would give a rather odd result.

In Metz's example the plurality of codes works, so to speak, horizontally. The addressee decodes the whole phrase with reference to one code, and then the second half with reference to another. But in our example (the signal AB) the plurality of the codes works, so to speak, vertically, superimposing many levels of signification upon the first and basic one.

2.5. Content and referent

2.5.1. The referential fallacy

Finally we face a problem which is mainly the concern of a theory of sign production and in particular a theory of mentions; but it is important to consider it at this point because its shadowy presence could disturb the proper development of a theory of codes. The problem in question is that of the *referent*, in other words the problem of the possible states of the world supposedly corresponding to the content of a sign-function. Although of considerable importance within its proper domain, the notion of 'referent' has most unfortunate results within the framework of a theory of codes, and to underestimate its malignant influence leads to a *referential fallacy*.

One may easily admit that the signs transmitted through the Watergate Model have a corresponding 'object', that is, the state of the water at the source. Likewise, one may admit that if the water (along with its possible states) were not there, at the source, then the entire Watergate Model would be without its *raison d'être*. Therefore the 'actual' water would seem to be a necessary condition for the entire model. But even though it certainly was a necessary condition for the *design* of the model, it is not a necessary condition for its semiotic *functioning*.

Since the model has been established, and relies on one or more given codes, a message like AB would work as a message (or a text) even if the water at the source actually was in another position, or if there was no water in the watershed, or if the watershed was the invention of a *malin génie*. It is not even necessary to disturb Descartes' *malin génie*; it is enough that somebody at the source, manipulating the transmitting device, should decide *to lie*. The semiotic functioning, the semantic import of the message AB, and the behavioral response of the addressee would not change at all. The same observations are also valid in many other cases. As was suggested in 0.1.3., if a liar pretends to be sick by behaving in a certain way, the semiotic functioning of this behavior can be analyzed irrespective of the fact that he is actually lying.

Every time there is possibility of lying, there is a sign-function: which is to signify (and then to communicate) something to which no real state of things corresponds. A theory of codes must study everything that can be used in order to lie. The possibility of lying is the *proprium* of semiosis just as (for the Schoolmen) the possibility of laughing was the *proprium* of Man as *animal rationale*.

Every time there is a lie there is signification. Every time there is signification there is the possibility of using it in order to lie. If this is true (and it is methodologically necessary to maintain that it is true) then semiotics has found a new threshold: between *conditions of signification* and *conditions of truth*, in other words the threshold between an *intensional* and an *extensional* semantics.

A theory of codes is concerned with an intensional semantics while the problems regarding the extension of an expression are bound up with a theory of t-values or with a theory of mentions. This threshold, however, is an 'internal' one, and it must only be considered, according to the present state of the art, a methodological boundary.

2.5.2. *Sinn* and *Bedeutung*

The semiotic study of content is often complicated by recourse to an over-simplified diagram which has rigidified the problem in an unfortunate way. The diagram in question is the well-known triangle, diffused in its most common form by Ogden and Richards (1923):

(1)

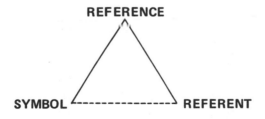

The triangle *apparently* translates Peirce's:

(2)

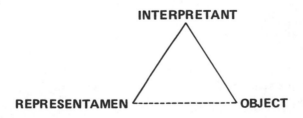

and is often considered to be equivalent to Frege's (1892):
(3)

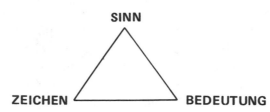

The first point to be made absolutely clear is that such triangles can indeed be useful in discussing a theory of sign production and particularly a theory of 'mentioning' (see 3.3), but they become something of an embarrassment when studying the problem of codes. As a matter of fact a model of a sign-function (such as the Saussurean dichotomy *'significant-signifié'* and the Hjelmslevian model outlined in 2.2) only concerns the left side of triangles (1) and (2), and can be of relevance to the whole of triangle (3) if and only if the notion of *'Bedeutung'* is not taken as strictly extensional.

The semiotics of Saussure and Peirce is a theory of the conventional (or at any rate strictly semiosical) relation between symbol and reference (or meaning) and between a sign and the series of its interpretants (see 2.7). Objects are not considered within Saussure's linguistics and are considered within Peirce's theoretical framework only when discussing particular types of signs such as icons and indices (for the elimination of the object within the framework of a theory of codes, even in such cases see 2.6. and 3.5.). Objects can be considered in the light of a 'narrow' Fregean reading only when the *Bedeutung* is understood as the real and actual object to which the sign can refer: inasmuch as the *Bedeutung* is regarded as a 'class' of actual and possible objects, not a 'token' but a 'type' object, it becomes very akin to the content in the sense that will be outlined in 2.6. From this intensional point of view the *Bedeutung* becomes something to be studied by a theory of interpretants (see 2.7).

It must be absolutely clear that the following argument has nothing to do with a theory of the t-values of an expression, that is, with an extensional semantics; within this framework, even if the meaning of an expression is independent of the actual presence of the objects it refers to, the verification of the actual presence of these objects (or states of the world) is necessary in order to satisfy the t-value of the given expression and thus to consider it within the framework of propositional calculus. But, from the point of view of the functioning of a code (or many codes), the referent must be excluded as an intrusive and jeopardizing presence which compromises the theory's theoretical purity. Thus, even when the referent could be the object named or designated by the expression when language is used in order to mention something, one must nonetheless maintain that an expression does not, in principle, designate any object, but on the contrary *conveys a cultural content*. To say that /Walter Scott/ and /the author of *Waverley*/ are two expressions that have the same *Bedeutung* but two *Sinn* concerns a theory of sign-function only insofar as: (i) the *Bedeutung* is intended as the definition of a historical entity that a culture recognizes as a single person, and is therefore a denoted content; (ii) the *Sinn* is a particular way of considering a given content, according to other cultural conventions, thereby including within one's consideration some of the connoted contents of the first denoted content.

If one assumes that the *Bedeutung* is an actual state of the world, whose verification validates the sign, one must ask oneself how this state of the world is usually grasped or analyzed, how its existence is defined or demonstrated when the sign-function is decoded. It will quickly be seen that, in order to know something about the *Bedeutung*, one must indicate it through another expression, and so on; as Peirce said, a sign can be explained only through another sign. Thus the *Bedeutung* is grasped through a series of its *Sinn*, and in this sense it is very imprudent to assume that the *Sinn* can be recognized as appertaining to the same *Bedeutung*, since it is the *Bedeutung* which is defined by the *Sinn* and not vice versa.

The central problem of the present chapter arises from the fact that 'meaning' really is a very complicated matter, but not in the way that the above triangles would suggest [3]. To say that a sign-vehicle necessarily corresponds to an actual object is a distinctly naive attitude and one that even a theory of t-values is none too eager to accept. The objection to it is well known: there exist sign-vehicles which refer to non-existent entities such as 'unicorn' or 'mermaid'. In these cases, a theory of t-values prefers to speak of terms with 'null-extention' (Goodman 1949) or of 'possible worlds' (Lewis, 1969).

Within the framework of a theory of codes it is unnecessary to resort to the notion of extension, nor to that of possible worlds; the codes, insofar as they are accepted by a society, set up a 'cultural' world which is neither actual nor possible in the ontological sense; its existence is linked to a cultural order, which is the way in which a society thinks, speaks and, while speaking, explains the 'purport' of its thought through other thoughts. Since it is through thinking and speaking that a society develops, expands or collapses, even when dealing with 'impossible' worlds (i.e. aesthetic texts, ideological statements), a theory of codes is very much concerned with the format of such 'cultural' worlds, and faces the basic problem of how *to touch* contents.

In order to understand the history of Christian theology, it is not necessary to know whether a specific actual phenomenon corresponds to the word /transubstantiation/ (even though for many people this belief was vitally important). But it is necessary to know which cultural unit (what intensionally analyzable set of cultural properties) corresponded to the content of that word.

The semiotic object of a semantics is the *content*, not the referent, and the content has to be defined as a *cultural unit* (or as a cluster or a system of interconnected cultural units). The fact that for many people /transubstantiation/ corresponded to an event or a thing may be grasped semiotically by maintaining that this event or thing was explicable in terms of cultural units. Otherwise there would never have been anything like a theological discussion and believers would have continued to receive the Holy Communion without wondering about those who did not believe in it. Whereas it was, on the contrary, necessary to conceive a world so organized that a cultural unit corresponding to /transubstantiation/ could find a place within it, i.e. could be a precisely segmented portion of the content of a given cultural background.

2.5.3. The extensional fallacy

The referential fallacy consists in assuming that the 'meaning' of a sign-vehicle has something to do with its corresponding object. Since the t-value theorists do not share this naive assumption, one could say that they do not concern themselves with the problem of the correspondence between signs and states of the world, either when discussing the meaning of a sign-vehicle such as /dog/ or /unicorn/, or when discussing the possible referent of a *description* such as /a glass of whisky and soda/ or /the King of France/. They are, on the other hand, concerned with the *extension of a sentence* or of its corresponding *proposition*: therefore two sentences like /all dogs are animals/ and /all dogs have four legs/ correspond to an actual state of the world and are to be considered true if and only if dogs really are animals and if they really have four legs. Since the theory of codes is only interested in sign-functions and the rules of their possible combination, sentences should only be a matter of sign production. Nevertheless there is a way in which the

extensional approach may disturb a theory of codes — thus producing an
extensional fallacy.

Let me anticipate a classification of various types of sentences
(following Katz, 1972) that should more properly be considered in ch. 3. If
sentences are considered as the vehicular form of propositions they can
convey various kinds of propositions:

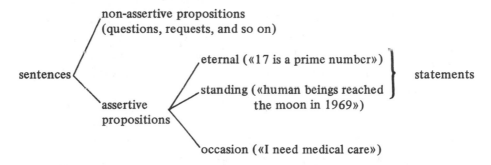

Even though 'standing' propositions rely on indexical elements (as do the
'occasion' ones) they can be considered 'statements' (along with 'eternal'
propositions). The extension of both 'standing' and 'occasion' propositions
can be detected; they therefore possess a t-value.

What renders statements of some purport to a theory of codes is the
fact that all or at least the greater part of them can be defined (see 3.2) as
semiotic statements, that is, judgments which attribute to a given expression
the content or the contents that one or several codes usually and
conventionally assign to it. Thus all (or at least many) statements are not to
be considered as the result of sign production, but rather as the proper object
of a theory of codes.

Since a theory of codes does not consider extension as one of its
categories (and similarly does not take referents into account) it is able to
consider, for instance, the so-called 'eternal propositions' while disregarding
their extensional value. If it does not disregard this factor, it falls, when
dealing with code theory, into the extensional fallacy. Since, in other words,
a theory of codes is interested in the definition of content as the functive of a
sign-function and as a unit of a semantic system, the fact of assuming (as a
theory of t-values correctly does) that $/p \supset q/$ is True if and only if (i) p and q
are both True; (ii) p is False and q is True; (iii) both p and q are False, does
not help one to make clear the notion of 'meaning'.

Suppose that one posits the following implication: /if Napoleon is an
elephant then Paris is the capital of France/. It is well known that, according

to the rules of sentential calculus, this implication is true even though Napoleon is not an elephant, and would be so even if Napoleon were an elephant, just as long as Paris is the capital of France, (it is also True if both the propositions are False). The propositional calculator would find nothing to laugh about in this implication: but the code theorist may be justifiably amused. The same would happen (to take another example, since propositions concerning proper names seem to have rather peculiar properties) if one said /if snow is made with peanut butter then dogs are animals/. The semiotician will laugh because it is rather difficult to imagine something which does not fit in with the common cultural notion of Napoleon or snow. Every English speaker can speak about snow and understand sentences concerning snow because he possesses a cultural competence assigning to the content-unit «snow» certain properties which do not include that of being made with peanut butter. The laughing response is the side-effect of a misuse of the code, or of a contradiction posited within the code. But it is both authorized and elicited by the code's existence. The code does not stop us from understanding a proposition which is commonly believed to be false. It allows us to understand it and to understand that it is 'culturally' false. It is possible that in a possible world or in our future world, because of the increasing water pollution, snow could be exposed to such an ecological tragedy. But even though it happened, the fact would still be semiotically ridiculous. Obviously in the latter case this sense of the ridiculous will quickly disappear, and a sense of fear will take its place. But both fear and amusement can, in this sense, be considered as the consequence of a particular contradiction within the code [4].

One laughs because even though one realizes that the situation is unthinkable, one understands the meaning of the sentence. One feels fear because, even though one realizes that the situation is possible, one does not like to accept such an alarming semantic organization of one's experience. The sentence appears to be ridiculously or tragically meaningful insofar as its meaning conflicts with the meaning-rules we possess. Its meaning is unacceptable not because it is incomprehensible but because − if accepted − it implies the restructurization of our codes.

The Schoolmen said that the *proprium* of human beings is to be *ridens*. Enlarging the remarks made in 2.5.1, we can now say that not only is semiotics the science of everything subject to the lie: *it is also the science of everything subject to comic or tragic distortion*. This definition covers the entire range of natural languages. An extensional semantics cannot help semiotics insofar as it does not deal with lying and laughing: logically speaking a proposition labelled as false can be 'comic' without having any effect on the correctness of the calculus. To explain the comic effect means to elaborate a complete intensional semantics, or a theory of content. To explain the semiotic import of the lie means to understand why and how a lie (a false statement) is semiotically relevant irrespective of the truth or the falsity of that statement.

Clearly it *cannot* be said that there do *not* exist statements to which we are induced to give the values of True or False, by comparing them to the 'real' events which we experience; and it *cannot* be said that the addressee of a message does *not* refer the message to the 'things' of which it speaks and about which he has been told (given that he is told about 'things').

Whoever receives the message /your house has burned down/ probably thinks of his house and if he is wise tries to check as to whether the statement is true or false, even if he is a code theorist who distrusts extensions. But these two facts are not pertinent to a theory of codes, which should only study the conditions under which the message may be communicated and comprehended. The reasons why a message acquires sense are independent of the fact that the addressee may have a house which is *actually* burning. The 'pragmatic' response to signals which produce behavior (the addressee running home) is independent of the truth or falsity of the assertion, as are all possible *translations* of the message (the addressee drawing a house for an illiterate friend).

Given two sentences such as /Napoleon died at Saint Helena on May 5, 1821/ and /Ulysses reconquered the kingdom by killing all the Proci/ it is irrelevant to a code theory to know that *historically speaking* the former is true and the latter is false [5]. This does not merely mean, as Carnap would say, that the analysis of their intensions must precede the verification of their extension. From the point of view of a code theory what matters is that: (a) in our culture there exist codes such as that through which the first sentence is understood, is studied in school and connotes «historical truth»; (b) in classical Greek society there existed codes such as that through which the second sentence was understood, was studied in school and connoted «historical truth». The fact that for us the second sentence connotes «legend» is semiotically analogous to the fact that it could yet be proven in some future civilization, on the basis of as yet unknown (or false) documents, that Napoleon died in a different place on a different day (or that he never existed). *Semiotics is mainly concerned with signs as social forces.*

When it is said that the expression /Evening star/ denotes a certain large physical 'object' of a spherical form, which travels through space some scores of millions of miles from the Earth (Quine, 1953, 1) one should in fact say that: the expression in question denotes 'a certain' corresponding *cultural unit* to which the speaker refers, and which he has accepted in the way described by the culture in which he lives, without having ever experienced the real referent. So much is this so that only the logician knows that the expression in question has the same denotatum as has the expression /Morning star/. Whoever emitted or received this latter sign-vehicle thought that there were *two different things*. And he was right in the sense that the cultural codes to which he referred provided for two different cultural units. His social life did not develop on the basis of things but on the basis of cultural units. Or rather, for him as for us, things were only known through cultural units which the universe of communication put into circulation *in place of things*.

We may commonly speak of a thing called /*Alpha Centauri*/, but we have never experienced it. An astronomer has occasionally experienced it with some strange apparatus. But we do not know this astronomer. We only know a cultural unit communicated to us by means of words, drawings or other means. For the defense or destruction of this cultural unit, as for others such as /freedom/, /transubstantiation/ or /free world/, men are even ready to go to their death. Yet death, once it has occurred, and only then, constitutes the one and only referent, or event which cannot be semioticized (in that a dead semiotician no longer communicates semiotic theories). But right up to a moment before it occurs, «death» is mainly used as a cultural unit.

2.6. Meaning as cultural unit

Let us try to understand the nature of the object that corresponds to an expression. Take the term /dog/. The referent will certainly not be the dog x standing by me while I am pronouncing the word. For anyone who holds to the doctrine of the referent, the referent, in such a case, will be all existing dogs (and also all past and future dogs). But «all existing dogs» is not an object which can be perceived with the senses. It is a set, a class, a logical entity.

Every attempt to establish what the referent of a sign is forces us to define the referent in terms of an abstract entity which moreover is only a cultural convention. But even admitting that one wants to establish that through the use of certain terms it is possible to indicate a real referent which can be perceived with the senses, whoever identifies the meaning with the referent (and makes the value of the sign-vehicle depend on the presence of the referent) is then forced to remove from a discussion of meaning all sign-vehicles which cannot correspond to a real object. For example all the terms which classical linguistics called *syncategorematic* as opposed to *categorematic* — terms such as /to the/, /of/ and /nevertheless/ — would not have referents. Since, however, they are fundamental elements in the process of signification it is necessary to accept the idea that the notion of referent, undoubtedly useful in other contexts, is useless and damaging in this one. So we shall have to free the term 'denotation' from its historical compromise with the referent (see 2.9).

What, then, is the meaning of a term? From a semiotic point of view it can only be a *cultural unit*. In every culture "a unit . . . is simply anything that is culturally defined and distinguished as an entity. It may be a person, place, thing, feeling, state of affairs, sense of foreboding, fantasy, hallucination, hope or idea. In American culture such units as uncle, town, blue (depressed), a mess, a hunch, the idea of progress, hope and art are cultural units" (Schneider, 1968: 2) [6]. We shall see later how a cultural unit can be defined semiotically as a semantic unit inserted into a system. A unit of this type might also be recognized as an intercultural unit which remains invariable despite the linguistic symbol with which it is signified: /dog/ denotes not a physical object but a cultural unit which remains constant or invariable even if I translate /dog/ by /cane/ or /chien/ or /Hund/. In the case of /crime/ I might find that the corresponding cultural unit in another culture has a broader or more restricted range; in the case of /snow/ it might be found that for the Eskimos there are in fact four cultural units which correspond to four different states of snow and which are conveyed by four expression-units. Since the problem of code is not here taken into account, I shall not consider the problem of whether a modification in the dictionary entails a different segmentation of the semantic field or vice versa: I only wish to observe that in some cultures the same semantic system is more finely analyzed than it is in others and that the unevenness of such analysis produces a series of uneven overlaps. Thus, for example, the expression /art/ within classical and medieval culture covers a wide range of contents that in contemporary Western culture are conveyed by other expressions such as /technique/ and /technics/; and when Anglo-Saxon culture apparently adapts itself to the classical segmentation of the field, speaking of /the state of the art/ when surveying the development of logic or theology, the super-imposition is only apparent, for though the Schoolmen did consider logic as an art, they did not consider theology as such (thus distinguishing the Faculty of Theology from the Faculty of Arts).

Recognition of the presence of these cultural units (which are therefore the meaning to which the code makes the system of sign-vehicles correspond)

involves understanding language as a social phenomenon. If I declare that
/There are two natures in Christ, the human and the divine, and one Person/ a
logician or scientist might observe to me that this string of sign-vehicles has
neither extension nor referent — and that it could be defined as lacking
meaning and therefore as a pseudo-statement. But they will never succeed in
explaining why whole groups of people have fought for centuries over a
statement of this kind or its denial. Evidently this happened because the
expression conveyed precise contents which existed as cultural units within a
civilization. Since they existed they became the supports for connotative
developments and opened up a whole range of semantic reactions of a type
that directly affected behavior. But behavioral reactions are not necessary in
order to establish that the expression has a content; the civilization itself
elaborated a series of definitions and explanations of the terms involved
(person, nature, etc.). Each definition was a new linguistic (or visual) message
whose meaning had in turn to be clarified by means of other linguistic
expressions which defined the cultural units carried by the preceding
expression. The series of clarifications which circumscribed the cultural units
of a society in a continuous progression (always defining them in the form of
sign-vehicles) represents the chain of what Peirce called the *interpretants*
(5.470 and ff.).

2.7. The interpretant

2.7.1. Peirce's theory

The interpretant is not the interpreter (even if a confusion of this type
occasionally arises in Peirce). The interpretant is that which guarantees the
validity of the sign, even in the absence of the interpreter.

According to Peirce it is that which the sign produces in the quasi-mind
which is the interpreter; but it can also be conceived as the *definition* of the
representamen (and therefore its intension). However, the most fruitful
hypothesis would seem to be that of conceiving the *interpretant as another
representation which is referred to the same 'object'*. In other words, in order
to establish what the interpretant of a sign is, it is necessary to name it by
means of another sign which in turn has another interpretant to be named by
another sign and so on. At this point there begins a process of *unlimited
semiosis*, which, paradoxical as it may be, is the only guarantee for the
foundation of a semiotic system capable of checking itself entirely by its own
means. Language would then be an auto-clarificatory system, or rather one

Theory of Codes

69

which is clarified by successive systems of conventions that explain each other. Therefore a sign is "anything which determines something else (its *interpretant*) to refer to an object to which itself refers (its *object*) in the same way, the interpretant becoming in turn a sign, and so on *ad infinitum*" (2.300). Thus the very definition of 'sign' implies a process of *unlimited semiosis*.

"A sign stands *for* something *to* the idea which it produces, or modifies . . . . That for which it stands is called its *object*; that which it conveys, its *meaning*; and the idea to which it gives rise, its *interpretant*" (1.339). This definition seems to leave too important a place for the object: but immediately afterwards Peirce adds: "The object of representation can be nothing but a representation of which the first representation is the interpretant. But an endless series of representations, each representing the one behind it, may be conceived to have an absolute object as its limit". Peirce later calls this absolute object not an object but a *habit*, understood as the *final interpretant* (see 4.536; 5.473-492). Anyway in this text he does not insist on this exigency; he continues to develop the doctrine of unlimited semiosis as follows: "The meaning of a representation can be nothing but a representation. In fact it is nothing but the representation itself conceived as stripped of irrelevant clothing. But this clothing never can be completely stripped off; it is only changed for something more diaphanous. So there is an infinite regression here. Finally, the interpretant is nothing but another representation to which the torch of truth is handed along; and as representation, it has its interpretant again. Lo, another infinite series".

This fascination with infinite regression appears in many other passages. For instance: "Now the Sign and the Explanation together make up another Sign, and since the explanation will be a Sign, it will probably require an additional explanation, which taken together with the already enlarged Sign will make up a still larger Sign; and proceeding in the same way, we shall, or should, ultimately reach a Sign of itself, containing its own explanation and those of all its significant parts; and according to this explanation each such part has some other part as its Object" (2.230). In this quotation the fascinating image of signs generating signs goes too far, indeed so far as to prevent Peirce from realizing that the final Sign of which he speaks is not really a sign, but is the entire semantic field as the structure connecting and correlating signs with each other. Whether such a global semantic field can exist, or whether the *structure of unlimited semiosis* (apparently a *contradictio in adjecto*) should be viewed in some other way, will all be discussed in 2.12-2.13.

2.7.2. Various sorts of interpretants

It is no chance that the idea of the interpretant frightened many scholars who proceeded to exorcise it by misunderstanding it (interpretant=

interpreter or receiver of the message). The idea of the interpretant makes a theory of signification a rigorous science of cultural phenomena, while detaching it from the metaphysics of the referent.

The interpretant can assume different forms:

a) It can be the equivalent (or apparently equivalent) sign-vehicle in another semiotic system. For example I can make the drawing of a dog correspond to the word /dog/.

b) It can be the index which is directed to a single object, perhaps implying an element of universal quantification («all objects like this»).

c) It can be a scientific (or naive) definition in terms of the same semiotic system, e.g. /salt/ signifies «sodium chloride».

d) It can be an emotive association which acquires the value of an established connotation: /dog/ signifies «fidelity» (and vice versa).

e) It can simply be the translation of the term into another language, or its substitution by a synonym.

At first glance, within the framework of the present approach, the interpretant could be equated with any coded intensional property of the content, i.e. with the entire range of denotations and connotations of a sign vehicle (see 2.9). This could in fact be a very suitable reduction of the vague concept of 'interpretant', but it would impoverish Peirce's suggestions. In his semiotics the interpretants are much more than this: they can be complex discourses which not only translate but even *inferentially* develop all the logical possibilities suggested by the sign; in other words the interpretant can also be the entire syllogism deduced from such premises as /all men are mortal/ or /Socrates is a man/.

Moreover, the interpretant can be a response, a behavioral habit determimed be a sign, and many other things. So I shall assume that all the denotations of a sign-vehicle are undoubtedly its interpretants, that a connotation is the interpretant of an underlying denotation, and that a further connotation is the interpretant of the one underlying it. But the category of 'interpretant' goes beyond those of denotation and connotation. Since in 2.9.1. I shall define both connotation and denotation as semantic markers, belonging to the semantic representation of a semantic unit called the 'sememe', I shall assume that the entire set of possible interpretants of a sememe is broader than the set of its semantic markers.

Insofar as a theory of codes provides a description of all the markers attributed by one or more codes to a single sememe, then the interpretant is clearly a category that may suitably take its place within the framework of a theory of codes, but at the same time its usefulness goes beyond such a theory; thus the interpretant also has to be considered as a category that may suitably find a place within the framework of a theory of sign production, for it also defines many kinds of proposition and argument which, beyond the rules provided by codes, explain, develop, interpret a given sign. In this sense one should even consider as interpretants all possible semiotic judgments that a code permits one to assert about a given semantic unit, as well as many factual judgments (see 3.2).

2.7.3. Unlimited semiosis

Because it is such a broad category, the interpretant may turn out to be of no use at all and, since it is able to define *any* semiotic act, may in the last analysis become purely tautological. Yet its vagueness is at the same time its force and the condition of its theoretical purity.

The very richness of this category makes it fertile since it shows us how signification (as well as communication), by means of continual shiftings which refer a sign back to another sign or string of signs, circumscribes cultural units in an asymptotic fashion, without ever allowing one to touch them directly, though making them accessible through other units. Thus a cultural unit never obliges one to replace it by means of something which is not a semiotic entity, and never asks to be explained by some Platonic, psychic or objectal entity. *Semiosis explains itself by itself*; this continual circularity is the normal condition of signification and even allows communication to use signs in order to mention things. To call this condition a 'desperate' one is to refuse the human way of signifying, a way that has proved itself fruitful insofar as only through it has cultural history developed.

In fact we can 'touch' interpretants (i.e. we can empirically test a cultural unit), for culture continuously translates signs into other signs, and definitions into other definitions, words into icons, icons into ostensive signs, ostensive signs into new definitions, new definitions into propositional functions, propositional functions into exemplifying sentences and so on; in this way it proposes to its members an uninterrupted chain of cultural units composing other cultural units, and thus translating and explaining them.

We can say that *cultural units are physically within our grasp*. They are the signs that social life has put at our disposal: images interpreting books, appropriate responses interpreting ambiguous questions, words interpreting definitions and vice versa. The ritual behavior of a rank of soldiers interpreting the trumpet signal /at-tention!/ gives us information about the cultural unit «at-tention» conveyed by the musical sign-vehicle. Soldiers, sounds, pages of books, colors on a wall, all these *etic* entities are physically, materially, *materialistically testable*. Cultural units stand out against society's ability to equate these signs with each other, cultural units are the semiotic *postulate* required in order to justify the very fact that society *does* equate codes with codes, sign-vehicles with meanings, expressions with contents. *Unseen* but *used* by the layman, they are not used but *seen* by semiotics, which is simply the science of this culturally performed (if unexpressed) competence.

Moreover, the idea of the interpretant again demonstrates that in cultural life every entity can aim at becoming independently both meaning and sign-vehicle. «Salt» is the interpretant of /NaCl/ but «NaCl» is the interpretant of /salt/. In a given situation a handful of salt can become the interpretant of /salt/, just as can the gesture imitating a person who is given a pinch of something salty on the tip of his tongue (as in a intracultural relationship between anthropologist and native informant).

2.7.4. Interpretants in a theory of codes

Therefore a definition of the interpretant which will function within the framework of a code theory (and will therefore be a restricted one) should cover the following three semiotic categories:

(i)   The *meaning* of a sign-vehicle, understood as a cultural unit displayed through other sign-vehicles and thus showing its semantic independence from the first sign-vehicle (this definition equating the one of 'synonymy' by which many semanticists [for instance Carnap, 1955; Quine, 1953] seek to define 'meaning');

(ii)   The *intensional* or componential analysis by which a cultural unit is segmented into its elementary semic components, or semantic markers, and therefore presented as a 'sememe' which can enter, by the amalgamation of its 'readings', into different contextual combinations (this definition equating the interpretant with the componential representation of a sememe, that is, with a 'tree' like the one proposed by Katz and Fodor, 1963);

(iii) Each of the *units* composing the componential tree of a sememe, every unit (or seme or semantic marker) becoming in its turn another cultural unit (represented by another sign-vehicle) which is open to its own componential analysis (in other words, can be represented by a new system of sign-vehicles; this definition is equal to that of the 'seme', or elementary and absolutely abstract semantic component, as discussed in *Sémantique structurale* by Greimas, 1966a) [7].

2.8. The semantic system

2.8.1. Oppositions in content

A cultural unit cannot be isolated merely by the sequence of its interpretants. It is defined inasmuch as it is *placed* in a system of other cultural units which are opposed to it and circumscribe it. A cultural unit 'exists' and is recognized insofar as there exists another one which is opposed to it. It is the relationship between the various terms of a system of cultural units which substracts from each one of the terms what is conveyed by the others. This translation of the meaning into the positional value of the sign becomes very clear in one of Hjelmslev's classic examples (1943:50).

In Table 8 we see how the French word /arbre/ covers the same area of meanings as the German word /Baum/, while the word /bois/ is used either to indicate what the Germans call /Holz/ or a portion of what they call /Wald/; in the same diagram we see how the French distinguish between «a little group of trees» (/bois/) and a bigger one (a /forest/, /forêt/); and so on.

Table 8

trae	Baum	arbre
	Holz	bois
skov	Wald	
		forêt

In a table of this kind we are not concerned with 'ideas', psychic entities, nor even referents as objects; *we are concerned with values which issue from the system*. The values correspond to cultural units but they can be defined as pure differences; they are not defined in terms of their content (and therefore of the possibility of intensional analysis) but in terms of the way in which they are opposed to other elements of the system and of the position which they occupy within it. As in the case of phonemes in a phonological system, we have a series of differential choices which can be described by binary methods. Therefore in Hjelmslevian terms an empty diagram like

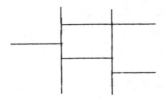

represents the content-form while such units as *«Baum», «Holz», «bois»* (and so on) are the content-substance [8].

As for the expression-form, given four 'etic' emissions like [b], [p], [d], [t], these are 'emically' generated as Table 9 shows:

Table 9

Labial		
Dental		
	Voiced	Unvoiced

Table 9 therefore provides four types for many etically variable tokens.

The difference between the two examples is that in the study of expression forms the structural boundaries between phonemes are strictly defined by a highly developed structural theory of the expression-form, such as phonology. Whereas the semantic boundaries, even in Hjelmslev's example, are still vague. In English, /wood/ seems to convey the same 'semantic space', as does the French sememe «bois» (both referring to a material of which objects can be made, and also to a collection of trees smaller than a forest). Nevertheless English is able to distinguish /wood/ as «timber» from /wood/ as «little forest» (in the expression /a walk in the woods/ the purposeful use of the plural form shows that the English semantic system is well aware of the difference between the two readings of /wood/), whereas it is not so clear whether a German speaker grasps the 'semantic' difference between a *«grosser Wald»* and a *«kleiner Wald»* (or /*Wäldchen*/). In the same way, a European when distinguishing «soft snow» from «melting snow», is predicating only two diverse 'states' of the same semantic entity — while sharply distinguishing «snow» from «water» and «ice», even if all three are H_2O in different physical states.

There is a considerable gap between the capacity that the expression sciences have for analyzing their systems and that of the content sciences for similar analytical procedures. The limited number of phonemes which operate in any language has allowed phonology to build extremely circumstantiated models of the expression-form. Some new approaches such as paralinguistics nowadays succeed in thoroughly analyzing such a form, minimizing the space occupied by what was formerly considered an unanalyzable continuum (Trager, 1964; Sebeok, Bateson, Hayes, 1964; etc.). All studies on syntactic

structures which limit themselves to surface structures, and to the phonological interpretation of underlying deeper structures, increasingly formalize
the universe of expression.

Yet the problem of the form of content remained at so imprecise a level
that it led many authors to think that linguistics (and therefore semiotics in
general) could not be concerned with the problem of meaning; they dealt
rather with the universe of objective referents, the universe of psychic events
and the social universe of uses (Antal, 1964).

Wittgenstein's *Philosophische Untersuchungen* basically represented the
most rigorous (and suggestively fertile) attempt to eliminate every formalized
discipline of meaning.

2.8.2. Sub-systems, fields, axes

Structural semantics has now taken up the ambitious task of elaborating a general system for the content-form. It is a universe which culture
structures into *sub-systems*, *fields* and *axes* (see Guiraud, 1955; Greimas,
1966; Todorov, 1966 *c*; Ullmann, 1962; Lyons, 1963).

Modern linguistics had already discovered that a given term can trigger
off a series of associations. Saussure gave the example of a term such as
/*enseignement*/ which in the one case evokes the sequence /*enseigner,
enseignons*/ in another /*apprentissage, éducation,* etc./, in a third /*change-
ment, armement,* etc./ and finally /*clément, justement,* etc./. This constitutes
a case in which we are not concerned with a structural field but with the
capacity of a term to be associated with another one by pure phonic analogy,
by homology of cultural classification, by the ability to combine various
morphemes with the same lexeme (in Martinet's sense) or vice versa. A more
coherent approach is achieved by Trier (1931) with the construction of
structured semantic fields, where the value of an idea is due to the limits set
on it by neighboring ideas — as happened with terms such as /*Wisheit*/
(wisdom), /*Kunst*/ (art) and /*List*/ (skill) in the thirteenth century.

The work of the lexicographers was next combined with that of the
anthropologists, who isolated systems of highly structured cultural units, such
as field of colors, terms of kinship, etc. (see Conklin, 1955; Goodenough,
1956). The most recent and far-reaching studies of structural semantics have
also made it possible for us to establish that one can even construct semantic
axes and fields for these semantic units which do not correspond to names of
objects. As a result the notion of 'meaning' as 'cultural unit' becomes
applicable not only to the *categorematic* terms but also to *syncategorematic*
ones. Instead of putting into structural relationship names of intellectual

qualities, names of colors, or terms of kinship, Apresjian (1962) indicated fields which place pronouns in opposition (pronouns which designate *animate* things vs. pronouns which designate *inanimate* things; also for instance the place occupied by /you/ in English compared with the place occupied by /tu/ /Lei/ /voi/ in Italian) or fields of verbs which designate different operations within the same sphere of operations (for example to advise, to assure, to convince, to inform etc., all of which belong to the sphere of transmission of information).

This enables us to face the problem of the possible content of syncategorematic terms and of the so-called 'functional monemes' (see for instance Leech, 1969). See on this subject 2.11.5., in which some suggestions for a componential analysis of syncategorematic terms are proposed.

Naturally structural semantics hopes to establish the Semantic Space (as the Form of Content in Hjelmslev's sense) in its totality. But this aim, which can constitute a general hypothetical framework for research, comes up against two obstacles; one empirical and the other inherent in the semiotic process.

The first obstacle is that until now such studies as have been undertaken only arrived at a structuring of very restricted subsystems, such as for example that of colors, of botanical classifications, of metereological terms, etc. The second obstacle is due to the fact that the life of semantic fields is briefer than that of phonological systems where the structural models attempt to describe forms which remain unchanged for long periods of time within the history of a language. Since semantic fields give shape to the units of a given culture and establish portions of the world vision belonging to that culture, movements of acculturation and critical revisions of knowledge are enough to upset a semantic field. If Saussure's metaphor of the chessboard is accurate, the movement of one piece will suffice to change all the relationships of the system. Therefore it is enough that as the culture develops, the term /Kunst/ be given areas of application which are much wider than usual, for the whole system of thirteenth-century relationships studied by Trier to be changed, thus depriving the term /List/ of its value.

2.8.3. The segmentation of semantic fields

In what sense does a semantic field show the world vision belonging to a culture? Let us go back to one of the classic examples of the theory of semantic fields and examine the way in which a European civilization analyzes the color spectrum by assigning names (and therefore establishing cultural units) to various wave-lengths expressed in millimicrons.

a.	red	800-650 mμ
b.	orange	640-590 mμ
c.	yellow	580-550 mμ
d.	green	540-490 mμ
e.	blue	480-460 mμ
f.	indigo	450-440 mμ
g.	violet	430-390 mμ

A preliminary and naive interpretation might propose that the spectrum, divided into wave-lengths, constitutes the referent, the object of experience to which the names of the colors refer. However, we know that the color was named on the basis of a visual experience (which the simple speaker would define as 'perceptual reality') which is only translated into wave-lengths by scientific experience. But let us assume that the wave-lengths are something absolutely 'real'. There is no difficulty in stating that the undifferentiated continuum of the wave-length constitutes 'reality'. Yet science comes to know that reality after having divided it into pertinent units. Portions of the continuum have been cut out (and as we shall see, they are arbitrary) so that the wave-length *d* (which goes from 540 to 490 millimicrons) constitutes a cultural unit to which a name is assigned. We also know that science has divided the continuum in such a way as to justify in terms of wave-length a unit which simple experience had already cut out of its own accord and given the name /green/.

The choice based upon naive experience *was not arbitrary*, in the sense that the exigencies of biological survival probably forced that unit to be termed pertinent rather than another (just as the fact that the Eskimos divide the continuum of experience into four cultural units in place of the one which we call /snow/ is due to the fact that their vital relationship with snow imposes distinctions on them that we can disregard without suffering any notable damage).

But it *was arbitrary* in the sense that another culture divided the same continuum in a different way, which means that the continuum is a content-stuff which can be cut into different formal systems. We are not lacking in examples: for the portion of continuum *e* (blue) Russian culture has two different cultural units (corresponding to /goluboj/ and /sinij/), while the Greco-Roman civilization probably had only one cultural unit for the various names (/glaucus/ /caerulus/) to indicate the portion *d* - *e* and the Hindus combine under a simple term (and thus a single cultural unit) the portion *a* - *b*. We can therefore say that a given culture has divided the continuum of experience (and it does not matter whether the continuum is seen in terms of perceptual experience or defined by means of oscillographs and spectographs), making certain units pertinent and understanding others merely as variants, 'allophones'. Thus to single out a shade such as «light blue» and another such as «dark blue» means for an English speaker isolating a free variant, in much the same way as when two idiosyncratic pronunciations are singled out from one phoneme which from the 'emic' point of view is considered a pertinent unit of the phonological system.

All this leaves unsolved a question which will appear clearer when the units of two different semantic fields are compared in two different languages, Latin and English (Table 10),

Table 10

Mus	Mouse
	Rat

which can be rendered as: "to the Latin word /*mus*/ correspond two different things which we shall call x_1 and x_2" (Table 11).

Table 11

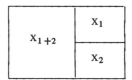

On the other hand, since the existence of x_1 and x_2 is only made evident by the comparison of the two semiotic systems, can we say that x_1 and x_2 exist independently of the names which a language has assigned to them and which establishes them as cultural units and therefore meanings of a certain sign-vehicle?

If we turn to colors the answer is simple. There is no reason why there must be a physical entity which begins at the wave-length 640 millimicrons and ends at the wave-length 590 millimicrons. In fact in Hindu culture the segmentation of the continuum occurs not at 640 but at 590 millimicrons. But why should there not be a cultural unit (and a unit of experience) which goes from 610 to 600 millimicrons? Actually a painter with an extreme sensitivity to colors who possesses a more carefully graded system would answer that such a unit exists and is present in his own special code, where a specific name would correspond to that portion of the wave-length continuum.

The problem concerning /*mus*/ is a different one. The zoologist would tell us that the x_1 and x_2 which correspond in English to /mouse/ and /rat/ exist as specific objects and that they can be analyzed in terms of properties and functions. But what Foucault (1966) has written on the 'epistemes' of different epochs and the variations in their segmentation of the universe, or what Lévi-Strauss (1962) has written on the taxonomy of primitive people, should suffice to make us aware that even on these points it is wise to proceed with caution. Since, after all, a study of codes should not be concerned with x_1 and x_2, which are referents, it should be enough to confirm that there exists in English a semantic field governing rodents, which is more analytic than its equivalent in Latin, and that therefore for the speaker of English there exist two cultural units where for the speaker of Latin there exists only one.

All this brings the problem of semantic fields back to the so-called Sapir-Whorf hypothesis and to the question of whether the form of communicative systems determines the world vision of a certain civilization. At this stage it does not seem appropriate to broach the question: it is enough to assume that (at least on the level of the segmentation of the experiential continuum into the *form* of the content) there exists a fairly close interaction between the world vision of a civilization and the way in which it makes its own semantic units pertinent. Given the elements in play – Y (material conditions of life), X (units of perceived experience), U (corresponding cultural units) and SV (the sign-vehicles which denote them) – it is not necessary to know at this point whether Y determines X, which generates U, assigning to it the name SV; whether Y strives to elaborate SV in order to segment the experience to which U corresponds; whether semiotic activity on a deeper level leads man to base his thoughts on SV, which not only produces U and X but directly conditions human beings to experience Y and so on. These are *still* extra-semiotic problems.

It would be more interesting, from a semiotic point of view, to understand within which civilizations a semantic field functions and at what point it begins to dissolve in order to make room for another; and how, in the same civilization, two or more semantic fields can coexist although in opposition, when different patterns of culture are superimposed.

A typical example is provided for us by the series of definitions which Aulus Gellius gave to colors in his *Noctes Atticae* (ii, 26) in the second century A.D.: he, for example, associated the term /rufus/, (which we would translate /red/) with fire, blood, gold and saffron. He stated that the term /xanthos/ (color of gold) was a variation of the color red, just like /kirros/ (which in the chain of interpretants reconstructed by philology must be understood as equivalent of our /yellow-orange/). He furthermore considered, as alternative names for the color red, /flavus/ (which we are also used to associating with gold, with grain and with the water of the river Tiber), and /fulvus/ (which is usually the color of a lion's mane). But Aulus Gellius calls the eagle, the topaz, sand, gold /fulva/ while he defines /flavus/ as a "mixture of red, green and white" and associates it with the color of the sea and of olive branches. Finally he states that Virgil, in order to define the color "greenish" of a horse, uses the term /caerulus/, which is commonly associated with the color of the sea. The extreme confusion which strikes the reader in this one page of Latin is probably due not only to the fact that Aulus Gellius' field of colors was different from ours, but also that in the second century A.D., in Latin culture, alternative chromatic fields coexisted owing to the influence of other cultures. Hence the perplexity of Aulus Gellius, who does not manage to arrange the material, which he takes from the works of writers of different epochs, into strict fields. As we have seen, the 'actual' experience which the author could feel from looking at the sky, the sea or a horse is here mediated by recourse to given cultural units, and his world vision is determined (in a rather incoherent way) by the cultural units (with corresponding names) which he finds at his disposition.

We could therefore state that: (a) *in a given culture there can exist contradictory semantic fields*: this is an aberrant cultural occurrence which semiotics must take into consideration rather than try to eliminate it; (b) *the same cultural unit can itself become part of complementary semantic fields* within a given culture. Carnap (1947, 29) gives the example of a double classification according to which animals are divided on the one hand into aquatic, aerial and terrestrial, and on the other hand into fish, birds and others. A cultural unit such as «whale» can then occupy different positions in the two semantic fields without the two classifications being incompatible. One must thus admit that the user of a language possesses within his 'competence' the possibility of coupling a given system of sign-vehicles with various systems of meanings: (c) *within a given culture a semantic field can disintegrate with extreme rapidity and restructure itself into a new field*.

Points (a) and (b) will be dealt with in 2.8.4, since they are matters for a theory of codes. But they also have direct consequences as far as sign production is concerned; mainly in the rhetorical and ideological treatment of discourse. So they will also be more deeply considered in 3.9. Likewise, point

(c) is the concern of a theory of code-changing, which is a branch of the theory of sign production. For an example of this see 3.8.5.

2.8.4. Contradictory semantic fields

As for a suitable example of contradicting semantic fields, I shall consider the problem of *antonymous* terms as pairs of oppositions constituting a semantic axis.

Lyons (1968) classifies three types of antonymy: (i) complementary antonyms such as 'masculine vs. feminine'; (ii) properly called antonyms, such as 'small vs. large'; (iii) antonyms by converseness, such as 'buy vs. sell'. Katz (1972), on the other hand, subdivides antonyms into: (a) contradictories, such as 'mortal vs. immortal', which have no possible mediation between them; (b) contraries, such as 'superior vs. inferior', and 'rich vs. poor', which have some possible mediation between or beyond them; (c) converses, such as 'husband vs. wife' or 'buy vs. sell', which, like the converses in Lyons, imply syntactic transformations and entail an inferential relation of the type 'if . . . then'.

Even a superficial glance at some pairs of antonyms reveals that: (1) The same term can entertain different relationships provided that it is inserted into different axes: thus «bachelor» can be considered the contrary of «spinster» but also of «married»; since «married» is at the same time the contrary of «spinster», there is a sort of rhetorical equivalence between contraries — which from a logical point of view does not make sense at all. (2) The same term can entertain a contradictory or converse or contrary antonymous relation depending on the rhetorical (and ideological) way in which these relations are viewed. Suppose that, according to the rhetorical premise "in an affluent society every poor man has the opportunity to become rich" a first speaker presents 'rich vs. poor' as a relation of contrariness: it only needs someone to change the rhetorical premise to "in a capitalist society one person's riches are the result of another's poverty, riches being the fruit of *plus value* extorted from the proletariat" for rich and poor to become converse antonyms, exactly like husband and wife. Suppose finally that a third, and rather reactionary, speaker objects that this 'radical' explanation does not hold, since richness and poverty are natural and hereditary boundaries of the human condition, established by the mysterious design of Divine Providence, and the relation between rich and poor will become to some degree a contradictory one.

If one considers 'buy vs. sell' following the rhetorical premise "one sells what one owns and buys what one needs", then the relation between buy, sell, own and need could take the form of a classical logical square (Table 12).

Table 12

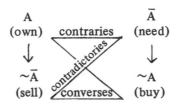

In Table 12 'own vs. need' represent two contraries; 'sell vs. need' and 'own vs. buy' represent contradictories; 'sell vs. buy' are classical converses; sell may imply own and buy may imply need.

But suppose that one now takes the rhetorical premise "anyone who buys receives something while anyone who sells gives something". The square then assumes the format suggested by Table 13.

Table 13

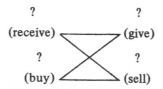

In Table 13 receive and give are no longer contraries but converses, as are buy and sell; 'give vs. buy' and 'receive vs. sell' are contradictories if the 'something' bought and received (or sold and given) always refers to a commodity; but if in the first case the 'something' refers to a commodity and in the second to a sum of money, then it is possible to sell a 'something-commodity' and to receive a 'something-sum of money' [9].

The correct explanation of such a problem is that in natural language (indeed in every kind of semiotic phenomena) the cultural units are very seldom formally univocal entities, and are very frequently what logic calls *'fuzzy concepts'* (Lakoff, 1972).

The fact that a study of semantic systems deals with fuzzy concepts demands many precautions. First of all, the units of a semantic system must be analyzed in all their equivocality, i.e. as sememes open to diverse 'readings'. Therefore the format of a semantic system seems to lose that crystal-like structure which the most optimistic theories seek to attribute to it. This inner contradictoriness of a Global Semantic System (on which many dialectic aspects of sign production and code changing rely) will be discussed in 2.13.

2.8.5. The methodological nature of a semantic system

Anyway the contradictory nature of semantic fields does at any rate allow one to solve an epistemological question that might otherwise have been surreptitiously left under cover during the following discussions.

The question is that of whether or not semantic fields 'really' exist. This is equivalent to asking: "Is there something in the mind of the person understanding the content of an expression which corresponds to a semantic field?". Insofar as a theory of codes has nothing to do with what may happen in the addressee's mind, semantic fields will be both a supposed cultural structure and the semiotic model of such a structure posited by the theorist. But I would like to stress the following methodological assumptions: (a) meanings are cultural units; (b) these units can be isolated thanks to the chain of their interpretants as revealed in a given culture; (c) the study of the signs in a culture enables us to define the value of the interpretants by viewing them in a system of positions and oppositions; (d) the postulation of these systems makes it possible to explain how meaning comes into existence; (e) following a method of this kind it could in theory be possible to construct a robot which possesses an assortment of semantic fields and the rules to link them to systems of sign-vehicles; (f) in the absence of a description of the Universal Semantic System (i.e. one which shapes a cultural world vision; an impossible operation because that world vision, in its interconnections and its peripheral manifestations, changes constantly), the semantic fields are *postulated* as useful tools to explain significant oppositions for the purposes of studying a given group of messages.

When Greimas (1966) elaborates a system of oppositions of meaning in order to explain the narrative structures in Bernanos, he undoubtedly brings to light the oppositions which can be found in the text on the level of a certain working hypothesis; but nothing prevents another reader, using that text in a different way, from singling out another key to reading and therefore of reducing it to different oppositional values. As will be seen in 3.7, the aesthetic text possesses such ambiguous qualities and allows such a variety of approaches that many possible choices can be justified. These observations are aimed at questioning the task that structural semantics has undertaken attempting to bring to light, immediately and without discussion, the immutable structures of meaning [10].

A cautious conclusion may be found in Greimas' introduction to his essay *La structure sémantique*: "Par structure sémantique on doit entendre la forme générale de l'organisation des divers univers sémantiques — donné ou simplement possible — de nature sociale et individuelle (cultures ou personnalités). La question de savoir si la structure sémantique est sous-tendue à l'univers sémantique, ou si elle n'est qu'une construction métalinguistique rendant compte de l'univers donné, peut être considérée comme non pertinente" (Greimas, 1970:39).

2.9. The semantic markers and the sememe

2.9.1. Denotative and connotative markers

We are now entitled to give a definite response to the question: what is the meaning of a sign-vehicle (or what is the functive 'content' of a sign-function)? It is a semantic unit posited in a precise 'space' within a semantic system. In this sense it would be easy to say that the content of the sign-vehicle /dog/ is a given sememe «dog» as opposed to other sememes within a given semantic subsystem.

But first one must face the question: which system? the one organizing animals? or that organizing living beings? or carnivores? or mammals? However these questions are answered, a further problem will arise: why should the sememe «dog» be opposed, let us say, to «cat» or to «kangaroo»? One suddenly realizes that this last question is the same as was posed by Jakobson (Jakobson and Halle, 1956) when asking why one phoneme should be opposed to another. In fact the definition of a phoneme as a minimal oppositional entity has to give way to a more analytical definition: a phoneme is a *bundle* of more analytical *distinctive features*, and the system of positions and oppositions is directly concerned with these features and not with the phoneme, which is only the result of a network of presences and absences of these features.

The same internal network of mutually opposed features should also rule the differences between two sememes. Thus, to say that a sign-vehicle conveys a given position within a semantic field constitutes a shorthand definition (as does saying that a phoneme is a position within a phonological system). As a matter of fact one must assume that a sign-vehicle may refer (i) to a network of positions within the same semantic system, (ii) to a network of positions within different semantic systems. These positions constitute the *semantic markers* of a given sememe. These markers can be either *denotative* or *connotative*.

Let me call denotative markers those whose sum (or hierarchy) constitutes and isolates the cultural unit which first corresponds to the sign-vehicle and upon which rely all the other connotations. Consequently, connotative markers are all those which contribute to the constitution of one or more other cultural units expressed by the preceding sign-function. As noted in 2.3 *à propos* of denotation and connotation, denotative markers differ from connotative markers only insofar as a connotation must rely on a preceding denotation; the former are not distinguished from the latter because of their greater stability; a denotative marker can be very short-lived if the code that institutes it lasts only *l'espace d'un matin* (as many secret agents, changing their ciphers day by day, know very well); while a connotative marker can be stably rooted in a social convention, thus lasting as long as the denotation upon which it is based.

So the following formal definition should suffice to distinguish denotative from connotative markers: (i) a denotative marker is one of the positions within a semantic system to which the code makes a sign-vehicle correspond without any previous mediation; (ii) a connotative marker is one of the positions within a semantic system to which the code makes a sign-vehicle correspond through the mediation of a preceding denotative marker, thus establishing a correlation between a sign-function and a new semantic unit.

Nevertheless such a definition results in being unsatisfactory, whether from the point of view of a theory of codes or from that of a theory of sign production, since it is difficult to distinguish a denotative marker from a connotative one. It is easy to assume that the sign-vehicle /dog/ denotes a given animal through certain physical properties or zoological features, and connotes, among many other things, «fidelity». But what about the marker «domestic»? When in 2.10.2 the problem of the sememe as 'encyclopedia item' is discussed, the difficulty of such a problem will become clearer. At present it would suffice to say that, within the framework of a theory of codes, the straightforward distinction between denotative and connotative markers still remains to be definitely established. Perhaps a tentative solution may be given through an empirical formulation of the problem into the terms of a theory of sign production.

From the point of view of a theory of sign production one should clearly distinguish denotation from connotation:

(a)   a denotation is a cultural unit or semantic property of a given sememe
      which is at the same time a culturally recognized property of its
      possible referents;
(b)   a connotation is a cultural unit or semantic property of a given sememe
      conveyed by its denotation and not necessarily corresponding to a
      culturally recognized property of the possible referent.

These two definitions allow us to understand why in the Watergate Model AB
denoted «danger level» and connoted «evacuation» or «flood». In fact
«danger level» was a cultural unit corresponding to a supposed actual state of
the water (even though this state, rather than constituting an actual event,
was already the result of a segmentation of the continuum performed by
another science, i.e. hydrography). «Evacuation», on the contrary, was not a
property of the supposed referent, but a meaning aroused by the signification
of the content corresponding to the supposed referent [11].

In any case it must be made clear that in the following pages *denotation
will not be taken as an equivalent of extension*. In the same way connotation
will not simply be an equivalent of intension. For intension and extension are
categories of a t-values theory, while denotation and connotation, in my
sense, are categories of a theory of codes. Thus denotation in the present
context is a semantic property, not a corresponding object. Denotation is the
content of an expression, connotation the content of a sign-function.

2.9.2. Denotation of proper names and of purely syntactic entities

Having made this much clear, one could now proceed to establish a
compositional theory of sememes. But first of all one must eliminate some
misunderstandings about proper names and sign-vehicles of purely syntactic
systems that lack any apparent semantic content, such as musical sounds, for
example. These problems must be clarified because in logical literature − for
instance − it is frequently asserted that proper names do not have a
denotatum and therefore an extension. Within the framework of a theory of
codes, to assume that an expression can and must have denotation means that
this expression does actually have a corresponding content, which can be
analyzed into more elementary semantic units.

The problem of proper names is similar to the problem of iconic signs,
which are commonly supposed to refer to someone without there being a
precise code to establish who this person is (for example, images of people).
Above all, we must try to understand what happens in the case of proper
names referring to known historical personages. We shall see later that the

other cases are not different structurally. The expression /Napoleon/ denotes a cultural unit which is well defined and which finds a place in a semantic field of historical entities. This field is common to many different cultures (there can be a very great variety of connotations attributed by different cultures to the cultural unit «Napoleon», but its denotations do not change). Thus the sememe «Napoleon» should have several markers including that of being a human person. It is because of this that it is semantically ridiculous to say "if Napoleon is an elephant" (see 2.5.3).

Now let us imagine a case where the author of this book receives the sign-vehicle /Stefano/. The author possesses a competence, shared with many people from his own environment, which provides for a field of cultural units that includes his own relations and friends, and the sign-vehicle /Stefano/ immediately denotes for him his own son. In this case we are dealing with a much more limited code than the one by which the message /Napoleon/ was decoded, but the semiotic mechanism has not changed. Spoken languages can exist that have very few speakers (idiolects). A possible objection is that /Stefano/ can also denote other individuals. But here we are simply faced with *a case of homonymy*. Homonymy often occurs in the use of language, and contextual situations exist which have to be specified, when term /x/, which can refer either to a meaning «X_1» or to a meaning «X_2», must be understood in one way or the other. The universe of proper names is simply a linguistically poor universe in which there are many cases of homonymy. The semantic universe of connected cultural units (the named human beings), is, however, quite rich and every unit in it is isolated by very precise systems of opposition.

Syncategorematic terms are homonymous in the same way. The /to/ of /to be/ is not the same as the /to/ of /to you/. However, Ullmann (1962:122) states that a proper name out of context does not denote anything, while a common noun out of context always has a lexematic meaning. But no sign-vehicle denotes, unless it is referred (on the basis of the context) to a specific code in which it appears primarily as an element of a repertoire of sign-vehicles. The graphic sign-vehicle /cane/, if it is communicated to me out of context and without any indication of code, can be either a Latin imperative, or an Italian common noun («dog») or an English common noun. Thus there must always be a code indication which refers to a precise vocabulary. The vocabulary may also include a section on first names which would tell me that a sign-vehicle such as /David/ is a proper name and therefore connotes a human being of the masculine sex.

Where *proper names of unknown persons* are concerned one would have to admit, however, that they connote but do not denote — reversing the opinion of J. S. Mill, for whom they could denote but not connote. These limitations should be admitted: proper names of unknown persons are sign-vehicles with an open denotation and can be decoded as one would decode an abstruse scientific term that one has never heard of, but that certainly must correspond to something precise. There is not much difference therefore between receiving the message /ascorbic acid/ and intuiting that it means a chemical compound (an imprecise connotation) without knowing which (no denotation), and receiving the message /David/ and knowing that it must refer to a man (imprecise connotation) without knowing whom (no denotation). These are two examples of imperfect possession of the codes of a group. In the first case I consult a chemist, in the second I ask to be introduced to David. But I could also want to know which is the position of «David» in a field of well-known cultural units: David is the son of John and the brother of Sheila.

Let us now turn to the case of the signs in those semiotic systems that are purely syntactic and have no apparent semantic depth. Music is a typical example. Let it be quite clear that there is no question of defining what is the meaning of the graphic sign

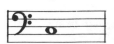

This sign-vehicle denotes «note C» in the middle register of the pianoforte, it denotes a position in the system of notes; it denotes a class of sound events which have for interpretants mathematical values and oscillographic and spectrographic measures.

The problem is instead *what* it denotes and *whether* it denotes the note C itself, emitted by a trumpet. In this connection it must be said that the sign-vehicles of syntactical systems have denotations inasmuch as they possess some interpretants. Thus the note C of the central octave, or that emitted by the trumpet, denotes a position in the musical system that will be maintained despite various transpositions. It could be said that the physical signal /note C/ denotes that position in the musical system which remains unvariable whether it is interpreted by the sign

or by the sign

In order to recognize the //note C// the musician must hear it in relation to some other note and therefore to its position in the system (this relation may be purely mnemonic in the rare cases of so-called "absolute pitch").

One may object that Hjelmslev (1943: 99, 100) has carefully distinguished between semiotic and non-semiotic systems, or "games". According to Hjelmslev "the decisive point for the question of whether or not a sign is present is not whether it is interpreted, i.e., whether a content purport is ordered to it" (for there exist "not interpreted but only interpretable systems"), but rather whether there are *two* planes and these planes are not *conformal*. "Two functives are said to be conformal if any particular derivate of the one functive without exception enters the same functions as a particular derivate of the other functive, and vice versa". In the case of "pure games", as well as of music, formal logic and algebra, "if the two planes are tentatively posited the functional net will be entirely the same in both". Therefore these structures are not called 'semiotic' for they are interpretable but not biplanar (while languages are biplanar and not conformal).

It should be enough to reverse Hjelmslev's position, therefore asserting that the decisive point of whether or not a sign is present *is whether it is interpreted* ('interpretable' systems being only signal systems, ready to be inserted within a coding correlation), but one should also explain why and how such a counter-proposal can improve the theory. The reason is the following.

To deny the nature of sign to conformal systems means to disregard a large portion of semiotic phenomena, first of all the entire range of so-called 'iconic' signs. It is not by chance that Hjelmslev finds some affinity between so-called symbolic systems and these entities "that are isomorphic with their interpretation, entities that are depictions and emblems, like Thorwaldsen's Christ as a symbol for compassion, the hammer and the sickle as a symbol of Communism, scales as a symbol for justice, or the onomatopoeia in the sphere of language". We will see that all these signs, even if in some way 'conformal', are not monoplanar at all: simply the relationship between expression and content is ruled by *ratio difficilis* (see 3.4.9. and 3.6.). When speaking of this problem it will be shown why it is possible to consider as signs even the units coming from *conformal but not monoplanar* systems in which the expression form coincides at some extent with the content form.

Hjelmslev classifies chess among "pure games", but this example is misleading and throws a shade of perplexity on many other so-called "symbolic" systems. In chess a given formal relationship between two different pieces on the board *does not* simply correspond to an equivalent relationship on the content plane: a given mutual position, let us say, between the black Queen and the white Bishop (both being correlated to the actual position of their own King and, in principle, of any other piece on the board) conveys — as the whole of its content — a series of optional moves, a set of possible responses, a chain of foreseeable (or unforeseeable) solutions and therefore a series of new interrelational positions of the entire set of pieces. In other words, even if one maintains that a given piece in a given position *denotes* only itself (a case of 'monoplanarity'), one should agree that the same piece *connotes* a series of possible moves — and in some way *stands for* them. Moreover, each position connotes *different* possibilities *for each* of the two players. Therefore the possible content of a single piece is independent of the piece taken as expression. A chess game is a semiotic system with *two* planes and its pieces act as functives of a sign-function.

Insofar as every situation in a musical piece may (or may not) announce a foreseeable but unpredicted musical solution, music offers another example of a semiotic system in which each situation could be differently *interpreted*.

2.9.3. The code and combinational rules

A sign-function can be defined in itself, and in relation to its combinational possibilities within a context. To maintain a sharp distinction between these two types of definition could clarify many unsolved problems in semantic analysis. At first glance it would seem that a theory of codes merely has to consider the sign-function in itself, for its combination within a context is a matter of sign production. But sign production is permitted by rules previously established by a code, for a code is usually conceived not only as a correlational rule but also as a set of combinational ones.

The fact that an expression like /Johnny found sad/ is unacceptable depends on the code. Obviously a decision as to whether /Johnny found sad/ can in certain circumstances be accepted as valid will depend on interpretive decisions connected to the practice of sign production. Thus the code states that /green colorless ideas sleep furiously/ is semantically anomalous, but an interpretive decision, within the context of a given text, can establish the legitimacy of such an expression — as when, for instance, it is viewed as a poetic device, a calculated and semantically interesting deviation from the norm. In any case it would be very restrictive to assert that a code is only concerned with establishing the isolated meaning of /sleep/ or of /furiously/, without providing any indications about its combinational possibilities.

At this point it may seem necessary to conceive of a code as a double entity establishing on the one hand correspondences between an expression and a content and, on the other, a set of combinational rules.

I believe, however, that the distinction between the definition of the *sign-function in itself* and the definition of the *sign-function as a combinational unit* does not imply this double definition of the code. A code provides: (i) a 'restricted description of a sign-function so that it can be easily understood in its biplanar format independently of any context; (ii) a more complex definition which also foresees some nodal points in which the sign-function, in both its functives, can amalgamate with other sign-functions. In this way the notion of independent combinational rules can be avoided, for they are a part of the coded representation of the sign-function.

Suppose for instance that the representation of /to love/ has a syntactic marker as $V(x,y)$ — which specifies that the verb is transitive — and at least a semantic marker such as Action (A + human, O ± human), or

$$d_{action} \text{---} d_{A + human} \text{---} d_{O \pm human}$$

Suppose then that the semantic representation of /to eat/ has semantic markers such as

$$d_{action} \text{---} d_{A + human} \text{---} d_{O + organic, -human} \ldots \ldots$$

At this point it is easy to see why /John loves his father/ is semantically acceptable and /John eats his father/ is semantically anomalous (except in a quite different cultural context in which even human beings are classified as possible food) [12]. Insofar as a single sign-function can be ruled by many codes or subcodes, one ought to admit that every code establishes its own combinational modes. When speaking of a complex social type of competence such as a language, one should be thinking not of a single code, but of a system of interconnected codes. If somebody prefers to call such a system of systems of sign-functions 'a language', then the proposal could be accepted, provided that one is able to apply this word to each semiotic code without ambiguity or metaphorical transferences.

2.9.4. Requirements of a compositional analysis

When considering the double definition of a sign-function (in itself and in its combinational capacities) one realizes that the expression plane has a privileged status: any expression unit can be defined in itself, not only independently of its combinational possibilities but also of its material quality as a functive. Thus an expression (for instance the word /dog/ or a red flag on a beach) can be analyzed into its articulatory formants:/dog/: three phonemes, each of them formed by a bundle of pertinent features; a red flag: a geometrical form (resulting from an articulation of Euclidean elements) and a color, resulting from a given spectral situation. These expression markers remain the same even though the vehicles are not taken as vehicles (and therefore semiotic functives); they are *structural properties* of the signal.

When on the contrary the expression is considered in its combinational capacities, it acquires so-called syntactic markers, such as Singular, Masculine, Verb, Adjective, etc., which are *grammatical properties* of the functive. They may or may not be represented, at the content level, by corresponding semantic features (/Sonne/ is, syntactically speaking, Feminine in German while /sole/ in Italian is Masculine; yet both expressions convey the same semantic unit, which has no sexual markers) [13].

It is now clear that the markers which must be considered relevant for a description of sign-function are only the markers of the functives as such. The following discussion can thus disregard the structural markers of the signal as such. They seem to be more relevant to a theory of sign production when this latter considers the 'labor' necessary to produce an utterance (see 3.1.).

One may now outline a first tentative analytical model of sign-function.

(i)   The sign-vehicle *possesses* certain syntactical markers (such as Singular, Count etc.) which permit its combination with other sign-vehicles, thus making some syntactically well-formed sentences acceptable even though they are semantically anomalous (for instance /the train delivers a beautiful baby/), and making some other sentences unacceptable even though, semantically speaking, they do make sense (for instance /je est un autre/) [14].

(ii)   A meaning as sememe is *formed* by semantic markers of different kinds (denotations and connotations) which may be arranged hierarchically. Some of these markers may or may not correspond to syntactic markers.

(iii)   In principle, no sign-function is performed by a simple syntactic marker, since the sign-function is established by the code between a given set of semantic markers and a given set of syntactic markers, both taken as a whole. This means that the sign-function *is not a marker to marker correlation*; therefore the sign-function is not established on the grounds of a strict and 'natural' homology between the two functives, but is the result of an arbitrary coupling [15]. Therefore the schematic representation of the meaning of a sign-vehicle (or of the sememe conveyed by a lexical item) should be as follows:

$$\text{/s-v/} \text{---sm----«S»----------} d_1, d_2, d_3 \text{ ----------} c_1, c_2, c_3 \ldots$$

(where /s-v/ is sign-vehicle, sm are the syntactic markers, «S» is the sememe conveyed by /s-v/ and the ds and the cs are the denotations and connotations which compose the sememe. Even if the representation of a sememe were that simple (and let us assume for the moment that it is) many problems would still arise as to the nature of the semantic components. Since a sememe is composed by a more or less finite and more or less linear set of elementary components (denotations and connotations), the problems that must be faced at this point are: (i) whether these components can be isolated; (ii) whether or not they are a finite set of semantic 'universals'; (iii) whether they are theoretical constructs which do not need further semantic definition, or constructs of the type given by a dictionary, that is, words, definitions, purely linguistic constructs; (iv) whether their interconnection is sufficient to define a sememe and the way in which it can be inserted into a discourse, i.e. the way in which a given meaning can be contextually and circumstantially disambiguated.

2.9.5. Some examples of compositional analysis

As regards point (i) Hjelmslev (1943) proposed the possibility of explaining and describing an unlimited number of content-entities by making use of a limited number of content-*figurae*, i.e. more universal combinatory features. Given four elementary features such as «ovine» and «porcine», and «male» and «female», it is possible to combine them into the sememes «ram», «ewe», «pig» and «sow», these primary universal features remaining at one's disposal for further combinations.

As to point (ii), according to Chomsky's first approach (1965), the syntactic markers are undoubtedly a finite set of components on which the so-called 'subcategorization rules' depend (for instance the subcategorization of verbs in Transitive and Intransitive explains why /John found sad/ is grammatically unacceptable). As for the semantic components, which give rise to the so-called 'selectional rules', Chomsky states that "the very notion of 'lexical entry' presupposes some sort of fixed, universal vocabulary in terms of which these objects are characterized, just as the notion of 'phonetic representation' presupposes some sort of phonetic theory"; thus selectional features are 'universal' and 'limited' or must be postulated as such. Unfortunately the only examples of such features so far distinguished are so 'universal' that they are just able to differentiate a bishop from a hippopotamus but do not succeed in differentiating a hippopotamus from a rhinoceros. This difficulty regards point (iv) and demands more analytical features.

For instance, according to Pottier (1965) the sememe «*fauteuil*» can be analyzed by the semes «*pour s'asseoir*», «*sur pied(s)*», «*pour une personne*», «*avec dossier*» and «*avec bras*», while the sememe «*canape*» has the first two semes, lacks the third and can or cannot have the last two. But since these 'semes' are highly analytical, they fail to be 'universal' and, as regards point (iii), need in their turn to be semantically analyzed.

Greimas' 'structural semantics' (Greimas, 1966) seeks to establish semantic features which are universal and are theoretical constructs which do not need a further analysis, or rather, which allow a further analysis but only in the sense that each feature, posited as one among the opposites relating to a dominating axis, can become the axis of an underlying opposition. Thus Greimas gives as an example the semic system of spatiality (Table 14).

Table 14

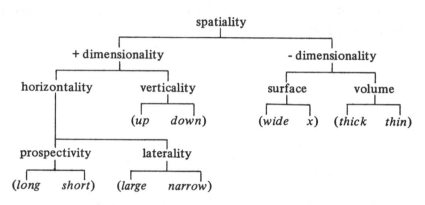

The bracketed words in italics are lexemes characterized by the presence of some semic element: thus the couple *long/short* is characterized by the semes «prospectivity, horizontality, dimensionality, spatiality». However, Greimas means by /lexème/ the manifestation of an expression insofar as it is characterized by the presence of many semes; he calls on the other hand /semème/ not the globality of these semes, as I am doing in the present book, but a given *effect de sens*, or a particular 'reading' of the *lexème*. The limitation of this system seems to be that the repertoire of these features is not a finite one. One only has to consider the system of temporality, or a system of values (Good, Bad, Acceptable, Unacceptable), in order to understand how such a system could develop like an expanding though structured galaxy.

Greimas' method is very useful for explaining how a sememe can permit many rhetorical substitutions; thus to demonstrate that a lexeme like /tête/ has a *'noyeau sémique'* with 'nuclei' such as «extrémité» and «spheroidité» helps one to understand why there exist such catachreses as /tête d'épingle/, /tête du convoy/ or /tête de pont/, depending on the seme made pertinent by the rhetorical substitution. Therefore a semantic representation (especially if trying to explain such problems of sign production as aesthetic texts) must take markers of this kind into account. But this, in itself, would not seem to be enough[16].

So it is necessary to enlarge the notion of semantic marker, even though this may be prejudicial to the postulates of universality and limitation.

2.9.6. A first approach to a definition of the sememe

A sign-vehicle denotes and connotes various cultural units, and some of these exclude each other. This means that among the various denotations and connotations that make up a sememe alternative, complementary or mutually exclusive readings may occur, thus producing semantic incompatibilities. While the decision as to which reading the sender of the message presumably chooses is a matter of sign production (and interpretation), a theory of codes must provide the structural conditions for such a choice. Thus a theory of the interpretation and disambiguation of sememes relies on a theory of their compositional nature.

/*Mus*/ can denote «living being» in respect to the axis 'animate vs. inanimate', «rodent» in respect to a zoological field, «harmful» in respect to the axis 'harmful vs. harmless' and so on. In other words a sign-vehicle s_2 may denote positions α_2 and β_2 in two different semantic axes and, because of these denotations, can connote the contradictory positions γ_1 and γ_3 in another semantic axis, further connoting, through γ_1, ϵ_1 and ζ_1 in two other axes.

Table 15

This is equivalent to Greimas' remark (1966:38) that "le lexème est le lieu de manifestation et de rencontre de sèmes provenant souvent de catégories et de systèmes sémiques différents et entretenant entre eux des relations hiérarchiques, c'est-à-dire hypotaxiques".

Thus s_2 branches out into various positions, not necessarily mutually compatible, in different semantic axes, fields or subsystems. This means that the codes provide the speaker with a competence which includes a large series of semantic fields. These can shift in many directions, and match up in various ways, so that, according to the above diagram, the following situations are possible:

(i)   a speaker A knows all the possible coded denotations and connotations of the sememe «S_2» conveyed by the sign-vehicle /s_2/ and therefore, when emitting or receiving it, takes care to avoid any ambiguity in his expression;

(ii)   a speaker B has a reduced and incomplete knowledge of the code and believes that sememe «S_2» is represented by «$\alpha 2$, $\gamma 1$, $\epsilon 1$» alone (thereby exposing himself to many misunderstandings when speaking or reading).

This apparently unsatisfactory definition of a semantic representation of a sememe could be either corrected by resorting to a strictly formalized semantic theory, or justified by defining the general competence of a social group as the truly vast range of all possible knowledge about the coding correlations, thereby resembling an *encyclopedia* more than a dictionary. These two positions will be discussed and compared in 2.10.2.

2.10. The KF model

2.10.1. Bachelors

One of the most interesting models of compositional analysis is undoubtedly the one proposed by Katz and Fodor (1963) and successively revised in Katz and Postal (1964); for the sake of convenience, I shall call it, from now on, the KF Model. In spite of its many weaknesses (which have been recognized and corrected by one of its authors, see Katz, 1972) this model has provoked such an impressive amount of discussion and refutation [17] that it would seem a convenient point of departure for a Revised Model.

Despite its universal familiarity, I reproduce in Table 16 that compositional analysis of the sememe «bachelor» which seems to have made the whole universe of semantics paranoically and obsessively concerned with the problems of unmarried males and sexually unlucky seals.

In the KF tree there are *syntactic markers* without brackets (which can include categories such as Animate, Count, Common Noun, etc.). Between the round brackets are the *semantic markers* which are very similar to those

Table 16

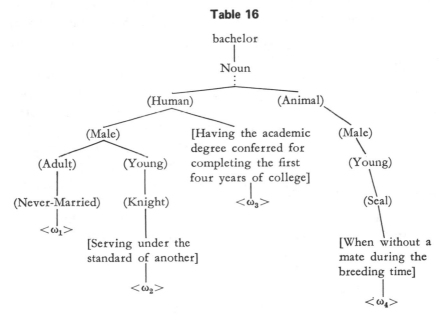

which other authors call "semes". Between square brackets are what the authors call *distinguishers*. Finally there are the *selection restrictions* (symbolized here by Greek letters between angular brackets): "a formally expressed, necessary and sufficient condition for that reading to combine with others" (Katz and Postal: 15). A "reading" is the choice of a "path" and therefore of a *direction*. According to the context, the various semantic components are combined with those of other expressions to make plausible or otherwise a sentence such as /a married man is not a bachelor any more/ or else /my husband is a Bachelor of Arts/.

The possibility of combining expressions is provided within the context by a series of *projection rules* analyzed in detail by Katz and Fodor, so that, faced with the sentence /the man hit the colorful ball/, once the proper semantic components have been assigned to each word, it is possible to construct a series of different readings for the sentence. In fact /colorful/ has two semantic markers («Color» and «Evaluative»); it has two distinguishers "Abounding in contrast or variety of bright colors" and "Having instinctive character, vividness or picturesqueness", and it has selection restrictions such "Physical Object" V "Social Activity" or "Aesthetic object" V "Social Activity". Only after it has been established with which semantic components of /ball/ this adjective should enter into contact will it be known which are the amalgamated paths that lead to the interpretation of the syntagm /colorful ball/ as: (a) «social activity dedicated to the dance, abundant in colors»; (b) «object of spherical shape rich in colors»; (c) "solid missile rich in colors projected by instruments of war»; (d) «social activity dedicated to the dance, vivacious and picturesque».

Sense is specified here as a binary choice which the addressee of the sentence (and the emitter when thinking about how it should be interpreted) makes between the various possible componential ramifications of the sememe.

Katz and Fodor specify that the semantic components should not depend for interpretation on the situation or circumstance (which they call 'setting') in which the sentence is pronounced. They actually indicate various possible readings but their semantic theory is not intended to establish when, how or why the sentence is used in a certain sense and when in another.

The theory is in a position to explain if and why a sentence has many senses but not in what circumstances it will lose its ambiguity nor in what sense.

The KF Model aims to explain semantic problems without resorting to a referential and extensional theory. But it refuses to countenance certain solutions that are strictly necessary in order to attain this end.

I shall try to draw up a sort of *cahier de doléances* about this model so that the more indispensable requirements for a Revised Model can be outlined. These *doléances* concern six points, namely:

(i)   a dictionary-like rigidity (see 2.10.2.);
(ii)   the Platonism of the markers (see 2.10.3.);
(iii)   the disregard of connotations (see 2.10.4);
(iv)   the refusal to consider settings (see 2.10.4);
(v)   the extensional impurity of the distinguishers (see 2.10.5).
(vi)   limitations to the verbal and the categorematic (see 2.10.5).

Let us examine these six points more analytically.

2.10.2. Dictionary and encyclopedia

Doléance (i) concerns the fact that the KF Model represents the ideal competence of an ideal speaker; in the last analysis it can only lead to the making of a very elementary dictionary unable to explain social competence in all its living contradictions, whereas such a competence would have to be acknowledged and explained if a semiotic theory of signification and communication were to be drawn up.

Thus the *doléance* (i) concerns the difference between the abstract dictionary and the concrete encyclopedia. In Katz (1972) there is a criticism of Wilson's critique (1967) of Katz and Fodor (1963). Wilson maintains that a semantic theory ought to concern not the ideal competence of an ideal speaker, but the factual beliefs that people share about things. Meanings are common social beliefs, sometimes mutually contradictory and historically rooted, rather than undated and theoretically fixed constructs. Thus "what takes the place in a dictionary entry in Wilson's theory is a special sort of encyclopedia entry which presents the common core of factual beliefs about the referents of a word" (Katz, 1972:73). In the light of the theory being here elaborated, one may justifiably accept Wilson's proposal provided that the "common core of factual beliefs" are not beliefs "about referents" but the actual cultural definition that a society conventionally accepts for a given content unit. That these beliefs represent different arrangements of markers, and that a code should foresee all of these possible arrangements, is better stated in 2.11.

Katz (1972:75) objects that "words must be seen as changing their tune-in entry continuously, since each time a new discovery is made about the world and speakers come to know about it, their belief in the newly discovered fact must be added to some tune-in entries and a related belief must be added to most". Which is, undoubtedly, a very hard job; unfortunately this job is the one actually performed by a society in using and enriching (by challenging) its codes, as will be discussed in chapter 3.

Thus the theory of the ideal competence of an ideal speaker, carefully defended against the disturbances of historical and social intercourse, has a good chance of being a perfect formal construct, but has very poor chances of being useful to anyone, not even a dictionary publisher, who is equally concerned with the continuous revision of his product. Although to some extent the history of a language is a function of the existence of dictionaries, the latter is more frequently a function of the former.

Katz is rightly preoccupied with the fact that the notion of factual belief does not introduce into semantic theory all the modifications introduced by the speakers' day-to-day factual experience. But it will suffice to reformulate Wilson's requirements as follows: factual beliefs, even if widespread, *must be coded*, or in some way conventionally recognized by a society. Katz asks on what basis they might be recognized. The reply is: on the same basis that allows the KF Model to assume that a /bachelor/ is an unmarried man and not a toothpaste; on the basis which allows not only an encyclopedia but also a dictionary to record that a given entry means one thing in a certain context or for given uses, and in other cases means another [18].

Obviously if one elaborates a semantic theory that resembles an encyclopedia rather than a dictionary, this has several consequences, one of them being a certain loss of crystal-like perfection in the description, as will be shown in 2.12. and 2.13. *à propos* of Model Q. Moreover it implies a theory of the *fuzzy concepts* and of the hedges, such as has been proposed by Lakoff (1972)[19].

2.10.3. Markers as interpretants

Doléance (ii) concerns the Platonism of the markers. We have already discussed in 2.9.5 how difficult it is to imagine a finite and universal set of theoretical constructs able to explain any shade of semantic difference.

The KF Model initially proposed semantic markers as purely theoretical constructs that should not, in principle, have been further analyzed since they were the *explicans* of the sememe and not another *explicandum*; nevertheless when positing *redundancy rules* (Katz, 1972:44) one postulates the further semantic analysis of each component, and so on *ad infinitum*, thus indirectly raising the question of the interpretation of the interpretants.

The redundancy rule states that given for instance a marker like «furniture» possessed by the sememe «chair», «furniture» must be further marked as «artifact» and this last, in its turn, must be further analyzed as «Object+Physical+Non-living». In Katz's mind the redundancy rules are operational devices, which serve to simplify a representation; theoretically speaking it must on the contrary be assumed that the redundancy principle is a requirement of a theory which seeks to complicate the analysis of the sememe, for it shows that every marker is in its turn the origin of a new sememic analysis. Thus every marker must be interpreted by other markers (its interpretants) and the problem that arises at this point is whether even in this sense the interpretants constitute a finite set or whether they are identical to the infinite and continuously self-renewing set of semiosic products that Peirce suggested (see 2.7.3).

2.10.4. Connotations as markers. Settings

Doléance (iii) concerns the problem of connotations. The KF Model, by stopping short at the distinguishers, does not give the measure of all the possible connotations that a sememe may have; thus it offers the semantic theory of a strictly denotative language, and give rules for a basic dictionary that might be useful for tourists who wanted to order lunch, but would be of little help if they really wanted 'to speak' a given language.

The KF Model fails to take into account an infinity of possible ramifications (or paths). Subcodes can exist in which /bachelor/ connotes «dissolute» or «charming young man», or even «libertine with an apartment of his own». As a result (for example in the universe of *pochade*) there are added emotive connotations of sympathy or antipathy and totally axiological connotations. /Bachelor/, understood simply as «unmarried», also connotes the negation of its antonym − i.e. «−married».

One must moreover take into consideration a series of interpretants which the expression connotes although they do not belong to the same semiotic system. The expression /dog/ often connotes − as we have already said − the *image* of a dog. To deny the existence and normality of such connotations signifies limiting the intensional analysis of the sememe to the linguistic environment alone.

The possible objection of 'mentalism' does not hold. We are not speaking of mental and psychological associations (even though they can occur as the result of a given cultural network of connotative equivalences); we are speaking of the correlation posited by a given culture, i.e. that between the word /dog/ and all the images depicting dogs. We are speaking of the fact that in every zoological handbook there is an image of a dog and, as its caption, the verbal graphic sign /dog/. Image and word are mutually implied in strictly abstract and cultural terms, independently of the fact that a human mind can realize that association.

In the case of /bachelor/ the conventional image of the young student who receives his final diploma or of the pageboy to a medieval knight can replace a verbal definition. Once having accepted the model of the KF tree one must allow the whole family of interpretants of a term to find room among its branches. If one arranges this family in all the variety of its ramifications then it becomes difficult to assign the responsibility for its semantic relations to its semantic markers alone (as did Katz and Fodor), regarding the distinguishers as end-points to which semantic relations lead. It is instead necessary to admit that the *amalgamation* of a path can be realized in any one of the tree's nodes.

À propos of connotations it has also been said (2.9.6.) that an expression can *fish* in different semantic axes which, being mutually incompatible, possess opposite connotations. The decision to 'read' the sememe according to one or other connotation will be motivated by contextual or circumstantial factors [20].

All this leads to *doléance* (iv). The KF Model refuses to consider 'settings'. In doing so it is unable to explain how a given lexical item, if uttered in a given circumstance, or if inserted into a specific linguistic context, acquires either of its possible readings. True, the authors announce that they are not concerned with such a matter; but it is equally true that they should be, if they are not, faced with a missing link between a theory of codes and a theory of linguistic performance (or of sign production). Rather than criticize the lack of a theory of settings, I prefer to show, in 2.11., how taking it into account can improve a theory of codes, thus introducing into the framework of a theory of codes many elements of a pragmatics.

2.10.5. Distinguishers as spurious elements

Doléance (v) concerns the nature of distinguishers. In the KF Model the distinguishers are spurious elements which seem to correct the insufficiency of the markers by a more complete and *ad hoc* definition: since a definition is something more complicated than a marker or an entire sememe, the model explains the simpler by the more complex.

When in Katz (1972) the distinguishers are somewhat better defined, they become an *extensional* element introduced into a purely *intensional* theory, with uneconomical results.

If the markers really were pure theoretical constructs which could not be further analyzed (although this is contradicted by the notion of redundancy), they could then be considered as purely intensional categories, thus preserving the non-extensional purity of the theory. But the distinguishers *are not* pure theoretical constructs but, on the contrary, complex definitions. What is their role within the theory? Katz (1972) is aware of this problem and replies that they are not intensional properties of the sememe, indeed they are no more than a description of the referents to which the reading can be applied. In other words, given a reading which provides the intensional description of an Animal Male Young Seal, the tree advises that it is possible to apply such a semantic entity to an actual seal which is without a mate during the breeding season. The first weakness of this solution is clearly due to the fact that an extensional indication is inserted into an intensional description; but the more dangerous result is that, without such an extensional description, there is nothing to distinguish a seal with a mate from a seal without one — except that the latter is called a /bachelor/. Thus the intensional theory contradicts itself by a *petitio principi*, since, without extensional indications, it is not the markers but the name coupled to a referent that characterizes the meaning of a sign. But, curiously enough, another reading of /bachelor/ states that it is a Human Male Adult

Never-Married. Why is «Never Married» a marker (and therefore a theoretical intensional construct), and «when without mate etc.» a distinguisher? «Never Married» is a marker which means «who has not found or does not want to find a wife» (its interpretant looks like a distinguisher); while «when without a mate etc.» is a distinguisher whose interpretant is «un-mated» (and therefore looks like a marker). Why is the former a theoretical construct and the latter not? Because an unmarried man is always such, while an unmated seal is such only during a certain period of the year? Evidently not, because both situations are provisional.

Thus the distinguishers would really seem to be an *ad hoc* solution introduced to cover certain weaknesses of the model.

Katz says that "distinguishers are purely denotative distinctions" (where 'denotative' is used in its extensional sense) which "mark purely perceptual distinctions among the referents of conceptually identical sense . . . . Consequently, only a general theory of linguistic performance, which incorporates and integrates accounts of linguistic competence and perceptual mechanisms, can connect the distinguishers in the vocabulary of semantic theory with the constructs in the vocabulary of perceptual theory that correspond to them" (1972:84).

Katz is right in assuming that a theory of competence (or of codes) can only provide for the use of words in order to refer to actual states of the world. But, to my mind, he anticipates these limits to a theory of competence somewhat hastily. Let us consider the phrase more attentively quoted above: what does "referent of conceptually identical sense" mean? A referent as such has no sense at all. It is a state of the world. At most it could be viewed as the sense of an otherwise empty sign which acquires meaning only when it is referred to it. But we know that Katz rejects this theory, according to which the meaning of a sign should be its referent. Therefore when he speaks of a "conceptually identical sense" he can only mean that a given referent, in order to be perceived as such, must be subsumed under a pre-established category, a cultural construct, i.e. a sememe (for the development of a semiotic theory of perception itself, see 3.3.). So this 'conceptually identical sense' must be analyzed *as a sense*, making use of all the paraphernalia of a semantic theory. Instead of distinguishers the tree must have intensional descriptions (and therefore a network of semantic markers), so that the distinguishers are submitted to the same redundancy rule as that which provides an underlying semantic analysis for each marker. Either the item of a perceptual theory is a construct or it is not; if it is (as Katz assumes), then it must be described by a semantic theory, on the grounds of that very 'effability principle' which Katz so strongly asserts (1972:19). If a perceptual construct cannot be described by a semantic theory, on what grounds could a word (along with its senses) then be used in order to name a perceptual construct? As will be seen in 3.3.5., even 'mentioning' (i.e. referring signs to things) consists in stating that a sign-vehicle to which a code assigns a given set of (semantic) properties can be applied to a perceptum to which another scientific 'code' assigns a given set of (perceptual or physical) properties, the latter being susceptible to naming by the former, or both being susceptible to naming by a common metalanguage [21].

Finally, there is a factor in Katz's (1972) theory which makes solving the problem of distinguishers extremely difficult: this is the lack of a more articulated notion of the interpretant.

Katz says that a distinguisher is not a conceptual construct because it can also be a sense datum like "red": "it is hard to imagine that a color quality like redness is susceptible to conceptual analysis" (1972:87).

Apart from the fact that if red is a "perceptual construct" studied by a perceptual theory, then there must be some way to analyze it conceptually (as in fact happens when the red cue is defined as the spectral space which goes from 650 to 800 millimicrons), it must clearly be maintained that the semantic markers are neither other words nor pure abstract theoretical constructs, but *interpretants*, so that semantic representations of the words /red/ and /cherry/ must include among their branches the image of a sense datum. This assumption does not compromise the theoretical purity of a theory of codes, for even «red» as a sense datum can be semantically defined as a cultural unit not only insofar as it may be completely analyzed into spectral formants, but also because it is culturally detectable as a *position in a color field* and thus culturally distinguishable from other colors: a color is simply a member of an antonymous *n*-tuple! A red cue cannot be understood if not inserted in a semantic field, just as «human» cannot be understood if not inserted into its own semantic frame of reference.

This incapability to accept as a marker what is not verbally translatable by synonyms or paraphrases leads to *doléance* (vi), which concerns the model's relevance to non-verbal, and to verbal but non-categorematic devices. The KF Model is neither applicable to syncategorematic terms nor to signs outside verbal language; it is not therefore suitable for a semiotic theory of codes. True, its authors never claimed to offer a general semiotic theory of semantics, but here I am not concerned with their intentions as much as with the usefulness of their proposals for my present purposes. So rather than criticize their weakness on this point, I prefer to show how a Revised Model could even take this important requirement for a theory of codes into account.

2.11. A revised semantic model

2.11.1. The format of the sememe

The Revised Model aims to insert into the semantic representation all coded connotations depending on corresponding denotations as well as *contextual* and *circumstantial selections*. These selections distinguish the different readings of the sememe as encyclopedia item and determine the assignment of many denotations and connotations. They are not matters of empirical and *ad hoc* knowledge of referents but rather pieces of coded information, in other words semantic units just like the others except that they perform a *switching function*.

Let us imagine in Table 17 a hypothetical sign-function so encyclopedically complex that it can show various types of differently organized 'readings':

Table 17

Here *sm* is the entire set of syntactic markers (which will not here be brought into question); *d* and *c* are respectively the denotations and connotations (in the sense of 2.9.1.); *(cont)* are contextual selections, giving instructions of the type: "when you find *(cont$_a$)*, use the following *d*s and *c*s when the sememe in question is contextually associated with the sememe «a»"; [*circ*] are circumstantial selections giving instructions of the type: "when you find [*circ$_\alpha$*] use the following *d*s and *c*s when the sign-vehicle corresponding to the sememe in question is circumstantially accompanied by the event or the object //α//, to be understood as the sign-vehicle belonging to another semiotic system".

A compositional tree like this one shows that:

(i) Syntactic marker, along with the subcategorization rules that they imply, pertain to the expression, not to the content; thus a sentence like /a gloop is a bloop/ is syntactically correct, even if you don't know what it means, provided that /gloop/ and /bloop/ are equally marked as Noun+Masculine+ Singular (in the same sense, a flagpole with a green square flag in which three yellow circles are inserted, is syntactically correct, outside verbal signs, even though no registered nation, state or association can be identified with this type of symbol);

(ii) A sememe may have (a, i) denotative markers which remain unchanged in every possible contextual and circumstantial selection, such as d_1 and d_2 (with some added connotation c_1 and c_2, depending on d_1) or may have (b, i) different ds and therefore different cs according to diverse contextual and circumstantial selections. Thus a /bachelor/ is conventionally «young» only if a contextual selection specifies ($cont_{chivalry}$), the denotation «young» releasing connotations such as «chastity»; in the above diagram a case like this is represented by the contextual selection ($cont_b$). The case of $[circ_\gamma]$ is instead one in which, granted the same circumstances, there can be different contextual selections; the case of ($cont_a$) is one in which, granted the same context, there can be different circumstantial selections;

(iii) Contextual selections record other sememes (or groups of sememes) *usually* associated with the sememe in question; circumstantial selections record other sign-vehicles (or groups of sign-vehicles) belonging to different semiotic systems, or objects and events taken as ostensive signs, *usually* occurring along with the sign-vehicle corresponding to the sememe in question; both act as *amalgamation switchers*. In this way, contextual and circumstantial selections do not require a specific type of instruction, for they are none other than cultural units or expressions, constituting the main node of other sememic representations or the elements of the compositional analysis of another sememe. Thus the same elements serve both as markers or as 'selection restrictions': the same kind of entity performing a double role according to its strategical position within the tree, an economical result has been attained (*entia non sunt multiplicanda praeter necessitatem*).

(iv) Selection restrictions are eliminated along with distinguishers. The former are in fact anticipated by both contextual and circumstantial selection, the latter dissolve into a complex network of semantic markers. Thus /bachelor/ could be approximately analyzed as «man+young+fulfillment+college+ . . .» .

This is a very rough suggestion about what a compositional analysis (able to eliminate distinguishers) should be, and the suggestion can be improved only after a more painstaking analysis of the underlying semantic fields. The postulation of such semantic fields is an indispensable requirement, even in the case of other semantic approaches such as the one proposed by Bierwisch (1970), who analyzed lexemes in this way:

/father/ = X parent of Y + Male X + (Animate Y + Adult X + Animate Y)
/kill/ = X_s Cause (X_d Change to (-Alive X_d)) + (Animate X_d)

(v) When analyzing verbs a particular series of denotative markers should represent the arguments of an n-places predicate, according to an inventory of *roles* or 'cases'. Those cases are semantic *actants* (in the sense of the *"analyse actantielle"* proposed by Greimas) rather than morphological cases (see also the suggestions of Fillmore, 1968 and 1971). In short, an action is accomplished by an Agent (A), by means of an Instrument (I), to reach an aim or a Purpose (P) and affecting an Object (O) — where Object still is an umbrella-category covering semantic roles implied by different morphological cases, such as 'dative' or 'accusative': therefore the Object should be more finely analyzed as Addressee, Experiencer, Object physically modified by the action, and so on. Let us assume that, when the verb is a locutionary one, there is a Topic (T) (*de te* (T) *fabula* (A) *narratur* (locutionary)).

Such an approach should take into account even the semantic presuppositions directly entailed by the sememe, without introducing new semantic categories such as 'focus' and 'presupposition' (PS). Obviously, in order to elaborate this kind of representation one should first of all distinguish between the various senses of the word /presupposition/ that in philosophical and logical literature sends back to radically different phenomena.

Referential presuppositions concern a theory of mentions (cf. 3.3.) and are the ones studied by Frege (1892): "if anything is asserted there is always an obvious presupposition that the simple or compound proper names used have a reference".

Contextual presuppositions are the ones studied by a text theory and concern both textual inferences and rules of overcoding (cf. 2.14.3.). Hiz (1969) calls these mutual textual occurrences 'referentials'' and says that, given the text /Two roads lead to John's house. One way goes through the woods. The other is shorter. Both are paved and he knows them very well/, /he/ refers to the occurrence /John/, /them/ refers to /two roads/, /way/ refers to /roads/, and so on.

Circumstantial presuppositions concern what both the sender and the addressee know or are supposed to know about coded or uncoded entities and events. Contextual and circumstantial presuppositions can be also called *pragmatic*.

Semantic presuppositions strictly depend on the format of the sememe: if one says that /John is a bachelor/ everyone understands that John is a male adult human being. But, insofar as they are directly *entailed* by the semantic organization (i.e., are analytically "included" as a necessary part of the complete meaning of a given expression, cf. Katz, 1972, 4.5.), let us define them rather than 'presupposition', as *semiotic entailment* (see the difference between semiotic and factual judgments in 3.2.) [22]. Therefore only semantic presuppositions (i.e., semiotic entailments) directly concern the theory of codes and must be recorded by the semantic representations as parts of the meaning. Once this granted, let us translate in terms of the Revised Model the representation of two verbs studied by Fillmore (1971), /accuse/ and /criticize/. Fillmore asserts that, as far as 'meaning' and 'presupposition' are involved, one verb asserts what the other presupposes and vice versa. In terms of the Revised Model this difference should be completely manifested by a series of denotations. Let us assume that /accuse/, syntactically marked as $/v(x,y,z,k,w)/$, is semantically analyzed as follows:

$$d_{action}, d_{claim}, d_{A:human}, d_{O:human}, d_{I:locutionary}, d_{T:action\ of\ O},$$
$$d_{T:bad}, d_{P:revelation} \cdots\cdots etc.$$

In fact (when accusing) an agent is claiming by linguistic devices that a human object (the Addressee of his locutionary act and the Experiencer of his attack) has done a supposedly bad action. The *performative* nature of the verb is given by the marker «claim», which, at the same time, analytically (or semiotically) *entails* the fact that the Topic has not a marker of «factuality»; the locutionary nature of the verb is given by the fact that the instrument is a verbal one.

Let us now assume that /criticize/ (having the same syntactical marker as a five places predicate) is semantically analyzable as follows:

$$d_{action}, d_{A:human}, d_{I:locutionary}, d_{O:human}, d_{T:action\ of\ O}, d_{P:censure}, d_{P:demonstration}$$

The representation shows that by means of language one can criticize a human being for an action which is not yet felt to be bad while the purpose of the agent is just to demonstrate that the action is censurable. It is not necessary to express the fact that the action or the object that constitutes the topic of the locutionary act are presupposed as 'real', for such a presupposition is a pragmatic and referential one, depending on conversational rules (see 2.14.5. and note 26): first of all the one of "Telling the Truth" (Cooperative Principle).

The representation of /accuse/ gives more interesting results if one analyzes the corresponding Italian expression /accusare/, since in Italian it is customary to say that an inanimate object (a clue, an imprint) 'accuses' someone, that is 'proves' without any doubt that someone has done something. Therefore the representation of the Italian /accusare/ should be:

$$d_{action}, d_{O\ human} < \begin{matrix} (cont_{A\ +\ human}) \text{---}d_{claim}, d_{l:locutionary}, d_{T:action\ of\ O}, d_{T:bad}\cdots \\ (cont_{A\ -\ human}) \text{---}d_{I=A}, d_{proof}, d_{T(O=A_2\ of\ O_2)}, d_{O_2\ bad}, \cdots \end{matrix}$$

Denotations depending on the second contextual selections sound rather unsatisfactory since the action, insofar as it is attributed to an object, cannot be viewed as a locutionary act, while in fact there is a sort of anthropomorphization of the object which is considered to 'speak'. In fact this second use of /accusare/ has to be viewed as a rhetorical figure (a *prosopopoeia*) even if it has been definitely catachresized by usage. In this sense the difficulty in representing this second sense works as an etymological clue and the structural and synchronic analysis asks for an historical one, showing that a process of *code changing* (cf. 3.1.) has occurred, leaving the semantic system somewhat unbalanced.

(vi) The tree may be simplified if we consider certain readings as the univocal paths of two or more *homonymous sememes*. Suppose for instance that there are two different sememes, «bachelor$_1$» with the immediate and omni-contextual denotation «Human», and a «bachelor$_2$» with the immediate and omni-contextual denotation «Animal». But in such a case one will have to give up one's grasp upon a lot of historical overlaps caused by metaphorical substitutions: a particular kind of seal, an unmarried man and a young knight are three different semantic units, but they have a component in common («no mate»). It has thus been metaphorically suitable to take the name (the lexeme) corresponding to one of the sememes (it does not matter which) and to assign it to the others. As we will see in 3.8., a metaphor is nothing more than the substitution of one sememe for another, through the innovatory amalgamation of one or several markers. When the metaphor becomes customary, a *catachresis* takes place: two sememes acquire the same corresponding lexeme (that is: two content units possessing some components in common accept the same expression).

The reduction of one complex tree (which takes into account metaphorical and catachresical homonymies) to several more simplified trees does not prevent one from considering this kind of rhetorical parenthood. But it does seem to be more convenient to conceive the trees in their most complex polivalence.

2.11.2. Coding contexts and circumstances

The only objection is the one already advanced by Katz and Fodor (1963): in order to establish a theory of contextual and circumstantial selection (that is a theory of settings) "it would be required that the theory represents *all* the knowledge speakers have about the world".

To this objection it must be answered that: (a) some of the tasks attributed by the KF Model to the theory of settings are in fact undertaken by a satisfactory compositional analysis of the sememe; (b) the theory does not have to list and to structure *all* the possible occurrences of a given item but only those which are *culturally* and *conventionally* recognized as the more statistically probable.

Let us examine these two important points.

Katz and Fodor show some perplexity about the correct disambiguation of an expression such as /our store sells alligator shoes/. They suggest that, granted the appropriate external circumstances (for instance a sign in a store window), the expression will undoubtedly mean «we sell shoes made from alligator skins», but they are in doubt as to whether the phrase could not also be read as «we are selling shoes for alligators». This perplexity conceals a double fallacy. If one possesses a suitable semantic representation, the cultural unit «shoe» must have been analyzed in such a way that its explicit semantic property of being worn by human beings will not allow one to amalgamate the sememe «shoe» with the sememe «alligator», which has the denotative marker «Animal». So, since one cannot read «shoes for alligators», one is left with only one correct solution. Therefore no ambiguity is possible, except in Disneyland (but Disneyland, and the world of fairy tales in general, is a semantically revised universe within which the usual denotative and connotative properties of sememes are upset — though not at random, but following the rules of a complete semantic restructuring). This once granted, it is not even necessary to confront, to disambiguate the expression, with a particular external circumstance: /we sell alligator shoes/ has the same univocal meaning even if written on the door of a zoological garden (though here the problem is whether to bring charges against the director of the zoo for professional misconduct). The other example Katz and Fodor give is a more puzzling one.

The two expressions (1) /should we take Junior back to the zoo?/ and (2) /should we take the lion back to the zoo?/ really seem to require some sort of extra-knowledge in order to be disambiguated. One needs to know that "lions . . . are often kept in cages", Katz and Fodor say. No doubt they are right; however, it is not by chance that the authors say that lions are "often" kept in cages. There may be lions circulating freely in the penthouse of some millionaire, but this fact is so idiosyncratic that society does not register it (and anyway the police usually forbid it). But society does record the fact that lions usually live: (a) in the jungle; (b) in cages at the zoo; (3) in circuses. A lion living free in the jungle conventionally connotes «freedom», «pride» (or «nobility»), «ferociousness» and «savageness» (leaving aside, for the moment, more elaborate legendary or allegorical connotations). A lion living in a zoo conventionally connotes (among other things) «captivity». A lion in a circus connotes «tamed» and «skilfulness» (though connotations such as «ferociousness» are not excluded but hang in the background — the pleasure of the circus being precisely due to this ambiguous interplay of antynomical connotations, which means that the circus performance has something in common with an aesthetic message). If we consider that /zoo/ also conveys a connotative mark of «captivity» there is only one correct amalgamation: a lion taken back to the zoo is an animal once again reduced to captivity (so that the very expression /to take back/ acquires a connotation of «repression»).

But /Junior/, understood as «son», does not possess these connotations, nor indeed does /zoo/ have any markers that can be amalgamated with it (the amalgamation takes place between «to move toward + human object + place»). Thus we are not sure whether it is a pleasant experience for Junior to be taken back to the zoo, and the sentence is open to various pragmatic evaluations, whereas we can be sure that the same experience is an unpleasant one for the lion. Let it be noted that in this case circumstances have not been involved; contextual selections alone have sufficed to disambiguate all the connotations implied by the use of the above sememes. Circumstances, and circumstantial selections, would have been involved if the expression /we should take back the lion/ had been pronounced in front of the door of the zoological garden, while walking the lion on a leash. Except that such a case is so unusual that there is no need to certify this type of circumstance. A case of coded circumstance is on the contrary provided by the image of a skull that if placed on a bottle means «poison» and if placed on an electric pylon means «high voltage».

In order to establish a theory of settings, one must assume that a semantics of verbal language cannot be outlined unless one accepts as a general background the intertwined influence of *many semiotic codes*. A theory of settings requires that external circumstances also be subject to semiotic convention.

Only if objects, images and actual experiences fall within the domain of a general semiotic theory is it possible to accept the idea that a coded external circumstance enters into the compositional spectrum of a sememe.

Only if the possible content of a verbal lexeme along with the possible content of another type of experience are both translated into abstract cultural units is it possible to outline the revised componential model that has been proposed here.

Is it possible to establish componential trees that take into account all coded contexts and circumstances? The question could only have sense if there existed a Global Semantic System correlating all possible interconnections between every one of its items. Otherwise it should be reformulated as follows: "Are there any cultural environments and precise universes of discourse in which this could be done?" It is always possible to isolate a cultural framework in which some contextual and circumstantial selections are coded, as in the example of alligator shoes in a Western culture. Obviously in a savage culture where shoes are scarcely known (and where the idea that the skin of an alligator serves to make shoes is absolutely unknown), the sentence quoted above could also be interpreted as referring to shoes for alligators, thereby appearing somewhat whimsical but at least less unacceptable than the idea of killing alligators in order to make Cinderella a present.

2.11.3. The sememe as encyclopedia

Therefore there can be cases of incomplete codes, of hierarchical scientific componential spectrums, of disconnected lists of semantic properties attributed to a sememe by the layman, and so on.

For a zoologist «whale» is a hierarchically and univocally organized sememe in which secondary properties depend on primary ones, thus producing the organization suggested by Table 18.

Table 18

$$/X/ = «X» \begin{cases} P \begin{cases} P \\ P \begin{cases} P \\ P \end{cases} \end{cases} \\ P \\ P \begin{cases} P \\ P \end{cases} \end{cases}$$

For the medieval author of a bestiary, «whale» may have had the same formal semantic structure, except that the content of the properties differed: the whale was a fish and not a mammal, and among the secondary properties he would have put a lot of allegorical connotations, such as the property of representing the Leviathan, the Devil, Sin and so on.

For a modern layman «whale» is probably a very disconnected sememe in which such properties as «fish» and «mammal» coexist and its semantic spectrum should probably be a network of superimpositions of possible readings in which the contextual selections are not very well established. An example of this kind of competence can be found in the way in which Melville, consciously interpreting the state of knowledge of the mariners of Nantucket, defines the whale as a big fish with a warm bilocular heart, lungs and a *"penem intrantem foeminam mammis lactantem"* (*Moby Dick*, ch. 32). We can now imagine a certain cultural level at which /whale/ gives rise to a contradictory sememe considering both the medieval, the scientific and the popular system of units (Table 19).

Table 19

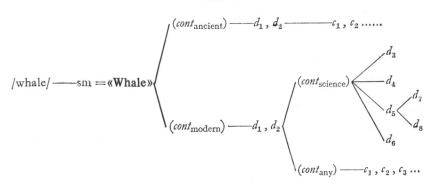

This exactly represents the sort of competence as 'encyclopedia' (instead of 'dictionary') that was outlined in 2.10.2. The fact that, in the above example, the encyclopedia seems closer to a medieval 'speculum mundi' than to the *Encyclopedia Britannica* suggests that the universe of natural languages is a rather unformalized and 'primitive' one, and thus far from being scientific or highly formalized.

The sign-vehicle /whale/ corresponds to a content unit (a sememe) «whale» which can be decomposed in different ways. It depends on the context whether a whale will be considered a fish or a mammal, and this decision precedes the isolation of the first immediate denotation. In fact, in order to conceive of a whale as being something like a fish, a culture must set it in a given semantic field in which «whale» is opposed and interconnected with «shark» and «dolphin» for example, those cultural units having certain elements in common and others in mutual opposition, exactly as in a structured field of phonemes, mutually correlated and opposed by means of distinctive features (Jakobson-Halle, 1956). If on the other hand a whale is viewed as a mammal (or at least as an aquatic animal although not a fish) it will have to be posited as the pertinent unit of another semantic field.

If the whale is viewed within a contemporary context, then there are two more contextual selections to be made. If the reading is a scientific one, it will have to consider a hierarchy of denoted properties, and if it is a popular one, it will have to choose between an array of non-coordinated connotations. This componential spectrum is a synchronico-diachronical one, and allows one not only to distinguish between the possible readings available for ancient and modern scientific texts, but also to accept the *double jeu* imposed by a text like *Moby Dick*, whose author deliberately tried to exploit our modern (indeed, rather contradictory) notion of «whale», speculating upon the overlapping of possible readings or paths whose programmed intertwining constitutes an aesthetic achievement.

2.11.4. Compositional analysis of non-verbal expressions.

Even non-verbal signs can have a semiotic representation according to the Revised Model. The two examples in Tables 20 and 21 may suffice:

Table 20

$$//red\ flag// \ — \text{sm} = \text{«red flag»} \begin{cases} [circ_{\text{highway}}] \ —— d_{\text{caution}} \\ [circ_{\text{railroad}}] \ —— d_{\text{stop}} \\ [circ_{\text{politics}}] \ —— d_{\text{communism}} \end{cases}$$

Table 21

$$//skull// — \text{sm} = \text{«skull»} — c_{\text{death}} \begin{cases} [circ_{\text{bottle}}] \ —— d_{\text{poison}} \\ [circ_{\text{flag}}] \ —— d_{\text{pirate}} \\ [circ_{\text{power plant}}] \ —— d_{\text{high voltage}} \ —— c_{\text{danger}} \\ [circ_{\text{shirt}}] \ —— d_{\text{fascist commandos}} \end{cases}$$

Obviously the above examples concern visual but strictly coded signs. One could object that the same procedure cannot be applied to the so-called 'iconic' signs. This particular problem is discussed in chapter 3. But for the moment let us test the model on other types of signs.

2.11.5. Compositional analysis of verbal shifters and other indices

The first signs to be tested are the so-called *syncategorematic* terms. It is not difficult to demonstrate that such terms as /away-off-out/ or /at-in-on/ and /with-without/ can be viewed as cultural units inserted into given semantic axes (see Leech, 1969). It is possible to compositionally analyze such items, demonstrating that they possess definite semantic markers which are independent of the context into which they are inserted. It is no more difficult to explain what it means to be /under (something)/ than to explain what it means to be /father (of somebody)/ (see Bierwisch 1970).

The problem becomes more awkward when examining the meaning of the so-called *deictic* or *anaphoric* verbal signs, such as /this-that/ or /here-there/. These signs seem to be very similar to non-verbal *pointers*, such as a pointing finger or a directional arrow. These latter deserve a further examination not only because of the content they convey but also because of their particular expressive features. But what will be said about the semantics of verbal pointers can be extended to the semantics of other kinds of non-verbal indices.

Peirce defined the index as a type of sign causally connected with its object, and recognized medical symptoms, tracks and so on as such, but was tempted to exclude both non-verbal pointers and deictic and anaphoric verbal shifters from this category; as a matter of fact though they do have a sort of causal connection with the object to which they refer, they are not natural signs and are artificially, indeed often arbitrarily, chosen. Peirce (2.283) called them both *subindices* and *hyposemes*. Inasmuch as they are connected with the object to which they point and from which they seem to receive their meaning, subindices should not adapt to a non-referential semiotics. If a sign is a correlation between an expression and a content (independently of the actual presence or existence of any referent) how can one call a shifter like /this/, which receives its semiotic character from the presence of the actual object, a 'sign'? The object can be either an extra-linguistic entity (as when replying to the question /which one would you like?/, one points one's forefinger toward an object and says /this one/) or another linguistic item to which the anaphoric verbal item refers, as in /I do not approve of a statement like that/.

But suppose that one says the above sentence when in fact nobody has recently stated anything. The hearers immediately notice a misuse of language, and begin to wonder what statement the speaker is talking about (maybe trying to recollect past conversations in order to place the presupposition that the speaker has so oddly recalled). This means that the speaker has more or less presupposed: «I am naming through the shifter something which is not here, and which preceded the present statement». And this meaning of /this/ or /that/ is understood even if the presupposed event or thing does not exist and never has existed.

Once again a lie is made possible by the fact that sign-vehicles always convey a content, even when there is no testable referent.

Neither the presence of the supposedly connected object nor of the supposedly connected contextual item is necessary to the comprehension of a verbal index. A verbal index is composed by an expression which conveys a denotation. In the case of /this/ the denotations are two: «closeness» and «to the speaker» (in the same sense in which the shifter /I/ primarily means «the logical subject of the sentence is the sender of the utterance»). If this is accepted, then the referential theory of indices (or subindices) is totally upset. According to the referential theory the verbal index indicated an object or another verbal item (therefore a referent) *because of its physical closeness to it*. Physical closeness was thus a marker of the sign-vehicle, but rather a curious one: the sign-vehicle was able to signify an object as its content because of the proximity of that object as an item of its own expression! On the contrary our theory *excludes* physical connection with the referent and considers *closeness as a signified content*. /This/ does not acquire a meaning because something is close to it; on the contrary it signifies that *there must be something close to it.*

This explains why, when responding to the question /which one?/ (and presupposing that there are none of the objects in question around), if I answer /this one/ the hearer will understand that I am signifying something very close to me and will therefore realize that, since there is nothing there, I am misusing language and performing an inappropriate referring act.

The expressive opposition /this vs. that/ relies upon a semantic opposition «closeness vs. distance» (or «+ close vs. - close»)which represents a precise segmentation of the content. It is worth noticing that if the question /which one?/ concerns two or more objects placed at the same distance from the speaker, the answer /this one/, if not accompanied by a pointing finger (or a movement of the eyes or head), does not work. The content of /this/ is equally comprehensible but the referring act is incomplete. One could say that: (a) in some cases the verbal shifters have a purely redundant function and what really does the indication is the pointing finger; (b) the pointing finger represents a sort of circumstantial selection prescribing that in cases of such a connection the meaning of /this/ is «the object toward which the finger points»; (c) there are two referring acts: first of all /this/ enhances a mention whose object is the finger, secondly the finger enhances a mention whose object is something else. Explanation (c) refers back to explanation (a) because once again /this/ has a purely redundant function.

Another problem is whether verbal indices really stand for a content which is *verbally* translatable. Does /this/ really mean something corresponding to the word /closeness/? Let us consider the possible anaphoric function of /this/. When used for deixis, /this/ gives rise to a referring act, but when it is used inside a verbal context it has an anaphoric function; in these instances the opposition between /this/ and /that/ practically disappears; one can say either /I do not like this/ or /I do not like that/, releasing the same immediate denotation of «the immediately preceding semantic unit». But this verbalization leaves many problems unsolved. The preceding semantic unit may be a word or an entire phrase, and does not, after all, necessarily have to be the 'immediately' preceding one. A crude but more satisfactory verbalization would be: /the last relevant portion of the content/. In fact /this/ or /that/ does indeed seem to demand that the hearer turn his mind backward. The rest should be a matter of contextual interpretation. Thus it would be more suitable to transcribe the content of /this-that/, in their anaphoric function, as ← . One could then transcribe their deictic function as → .

We must remember what has been stressed in 2.7.2. and 2.10.4: it is not claimed that the interpretant of a sign ought to be another sign of the same type; it is not claimed that the denotation or the connotation of a word ought to be something that can only be translated by another word. To come in, to come out, to climb, to lean, to lie on the ground, are all portions of a highly segmented content field concerning body behavior. This behavior is not only segmented, but the segments are culturally recognized as such and named. However, the most recent experience in kinesic research shows not only that a gesture is best described (as far as the expression plane is concerned) by a non-verbal shorthand, but also that the content of this gesture can be best interpreted by a movie recording or a behavioral response. When Morris (1946) says that the 'significatum' of a sign is our disposition to respond to it (therefore reducing the theory of meaning to the behavioral verification of the effects of the sign-vehicle) he deprives the theory of meaning of a lot of opportunities that a theory of interpretants and of cultural units can restore to it; however, he does suggest that some sign-vehicles need to be interpreted by a behavioral response.

Let us therefore assume that one of the primary denotations of /this/ and /that/ is a behavioral attitude. They are both 'imperative' and 'referential' expressions (or in Morris' terms, *designators* and *prescriptors*). This makes better sense than saying (as does Morris) that they are *identifiors* and thus similar to logical proper names (in Russell's sense).

When deictically used, /this/ means: «→ (or «look at!») + close + speaker». When anaphorically used, /this/ means: «← + close + context». Thus the compositional analysis of /this/ should, according to our revised compositional model, be represented as in Table 22.

Table 22

(a)

$$/this/ \text{ ———sm} = \text{«This»} \text{ —— } d_{close} \begin{cases} [circ_{+pointer}] \text{ —— } d_{speaker} \text{ —— } d_{\rightarrow} \\ [circ_{-pointer}] \text{ —— } d_{context} \text{ —— } d_{\leftarrow} \end{cases}$$

(b)

$$/that/ \text{ ———sm} \rightarrow \text{«That»} \begin{cases} [circ_{+pointer}] \text{ —— } d_{speaker} \text{ —— } d_{distant} \text{ —— } d_{\rightarrow} \\ [circ_{-pointer}] \text{ —— } d_{context} \text{ —— } d_{\leftarrow} \end{cases}$$

Table 22 may be read as follows:

(a): /this/ always has a denotation of proximity; when connected with a kinesic pointer it also denotes physical proximity to the speaker and obligation to focus one's attention prospectively; when without kinesic pointers it means that attention must be directed retrospectively within the context.

(b): on the contrary /that/ does not have an immediate denotation of distance; it acquires this only if circumstantially connected with a kinesic pointer, in this case meaning something far from the speaker; if without such a pointer it has the same path as /this/.

One realizes that, whether or not one accepts that some semantic markers can be non-verbally represented, the representation of /this/ or /that/ follows the same procedure as did that of /whale/ or any other categorematic term [23].

The above representation may be verified by the compositional analysis of the kinesic pointers circumstantially connected with the verbal shifter. Such an analysis will appear a little more complex because, while in analyzing verbal lexemes, within the present context, we have taken for granted the representation of the syntactic markers (*sm*), when analyzing a pointing finger these markers must be explicitly analyzed. The reason for this will be clarified below. Obviously these features are not of the same nature as the verbal ones, for different types of expressions are produced according to different physical parameters (as will be shown in 3.4.2); and different

physical parameters generate different formal features. So a pointing finger
has at least four pertinent syntactic features: two dimensional markers and
two kinesic markers. First of all a pointing finger possesses *//longitude//* and
//extremity// (or *//apicality//*). It is longer than it is bulky and 'stops' at
the top of the fingernail. This observation might seem rather obvious, but
suffice it to think of an iconic surrogate of the pointing finger (for instance,
of the image of an arrow in a road signal) to discover that these features are
indispensable. As a matter of fact, the arrow 'iconically' reproduces not only
the longitudinal feature but also the apical one: the arrow is not supposed to
stop at its apex but rather 'to travel' (and irreversibly) in a given direction,
but this suggested movement helps one to distinguish between the point from
which the arrow is 'generated' and the one toward which it 'grows' or
'springs'. What this means is that the arrow, like the finger, has a 'root' and an
'apex', and in both cases it is the apex that is marked. Nevertheless a road
arrow is not really moving, whereas a pointing finger is. However, it is not by
chance if, in order to imitate a pointing finger, the image of an arrow has
been chosen: the arrow suggests the idea of a movement toward something.

In fact the third feature of the pointing finger is a *//movement toward//*.
This feature must always exist, even if imperceptible. In some other kinesic
expressions it is absolutely indispensable, as occurs when somebody 'turns'
his head or glances toward something. In these cases the features *//movement
toward//* and *//apicality//* suffice, and *//longitude//* is not needed.

On the contrary with pointing fingers (as well as with arrows) it is
longitude that seems to be a basic feature: if, instead of indicating something
with a single forefinger, one points two parallel forefingers separated by a
distance of two or three inches, the *//longitude//* of the single finger is
neutralized by the *//latitude//* of the entire gesture; what is then suggested is
not «direction» but «dimension» (the size of an object is expressed). But if
one reduces the distance between the forefingers to half an inch, *//latitude//* is
neutralized and *//longitude//* emerges again, thus expressing a semantic marker
of «direction».

The fourth necessary feature is again a kinesic one, and is a *//dynamic
stress//*. It is fairly difficult up to now to exactly record this feature, but it
represents the syntactic marker which conveys semantic markers of «closeness» or «distance» (thus kinesically distinguishing what could be verbally
interpreted by the opposition 'this *vs.* that'). When the finger points with
comparatively little energy it means «close», and when pointing with greater
energy (the gesture being more ample and abundant, with the arm itself
participating in 'propelling' the finger) it means «distance».

So in cases of indeterminate stress, the gestural pointer must be helped along by a verbal shifter (/this/ or /that/), just as the verbal shifter usually has to be helped by a gestural pointer (as noted in Table 22). When responding to the question /which one?/ one cannot answer /this/ or /that/ without accompanying the verbal expression with a pointer, unless the question regards two objects of which one is present and the other absent. The presence of the verbal expression constitutes a typical case of circumstantial selection (the kinesic pointer constituting, on the contrary, circumstantial selection for the verbal one). Thus the relationship between content and expression, in the case of a pointing finger, can be viewed as shown in Table 23.

Table 23

$$
//pointing\ finger// \longrightarrow
\begin{cases}
+ & \text{longitude} \\
+ & \text{apicality} \\
+ & \text{movement toward} \\
+ & \text{dynamic stress}
\end{cases}
\longrightarrow d_{direction} \longrightarrow d_{distant} \longrightarrow d_{sender}
$$

$$
//pointing\ finger// \longrightarrow
\begin{cases}
+ & \text{longitude} \\
+ & \text{apicality} \\
+ & \text{movement toward} \\
- & \text{dynamic stress}
\end{cases}
\longrightarrow d_{direction} \longrightarrow d_{close} \longrightarrow d_{sender}
$$

$$
//pointing\ finger// \longrightarrow
\begin{cases}
+ & \text{longitude} \\
+ & \text{apicality} \\
+ & \text{movement toward} \\
{}^{+}_{-} \} & \text{dynamic stress}
\end{cases}
\longrightarrow d_{sender}
\begin{cases}
[circ\ _{/this/}] \longrightarrow d_{close} \\
[circ\ _{/that/}] \longrightarrow d_{distant}
\end{cases}
$$

One could at this point observe that, when considering verbal pointers, syntactic markers were absolutely independent of semantic ones (and therefore in Table 22 they were not analytically recorded), while in kinesic pointers the presence or absence of a given syntactic marker determined the corresponding semantic feature. It could then be said that in non-verbal signs the format of the sememe is determined by the format of the sign-vehicle — or vice-versa. This particular link of *'motivation'* will be discussed in 3.4.10, for it cannot be explained without having recourse to a theory of the modes of physical production of sign-functions.

A theory of codes may well disregard the difference between motivated and arbitrary signs, since it is only concerned with the fact that a convention exists which correlates a given expression to a given content, irrespective of the way in which the correlation is posited and accepted.

2.12. The model "Q"

2.12.1. Infinite semantic recursivity

The Revised Model does not escape a criticism to which the model KF has also been subjected. Componential analysis isolates within the sememe paths or readings composed of different nodes representing semantic markers. In the KF model these markers could still at times be complex definitions (the distinguishers); in the Revised Model they have been reduced to elementary cultural units such as «fish» or «close».

At this point one has to specify what kind of theory will explain the semantic content of the expressions /fish/ or /close/ used in order to interpret /whale/ or /this/. One could say that insofar as they are not 'words' but *meta-semiotic constructs* they do not have to be semantically explained because they are just *posited as explainers*. But this answer could only hope to partially hold if one were able to use a very reduced and strictly structured number of semantic universals in order to analyze thousands and thousands of lexemes. Unfortunately, as soon as the semantic universals are reduced in number and made more comprehensive (of Greimas' semic analysis using categories such as «verticality») they become unable to mark the difference between different sememes. And as soon as their number is augmented and their capacity for individuation grows, they become *ad hoc* definitions, like the distinguishers. The real problem is that *every semantic unit used in order to analyze a sememe is in its turn a sememe to be analyzed*.

Thus, given an elementary tree like the one represented in Table 24 d_1, d_2, d_3, d_4, plus c_1, c_2, c_3 and c_4 all ought, in turn, to become the starting-points for new compositional analyses. Each of them should constitute, inside the tree, a sort of *embedded sememe* generating its own tree, and so on *ad infinitum*, each of their semantic markers in turn generating another tree. The graphic representation of such a landscape of everlasting recursivity cannot be imagined, if only because such a representation would have to take into account the fact that each unit acquires a semantic value only insofar as it is inserted into a semantic axis, and thus opposed to another unit. How then can one represent this type of semantic universe (which happens to be the one in which human beings live)?

Table 24

$$/s\text{-}v/ \text{ —— } sm = «sememe» \text{ —— } d_1, d_2 \begin{cases} (cont_a) \; c_1, c_2 \\ (cont_b) \; d_3, d_4, \text{ —— } c_3, c_4 \end{cases}$$

Let us examine an indirect proposal, coming from M. Ross Quillian's model for a semantic memory (1968).

2.12.2. An *n*-dimensional model

Quillian's model (which will from now on be called Model Q) is based on a mass of nodes interconnected by various types of associative links. For the meaning of every lexeme there has to exist, in the memory, a node which has as its "patriarch" the term to be defined, here called a *type*. The definition of a type A foresees the employment, as its interpretants, of a series of other sign-vehicles which are included as *tokens* (and which in the model are other lexemes). The configuration of the meaning of the lexeme is given by the multiplicity of its links with various tokens, each of which, however, becomes in turn a *type* B, that is, the patriarch of a new configuration which includes as tokens many other lexemes, some of which were also tokens of type A, and which can include as token the same type A. Let us give an example here, the definition of /plant/ which is reproduced graphically in Table 25. A token such as /grow/ can become the type of a new branch (or plane) which includes among its tokens many of those which go with /plant/ (as for example /air/ or /water/ and indeed /plant/ itself). "The over-all structure of the complete memory forms an enormous aggregation of planes, each consisting entirely of token nodes except for its 'head node'." As can be seen, this model anticipates the definition of every sign, thanks to the interconnection with the universe of all other signs that function as interpretants, each of these ready to become the sign interpreted by all the others; the model, in all its complexity, is based on a process of *unlimited semiosis*. From a sign which is taken as a type, it is possible to penetrate, from the center to the farthest periphery, the whole universe of cultural units, each of which can in turn become the center and create infinite peripheries.

Table 25

PLANT: 1. Living structure which is not an animal, frequently with leaves, getting its food from air, water, earth.
2. Apparatus used for any process in industry.
3. Put (seed, plant, etc.) in earth for growth.

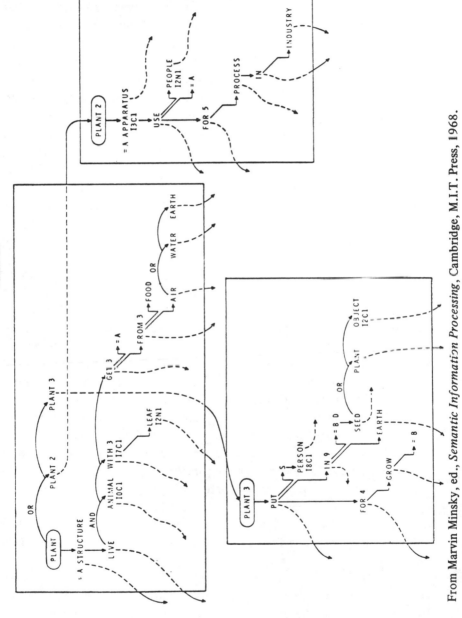

From Marvin Minsky, ed., *Semantic Information Processing*, Cambridge, M.I.T. Press, 1968.

A similar model can still receive a bidimensional graphic configuration when one part of it is examined (and it is understandable that in its mechanical simulation, thanks to the limited number of tokens included, it may be possible to confer on it a structure which can be described). But *actually no graph is in a position to represent it in all its complexity*. It must appear as a sort of polydimensional network, equipped with topological properties, in which the distances covered are abbreviated or elongated and each term acquires proximity with others by means of short-cuts and immediate contacts, meanwhile remaining linked with all the others, according to continually changing relationships.

We can imagine all the cultural units as an enormous number of marbles contained in a box; by shaking the box we can form different connections and affinities among the marbles. This box would constitute an informational source provided with high entropy, and it would constitute the abstract model of semantic association in a free state. According to his disposition, his previous knowledge, his own idiosyncrasies, each person when faced with the sign-vehicle /centaur/ could arrive at the unit «atomic bomb» or «Mickey Mouse».

But we are looking for a semiotic model which justifies the *conventional* denotations and connotations attributed to a sign-vehicle. And so we should think of magnetized marbles which establish *a system of attraction and repulsion*, so that some are drawn to one another and others are not. A similar magnetization would reduce the possibility of interrelation. *This would constitute an s-code*. Still better, we could consider every cultural unit in this Global Semantic Universe as emitting given wave-lengths which put it in tune with a limited (though possibly very large) number of other units. Except that we have to admit that the wave-lengths can change according to new messages emitted and that therefore the possibilities of attraction and repulsion change in time; in other words, that a componential tree may change and enrich its markers, proving the hypothesis of De Mauro (1970) that the components of the meaning are not closed in number, frozen into a system of relevant units, as happens with the units of expression, but form an open series. In effect the model Q supposes that the system can be nourished by fresh information and that further data can be inferred from incomplete data.

The model Q is a model of linguistic creativity. Moreover, it also gives a comprehensive image of Wittgenstein's discussions on meaning. When Wittgenstein (1953, I, 67) mentioned the existence of 'family resemblances' he gave /game/ as an example. The idea of game refers to a family of extremely disparate activities, stretching from chess to ball — games which can have components in common (chess and a ball game between two people have in common the idea of winning and losing), and can be separated by radical dissimilarities (a game of chess and the solitary game of a child throwing the ball against a wall, or a game of chess and ring around the roses). Wittgenstein concludes that "something runs through the whole thread — namely the continuous overlapping of those fibres". This image of a continuous super-imposing of correlations recalls that of model Q; model Q is already, in the phase in which Quillian presents it, a portion of the Semantic Universe in which a system has intervened in order to establish attractions and repulsions.

2.13. The format of the semantic space

All that has been said about the semantic system finally forces us to look once more at the idea of a code. A code is commonly supposed to render the elements of two systems equivalent, term by term (or strings of units by strings of units). But the study of semantic fields shows that (when speaking for instance of a 'language' as a code) it is necessary to consider a vast series of partial content systems (or fields) which are matched in different ways with the expressive units. This fact engenders a situation in which many compositional trees may exist for every sign-vehicle, simultaneously connecting it to different positions in different semantic fields. Thus the system of semantic fields, involved as it is in multiple shiftings, becomes crossed (along another dimension which no graph will succeed in homogenizing with the preceding one) by various paths from each sememe. The sum of these crossings makes up Model Q.

A code as *'langue'* must therefore be understood as a sum of notions (some concerning the combinational rules of the expression items, or syntactic markers; some concerning the combinational rules of the content items, or semantic markers) which can be viewed as the *competence* of the speaker. However, in reality this competence is the sum of the individual competences that constitute the code as a collective convention. What was called 'the code' is thus better viewed as a *complex network of subcodes* which goes far beyond such categories as 'grammar', however comprehensive they may be. One might therefore call it a *hypercode* (following the etymology of 'hypercube') which gathers together various subcodes, some of which are strong and stable, while others are weak and transient, such as a lot of peripheral connotative couplings. In the same way the codes themselves gather together various systems, some strong and stable (like the phonological one, which lasts unchanged for centuries), others weak and transient (such as a lot of semantic fields and axes).

This difficulty in defining all the tasks performed by the codes does not depend only on the fact that research is still on a primitive level. It also depends on the fact that *the code is not a natural condition of the Global Semantic Universe nor a stable structure underlying the complex of links and branches of every semiosic process.*

Let us go back to the metaphor of the box of marbles. If the marbles, when free, represent a model of an informational source with high entropy, a system is a rule which magnetizes the marbles according to a combination of mutual attractions and repulsions on the same plane. The code which, on the other hand, couples different systems is a *biplanar rule* establishing new attractions and repulsions between items from different planes. In other words, every item in the code maintains a double set of relations, a *systematic* one with all the items of its own plane (content or expression) and a *signifying* one with one or more items from the correlated plane.

Now, to maintain that there exists a structure of the Human Mind or a sort of ontological system of Essences, on which signification and communication rely, means that the magnetization *is inherent* in the marbles as a 'property'. If, on the other hand, the code is a social convention, the magnetization is a *transitory* (that is, a *historical*) condition of the marbles box.

The approach adopted in the present work is that the magnetization must be understood as a cultural phenomenon and that the box-source must be at best considered as *the site of a combinational interplay*, of a highly indeterminate *game*. A semiotics of the code is only interested in the results of this game, after the intervention of the magnetization. A semiotics of sign production and of code-changing is interested in the process by which a rule is imposed upon the indeterminacy of the source (see chapter 3).

If this is true, it would then be necessary to admit that any subcode (for example a certain type of connotative association between two elements of two semiotic fields) is a comparatively transitory phenomenon which it would be impossible to establish and describe as a stable structure (except in cases of 'strong' magnetization, i.e. scientific definitions). Moreover the fact that every item of the game can simultaneously maintain relations with many other elements makes it difficult to draw explanatory but simplifying graphs such as a compositional tree.

A compositional tree should thus be viewed as a purely temporary device *posited* in order to explain a certain message, a working hypothesis that aims to control the immediate semantic environment of given semantic units. Let us consider the case of the very simple message emitted by a traffic light. According to an international code, *//red//* means «stop» and *//green//* means «go». But «stop» may also connote «obligation», while *//green//* − at least to a pedestrian − also denotes «free choice». At a higher connotative level «stop» may connote «fine» while *//green//* may connote «hurry», especially if the signal is received by a driver. A compositional representation of *//green//* and *//red//* would then be as follows (Table 26):

Table 26

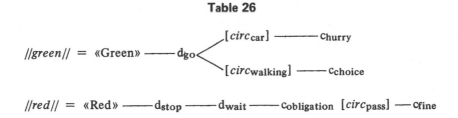

Both trees explain how the traffic lights mean something. But on what semantic subsystem do these sign-functions rely? If we use a classical Hjelmslevian representation we are tempted, for the sake of symmetry, to represent the underlying fields as follows (Table 27):

Table 27

«fine»	expression of		expression of		«hurry»
	«obligation»	expression of	expression of	«free choice»	
		«stop»	//red//	//green//	«go»

But this would be a misleading solution. Although there is an axis «go vs. stop» establishing the differences in denotation, and although it is possible to isolate an opposition «obligation vs. choice», there is no opposition between «hurry» and «fine». Again it is possible to assume that: a) a given sememe *fishes*, in order to find its interpretants, in different semantic axes while the sememe immediately opposed to it at the level of primary denotation, may, as far as further connotations are concerned, fish in different positions in different axes; b) two different sememes can maintain an oppositional relation as regards primary denotation and at the same time have some connotations in common; c) the same sememe may derive two of its connotations from two opposed positions in a given semantic axis; d) etc. For example «red», at its extreme compositional periphery, fishes in the position «fine» (in the axis «fine vs. award») while «green» is not concerned with that axis. But there could be another sememe which directly occupied the position «award» without having an oppositional unit which fishes, for its interpretation, in the position «fine». For instance, «bachelor» (as B.A.) connotes «award» and also «go» or «right of way» (it is indeed a *rite de passage*!). Therefore another *ad hoc* representation of this puzzling network of intertwined oppositions, homologies and discrepancies could take the tentative form of Table 28 (which somewhat recalls model Q):

Table 28

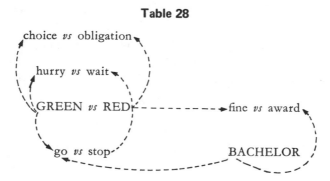

The creation of a complete semantic structure *must thus remain a mere regulative hypothesis*. Even if one ever managed to describe a system of this kind, it would already have changed, and not merely because of the influence of various historical factors, but also because of the critical erosion to which it would have been submitted by the analysis itself. Whereas in the case of a phonological system this will not be the case because of the restricted number of pertinent items and combinational rules.

There must therefore be a methodological principle of semantic research whereby, in almost all cases, the description of fields and semantic branches can only be achieved *when studying the conditions of signification of a given message*.

A *semiotics of the code* is an operational device in the service of a *semiotics of sign production*. A semiotics of the code can be established — if only partially — when the existence of a message *postulates it* as an explanatory condition. Semiotics must proceed to isolate structures *as if* a definitive general structure existed; but to be able to do this one must assume that this global structure is a simply regulative hypothesis and that *every time a structure is described something occurs within the universe of signification which no longer makes it completely reliable*.

But this condition of imbalance and apparent lack of stability puts semiotics on a par with other disciplines such as physics, governed — as this latter is — by such methodological criteria as the indeterminacy or complementarity principles. Only if it acquires this *awareness of its own limits*, and avoids aspiring to an absolute form of knowledge, will one be able to consider semiotics as a *scientific discipline*.

2.14. Overcoding and undercoding

2.14.1. The uncoded determinants of interpretation

The mobility of semantic space makes codes change transiently and processually. But at the same time it imposes on the activity of sign production and text interpretation itself the necessity of a continuous *extra-coding*.

The interpreter of a text is at the same time obliged both to challenge the existing codes and to advance interpretive hypotheses that work as a more comprehensive, tentative and prospective form of codification. Faced with uncoded circumstances and complex contexts, the interpreter is obliged to recognize that the message does not rely on previous codes and yet that it must be understandable; if it is so, non-explicit conventions must exist; if not yet in existence, they have to exist (or to be posited). Their apparent absence postulates their necessity.

Let us try to clarify this border-line situation, in which the very activity of sign production and interpretation nourishes and enriches the universe of codes. The theory of codes explains how one possesses rules of competence that permit one to disambiguate or to overambiguate, to form and to interpret given messages or texts. The example of the traffic light (given in 2.13.) has shown that there exists a system of possible subcodes and some contextual and circumstantial selections that the code foresees insofar as they are commonly recognized as institutionally connected with certain sign-events. In the case of the traffic lights, the proposed circumstantial selections (along with the most direct denotations and connotations) are sufficient in order to understand these signs. But in some other cases there are (besides the possible contexts which can be foreseen but cannot be coded) possible circumstances which are either unforeseeable or excessively complex and which make up a cluster of different extra-semiotic factors. In all these cases one is entitled to speak of extra-semiotic and *uncoded determinants of the interpretation.*

A typical case of uncoded context is the one proposed by Katz and Fodor in order to demonstrate the impossibility of a theory of settings. The expression /he follows Marx/ can be read as:

(i) «he follows Karl» ⟨ «he is a disciple of Karl»
                          «he postdates Karl»

(ii) «he follows Groucho» ⟨ ......
                             ......

Readings (i) and (ii) are two denotative meanings of the sentence; each of them may also connote a double further reading. Connotations may be disambiguated by making recourse to a possible contextual selection provided by the componential tree of /to follow/: the verb has a 'physical' reading when followed by a concrete noun, a metaphorical one («to be a disciple of») if followed by an abstract noun. What remains ambiguous is the case of personal proper names which can be metonymically taken as the substitute for the ideas or methods proposed by a given person. We can, however, suppose that there exists another contextual selection of the form ($cont_{style}$) that prescribes the reading of /follows/ as «to imitate» or «to agree with» when the verb is used in a theoretical context concerning styles of thinking or habits. No problem exists as for the possibility of understanding if one is speaking of Karl or of Groucho: if the sememe corresponding to names of persons can be semantically analyzed (as assumed in 2.3.2.) «Marx (Karl)» should have a marker «politics» and «Marx (Groucho)» a marker «movies» so that both can find their correct amalgamation with other units from the context.

But something else remains to be disambiguated: the 'ideological' connotation attributed to that philosophical definition. Is it good or bad to follow Marx? If a member of the John Birch Society says /look at this man: he follows Marx/ the sentence represents more than a philosophical attribution; and this kind of ideological connotative meaning must also be grasped, constituting as it does a part of the content of the expression. Here again only a survey of the uncoded context or circumstances can help the addressee to disambiguate the message. This kind of disambiguation does not represent an act of decoding in its stricter sense insofar as the code does not provide any clue. So how can this kind of "interpretation" be semiotically defined?

2.14.2. Abduction

In this context the term /interpretation/ has not been employed in the sense of «decoding». It has rather been taken to mean understanding, on the basis of some previous decoding, the general sense of a vast portion of discourse. So /interpretation/ has here the sense it acquires in hermeneutic discussion, or in literary and artistic criticism. Logically speaking this kind of interpretation is more akin to *inference*. Moreover, it is similar to that specific type of inference that Peirce called *abduction* (and at other times *hypothesis*): "Suppose I enter a room and there find a number of bags, containing different kinds of beans. On the table there is a handful of white beans; and, after some searching, I find one of the bags contains white beans only. I at once infer as a probability, or as a fair guess, that this handful was taken out of that bag. This sort of inference is called *making an hypothesis*" (2.623).

In the case of logical *deduction* there is rule from which, given a case, I deduce a result: *All the beans from this bag are white — These beans are from this bag — These beans are white*.

In the case of *induction*, given a case and a result, I infer a rule: *These beans are from this bag — These beans are white — All the beans from this bag are white* (probably).

In the case of hypothesis or *abduction* there is the inference of a case from a rule and a result: *All the beans from this bag are white — These beans are white — These beans are from this bag* (probably).

Abduction is a case of synthetic inference "where we find some very curious circumstances, which would be explained by the supposition that it was a case of a certain general rule, and thereupon adopt that supposition" (2.624). "I once landed at a seaport in a Turkish province; and, as I was walking up to the house which I was to visit, I met a man upon horseback, surrounded by four horsemen holding a canopy over his head. As the governor of the province was the only personage I could think of who would be so greatly honored, I inferred that this was he. This was an hypothesis" (2.265). Peirce did not know that (or whether) a canopy was the ritual sign distinguishing a governor (in which case there would have been a simple decoding). He invented or *supposed a general rule* [24]. This case seems not to be very different from a case of contextual interpretation when contextual selections are lacking. In fact, supposing that there existed an unexpressed but commonly shared semantic rule providing

$$//canopy// — d_x — (cont_{over\ head}) — c_{honor}$$

Peirce dared to add an *ad hoc* circumstantial selection:

$$[circ_{when\ in\ this\ province}] — d_{governor}$$

At first glance abduction seems to be a free movement of the imagination, more endowed with emotion (more similar to a vague 'intuition') than a normal decoding act. And as a matter of fact Peirce underlines its emotional nature: "Hypothesis substitutes, for a complicated tangle of predicates attached to one subject, a single conception. Now, there is a particular sensation belonging to the act of thinking that each of these predicates inheres in the subject. In hypothetic inference this complicated feeling so produced is replaced by a single feeling of greater intensity, that belonging to the act of thinking the hypothetic conclusion . . . . Thus, the various sounds made by the instruments of an orchestra strike upon the ear, and the result is a peculiar musical emotion, quite distinct from the sounds themselves" (2.643). What has to be retained from this quotation is not the picture of a particular emotional state, but rather the idea that the hearer, hearing music, grasps something more than the single 'meaning' of each sound. If this interpretive movement stopped at the enjoyment of such an imprecise emotion, there would be neither abduction nor anything else relevant to our present purposes. But the hypothetical movement is fulfilled when a new sense (a new combinational quality) is assigned to every sound, inasmuch as they compose the new contextual meaning of the musical piece.

This last example is a very complex instance of aesthetic interpretation, but the one about the Turkish governor is more transparent. At the end of the abductive effort Peirce was able to assign to /canopy/ the as yet uncoded denotation «governor». Peirce repeatedly asserts that even inferences are semiotic phenomena, that a rule can be the sign for its deduced result just as much as a specific case can be the sign for its deduced rule; however, it would be difficult to recognize as a sign the rule in the light of which the hypothesis interprets the case, *unless the abduction once performed becomes a customary social reflex*.

Thus abduction, like every other interpretation of uncoded contexts and circumstances, represents the first step of a metalinguistic operation destined to enrich a code. It is the more evident instance of *production of a sign function*. A consistently interpreted ambiguous uncoded context gives rise, if accepted by a society, to a convention, and thus to a coding coupling.

That context becomes, step by step, a ready-made sentence, just as a metaphor, which at first has to be abductionally interpreted, becomes step by step a catachresis. A semiotic theory must not deny that there are concrete acts of interpretation which produce senses that the code could not foresee, otherwise the principle of the flexibility and creativity of language would not hold. But these interpretations sometimes produce new portions of the code inasmuch as they constitute embryonic processes of *overcoding* and *undercoding*.

2.14.3. Overcoding

If one considers the two examples borrowed from Peirce (that of the Turkish governor and that of the musical piece), one perceives that Peirce has in fact subsumed under the heading of 'abduction' *two* different hypothetical movements. In the case of the Turkish governor Peirce was basing his abductional movement upon a previous system of conventions: the fact that a canopy over the head of somebody meant «honor» was an already acquired matter of convention; a sign-function already existed. Peirce has simply complicated the code by adding a circumstantial selection [*circ* when in the province so and so]. Therefore he has accomplished an operation of *overcoding*: on the basis of a pre-established rule, a new rule was proposed which governed a rarer application of the previous rule.

But frequently overcoding records commonly used ready-made syntagms, such as /how are you/, /I beg your pardon/ or /closed on Sundays/ which work as minimal units, single 'signs' endowed with an 'atomic' meaning. In this sense the whole series of *stylistical* and *rhetorical* rules operating in verbal language are cases of overcoding. A basic code establishes that a certain grammatical disposition is understandable and acceptable (how and why) and a further rule (which, far from denying the previous one, assumes it as a starting-point) establishes that the disposition in question has to be used under given circumstances and with a certain stylistical connotation (for example, «epic style» or «poetic dignity»). Overcoding works even at the level of grammatical rules such as the 'will-deletion' in sentences where it is presupposed that "the event is one that the speaker can be sure of" (Lakoff, 1971 b): one can say that /The Yankees *play* the Red Sox *tomorrow*/ but must say that /The Yankees *will* play *well* tomorrow/. Lakoff suggests that the deletion *of* /*will*/ is determined by a previous presupposition: I prefer to say that *the deletion of* /*will*/ (by an overcoded rule) *determines the presupposition* (i.e. 'means' that the future event will 'surely' happen). Therefore the deletion of /will/ along with the occurrence of the expression /tomorrow/ endows the event (by overcoding) with a marker «sure».

Outside the range of verbal language, all iconological entities are the result of overcoding. If we suppose that there is a code allowing one to recognize as such the representation of a woman bearing her eyes on a saucer, then an operation of iconographical overcoding will establish the correspondence between that woman and St. Lucy.

Overcoding proceeds in a twofold direction. It may be that, given a code assigning meaning to certain minimal expressions, overcoding will assign additional meanings to more macroscopic strings of these expressions. Rhetorical or iconological rules are of this sort. But it may also be that, given certain coded units, overcoding will analyze these units into more analytical entities, as when, given a word, paralinguistics establishes that different ways of pronouncing it (of a stressing on its various syllables, or of insisting on a particular kind of phonetic emission) correspond to different shades of meaning. All of the courtesy formulas come from an overcoded everyday language: the expression /s'il vous plaît/ (see Metz's discussion on messages and texts quoted in 2.4.) is understood in terms of its real signification on the basis of an accepted and traditional overcoding. Obviously the operations of overcoding, when completely accepted, produce what has been called (in 2.3.) a subcode: in this sense overcoding is an innovatory activity that increasingly loses its provocative power, thereby producing social acceptance.

But more frequently the overcoded entities float — so to speak — among the codes, on the threshold between convention and innovation. It is by a slow and prudent process that a society admits them to the ranks of the rules upon which it bases its own very *raison d'être*. Frequently a society does not recognize overcoded rules that in fact allow the social exchange of signs. A typical example is provided by the narrative rules, as outlined by Propp: for many hundreds (and perhaps thousands) of years, primitive societies allowed their members to tell and to understand stories which were based on narrative functions, (thus transphrastically overcoding the everyday language when using it for narrative purposes); but the plot laws introduced by Propp were an abductive proposal that brought to light the existence of an overcoded language. These laws are now universally accepted as the items of a recognized narrative subcode. But the present trends in typology of texts and text-grammar are toward further overcoding of more macroscopic portions of the discourses.

In the same way the 'ideological' system of expectations by which a member of the John Birch Society immediately assigns to the expression /he follows Marx/ the connotation of «dangerous adversary of my country» is an instance of overcoding valid inside a given group. Likewise all the stylistically ready-made devices that allow a critic to dismiss a page, a passage, or indeed an entire text by means of such damning critical judgments as *"déjà vu"*, "typical midcult", "a Tin Pan Alley melody, indeed", "mere advertising", "a soap opera", and so on, rely on previous operations of stylistical over-coding [25].

2.14.4. Undercoding

Let us now return to Peirce's second example. What happens when the hearer gets, from the various distinguishable sounds of a new musical composition, "a peculiar musical emotion", that is, the feeling of organization that permits one to speak of a significant whole? And what happens when, listening to new pieces by two different composers, one detects in them the same style or the same significant purpose, even if that style has not yet been recorded, analyzed and recognized by\a previous critical operation?

This seems to me to be a case of a sort of imprecise coding, a tentative hypothetical 'gesture' subsuming one or more large-scale portions of text under a given heading.

Suppose, in order to clarify this sort of movement from unknown texts to codes, that I visit a foreign country whose language I do not know. Step by step I begin to understand something: not really a precise grammar, but some general trends, some behavioral items composed of sounds, gestures, visual expressions and so on. After a while I begin to decide that a set of different textual expressions (of intertwined visual, verbal and corporal signs) corresponds to a very general meaning. Suppose that I detect that, when accompanied by a smile, an expression like /I love you/, /I like you/, /I am fond of you/, /I adore you/, /Hi, man!/, /Hello, my friend!/ and /How are you?/ roughly mean «friendship». Since these examples are provided in English we know that, grammatically and conversationally speaking, they have different meanings; but one could say that, in order to make general previsions about my possible social interactions in that country, the sort of rough coding that I have performed should prove reasonably successful. I call this kind of rough coding an operation of *undercoding*.

So undercoding may be defined as the operation by means of which in the absence of reliable pre-established rules, certain macroscopic portions of certain texts are provisionally assumed to be pertinent units of a code in formation, even though the combinational rules governing the more basic compositional items of the expressions, along with the corresponding content-units, remain unknown.

As we will see in 3.6.7., various kinds of texts, such as the images produced by an alien civilization, are understood by way of undercoding.

Thus overcoding proceeds *from existing codes* to *more analytic subcodes* while undercoding proceeds *from non-existent codes* to *potential codes*. This double movement, so easily detectable in various cases (paralinguistics is a clear case of overcoding, aesthetic judgments — beautiful vs. ugly — are very deceptive cases of undercoding), is frequently intertwined in most common cases of sign production and interpretation, so that in many instances it seems difficult to establish whether one is over or undercoding. In such threshold-cases (in which the programmed march toward codes is mixed with the free activity of semiosic production and innovation) it would be wiser to speak of *extra-coding* (such a category covering both movements at once). The movements of extra-coding are the subject matter of both a theory of codes and a theory of sign production.

2.14.5. Discoursive competence

Even in the idiosyncratic personal activity of memorizing previous semiotic experience, there is a continuous activity of extra-coding. There are a lot of phrases and indeed entire discourses that one no longer has to interpret or decode because one has already experienced them in analogous circumstances or contexts. There are a lot of circumstances in which the hearer already knows what the speaker is going to say. Interactional behavior is based on redundancy rules of this type, and if people had to listen to (or read, or look at) every expression they received, analyzing them item by item, communication would be a pretty tiring activity. As a matter of fact one is continuously anticipating expressions, filling up the empty spaces in a text with the missing units, forecasting a lot of words that the interlocutor may have said, could have said, will certainly say, or has never said.

A lot of the logic of presuppositions depends on the activity of extra-coding, as well as many of the *conversational rules*, and interpretive procedures, that assure a correct exchange of information between communicators (Austin 1962; Searle, 1969; Ducrot, 1972; Goffman, 1971; Veron, 1973; Cicourel, 1969; Gumperz, 1971; Hymes, 1971).

The whole of the psychology and the sociology of systems of expectations can be retranslated in terms of extra-coding. All the ellipses used in common discourses as well as the use of anaphoric devices (/give it me/, /remember tomorrow!/, /he is one of them . . . /, etc.) always rely on operations of abductions but are frequently made more understandable by previous extra-codings. And this happens not only with the verbal discourse, but also with a lot of other semiotic devices; many stylistic procedures in painting, whereby a part of a thing is suggested by few strokes, depend on this mechanism.

Obviously there is a difference between a strong extra-coding by which a social group explicitly and publicly establishes that a ready-made message, circumstance, or context must definitely be coded, and a weak extra-coding depending on the individual memory, on an imprecise and non-explicit rule, on a weakly contracted convention, on a silent agreement or on the intuitive assumption of such a silent and unconscious agreement. There is a scale of extra-codings, ranging from socially defined procedures (such as the hero's obligatory death in classical tragedy) to a sort of *discoursive competence* whereby anyone can guess that a phrase spoken in the context of a conversation implies such and such a presupposition. In other words there is a difference between what is *conventionally implicated* and what is *conversationally implicated* (Katz, 1972; Grice, 1968).

For these reasons overcoding and undercoding remain half-way between a theory of codes and a theory of sign productions and interpretation, producing (i) meta-semiotic statements (and therefore introducing into the codes new macroscopic sign-functions), (ii) simple *ad hoc* conversational abductions (socially shared but not firmly accepted and recorded), (iii) personal storages of tentative presuppositions (thereby forming idiolectal concretions that quite often lead to unfortunate misinterpretations) [26].

2.14.6. Grammars and texts

The notion of extra-coding, and the difference between coding and overcoding on the one hand, and undercoding on the other, permit one to define correctly, in terms of a theory of codes, the difference, proposed by Lotman, between *grammar-oriented* and *text-oriented* cultures. This indicates the different ways in which two cultures may organize their codes, but the same categories will help us to distinguish different types of sign production in the next chapter (see 3.6.).

The difference between a grammatically oriented and a textually oriented culture has been set out by Lotman (1969, 1971) and is of the greatest importance to the present argument. There are cultures governed by a *system* of rules and there are cultures governed by a *repertoire* of texts imposing models of behavior. In the former category texts are generated by combinations of discrete units and are judged correct or incorrect according to their conformity to the combinational rules; in the latter category society directly generates texts, these constituting macro-units from which rules could eventually be inferred, but that first and foremost propose models to be followed and imitated.

Lotman suggests that text-oriented societies are at the same time expression-oriented ones, while grammar-oriented societies are content-oriented. The reason for such a definition becomes clear when one considers the fact that a culture which has evolved a highly differentiated content-system has also provided expression-units corresponding to the content-units, and may therefore establish a so-called 'grammatical' system — this simply being a highly articulated code. On the contrary a culture which has not yet differentiated its content-units expresses (through macroscopic expressive groupings: the texts) a sort of *content-nebula*.

It is not by chance that Lotman describes a grammar-oriented culture depending on 'Handbooks' while a text-oriented culture depends on 'The Book'. A handbook is in fact a code that permits further messages and texts, whereas a book is a text, generated by an as yet unknown rule which, once duly analyzed and reduced to a handbook-like form, can suggest new ways of producing further texts.

Lotman recalls the customary twofold experience of language teaching. Adults are usually introduced to an unknown language by means of rules; they receive a set of units along with their combinational laws and they learn to combine these units in order to speak; a child, on the other hand, is trained through exposure to a continuous textual performance of pre-fabricated strings of that language, and he is expected to absorb his competence even though not completely conscious of the underlying rules. It is conceivable that the process of language acquisition, for a child learning its native language, proceeds first by acts of undercoding, then by a successive coding, and finally by acts of overcoding (this latter activity continuing through the adult life, inasmuch as society is involved in a continuous process of complicating existing codes).

Insofar as it is admissible to think of cultural phylogenesis in terms of cultural ontogenesis, it should be supposed that in some respects the same thing happens with societies. If primitive societies are text-oriented, then they should be conceived as being based on the preliminary processes of undercoding. The more akin to a 'scientific' society they become, the more they code and overcode. But the distinction is not that simple. A scientific society is a society of compulsory overcoding only on the conceptual level. On the behavioral level — on the contrary — primitive societies, with their repertoires of etiquette rules, seem to be more grammar-oriented than do modern ones, in which mass civilization increasingly proposes (through the media) undercoded texts, freely interpretable patterns of public behavior, permissive models (cf. Fabbri, 1973). Nevertheless, undercoding and overcoding, on the one hand, and grammar- and text-orientation on the other, are not to be considered as coincident categories.

The activity of extra-coding is connected with the movement that goes from sign production and interpretation toward codes, and is a category of a theory of codes (or at best of that branch of a theory of sign production which deals with code-making). On the other hand grammar- and text-orientation are categories of a theory of sign production, and as such we shall return to them in chapter 3.

2.15. The interplay of codes and the message as an open form

The activity of extra-coding (along with the interpretation of uncoded circumstances) not only impels one to select the most appropriate code or to isolate a given subcode (thereby governing the choice of connotations). It also changes the informative impact of signs: a skull on a bottle conventionally means «poison», but the amount of information I receive from such a bottle grows if, instead of finding it in a bathroom cupboard, I find it among my liqueurs.

Thus the criss-cross play of circumstances and abductive presuppositions, along with the interplay of various codes and subcodes, makes the message (or the text) appear as an *empty form to which can be attributed various possible senses*. At this point it is clear that the Watergate Model, which presupposed a common code for the sender and the addressee, is revealed as being rather summary. The multiplicity of codes, contexts, and circumstances shows us that the same message can be decoded from different points of view and by reference to diverse systems of conventions. The basic denotation of a sign-vehicle can be understood just as the sender intended it to be, but different connotations can be attributed to it simply because the addressee follows another path on the compositional tree to which the sender referred (both paths being legitimately accepted by the culture in which both sender and addressee live).

When receiving the message /he follows Marx/ a series of circumstances directs the addressee to presuppose the ideological bias of the sender and therefore *to abduce* the overcoded subcode to which he might have referred; the fact remains that an addressee who subscribes to an anti-Communist ideology can receive the message emitted by a Marxist and, while grasping exactly the right denotation, will load his own sememe with negative connotative markers, thus receiving a different and idiosyncratic message after all.

There is the extreme possibility that even the basic denotations may be different for sender and addressee but that the message may nonetheless be able to convey a sense in both cases. A paradoxical example is provided by the sentence /i vitelli dei romani sono belli/ which can be read either as a Latin one («Go Vitellius, to the sound of war of the Roman god») or as an Italian one («the calves of the Romans are beautiful»). However paradoxical, this example should be taken as the allegory or emblem of the basic nature of every message. We are thus obliged to reformulate even the informational and communicational definition of 'message'.

Message, as considered in chapter 1, seemed to constitute a reduction of information (and, as physical signal, does so − since it represents a selection of some among many equiprobable symbols). However, as it comes from the channel, and is received by the addressee as an expression, it appears as a source of further information. It possesses the same characteristics of equiprobability as belonged to the source. It becomes the source of different possible contents. In this sense it is correct to speak of *information of the message* (along with 'information of the source' and 'information of the code' − see 1.4.4.). Information is a value depending on the richness of possible choices; the different coded readings of the sememes, along with the manifold contextual and circumstantial interpretations, constitute multiple choices which can even be reduced to a binary selection.

This information of the message is only *reduced* by the addressee when he selects a definitive interpretation. In the case of aesthetic messages which require the simultaneous grasping of multiple senses, this informational quality of the message remains *unreduced*.

Even if it is doubtful that, once given a complete structure of a Global Semantic System, the information of the message might be computed quantitatively, nevertheless the information of the message constitutes a range of probabilities: not a total statistical equiprobability, as was the case with the information of the source, but all the same a vast if not indeterminate probabilistic matrix.

Both information of the source and information of the message can be defined as a state of disorder in relation to a successive order; as an ambiguous situation in relation to an ulterior elimination of ambiguity; as a possibility of alternative choices in relation to a system of definitely realized choices. Moreover what one usually calls 'message' is rather a text: a network of different messages depending on different codes, sometimes correlating different expressive substance with the same content (for example, a verbal message is always accompanied by paralinguistic, kinesic or proxemic devices), sometimes making different contents depend on the same expressive substance (by virtue of intertwined subcodes). Thus the usual communicational model should be rewritten in this way (Table 29):

Table 29

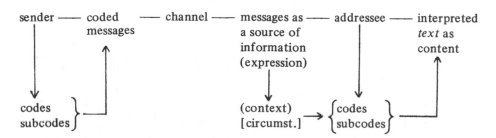

Thus the message as source constitutes a sort of network of constraints which allow certain optional results. Some of these can be considered as fertile inferences which enrich the original messages, others are mere 'aberrations'. But the term 'aberration' must be understood only as a betrayal of the sender's intentions; insofar as a network of messages acquires a sort of autonomous textual status, it is doubtful whether, from the point of view of the text itself (as related to the contradictory format of the Semantic Space), such a 'betrayal' should be viewed negatively.

Sometimes the addressee's entire system of cultural units (as well as the concrete circumstances in which he lives) legitimate an interpretation that the sender would have never foreseen. This kind of phenomenon is widely known by the sociology of mass communications, which has increasingly recognized the existence of such phenomena as the 'boomerang effect', the "two step flow" governing the passage of information from the sender to the addressee, the filter constituted by the opinion leaders, etc.

Because of such unpredictable decoding, the text may be 'consumed' at only one of its content levels, while the other (equally legitimate) levels remain in the background. Greimas (1966) calls these parallel and autonomous levels of sense the text's *'isotopies'*. But usually, however 'aberrant' the interpretation may be, the various *isotopies* differently interact with one another, through a process that can be schematically suggested by Table 30. When the addressee does not succeed in isolating the sender's codes or in substituting his own idiosyncratic or group subcodes for them, the message is received as pure noise. Which is what frequently happens with the circulation of messages from the centers of communicational power to the extreme subproletarian peripheries of the world.

Table 30

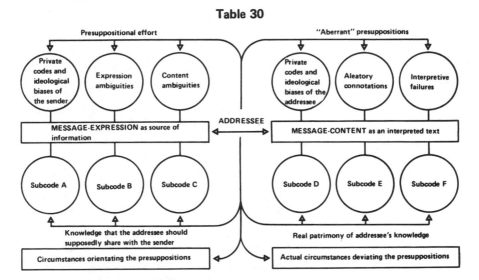

New semiotically oriented sociological studies (see Fabbri, 1973) are now beginning to enquire whether by chance it is not precisely that noise which produces a new 'culture', the unpredictable reorganizations of a sort of 'third semantic world' [27].

But in examining these problems the present discussion has trespassed the border-lines of a theory of codes; what one can make of the received message is the proper matter for a theory of sign production and interpretation (which could, from a certain point of view, be regarded as a more highly articulated pragmatics, even if it covers many items of a traditional semantics).

The purpose of the present chapter was to demonstrate that the very complexity and unpredictability of sign production springs from the format of the semantic universe as it must be outlined by a theory of codes.

NOTES
1. The Italian version of Hjelmslev (1943) by Giulio Lepscky translates /mening/ as /materia/ (matter). I agree with this interpretation.
2. In contemporary logical and semantic discussion the term 'pragmatics' has perhaps been allowed to assume too many senses. For instance: (i) pragmatics concerns the entire set of idiosyncratic responses that the addressee elaborates once the message is received (the engineer detects danger level and decides to take the first available plane to Florida for a holiday); (ii) pragmatics concerns the *interpretation* of all the semantic choices offered by the message; (iii) pragmatics concerns the entire set of presuppositions entailed by the message. While sense (i) really goes beyond our present concern, senses (ii) and (iii) can be subsumed within the framework of a more comprehensive semantic theory; see 2.11 and 2.14.
3. This bifurcated notion of meaning has penetrated the whole of modern thought on signs, whether it is presented as an opposition between *denotatum* and *designatum* (or *significatum*) (Morris, 1938, 1946) or between *extension* and *intension* in logical thought (Carnap, who also speaks of *nominatum* and *sense*) or as a difference between *denotation* and *connotation* (Stuart Mill), as *denotation* and *meaning* (Russell), etc. For the purposes of this discussion, let us posit the following equation: *meaning=intention=significatum=sense*. The so-called 'meaning' is then the signified or the content of an expression.
4. Fear and laughter can also be elicited by actual events (one laughs when tickled with a feather); but the types of fear and amusement considered by psychology as opposed to physiology have something to do with a contradiction within the code. Thus a theory of the tragic and the comic could rely on a theory of codes: tragic and comic feelings have semiotical roots.
5. It is obviously semiotically relevant if the phrase about Ulysses conventionally connotes «legend», not because it is a legend but because it is believed to be a legend. Therefore the activity of the historian, distinguishing False statements about the past from True ones (as well as that of the newsman regarding the present) is a matter of experience, and of various kinds of inference. A theory of codes does not deny the importance of such empirical necessities; but it will only become actively concerned with them when they have produced a statement that a society assumes as an *endoxon*, a matter of coded and accepted opinion or belief. See the discussion about the code as encyclopedia in 2.10.2.
6. Adopting a semiotic rather than a strictly linguistic criterion, we could even say that ready-made expressions can be considered corresponding to semantic units (equivalent in practice to lexemes): a case in point is the 'idioms' which language presents to us ready-made and which institutionally possess a fixed meaning. These expressions (which Lyons (1963) attributes to a factor of "recall" in the learning and use of language) range from /how do you do/ to /allons donc/. Greimas (1966) gives the name of 'paralexemes' to those expressions which, although constituting a syntagm formed by several

lexemes, conventionally transmit a meaning conceived as unique: for example
/pomme de terre/.

7. On the other hand, every time the functioning of natural language is
considered by formal logic, the idea of a chain of interpretants can hardly fail
to appear, even if any direct reference to Peirce is lacking. When Carnap
(1947) tries to explain what he means by the intensions of an expression, he
speaks in terms of properties. Properties are neither linguistic expressions nor
images nor sense-data; they are rather conceived as objective properties of a
thing. However, Carnap points out that he regards as properties not only
qualitative properties in the narrower sense (such as Blue, Hot, Hard) but also
quantitative properties (Weighing Five Pounds), relational properties (Uncle
of Somebody), spatiotemporal properties (North of Chicago). These 'properties' seem to be something very akin to a cultural unit and seem to be
expressed through interpretants of the given expression. In fact, when Carnap
tries to establish the scientific possibilities of determining the intensions of an
expression (1955) and when he presents the problem of how to instruct a
robot to understand a series of expressions and to apply a predicate C to an
object A on the basis of a previously received intensional description B of the
same object, the kinds of instruction the robot receives (as regards objective
properties) are: (a) visual images of the object described; (b) its verbal
description; (c) predicates of the object itself. The robot is nourished by
means of interpretants, and these interpretants are not simply synonyms.

The problem does not appear so clearly in Carnap's work because he is
unable to accept the determination of an intension as separated from the idea
of extension; his intensionalist thesis is always linked to an extensionalist
approach so that intensions serve to establish to which possible objects the
word can be applied (cf. Winter, 1973). Nevertheless Carnap insists on the
fact that the problem of meaning (and of intension) is independent of the
empirical truth-conditions of the expression, and thus of the existence or
non-existence of the referent. His robot can also receive descriptions of
expressions such as /unicorn/. As for compound predicators, a predicator
such as 'H.T.' (Human and Twenty Feet High) also has a meaning because it
expresses a property even if this property has no specific application. Shifting
continuously from statements such as "the tests concerning intension are
independent of the question of existence" to others such as "the intension of
a predicate may be defined as its range, which comprehends those possible
kinds of objects for which the predicate holds" (1955,3), Carnap shows how
difficult it is to insert a theory of interpretants into the framework of a
referential semantics; at the same time these shiftings suggest that one must
radicalize Peirce's approach and insert the notion of interpretant into the
framework of a non-referential and structural theory of codes and of
semantic systems.

8. «Baum», «Holz», etc. are written in guillemets and not between
slashes because in this case they are not words but semantic entities,
units filling the space provided by the system.

9. Those problems will be clarified by a compositional analysis.
Provided a verb, as /buy/, be characterized as an n-arguments predicate — i.e.: Buy(A, O, G, C, I . . . .) — it will be clear that when one buys
we have to detect the Agent, who receives an Object in order to attain a
certain Goal (to satisfy a need), from a Counter-Agent, by means of an
Instrument (money) and so on. cf. 2.11.1.

10. One example of this temptation within structural semantics is to be found in the criticism which Bremond (1966*a*) makes of an analysis on punched cards of the ideas contained in the Koran. Bremond observed that this study brings to light hidden interconnections between disconnected notions and isolated unexpected clusters springing from the very structure of the text; but the authors echo their own codes in the message and form a system not from the "objective" ideas within the Koran, but from "the ideas held by the contemporary scientific West concerning the Koran." Bremond instead proposes objective research which would strive to bring to light a system of ideas "immanent in the text" taking inspiration not from a more convenient *coding* but from a "more exact" *decoding*. The objection presumes that every sign refers to a univocal position in the Universal Semantic System, because of the existence of a single code. But if there are many contradictory semantic fields, their choice depends on the point of view controlling one's approach to the text. What one supposes to be a system of semantic units inherent in the Koran may be a system of ideas which the scientific West holds in respect to the Koran, or a system of ideas which a study of the history of culture shows to be present in the Arab world at the time of the Koran. It is unlikely that an interpretive reading will succeed in avoiding a dialectic between these two moments (quite apart from the fact that the semantic fields of the civilization of the Koran can also be found to be contradictory and intricate). A rereading of the *Poetics* of Aristotle (on which so many of the discussions of narrative depend) could help us avoid many mistakes. Certainly a plot can be seen as a series of *functions*, or a structured matrix of functions in alternate opposition, but the isolation of these functions cannot be freed from the preliminary attribution of pertinence (and therefore of meaning) to each of these. What, for example, does it mean when one says that something terrible or pitiful happens to a certain character? Does it mean that something happens which (in the light of the common opinion prevalent in a given society) will arouse pity or terror? Does the fact that a character is unwittingly induced to eat the flesh of his own son arouse terror? For a Greek, yes, and generally speaking, for a Westerner. But we could imagine a model of culture in which this ritual behavior would not seem terrible. It is understandable that a Greek should be inclined toward pity when confronted with the fact that Agamemnon *had* to sacrifice Iphigenia, whereas for us, if the fact were described outside its original context, an individual who, for purely superstitious reasons, had agreed to kill his daughter would seem to us merely disgusting, and we would not feel pity for Agamemnon but rather scorn and a desire to punish him. The *Poetics* cannot be understood without recourse to the *Rhetoric*; the functions of plot acquire value only when measured against the *value* systems of a given group. A fact cannot be defined as 'unexpected' if we do not know the *systems of expectation* of the addressee. Thus even the researches into the structure of narration refer to a socio-historical definition of semantic systems.

11. But this definition does not explain the denotation of syncategore-matic (and therefore non-referential) terms, such as /by/ or /however/. In these cases we have to hold the preceding definition, according to which denotation is the marker to which the sign-vehicle corresponds without any previous mediation. But saying 'without previous mediation' one should specify: 'except in cases of meaning requisites, i.e., semantic presuppositions,

(cf. 2.11.1.). If /dog/ is marked as «mammal», this marker entails the marker «animal», which can be disregarded by the representation according to redundancy rules; therefore «mammal» is 'mediated' by «animal» but such a mediation is requested as a meaning requisite (by a mechanism of *pars pro toto* or *species pro genere*, i.e., hypotactical relations). On the contrary «fidelity» may be mediated by «domestic» but without direct entailment; therefore it constitutes a connotation.

12. According to Fillmore (1971a) "a lexicon as a part of the apparatus of a generative grammar must make accessible to its users, for each lexical item: (i) the nature of the deep-structure syntactic environments into which the item may be inserted; (ii) the properties of the item to which the rules of grammar are sensitive; (iii) for any item used as a 'predicate', the number of 'arguments' that it conceptually requires; (iv) the role(s) which each argument plays in the situation which the item, as a predicate, can be used to indicate; (v) the presuppositions or 'happiness conditions' for the use of the item, the conditions which must be satisfied in order for the item to be used 'aptly'; (vi) the nature of the conceptual or morphological relatedness of the item to other items in the lexicon; (vii) its meaning; and (viii) the phonological and orthographic shapes which the item assumes under given grammatical conditions" (p. 370). In 2.11., presenting our Revised Model, granted that the semantic markers will be what Fillmore calls "meaning", we shall try to satisfy all the other seven requisites or, at least, to posit the possibility of satisfying them. In other words, the semantic representation will try to solve also the problem of combinational rules. /John is the son of a stone/ has to be considered as semantically anomalous, for the semantic representation of /son/ must consider a marker such as $S(x,y)$ in which both x and y are characterized as «human».

13. The fact that in German /sun/ provokes certain connotative associations, whereas in Italian it provokes others, only means that sometimes a given syntactic marker induces semantic connotative markers in the corresponding sememe. All English it-names are he-names or she-names in Italian and this naturally has its consequences in fairy tales. But these connotations are due to a rhetorical process of personification relying on the semantic markers.

14. To assume that syntactic markers must allow the correct combination of the given expression within the right context does not mean that the code should consider a sort of general rule (apart from the semantic representation of the given item) establishing, for instance, that NP = D+N(+A). It is enough that the syntactic representation of a lexical item as /dog/ establishes N(+D−,±A−), specifying whether the item has to be inserted before or after D and A. Obviously the semantic marker N entails, by redundancy rules, the following combinational description. The general grammatical rule, at this point, is no more than a statistical extrapolation.

15. This assumption may be challenged as far as so-called 'iconic' signs, which are considered 'naturally' correspondent to a given object, are concerned. A tentative solution of the problem is given in 3.5 and 3.6. As for clearly recognized arbitrary signs (such as those of natural languages), De Mauro (1968, 3.4.19.1 and 3.4.27) states that, whereas a phonological system is composed of pertinent elements, the systems of content units (which he calls "lexical noemes", which can be decomposed into minor significant units

such as the "hyposemes" equivalent to lexemes) do not have relevant semiotic components, except in specific cases (such as scientific systems) where they are established by very precise selective rules and by terms with unambiguous meanings. In my opinion this is too radical a thesis. To deny the marker to marker correspondence does not mean to deny that sememes are semically articulated.

16. The system of semes can be even more unsystematically listed, for empirical purposes. Thus for some authors who consider the problem in operative terms (the construction of thinking machines) the classification and hierarchy of the semantic components do not aim to realize an absolute classification but are dependent on an empirical choice. Thus we see how Bertram Raphael (in Minsky, 1968) can describe the class «cats» with features such as «Sound, Mew, Color (Black, White, Yellow, Brown), Leggedness, 4 . . . ».

17. See for instance Weinreich (1965). A challenging landscape of alternatives to the KF model may be found in Steinberg and Jakobovits (1971), mainly in the contributions of McCawley, Lakoff, Fillmore, Bierwisch. See also Fillmore and Langendoen, 1971.

18. Katz (1972), following Frege, says that if someone asserts that «Kepler died in misery», then the use of the name /Kepler/ presupposes that the name designates someone; nevertheless the possibility exists that the speaker or the hearer of such a sentence believes that Kepler was a German wurst-maker living on the lower East Side of New York. This detail is not relevant for Katz's purposes but it is so for mine. If that person's belief is an idiosyncratic matter of personal illiteracy, obviously that presupposition should not be taken into account by a theory of codes. But what if many members of a given society (let us suppose 60%) believe that Kepler was the wurst-maker?

19. 'Fuzzy concepts' seem to have vague boundaries for all members of a social group and therefore need to be gradated according to a universally accepted scale. On the contrary 'hedges' (expressions like "a sort of" or "technically speaking") seem to me to acquire different values according to different speakers or contexts; they would therefore be the proper subject for an encyclopedia recording different 'technical' uses of an expression.

20. For example /chair/ bears the marker «Inanimate», which from the point of view of the markers makes sentences such as /the chair has given birth/ impossible. But in the right context, it becomes possible to make a sentence of the type /the chair of St. Peter has given birth to an encyclical, illuminated by the Holy Spirit/. Here we have reached the level of rhetorical figures. But rhetorical convention is what assigns to the term /chair/ (even if only in the context of the syntagm /chair of St. Peter/) a connotative meaning of «Pope». And so it becomes possible, because of this reading, to assign a marker "Animate" to /chair/. Moreover, the reference to the Holy Spirit creates a presupposition which refers to the Virgin Birth. Because of this, /chair/ even acquires an indirect and indeed peripheral connotation «Feminine» which facilitates its amalgamation with /to give birth/. As may be seen, it is the correlation between peripheral nodes of the tree which determines the shifts and the compatibility with the original nodes. A competence which does not also take into account the coded possibility of rhetorical use of the lexeme does not allow any articulated and rich use of the

language. The KF tree is condemned to be complicated even if it can be simplified for experimental reasons.

21. Katz (1972:85) says: "If the elements concerned are semantic markers then the distinction marked by these elements is a conceptual one. If on the other hand, they are distinguishers, this distinction is a (linguistically reflected) perceptual one". But if a perceptual distinction can be linguistically reflected it must be a conceptual element! Katz could reply: there are some perceptual elements that are named by a word but are not conceptually explained by it, such as /red/ for instance. This response would be very dangerous, for it would imply that there exist words that 'reflect' concepts and that are susceptible to semantic analysis, and others that only 'reflect' sense data and which are not semantically analyzable. Which would bring the project for a semantic theory to complete bankruptcy. Moreover, why should /young knight/ refer only to a perceptual experience, and /human/ and /object/ not?

22. Conversely, let us call pragmatic and referential presuppositions, *factual implications*. They should be the object both of a practice of overcoding and of a theory of sign production and interpretation. As for recent literature on presuppositions in linguistic theory, see Fillmore, 1971, a and b; Langendoen, 1971; Lakoff, 1971b; Garner, Keenan, Langendoen and Savin in Fillmore and Langendoen, 1971). Fillmore (1971a) says that /bachelor/ presupposes «adult, male, human» so that the sentence /That person is not a bachelor/ "is only used as a claim that the person is or has been married, never as a claim that the person is a female or a child" (p. 382). But let us go back to our note 11: the semantic representation must display hierarchical relationships and to deny the property of being «never married» does not imply the refusal of broader properties such as «male» and «adult». Thus the notion of semiotic entailment has the same logical advantages as that of presupposition, without suggesting a shade of extra-semantic or factual implication.

23. All this gives rise to the question: if even syncategorematic relations such as /if/ or /then/ should be considered signs to compositional analysis (thus also reducing the combinational rules to a sememic description, see 2.9.3.), what about the order or the syntactic position of a sign-vehicle? In /Paul loves Mary/ it is the position that makes Mary the object of Paul's passion: Morris (1938) defined the word-order as a type of sign, that is a "formator". See, for a tentative answer, 3.6.5.

24. Abduction not only allows us to intepret a message referred to an uncoded context or circumstance. It also helps us to select the appropriate code or subcode for an imprecise message. Suppose we have three cards on which are written: (i) /cane/; (ii) /e gatto/; (iii) /sugar/. We do not know if /cane/ represents the graphic transcription of the English word [*kan*] or of the Italian word [*kane*] (dog). Provided that the graphic item may freely associate either with /e gatto/ (giving "cat and dog") or /sugar/ (giving "sugar cane"), the choice of the more suitable combination can only be suggested by some surrounding context or circumstance. And the comparison between these and the graphic items is quite simply a new act of abduction. Considering that, in principle, every time we hear a word we must decide to which code it has to be referred, *abduction would seem to enter into any act of decoding*, and moreover into every act of recognizing the 'emic' nature of an 'etic' utterance.

25. Verón (1973a) recalls the principle of 'inter-textuality' already held by Kristeva (1969) and by Metz (1968). This principle seems to me to join the one of overcoding, because only by means of overcoding is one able to refer an actual text to a series of previous texts in which something similar 'happened': "Un autre exemple: une bonne partie des propriétés du discours des hebdomadaires d'information restent incompréhensibles si l'on ne tient pas compte de leurs rapports systématiques avec le discours des quotidiens; de ce point de vue, les hebdomadaires constituent un véritable "méta-langage" dont les presupposés ne peuvent être décrits que comme des opérations intertextuelles. *Troisièmement*, il y a un rapport intertextuel auquel on n'a pas prêté autant d'attention qu'au deux précédents. Il s'agit du rôle, dans le processus de production d'un certain discours, d'autres discours relativement autonomes, qui, tout en fonctionnant comme des moments ou étapes de la production, n'apparaissent pas à la surface du discours 'produit' ou 'terminé'. . . . L'analyse de ces textes et de ces codes qui n'apparaissent pas à la surface d'un discours donné mais qui cependant ont fait partie du processus de production de ce dernier, me semble essentielle: leur étude peut nous offrir des éclaircissements fondamentaux sur le processus de production lui-même et aussi sur la lecture du discours au niveau de la reception . . . . Ces discours 'cachés' (l'on peut songer aussi, par exemple, aux croquis et dessins des projets d'architecture) jouent un rôle instrumental dans la production d'un certain objet discursif et par là même constituent un lieu privilegié où transparaissent certains des mécanismes idéologiques à l'oeuvre dans la production. Ils relèvent, si l'on peut dire, d'une intertextualité 'en profondeur', puisque ce sont des textes qui, faisant partie du processus de production d'autres textes, n'arrivent jamais eux-mêmes (ou très rarement, ou par des canaux très restreints) à la consommation sociale des discours."

26. The notion of extra-coding finally allows us to clarify many of the meanings of /presupposition/ (see note 22). It seems that pragmatic presuppositions (whether contextual or circumstantial) are usually matter for a free inferential labor, but sometimes they are extra-coded. When ethnomethodologists postulate "interpretive procedures" they are probably thinking of extra-coded rules. See for instance in Cicourel (1971:52) the procedures listed as 'the reciprocity of perspectives', 'the et cetera assumptions', and so on. Everything we take for granted in communicative interaction goes back to pieces of institutionalized knowledge. According to Fillmore (1971a), Garner (1971), Ducrot (1972) and others, an expression such as /please open the door/ presupposes that: (i) there is a particular relation between sender and addressee; (ii) the addressee is able to obey the order; (iii) the addressee has precise ideas about the existence and the specificity of the door; (iv) the door is closed when the sentence is uttered; (v) the sender wants the door open; etc. Requirements (i), (ii) and (v) are a matter of overcoding: there are discoursive rules that establish the circumstances in which one can command and the condition of reliability of one's statements, requests, and so on ('good faith' in communication). Requirements (iii) and (iv) should be considered as typical semantic presuppositions (or meaning requisites, or semiotic entailments) for "the presupposition about the closed state of the door is a property of the verb *open*" and "the presupposition about the existence of the door relates to the use of the definite article". One could suggest that even requirement (v) belongs to this type, since the will of the sender is expressed by /please/. Naturally

requirement (iii) is initially satisfied by a semantic presupposition but, insofar as the definite article is a pointer (see 2.11.5.), it asks for a referential presupposition and goes back to a mention (see 3.3.).

27. In Table 30 both the orienting and the deviating circumstances represent the *uncoded* complex of biological factors, economic occurrences, events and external interferences which appear as the unavoidable framework of every communicative relationship. They are almost like the presence of 'reality' (if so ambiguous an expression is permissible) which flexes and modulates the processes of communication. When Alice asks: "The question is whether you *can* make words mean so many different things," Humpty Dumpty's answer is: "The question is *who is to* be the master". Once this point of view is accepted, one might well ask whether the communicative process is capable of subduing the circumstances in which it takes place.

Communicative experience enables us to answer positively, if only insofar as circumstance, understood as the 'real' basis of communication, is also translated constantly into a universe of coding while for its own part communication, in its pragmatic dimension, produces behavioral habits which contribute to the changing of the circumstances.

But there is one aspect which is more interesting from the semiotic point of view, according to which the circumstance can become an intentional element of communication. If the circumstance helps one to single out the subcodes by means of which the messages are disambiguated this means that, rather than change messages or control their production, one can change their content by acting on the circumstances in which the message will be received. This is a 'revolutionary' aspect of a semiotic endeavor. In an era in which mass communication often appears as the manifestation of a domination which makes sure of social control by planning the sending of messages, it remains possible (as in an ideal semiotic 'guerilla warfare') to change the circumstances in the light of which the addressees will choose their own ways of interpretation. In opposition to a *strategy* of coding, which strives to render messages redundant in order to secure interpretation according to pre-established plans, one can trace a *tactic* of decoding where the message as expression form does not change but the addressee rediscovers his *freedom of decoding*.

3: THEORY OF
SIGN PRODUCTION

3.1. A general survey

3.1.1. Productive labor

What happens when I produce a sign or a string of signs? First of all I
must accomplish a task purely in terms of physical stress, for I have to 'utter'.
Utterances are usually considered as emissions of sounds, but one may enlarge
this notion and consider as 'utterances' any production of signals. Thus I
utter when I draw an image, when I make a purposeful gesture or when I
produce an object that, besides its technical function, aims to communicate
something.

In all cases this act of uttering presupposes *labor*. First of all the labor
of *producing* the signal; then the labor of *choosing*, among the set of signals
that I have at my disposal, those that must be articulated in order to compose
an expression, as well as the labor of isolating an expression-unit in order to
compose an expression-string, a message, a text. Fluency or difficulty in
speaking, insofar as it depends on a more or less perfect knowledge of
linguistic codes, must be examined by semiotics, although I do not propose to
go into the matter here. Rossi-Landi (1968) has dealt with this aspect of
performance.

151

Suppose now that, instead of uttering words, I draw an image corresponding to an object, as when I draw a dog in order to advise people to 'beware' of the dog in my garden. This kind of sign-vehicle production seems to be rather different from choosing the word /dog/. It implies extra work. Moreover, it might be pointed out that, in order to say /dog/, I had only to choose among a repertoire of established types, and to produce a single occurrence of that type, while in order to draw the image of a dog I have to *invent* a new type. Thus there are different sorts of signs, some of them entailing a more laborious mode of production than others.

Finally, when I 'utter' words or images (or whatever else), I have to labor in order to articulate them in 'acceptable' strings of sign-functions; thus I have to labor on their semantic acceptability and *understandability*. In the same way, when receiving a sentence, even though I do not have to labor in order to produce the sign-vehicles, I do have to labor in order to *interpret* them. Obviously I can send my messages in order to *mention* things and states of the world, in order to assert something about the organization of a given *code*, in order to *question* or to *command*. Either to send or to receive these messages (or texts) requires that the sender should foresee, and the addressee isolate, a complex network of *presuppositions* and of possible inferential *consequences*. In exchanging messages and texts, judgments and mentions, people contribute to the *changing* of codes. This social labor can be either openly or surreptitiously performed; thus a theory of code-changing must take into account the public reformulation of sign-functions and the surreptitious *code-switching* performed by various rhetorical and ideological discourses.

Many of these activities are already studied by existing disciplines; others will have to constitute the object of a new general semiotics. But even those already studied by pre- or extra-semiotic disciplines will then have to be included as branches of a general semiotics, even if it proves convenient to preserve their present affiliation for the time being.

3.1.2. Types of labor

Whereas a theory of codes was concerned both with the structure of sign-function and with the general possibility of coding and decoding, a theory of sign production will thus be concerned with all the problems outlined in Table 31. This table concerns the kind of labor required in order to produce and interpret signs, messages or texts (physical and psychological effort in manipulating signals, in considering, or disregarding, the existing codes; time needed, degree of social acceptance or refusal, energy expended in comparing signs to actual events; pressure exerted by the sender on the addressee, and so on).

The interconnecting arrows linking the various kinds of labor try to correct the oversimplification due to the bi-dimensional format of the diagram; each kind of labor interacts with many others and the process of sign production — in its relationships with the life of codes — represents the result of a network of interacting forces. On the right side are listed the various different approaches that may be applied to the different areas of study, and are in fact actually adopted irrespective of the general semiotic framework that the table proposes. The existence of such a diversity of approaches should not be regarded as a methodological limitation for semiotics; it must simply be listed among the so-called 'political' boundaries mentioned in 0.4.

Let us now examine the items of Table 31 one by one.

(i) There is a labor performed on the expression continuum in order to physically *produce* signals. These signals may be produced as mere physical entities without semiotic function; but as soon as they are produced — or selected among pre-existing entities — as the expression-plane of a sign-function, their mode of production directly concerns semiotics. They may be either already segmented discrete units or material clusters *somewhat* correlated to a content. In both cases their production presupposes different modes of labor or different techniques of production. These modes of production will be listed in Table 39.

(ii) There is a labor performed in order to articulate *expression-units* (either already established by an expression system or proposed as the somewhat segmented functives of a new coding correlation). This kind of labor concerns the choice and the disposition of sign-vehicles. There can be expression articulation during the act of constituting (or *making*) an innovatory code; during a discourse in which the senders try to *observe* all the laws of the existing codes; within a text where the sender invents new expression units, therefore enriching and *changing* the system (for example when Laforgue invents the word '*volupté*' or Joyce 'meandertale'; see for instance Eco, 1971). Obviously the modification on the expression-plane must be correlated with a modification on the content-plane, otherwise it becomes mere grammatical nonsense; therefore the labor of system observing, system making and system changing on the expression-plane must be considered in relation to the corresponding labor on the content-plane, through the mediation of a labor on the correlation of functives (item iii).

(iii) There is labor performed in order to correlate for the first time a set of functives with another one, and thus making a code; an example of such *code making* is given by the operation constituting the Watergate Model in chapter 1.

Table 31 Labor presupposed in the process of sign production

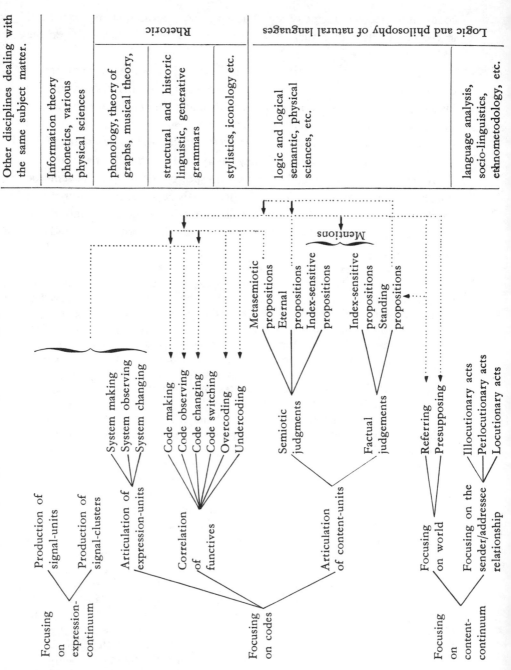

(iv) There is labor performed when both the sender and the addressee emit or interpret messages *observing* the rules of a given code, as in the case of 'common' semiotic acts such as the expression /the train from London will arrive at 6.00 P.M./. This kind of disambiguation of expressions was dealt with in chapter 2.

(v) There is a labor performed in order to *change* the codes shared by a given society. It is a complex process which involves both semiotic and factual judgments (see 3.2.) and other forms of textual manipulation; in this sense it directly involves the aesthetic manipulation of codes (see 3.7.).

(vi) There is labor performed by many rhetorical discourses, above all the so called 'ideological' ones (see 3.9.) in which the entire semantic field is approached in apparent ignorance of the fact that its system of semantic interconnections is more vast and more contradictory than would appear to be the case. In order to avoid openly acknowledging the contradictory nature of the Global Semantic System (see 2.13.) ideological discourse must *switch* from one code to another without making the process evident. Code switching is also performed in aesthetic texts, not as a surreptitious device but as a manifest procedure, in order to produce planned ambiguities and multi-levelled interpretations (see 3.7.1.).

(vii) There is labor performed in order to interpret a text by means of a complex inferential process. This process is mainly based on *abductions* and produces forms of *overcoding* (on the basis of a first level of pre-established rules new rules are proposed which articulate more macroscopic portions of the text) and of *undercoding* (in the absence of reliable pre-established rules, certain macroscopic portions of the text are assumed to be the only pertinent units even though the more basic combinational rules and their corresponding units remain unknown). To this important aspect of text interpretation the whole of section 14 of chapter 2 has been devoted.

(viii) There is labor performed by both the sender and the addressee to articulate and to interpret sentences whose content must be correctly established and detected. Section 2 of the present chapter will deal with these propositions (such as meta-semiotic, eternal and standing propositions) commonly called 'statements', while section 3 will deal with the index-sensitive sentences used in mentioning or referring, and will therefore also deal with many problems regarding item (ix).

Semiotic judgments predicate of a given semiotic item what is already attributed to it by a code (see 3.2.). They can assume three forms: (a) *meta-semiotic* propositions presupposing a 'performative' format («I state that from now on the word 'ship' can also be applied to vehicles for space-travel»); (b) *eternal* propositions of the type «bachelors are males»; (c) *index-sensitive* propositions coupling certain objects, taken as representative of a bunch of properties, to certain words («this object is a pencil»); this last kind of semiotic judgment, insofar as it is pronounced about actual objects, is also called a *'mentioning or referring* act' and can be studied under the same profile as index-sensitive factual propositions (see 3.3.1.).

Factual judgments predicate of a given semiotic item what was not attributed to it by the code. This judgment can be of two types: (a) *index-sensitive* propositions that attribute to a token occurrence of a semiotic type a factual property that, by definition, does not pertain to other 'tokens' of the same 'type' ("this pencil is black"); this kind of judgment, otherwise called 'occasion proposition' (see 2.5.3.), does not modify the semantic representation of a given semiotic item and in this sense it could be left aside by a semiotic inquiry, being better dealt with by a theory of the extensional verification of correspondences between propositions and states of the world; but all the same it has some semiotic purport insofar as, in order to predicate a semantic item as the property of an object, one will need a survey and a definition of this object's properties and such an operation has a semiotic aspect (see 3.3.3. − 3.3.6.); (b) *Standing* non index-sensitive propositions like "The moon has been walked on by human beings": as will be seen in 3.2.2, this kind of judgment when pronounced for the first time is a factual index-sensitive proposition (something is predicated of a given semantic item that no code attributed to it, and it is asserted for the first time by means of an indexical device of the type "in this moment" or "from now on"); but when these judgments are accepted by a society as true, then they assume a meta-semiotic function and gradually become semiotic judgments.

(ix) There is labor performed in order to check whether or not an expression *refers* to the actual properties of the things one is speaking of. This labor is strictly linked to the one performed in order to grasp the content of the index-sensitive semiotic and factual sentences, or mentions. To this problem section 3 is devoted.

(x) There is labor performed in order to interpret expressions on the basis of certain coded or uncoded circumstances. This labor of *inference* is linked both to the inferential labor required in order to understand something (thereby becoming the proper concern of a theory of perception and intelligence) and to the inferential labor performed within the text (see vii) which must be considered as an aspect of the labor of over- and undercoding (see 2.14.).

(xi) There is labor that the *sender* performs in order to focus the attention of the *addressee* on his attitudes and intentions, and in order to elicit behavioral responses in other people. This kind of labor (which will be considered in many of the following sections) was usually studied by the so-called theory of speech acts. Provided that in the present perspective the notion of 'speech act' is taken as concerning not merely verbal acts but every kind of expression (images, gestures, objects), it may be noted that among these various *communicational acts* figure not only the so-called *locutionary* ones, which may correspond to semiotic and factual judgments, but also all those types of expression that do not express any assertion but on the contrary perform an action or ask, command, establish a contact, arouse emotions and so on (*illocutory* and *perlocutory* acts). [1]

3.1.3. How to read the following sections

The present chapter 3 will not deal with all problems concerning a theory of sign-production; it will only deal with such specific problems as require direct, immediate and exclusive attention from a semiotic point of view. Let me stress the order of priorities which governs the organization of the eight following sections.

The labor performed in shaping the expression-continuum in order to produce the concrete occurrence of a given sign brings into immediate evidence the fact that there are different kinds of signs. If a general theory of codes, providing the notion of sign-function along with the notion of segmentation of both the expression and the content levels, seemed to offer a unified definition for every kind of sign, the concrete labor of producing these signs obliges one to recognize that there are different modes of production and that these modes of production are linked to a triple process: (i) the process of shaping the expression-continuum; (ii) the process of correlating that shaped continuum with its possible content; (iii) the process of connecting these signs to factual events, things or states of the world. These processes are strictly intertwined; once the problem of shaping the continuum is posed, that of its relationship with the content and the world arises. But at the same time one realizes that what are commonly called types of sign are not the clear-cut product of one of these operations, but rather the result of several of them, interconnected in various ways.

One also realizes that there are some signs that seem better adapted to the expression of abstract correlations (like *symbols*) and others that would appear to be more useful in direct reference to states of the world, *icons* or *indices*, which are more immediately involved in the direct mentioning of actual objects. In order to understand these points it would seem more profitable to tackle the problem of the various kinds of judgments pronounced about the world or codes and acts of mentioning things straight away. So instead of following the theoretical order outlined in Table 31 I will follow a sort of phenomenological order: in pronouncing judgments and performing mentions one discovers how one is using both verbal devices and other sorts of signs, such as for example, a pointing finger or an object taken as an example; at this point one should be able to single out both their differences and their similarities, and to realize that these differences do not characterize the various kinds of signs in themselves but rather discriminate between modes of sign production, every so-called sign being the result of many such operations.

Thus a typology of signs will give way to a typology of modes of sign production, thereby showing, once again, that the notion of 'sign' is a fiction of everyday language whose place should be taken by that of sign-function.

3.2. Semiotic and factual statements

3.2.1. Analytic vs. synthetic and semiotic vs. factual

To communicate means to concern oneself with extra-semiotic circum-stances. The fact that they can frequently be translated into semiotic terms does not eliminate their continuous presence in the background of any phenomenon involving sign production. In other words, signification is confronted with (and communication takes place within) the framework of the global network of material, economic, biological and physical conditions then prevalent. The fact that *semiosis lives as a fact in a world of facts* limits the absolute purity of the universe of codes. Semiosis takes place among events, and many events happen that no code could have anticipated. The semiotic creativity allowed by codes thus demands that these new events be named and described. The structure of codes can sometimes be upset by an innovatory statement concerning events which do not fit in with the organization of the content. What happens when messages state something concerning an as yet unorganized and non-segmented content? Does the new set of cultural units thus introduced into the social competence modify the pre-established semantic field? And how? This point prompts a return to an old philosophical distinction, widely discussed in logic and linguistic analysis, between *analytic* and *synthetic* judgments.

Considered from the point of view of a referential semantics this distinction is open to the broadest criticism. One might well wonder (cf. White, 1950) why such a statement as «all men are rational animals» is considered by traditional philosophers to be an analytic judgment and «all men are bipeds» a synthetic one. In effect, if one predicates the 'objectivity' of certain properties, the reason for the distinction between these two types of judgments is not evident. But Cassirer has already given an answer to this problem in *Das Erkenntnisproblem in der Philosophie und Wissenschaft der neueren Zeit*, II, 8, II. The analytic judgment is the one in which the predicate is contained implicitly in the concept of the subject, and the synthetic judgment is that in which the predicate is added to the subject as an entirely new attribute, due to a synthesis obtained from the data of experience.

Why then, according to Kant, is «all bodies are extensive» analytic and «all bodies are heavy» synthetic? Simply because Kant referred to the 'patrimony of thought' which he presumed to be known to his contemporaries. It is worth noting that «body» for him was not a referent but above all a cultural unit. And from the time of Descartes up to Newton and the encyclopedists, «extension» was attributed to this cultural unit as an essential quality which was a part of its definition, whereas «weight» was considered an accessory and contingent quality which did not therefore enter into the same definition. *Judgments are either analytic or synthetic according to the existing codes and not according to the presumed natural properties of the objects.* Kant explicitly states in the first *Kritik* that "the activity of our reason consists largely . . . in the analysis of ideas which we already have with regard to objects". Since, however, the opposition 'analytic vs. synthetic' co-involves too many philosophical problems, let us develop the above suggestion within a more specific semiotic context, in this way proposing a more suitable opposition.

Let us call *semiotic* a judgment which predicates of a given content (one or more cultural units) the semantic markers already attributed to it by a previous code; let us call *factual* a judgment which predicates of a given content certain semantic markers that have never been attributed to it by a previous code. Therefore /every unmarried man is a bachelor/ is a semiotic judgment solely because there exists a conventional code which refers to a compositional tree which possesses among its markers «never married». Instead /Louis is a bachelor/ is undoubtedly a factual judgment. On May 5, 1821, /Napoleon died on Saint Helena/ constituted a factual judgment. But from that moment on, the same statement has constituted a semiotic judgment because the code has fixed in the compositional tree of /Napoleon/ the definitional connotation «died on Saint Helena». On the other hand /Napoleon, after the battle of Marengo, drank a cup of coffee/ is a factual statement that can hardly be transformed into a semiotic one. Thus White (1950), criticizing the analytic-synthetic distinction, rightly affirms that a judgment is analytic on the basis of a convention and that, when the convention changes, the judgments which were once analytic can become synthetic, and vice versa. But what he intended as a limitation of the logical distinction between analytic and synthetic is instead the condition for the validity of the semiotic distinction between semiotic and factual judgments.

3.2.2. Statements

I shall briefly consider a particular example of these judgments, that is, semiotic (or meta-semiotic) and factual *statements*, granted that these are not to be confused with index-sensitive judgments or mentions (see 2.5.3., where non-statements are called 'occasion propositions'; mentions will be examined in 3.3.). It should be recalled that:

a) /This is a one dollar bill/ is not a statement: it is a *mention* (see 3.3).

b) /One dollar is worth 625 lire/ was a semiotic statement in 1971, thereby expressing a coded signifying relationship.

c) /One dollar is worth 580 lire/ was an astonishing factual statement emitted in a given day during 1972.

d) /One dollar is worth 580 lire/ became a semiotic statement of type (b) during 1972.

e) In order to make the factual statement (c) become the new semiotic statement (d) it was necessary that (c) should take the form of a meta-semiotic statement, presupposing or explicitly stating a performative formula such as: /The President of the United States (or the Bank of Italy, or the European Common Market) establishes that, from today on, everybody must accept the financial convention that one dollar is worth 580 lire/. The fact that since 1972 such a meta-semiotic statement has changed so many times only confirms yet again that many codes are very weak and transient, thus lasting *l'espace d'un matin*, like the rose. But a rose is no less a rose — witness Gertrude Stein — because it is so short-lived; in the same way a code is a code (is a code is a code) provided that a meta-semiotic statement has conventionally established a certain equivalence and a society has accepted it, and remains so until the arrival of another code-changing meta-semiotic adjustment.

Finally, the example of the dollar is particularly apposite, because the financial market represents a perfect case of coupling between units from different content systems, each unit being semantically defined by the opposition it entertains with every other unit. Therefore factual statements sometimes upset and restructure the codes [2].

3.2.3. Non-verbal statements

Even though to designate these operations of content-articulation I have employed terms borrowed from logic (which is mainly concerned with verbal expressions), all these types of propositions also concern non-verbal expressions. The Encyclopaedia Britannica is a text which sets out a lot of meta-semiotic and semiotic statements not only because it records many verbal definitions of various semantic units but also because it uses drawings and photographs in order to analyze the components of the same semantic units (for example visually describing the parts of human body or the elementary components of a four-stroke engine). The *New York Times* sets out a lot of factual statements not only by means of words but also of photographs or diagrams.

The visual demonstration of the theorem of Pythagoras is a semiotic statement. A road signal announcing a dangerous crossing is at the same time a factual statement and a mention. Other road signals commanding one to «stop» or «beware!» or forbidding right of way are communicational acts that are listed under item (xi). The drawing of a horse with the caption /horse/ represents an index-sensitive semiotic judgment; the portrait of the last winner of the Nobel Prize with the caption /this man has won the Nobel Prize/ constitutes an index-sensitive factual judgment. The Neapolitan gesture meaning «I am hungry» is an index-sensitive factual judgment. And so on.

3.2.4. Other questions

This dialectic between codes and messages, whereby the codes control the emission of messages, but new messages can restructure the codes, constitutes the basis for a discussion on the creativity of language and on its double aspect of 'rule-governed creativity' and 'rule-changing creativity'.

Factual statements, as usually performed, are an example of creativity permitted by the rules of the code. One can verbally define a new physical particle using and combining pre-established elements of the expression-form in order to introduce something new in the content-form; one can technically define a new chemical compound using and combining pre-existing content-units in a new way, in order to fill up an empty space within a pre-established system of possible semantic oppositions; one can thus alter the structure of both the expression and the content-system following their dynamic possibilities, their combinational capacities — as if the whole code by its very nature demanded continual re-establishment in a superior state, like a game of chess, where the moving of pieces is balanced out by a systematic unit on a higher level. Thus the possibility of meta-semiotic statements which alter the compositional spectrum of a lexeme and reorganize the readings of the sememe is also based on the pre-established elements and combinational possibilities of the code [3].

3.3. Mentioning

3.3.1. Index-sensitive judgments

Signs are used in order to name objects and to describe states of the world, to point toward actual things, to assert that there is something and that this something is so and so. Signs are so frequently used for this end that many philosophers have maintained that a sign is only a sign when it is used in order to name things. Therefore these philosophers have tried to demonstrate that a notion of meaning as separated from the 'real' and verifiable 'denotatum' of the sign, that is, the object or the state of the world to which the sign refers, is devoid of any real purport. Thus, even when they accept a distinction between meaning and referent (or denotatum) and do not equate the former with the latter, their interest is exclusively directed toward the correspondence between sign and denotatum; the meaning being taken into account only insofar as it can be made to correspond to the denotatum in specular fashion.

The theory of codes outlined in chapter 2 not only tried to restore the meaning's autonomous status, but even deprived the term /denotation/ of any extensional or referential relevance. The foregoing section, even though it has considered factual statements, has not linked these judgments to the facts about which they are stated. What is characteristic of a factual judgment of the kind examined in the above section is that although it seems to concern facts it can also be used in order to assert non-existent factual states, and therefore to lie.

If I assert that 'the man who invented eye-glasses was not Brother Alessandro della Spina but his cell-mate', I do not challenge an established semiotic statement, for the inventor of eye-glasses is a decidedly imprecise historical entity and the encyclopedias are rather vague and cautious on this subject, but I do make a factual statement, or a 'standing proposition'. It would be very difficult to check whether my judgment is true or false, and some documentation would clearly be needed; but all the same what I have produced is a factual statement (whether true or false) insofar as it does not assert something definitely recorded by a cultural code. Thus factual judgments of this type are not necessarily verified by an actual state of the world or a present entity. In this sense it is possible to assume that they have a meaning irrespective of their verification, and yet once their meaning is understood they demand verification.

Let us now consider another type of factual judgment, the *index-sensitive* one, i.e. the act of mentioning something actually present, as in /this pencil is blue/ or /this is a pencil/. As was suggested in 3.1., there is a difference between the two examples, and the second can be registered as index-sensitive but semiotic. Nevertheless both seem to be acts of mentioning (or of referring to) something. It may be assumed that in this case their meaning depends directly on the actual thing they refer to, but such an assumption would challenge the independence of meaning from referent maintained in chapter 2.5.

3.3.2. Meaning and referring

Strawson (1950) says that "mentioning or referring is not something an expression does; it is something that someone can use an expression to do". From this point of view 'meaning' is the function of a sentence or expression; mentioning and referring, and truth and falsity, are functions of the *use* of the sentence or expression. "To give the meaning of an expression . . . is to give *general directions* for its use to refer to or mention particular objects and persons; to give the meaning of a sentence is to give *general directions* for its use in making true or false assertions". [4] Let us try to translate Strawson's suggestions into the terms of a theory of codes. To give general directions for the use of an expression means that the semantic analysis of a given sememe establishes a list of semantic properties that should correspond to the supposedly extra-semiotic properties of an object. If this sounds somewhat Byzantine, one could reformulate it as follows: to give general directions for the use of an expression in referring means to establish to which actual experiences certain names, descriptions or sentences can be applied. Clearly this second definition, despite its correspondence to our normal way of speaking, says very little. Moreover, one has to face the question: how does one establish the rules of such an application?

So one must return to the first formulation of the problem. But at this point a new problem arises: how does one establish a correspondence between the semantic properties of a sememe (which clearly is a matter for semiotics) and the supposedly non-semantic properties of a thing? Can the mentioned thing assume the status of a semiotically graspable entity? For, either semiotics cannot define the act of mentioning or in the act of mentioning the thing mentioned should be viewed in some way as a semiotically graspable entity. So we must re-examine the whole process of mentioning.

3.3.3. The process of mentioning

The act of *referring* places a sentence (or the corresponding proposition) in contact with an *actual circumstance* by means of an *indexical device*. We shall call these indexical devices *pointers*. A pointing finger, a directional glance, a linguistic shifter like /this/ are all pointers. They are apparently characterized by the fact that they have as their meaning the object to which they are physically connected. I have shown in 2.11.5. that this is not true. Any pointer has first of all a content, a marker of «proximity» or «closeness» independently of the actual closeness of an object. But for the sake of the present analysis let us retain the common notion of pointer as something pointing toward something else.

Suppose now that I point my forefinger toward a cat, saying: /This is a cat/. Everybody would agree on the fact that the proposition «The object I have indicated by the pointer is a cat» is true (or that the proposition «The *perceptum* at which I pointed at moment x was a cat» is true; to put the matter simply, everyone would agree that what I had called a cat was a cat). In order that the above propositions be true I must be able to translate them as follows: "The *perceptum* connected with my forefinger at moment x represents the token occurrence of a perceptual type so conceptually defined that the properties possessed by the perceptual model systematically correspond to the semantic properties of the sememe «cat», and both sets of properties are usually represented by the same sign-vehicles".

At this point the referent-cat is no longer a mere physical object. It has already been transformed into a semiotic entity. But this methodological transformation introduces the problem of the semiotical definition of the *percepta* (see 3.3.4.). If the sentence was a semiotic act and the cat an empirical *perceptum* it would be very difficult to say what the expression /is/ was. It would not be a sign, since /this is/ is the connecting device joining a complex sign (the sentence) to an actual *perceptum*. It would not be a pointer, inasmuch as the pointer points toward the *perceptum* to be connected with the sign, while /is/ seems to actually perform the connection itself. The only solution seems to be: /this is a cat/ means «the semantic properties commonly correlated by the linguistic code to the lexeme /cat/ coincide with the semantic properties that a zoological code correlates to that *perceptum* taken as an expressive device». In other terms: both the word /cat/ and that token *perceptum* //cat// culturally stand for the same sememe. This solution undoubtedly looks rather Byzantine — but only if one is accustomed to think that a 'true' perception represents an *adaequatio rei et intellectus* or is a *simplex apprehensio* mirroring the thing, as the Schoolmen maintained. But let us simply suppose that the expression /this is a cat/ is uttered in the presence of an *iconic representation* of a cat. All the above reasoning immediately becomes highly acceptable; we have a sign-vehicle (a) which is a linguistic expression to which a given content corresponds; and we have a sign-vehicle (b) which is an iconic expression to which a given content also corresponds. In this case we are comparing two sets of semantic properties and /is/ can be read as /satisfactorily coincides/ (that is: the elements of the content plane of a code coincide with the element of the content plane of another code; it is a simple process of transliteration) [5]. Why does the mentioning act in the presence of a real cat seem so different to us? Clearly because we do not dare to regard perception as the result of a preceding semiotic act, as had been suggested by Locke, Peirce and many other philosophers.

3.3.4. Ideas as signs

There is a brief passage from Peirce (5.480) which suggests a whole new way of understanding real objects. Confronted with experience, he says, we try to elaborate ideas in order to know it. "These ideas are the *first logical interpretants* of the phenomena that suggest them, and which, as suggesting them, are signs, of which they are the . . . interpretants". This passage brings us back to the vast problem of *perception as interpretation of sensory disconnected data* which are organized through a complex transactional process by a cognitive hypothesis based on previous experiences (cf. Piaget, 1961). Suppose I am crossing a dark street and glimpse an imprecise shape on the sidewalk. Until I recognize it, I will wonder "what is it?" But this "what is it?" may be (and indeed sometimes is) translated as "what does it *mean*?" When my attention is better adjusted, and the sensory data have been better evaluated, I finally recognize that it is a cat. I recognize it because I have already seen other cats. Thus I apply to an imprecise field of sensory stimuli the cultural unit «cat». I can even translate the experience into a verbal interpretant (/I saw a cat/). Thus the field of stimuli appears to me as the sign-vehicle of a possible meaning which I already possessed before the perceptual event.

Goodenough (1957) observed that: "a house is an icon of the cultural form or complex combination of forms of which it is a material expression. A tree, in addition to being a natural object of interest to a botanist, is an icon signifying a cultural form, the very same form which we also signify by the word *tree*. Every object, event or act has stimulus value for the members of a society only insofar as it is an iconic sign signifying some corresponding form in their culture . . . . " Clearly from an anthropological point of view this position is close to what was said in the Introduction and to what will be said in 3.6.3. on the way in which every object may potentially become a sign within the environment of a given culture; and clearly the theory developed here finds many points of contact with the ideas suggested by Peirce.

As Peirce writes: "Now the representative function of a sign lies neither in its material quality nor in its pure demonstrative application; because it is something which the sign is, not in itself or in a real relation to its object; but which it is *to a thought*, while both of the characters just defined belong to the sign independently of its addressing to any thought. And yet if I take all the things which have certain qualities and physically connect them with another series of things, each to each, they become fit to be signs. If they are not regarded as such they are not actually signs, but they are so in the same sense, for example, in which an unseen flower can be said to be *red*, this being also a term relative to a mental affection" (5.287).

In order to assert that objects (insofar as they are perceived) can also be approached as signs, one must also assert that even the concepts of the objects (as the result or as the determining schema of every perception) must be considered in a semiotic way. Which leads to the straightforward assertion that *even ideas are signs*. This is exactly the philosophico-semiotical position of Peirce: "whenever we think, we have present to the consciousness some feeling, image, conception, or other representation, which serves as a sign" (5.283). But thinking, too, is to connect signs together: "each former thought suggests something to the thought which follows it, i.e., is the sign of something to this latter" (5.284).

Peirce is in fact following a very ancient philosophical tradition. Ockham (in *I Sent.*, 2,8; *Ordinatio*, 2,8; *Summa totius logicae*, 1, 1) insists on the fact that if the linguistic sign points back to a concept (which is its content), alternatively the concept is a sort of sign-vehicle able to express (as its content) singular things. The same solution can be found in Hobbes (*Leviathan*, i, 4), not to speak of Locke's *Essay concerning Human Understanding*: here Locke explicitly asserts *the identity between logic and semiotics* (IV,20) and the semiosic nature of ideas. These ideas are not (as the Schoolmen believed) a mirroring image of the thing; they too are the result of an abstractive process (in which — let it be noted — only some pertinent elements have been retained) which gives us not the individual essence of the named things but their *nominal essence*. This nominal essence is in itself a digest, a summary, a elaboration of the signified thing. The procedure leading from a bunch of experiences to a name is the same as that which leads from the experience of things to that *sign* of things, the idea. *Ideas are already a semiotic product.*

Obviously in Locke's system the notion of idea is still linked to a mentalistic point of view; but it is sufficient to replace the term 'idea' (as something which takes place in the mind) by 'cultural unit' (as something which can be tested through other interpretants in a given cultural context) and Locke's position reveals itself as very fruitful for semiotic purposes. Berkeley too (*Treatise*, Intr., 12) speaks of an idea as *general* when it represents or stands for all particular ideas of the same sort.

Obviously this interesting chapter of a future history of semiotics deserves a more careful elaboration. But it was in any case important to undertake this first tentative exploration in order to find some historical roots for the approach here proposed. It will help one to understand why throughout the entire history of philosophy the notion of *linguistic meaning* has been associated with that of *perceptual meaning*, by means of an identical term (or of a pair of homonymous terms.)

According to Husserl (*Logische Untersuchungen*, I, IV, VI) the dynamic act of knowing implies an operation of "filling up" which is simply an *attribution of sense* to the object of perception. He says that *to name* an object as /red/ and *to recognize* it as red are the same process, or at least that the manifestation of the *name* and the intuition of the *named* are not clearly distinguishable. It would be worth ascertaining to what extent the idea of 'meaning' found in the phenomenology of perception agrees with the semiotic notion of a cultural unit. A rereading in this light of Husserl's discussions might induce us to state that semiotic meaning is simply the socialized codification of a perceptual experience which the phenomeno-logical *epoché* should restore to us in its original form. And the significance of daily perception (before the *epoché* intervenes to refresh it) is simply the attribution of a cultural unit to the field of perceptual stimuli as has been said above. Phenomenology undertakes to rebuild from the beginning the conditions necessary for the formation of cultural units which semiotics instead accepts as data because communication functions on the basis of them. The phenomenological *epoché* would therefore refer perception back to a stage where referents are no longer confronted as explicit messages but as extremely ambiguous texts akin to aesthetic ones.

This is not the place to study this problem in greater depth. Suffice it to say that we have indicated another of semiotics' limits, and that it would be worth while to continue research on this in relation to the genesis of perceptual signification.

3.3.5. /Is/ as a metalinguistic device

Let us now return to our example of the expression /this is a cat/. One is now ready to accept the idea that an act of mentioning or referring is made possible by a very complicated previous semiosic process which has already constituted the perceived object as a semiotic entity: (i) I *recognize* the cat as a cat, that is, I apply a cultural schema (or idea, or concept) to it; (ii) I understand the *token* cat as the sign-vehicle of the *type* cat (the corresponding cultural unit) concerning myself only with its semantic properties and excluding individualizing physical properties which are not pertinent (clearly the same happens, with some other mediating processes, when I say /this cat is big, black and white/); (iii) among the semantic properties of the cultural unit «cat» I select the ones which are in accordance with the semantic properties expressed by the verbal sign-vehicle.

I thus compare two semiotic objects, that is, the content of a linguistic expression with the content of a perceptual act. At this point I accept the equation posited by the copula /is/. Inasmuch as the equation represents a sort of metalinguistic act, associating a linguistic expression with the living 'expression' of a cultural construct (and thereby trying to establish an equivalence between sign-vehicles coming from different codes), it can either be accepted or refused — insofar as it does or does not satisfy the semantic rules imposing as predicates of a given item certain other items, able to amalgamate together through some common semantic properties. So the copula /is/ is a metalinguistic sign meaning «possesses some of the semantic properties of». (6) In some circumstances the metalanguage might not be a verbal one: as when /is/ is replaced by a pointing finger meaning both «this» and «is».

3.3.6. Predicating new properties

The above discussion (from 3.3.3. to 3.3.5.) has made clear the status of *semiotic* index-sensitive judgments. But perhaps the nature of *factual* index-sensitive judgments, such as /this cat is one-eyed/ remains more obscure. In this case I assign to the token of the type-cat a property which is not recognized by the code, so that we would seem to be back with the problem of the relation between on the one hand two semiotic constructs (the sememe «cat» and the conceptual type «cat») and on the other a mere *perceptum*. Except that the property of being one-eyed is not a mere *perceptum*, but rather a sort of 'wandering' semantic property, coming from some organized subsystem, which is recognized as such and attributed to this one cat, viewed as the occurrence of a more general model. The single occurrence of a type can have more characterizing properties than its model (thus the occurrence of a word shows a lot of free variants), it cannot however have properties which are incompatible with its type.

To predicate new properties of an object is not so different from producing phrases which are semantically acceptable. I can accept well-formed phrases like /the pencil is green/ or /the man sings/ and I must usually refuse phrases like /the pencil sings/ or /the man is green/; it is simply a matter of semantic amalgamation.

Therefore I can accept factual judgments like /*this* pencil is blue/, for pencils are usually either black or colored, /*this* pencil is long/ because pencils are physical objects possessing dimensional properties, and /*this* man sings/ because men can emit sounds. All of them are acceptable factual index-sensitive judgments. On the contrary /*this* pencil is two miles long/, /*this* pencil is vibrating at the speed of 2,000 w.p.s./ or /*this* man is internally moved by a four-stroke engine/ are abnormal factual judgments for they nourish an inner semantic incompatibility. Thus if I said /this cat is four feet long/ there would be two possibilities: either I *see* that the cat is not actually that long, and in this sense I am simply associating unappropriate words with the living expression of a semantic property that I can conceptually detect and that I could verbally express in another way; or I am really 'telling the truth'. But if I have told the truth, I am obliged to ask myself: do four-foot-long cats really exist? All my knowledge about cats tells me that they do not usually share such a property, i.e. that the conceptual construct «cat» (corresponding to the sememe «cat») does not possess such a property. Therefore I must assume that what I have seen is perhaps not a cat but a panther. Suppose that I now check and I discover that it has all the properties of a cat and none of the properties of a panther, but that all the same it really is four feet long; then my perception, once it is conceptualized, does not coincide with the conceptual construct that made it possible. I must therefore reformulate the conceptual construct (and therefore the corresponding sememe); it is possible that a mutation may have changed the size of some cats. So I must emit a factual statement (/some cats are four feet long/) after which, by means of a meta-semiotic judgment, I can change the code.

3.3.7. Is the present king of France a bachelor?

The case of the four-foot-long cat is one of an actually perceived subject of which a puzzling property must be predicated. There are cases of predication in which the property does not create problems, but the subject does. Such is the case of the famous sentence /the present king of France is bald/. To engage in the Olympic Games that this sentence has provoked in contemporary semantics may help to solve the final problem about mentioning.

Everyone is agreed that the sentence in question, if uttered in the present century, is rather puzzling. It may also be suggested that the sentence is meaningless since 'definite descriptions' have a meaning only when there is a single object for which they stand. We have already provided the answer to such an assumption, and a theory of codes demonstrates that a description like /the king of France/ is fully endowed with meaning. It is not necessary to assume that a description like /the king of France/ must be verified by a presupposition, thus asking for an existential verification. This theory holds good when attributing a truth value to a proposition; so that if the description /the husband of Jeanne d'Arc/ does not have a 'referential index' a statement like /the husband of Jeanne d'Arc came from Brittany/ arouses a lot of interesting questions in terms of extensional semantics. But /the king of France/ stands for a cultural unit, not a person; not only does it share with /the husband of Jeanne d'Arc/ the quality of meaning something, but also it can correspond or not correspond to somebody who actually existed and who, in a possible world, could continue to exist.

So suppose then that someone states that /the king of France is wise/ as Strawson suggests; the expression is endowed with meaning, so the problem is to know under what circumstances it is uttered; if it is used in order to mention Louis XIV, it can be said to be acceptable, but if used in order to mention Louis XV some might judge it rather over-evaluative.

Suppose that I now say /this is the king of France/ pointing with my forefinger toward the President of the French Republic. This is the same as saying /this is a cat/ while indicating a dog. There is a semantic incompatibility between the properties of the sememe and the properties of the cultural unit represented by the indicated person, taken as an occurrence of a conceptual construct.

Suppose that I now say /this man is bald/ when referring to a long haired pop-singer; this represents a typical case of misuse of language. One need only translate the expression as /this man is a bald man/ for it to become clear that I am attributing certain semantic properties to a percept that cannot be taken as an occurrence of a more general model for bald men.

Suppose that I now say /the king of France is bald/; in itself the expression is meaningful and may become true when I use it in order to mention Charles the Bald, who was elected emperor in 875 A.D. If I use the sentence in order to mention Louis XIV the sentence is false. However, both mentions presuppose an indexical device; if I utter them I must in some way indicate which king I am referring to. The same happens when I say /the present king of France is bald/. The word /present/ is in fact a pointer, and as a pointer is a shifter (see 2.11.5.).

What does /the present king of France is bald/ mean? It has the following deep semantic structure: «there is a king of France. The king of France is bald». But /there/ is an ambiguous device: it has the sense of /there/ in /there are many books in the world/ and that of /there/ in /they are *there*/.. The first /there/ has an imprecise adverbial function, the second has the meaning «in this precise place» and an almost substantive function as in /he is in *there*/.

One should thus say: /there is *there* a king of France/, which would mean: «in the precise historical moment (or in the precise spatial environment) within which the sender of the message is speaking». And this is exactly the meaning of /present/, whose compositional tree could be represented as in Table 32 (according to 2.11.5.)

Table 32

$$/present/—sm—«present»-d_{time}—d_{close}—d_{immediately} \left\langle \begin{array}{l} [circ_{+index}] \longrightarrow \\ \\ [circ_{-index}] \end{array} \right.$$

where the absence of an index suggests an imprecise and multidirectional closeness. In terms of *meaning* the addressee receives the imperative content «point your attention toward the immediate temporal context». In terms of *mentioning* the addressee does not discover in such a temporal context a possible *perceptum* that could correspond to a conceptual type having the properties assigned by a code to a «king of France». Therefore the communication 'miscarries'; this proposition is neither true nor false, but simply inapplicable to any circumstance, and therefore misused. It is the same when I say /this is the king of France and he is bald/ while pointing my finger toward nothing.

Thus /the present king of France is bald/ is a meaningful sentence that, when considered as a mention, is an example of a misuse of sign production. Whereas /the king of France is bald/ is a meaningful sentence that, when used for imprecise mentions (for instance when uttered without specifying or presupposing any uncoded contextual selection) is simply useless. The proof is that,, when hearing it, people will ask: "which one?", thus demanding an indexical circumstantial marker [7].

3.4. The problem of a typology of signs

3.4.1. Verbal and non-verbal signs

Even though a definition of sign-function for every type of signs has been given in 2.1. and the process of sign production has also been examined from the point of view of many non-verbal signs, it would nevertheless be somewhat reckless to maintain that there is no difference between various types of signs. It is indeed possible to express a given content both by the expression /the sun rises/ and by another visual expression composed of a horizontal line, a semicircle and a series of diagonal lines radiating from the imaginary center of the semicircle. But it would seem more difficult to assert that /the sun *also* rises/ by means of the same visual device and it would be quite impossible to assert that /Walter Scott is the author of *Waverley*/ by visual means. It is possible to assert both verbally and kinesically that I am hungry (at least in Italian!) but it is impossible to assert by means of kinesic devices that «The *Kritik der reinen Vernunft* proves that the category of causality is an *a priori* form while space and time are pure intuitions» (even if Harpo Marx got remarkably near it). The problem could be solved by saying that every theory of signification and communication has only one primary object, i.e. verbal language, all other languages being imperfect approximations to its capacities and therefore constituting peripheral and impure instances of semiotic devices.

Thus verbal language could be defined as the *primary modelling system*, the others being only "secondary", derivative (and partial) translations of some of its devices (Lotman, 1967). Or it could be defined as the primary way in which man specularly translates his thoughts, speaking and thinking being a privileged area of a semiotic enquiry, so that linguistics is not only the most important branch of semiotics but the model for every semiotic activity; semiotics as a whole thus becomes no more than a derivation from linguistics (Barthes, 1964).

Another assertion, metaphysically more moderate, but possessing the same practical import, might consist in maintaining that only verbal language has the property of satisfying the requirement of *'effability'*. Thus not only every human experience but also every content expressed by means of other semiotic devices can be translated into the terms of verbal language, while the contrary is not true. The effability power of verbal language is undoubtedly due to its great articulatory and combinational flexibility, which is obtained by putting together highly standardized discrete units, easily learned and susceptible to a reasonable range of non-pertinent variations.

An objection to this approach might run as follows: it is true that every content expressed by a verbal unit can be translated into another verbal unit; it is true that the greater part of the content expressed by non-verbal units can also be translated into verbal units; but it is likewise true that there are many contents expressed by complex non-verbal units which cannot be translated into one or more verbal units (other than by means of a very weak approximation). Wittgenstein underwent this dramatic revelation (as the *Acta Philosophorum* relate) when during a train journey, Professor Sraffa asked him what the 'meaning' of a certain Neapolitan gesture was.

Garroni (1973) suggests that there is a set of contents conveyed by the set of linguistic devices *L* and a set of contents that are usually conveyed by the set of non-linguistic devices *NL*; both sets contribute to a subset of contents which are translatable from *L* into *NL* or vice versa, but such an intersection leaves aside a vast portion of 'unspeakable' but not 'unexpressible' contents.

Table 33

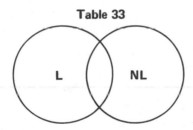

There are many proofs to support this theory. The power of verbal language is demonstrated by the fact that Proust successfully created the impression of rendering through words almost the entire range of perceptions, feelings and values embodied in an impressionist-like painting; but it is no chance that he was obliged to analyze an imaginary painting (by Elstir) for even a summary survey of a real painting could have suggested the existence of portions of content that the linguistic description did not cover. On the other hand it is quite clear that no painting (even if organized as some sort of supremely skillful comic strip with thousands and thousands of frames) could get across all that is conveyed by the *Recherche*. [8]

Whether there are *NL* semiotic systems; whether what they convey might be or ought to be called 'content' in the sense used up to now; whether as a result semantic markers and their interpretants have to be not only verbal devices but also organized and structured perceptions, habits, behaviors and so on; all this constitutes one of the most fascinating empirical boundaries of the present state of the semiotic art, and demands a great deal of further research.

In order to pursue this research it is absolutely necessary to demonstrate that (i) there exist different kinds of signs or of modes of sign production; (ii) many of these signs have both an inner structure and a relation to their content which is not the same as that of verbal-signs; (iii) a theory of sign production must and can define all of these different kinds of signs by having recourse to the same categorial apparatus.

Such is the aim of the following sections. I shall not attempt an exhaustive coverage of the entire field, but will instead try to define different types of signs, to analyze their constitutive differences and to insert them within the framework of the theory of sign-functions and codes. The conclusion to be drawn from this exploration will be that without doubt verbal language is the most powerful semiotic device that man has invented; but that nevertheless other devices exist, covering portions of a general semantic space that verbal language does not. So that even though this latter is the more powerful, it does not totally satisfy the effability requirement; in order to be so powerful it must often be helped along by other semiotic systems which add to its power. One can hardly conceive of a world in which certain beings communicate without verbal language, restricting themselves to gestures, objects, unshaped sounds, tunes, or tap dancing; but it is equally hard to conceive of a world in which certain beings only utter words; when considering (in 3.3.) the labor of mentioning states of the world, i.e. of referring signs to things (in which words are so intertwined with gestural pointers and objects taken as ostensive signs), one quickly realizes that in a world ruled only by words it would be impossible to mention things. In this sense a broader semiotic inquiry into various equally legitimate types of signs could also help a theory of reference, which has so frequently been supposed to deal with verbal language, as the privileged vehicle for thought alone.

3.4.2. Channels and expression parameters

Many different classifications of the various types of signs have been put forward during the development of the philosophy of language, linguistics, speculative grammar, semiotics, etc. All of these classifications served the purposes for which they were established. I shall limit myself here to a brief outline of those that are most relevant to the purpose of the present discussion. First of all, signs may be distinguished according to their *channel*, or expression-continuum. This classification (Sebeok, 1972) is useful for distinguishing many zoosemiotic devices and examines the human production of signs according to the different techniques of communication involved (Table 34).

Table 34

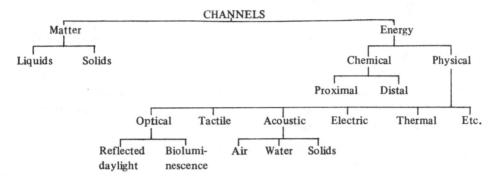

This distinction does not seem particularly useful for our present discussion, since it would seem pretty vague to place both Beethoven's *Ninth Symphony* and Dante's *Divina Commedia* among the acoustically channelled signs, and both a road signal and Manet's *Le déjeuner sur l'herbe* among the optical signs reflected by daylight.

Nevertheless it does permit one to isolate a set of important semiotic problems. There is a way in which Beethoven's music and Dante's poetry may be considered under the same heading. Both musical notes and words may be defined by means of sound parameters; the difference between a C emitted by a trumpet and a D emitted by a fiddle is detectable through reference to the parameters of pitch and timbre; the same happens for the difference between a velar voiced stop consonant (such as [g]) and a labial nasal one (such as [n]): in both cases, the decisive parameter is timbre. When distinguishing an interrogative utterance from an affirmative one, the essential parameters are pitch, dynamics and rhythm, as happens when distinguishing two different melodies.

On the other hand, in order to distinguish two road signals or two Manet paintings one resorts to both space and color parameters. In the first case the pertinent elements are the normal spatial dimensions, with features such as 'up/down', 'right/left', 'larger/smaller' and so on; in the second one, pertinent elements are wave-lengths, frequencies or, more commonly speaking, cues. The fact that a road signal is enormously simpler than a Manet painting does not matter. Thus in detecting two tactile signals, one has recourse to certain thermal and pressure gradients, while in detecting the difference between two signs channelled through a solid matter, like two gestural signals, one relies on positional or kinesic parameters such as the direction of the gesture, its stress, and so on.

3.4.3. Discreteness and gradated continua

One of the most disturbing features of a lot of semiotic studies past and present has been the interpretation of various signs on the basis of the linguistic model, and thus the attempt to apply to them something metaphorically similar to the sound parameters or the model of double articulation, etc. As a matter of fact we know very little about other parameters, for instance those that govern the distinction between the olfactory signs, which are based on chemical features. Semiotics has a long way to go if it is to clarify all these problems; but even if one cannot map them entirely, one must nevertheless trace their outlines. For instance, the notion of *binarism* has become an embarrassing dogma only because the only binary model available was the phonological (and therefore the phonetic) one. Thus the notion of binarism has been associated with that of absolute *discretedness*, since in phonology the binary choice was applied to discrete entities. Both notions were associated with that of *structural* arrangement, so that it looked to be impossible to speak of a structural arrangement for phenomena that appeared to be continuous rather than discrete.

But 'structure' does not only mean opposition between the poles of a *two*-tuple of discrete elements. It also means opposition between an *n*-tuple of gradated entitites, resulting from the conventional subdivision of a given continuum, as happens with the color system. A consonant is either voiced or not, but a shade of red is not opposed to its absence; instead it is inserted within a gradated array of pertinent units cut from a wave-length continuum. Frequency phenomena do not allow the same kind of pertinentization as do timbre phenomena. As has been already said *à propos* of a theory of codes (see 2.8.3.), there is structure when a continuum is gradated into pertinent units and the array of these units has precise boundaries.

Moreover, nearly all the non-verbal signs usually rely on more than one parameter; a pointing finger has to be described by means of three-dimensional spatial parameters, vectorial or directional elements, and so on. So an attempt to establish a complete set of semiotic parameters will involve the entire physical conditioning of human actions, inasmuch as they are conditioned by the structure of the human body inserted within its natural and artificial environment. As will be shown in 3.6., it is only by recognizing such a range of parameters that it is possible to speak of many visual phenomena as coded signs; otherwise semiotics would be obliged to distinguish between signs which are signs (because their parameters correspond to those of verbal signs, or can be metaphorically viewed as analogous to them) and signs which are not signs at all. Which may sound paradoxical, even though it is upon such a paradox that many distinguished semiotic theories have been established.

3.4.4. Origins and purposes of signs

Signs are also distinguished according to whether they originate from a *sender* or a natural *source*. Insofar as there exist a lot of signs that are without a human sender, occurring as natural events but being interpreted as semiotic devices, this classification, also summarized by Sebeok (1972), can be useful for the analysis of communicational processes (Table 35).

Table 35

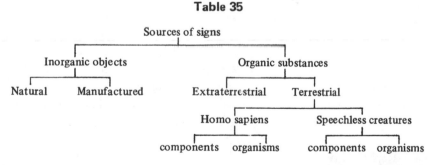

Signs are also distinguished according to their *semiotic specificity*. Some signs are objects explicitly produced in order to signify, others are objects produced in order to perform a given function. These latter can only be assumed as signs in one of two ways; either they are chosen as representatives of a class of objects (see 3.6.3.) or they are recognized as forms that elicit or permit a given function precisely because their shape suggests (and therefore 'means', 'signifies') that possible function. In this second case they are used as functional objects only when, and only because, they are decoded as signs.

There is a difference (as regards sign-specificity) between the injunction /sit down!/ and the physical form of a chair which permits and induces certain functions (among others, that of sitting down); but it is equally clear that they can be viewed under the same semiotic profile.

3.4.5. Symbols, Icons, Indices: an untenable trichotomy

At this point it would seem advisable to examine what is, perhaps, the most popular of Peirce's trichotomy, that by which signs are classified as *symbols* (arbitrarily linked with their object), *icons* (similar to their object) and *indices* (physically connected with their object).

This distinction is so widely accepted that we have used it in the preceding pages in order to indicate certain processes, so that they could be immediately, if vaguely, grasped by everyone. It is nevertheless the basic assumption of the following pages that notions such as 'icon' or 'index' are all-purpose, practical devices just as are the notions of 'sign' or 'thing'. They can undoubtedly be used for normal purposes, but no satisfactory definition can be found for them in the present context.

The reason is simple: such a trichotomy postulates the presence of the referent as a discriminant parameter, a situation which is not permitted by the theory of codes proposed in this book. The trichotomy could obviously be used in order to discriminate between different kinds of mentions (as indeed it was within that context), but it becomes more disturbing in a classification of modes of sign production which tries to focus exclusively upon the shaping of the signal (i.e. the expression continuum) and the correlation of that signal (as expression) with a content. Thus the following pages represent a critique of the naive notion of index and icon, and the new classification proposed in 3.6. aims to supersede these categories.

3.4.6. Replicability

A final distinction concerns the *replicability* of sign vehicles. The same word can be replicated an infinite number of times, but each replica is without economic value, whereas a coin, even though a replica, has a material value of its own. Paper money has a minimal material value but receives a sort of legal value by a convention, so that it cannot be indefinitely replicated; moreover, the process of replication is so technically difficult that it requires special techniques (the reasons of that difficulty are similar to those which seemingly forbid the reproduction of Michelangelo's *Pietà*; oddly enough this, too, has received a sort of conventional and 'legal' investiture whereby a replica, no matter how perfect, is refused as a fake). Finally a Raphael painting is commonly considered beyond replication except in cases of exceptional skillfulness — and even in these cases the replica is considered imprecise and unable to deceive a well-trained eye. [9] Thus it seems that there are three kinds of relationship between the concrete occurrence of an expression and its model: (a) signs whose tokens can be indefinitely reproduced according to their type; (b) signs whose tokens, even though produced according to a type, possess a certain quality of material uniqueness; (c) signs whose token is their type, or signs in which type and token are identical.

This distinction can be easily reduced to that proposed by Peirce's trichotomous distinction between *legisign*, *sinsign*, and *qualisign* (2.243.ff.): signs of type (a) are pure sinsigns; signs of type (b) are sinsigns which also are qualisigns; signs of type (c) are sinsigns which also are legisigns.

If these distinctions are considered from the point of view of the commercial value of the replica, then they are more a matter for Treasury Departments, income tax inspectors, art dealers and organized crime than for a theory of sign-functions (in which an object's only recognized value is its quality as a functive). From the semiotic point of view, the fact that a hundred dollar bill is counterfeit does not matter: every object looking like a hundred dollar bill will stand for the equivalent amount of gold to its addressees: the fact that the bill is a fake merely means that this is a case of lying.

A perfect replica of Michelangelo's *Pietà* which rendered each nuance of the material texture of the original with great fidelity would also possess its semiotic properties. Therefore the value accorded to the 'authenticity' of the original statue has more relevance for a theory of commodities, and when given undue importance on the aesthetic level it is a matter for social scientists or critics of social aberrations. The lust for authenticity is the ideological product of the art market's hidden persuaders; when the replica of a sculpture is absolutely perfect, to privilege the original is like giving more importance to the first numbered copy of a poem than to a normal pocket edition. But when one considers the same problem from the point of view of sign production, other factors have to be considered. Differing modes of production of the expression, along with the necessary type/token-ratio, determine a fundamental difference in the physical nature of various types of signs.

At this point we must make a clear distinction between absolute duplicative replicas which produce a *double*, and partial replicas, which will simply be called *replicas*.

3.4.7. Doubles

I mean by an absolutely duplicative replica a token which possesses *all* the properties of another token. Given a wooden cube of a given size, matter, color, weight, surface structure and so on, if I produce another cube possessing all the same properties (that is, if I shape the same continuum according to the same form) I have produced not a sign of the first cube, but simply *another* cube, which may at most represent the first inasmuch as every object may stand for the class of which it is a member, thus being chosen as an example (see 3.6.3.).

Obviously, as Maltese (1970:115) suggests, an absolute replica is a rather utopian notion, for it is difficult to reconstruct all the properties of a given object right down to its most microscopic characteristics; but there is a threshold fixed by common sense which recognizes that, when a maximum number of parametric features have been preserved, a replica will be accepted as another exemplar of the same class of objects and not as an image or representation of it. Two Fiat 124 cars of the same color are not each other's icon but two doubles.

In order to obtain a double it is obviously necessary to re-produce — to a given extent — all the properties of the model-object, maintaining their original order and interrelationships. But in order to do so it is necessary to know the *rule* which governed the production of the model-object. To duplicate is not to represent, to imitate (in the sense of making an image of), to suggest the same appearance; it is a matter of equal production *conditions* and *procedures*.

Suppose one has to duplicate an object devoid of any mechanical function, such as a wooden cube: one has to know (a) the modalities of production (or of identification) of the material continuum, (b) the modalities of its formation, i.e. the rules governing the relationships between its geometrical properties. Suppose now that one has to duplicate a functional object, such as a knife. One must *also* know its functional properties. A knife is the double of another knife if, *ceteris paribus*, it has the edge sharpened to the same degree. This being so, even if there were some microscopis difference in the surface texture of the handle, which could not be detected by sight, touch or a sensitive weighing machine, everybody would say that the second knife was the double of the first.

If the object is a very complex one, the principle of duplication does not change; what changes is the number of rules and the technical difficulties involved, as would be the case when trying to make the double of a Chevrolet, clearly no matter for the 'do it yourself' enthusiast.

An object as functionally and mechanically complex as the human body is not duplicable precisely because we are ignorant of many of its mechanical and functional rules, and first and foremost those required in order to produce living matter. Any duplication which does not follow all the rules of production and which therefore produces only a given percent of the mechanical and the functional properties of the model-object is not a double, but at best a partial replica (see 3.4.8.).

In this sense an uttered word is not the absolute duplicative replica of another word of the same lexicographic type, but rather, as we shall later see, a partial replica. If, however, I print the same word twice (for example: /dog/ . . . /dog/) I can say that one is the double of the other (microscopic differences in inking or in the pressure of the type on the paper being more a matter for metaphysical doubts about the notion of identity or equality).

According to this notion of double, it is commonly supposed that a painting is not truly duplicable. This is not completely true for, under given technical conditions, and using the same materials, one could theoretically establish a perfect double of the Mona Lisa by means of electronic scanners and of highly refined plotters. However, the perfection of such a double is determined by a perfect knowledge of even the microscopic texture of the artifact, which is usually unattainable.

Since we have defined as duplicable an object whose productive rules one knows, a painting will not usually qualify as such. What will qualify are such craft products as are traditionally duplicated without appreciable differences, so that nobody will be tempted to consider the duplicate as an iconic reproduction of the original; the duplicate is as much original as is its model. The same happens in civilizations where the representative rules are strictly standardized, so that an Egyptian painter might quite possibly have been able to duplicate a mural painting.

If Raphael's painting seems beyond duplication, this is because he *invented* his rules as he painted, proposing new and imprecise sign-functions and thereby performing an act of code-making (see 3.6.7.). The difficulty in isolating productive rules is due to the fact that, while in verbal language there are recognizable and discrete *signal-units*, so that even a complex text may be duplicated by means of them, in a painting the signal looks 'continuous' or 'dense', without distinguishable units. Goodman (1968) remarks that the difference between representative and conventional signs resides in this opposition (dense vs. articulate) and it is to this difference that the difficulty in duplicating paintings is due. As we shall see later (3.5.) this opposition is not sufficient to distinguish the so-called "iconic" or "representative" signs, but it may be retained for the moment.

A painting does in fact possess qualisign elements; the texture of the continuum from which it is made *counts* for a great deal, so that a dense signal is not reducible to a distinction between pertinent recognizable elements and irrelevant variations; even minimal material variations count. It is this quality which makes a painting into an aesthetic text, as will be better explained in 3.6.7. This is undoubtedly one of the reasons why the duplication of a painting is well-nigh impossible and why its rules of production are hardly detectable.

But the other depends on the particular type/token-ratio realized by a painting. In order to make this point clear, we must now consider the case of partial replicas.

3.4.8. Replicas

In replicas the type is different from the token. The type only dictates those essential properties that its occurrences must display in order to be judged a good replica, irrespective of any other characteristic that they may possess. Thus tokens of the same type can possess individual characteristics, provided that they respect the pertinent ones fixed by the type. It is this kind of type/token-ratio, for example, that rules the production of phonemes, words, ready-made expressions, etc. Phonology establishes certain phonetic properties that a token phoneme must have in order to be recognized as such; everything else is a matter of free variation. Regional or idiosyncratic differences in pronunciation do not matter, provided they do not affect the recognizability of the pertinent properties.

The type/token-ratio obeys different parameters and rules of fidelity according to different sign systems. Maltese (1970) lists ten kinds of ratio, from the absolute duplicate (which, given six properties of the visual-tactile experience of a given object, reproduces all of them) down to the reproduction of a unique property, as happens in a symbolic and schematic representation on a plane surface. This list coincides in some respects with the various 'scales of iconicity' (such as that proposed by Moles) and problems connected with these scales will be considered in 3.6.7.; but at present we are concerned with the three first degrees of Maltese's scale: between the first

(6/6), second (5/6) and third (4/6) one could easily classify the various kinds of type/token-ratio operating within the relationship between an expression and its type. For instance a road signal commanding "stop" is a 6/6 reproduction of its type; it is the absolute duplicative replica of many other signs of the same class. As an object, it is simply a double, but inasmuch as it is a sign it is one in which the fidelity of token to type must be absolute; the type prescribes form, size, painted lines and colors, material smoothness of surface, weight, etc. without permitting free variations. Free variations might well allow one to recognize the sign as such, but would induce a sharp observer (such as a policeman) to suspect a fake.

A phoneme does not have to be so faithful to its expressive type: or rather, it has to respect the dictates of its type, but its type does not dictate every material nuance of its occurrences. The type prescribing the form of the image of the King of Spades in playing cards offers many more possibilities for free variation (indeed this sort of stylization will be considered as something half way between replica and invention in 3.6.5.) [10].

3.4.9. *Ratio facilis* and *ratio difficilis*

Every replica is a token accorded to a type. Thus every replica is governed by a *type/token-ratio*. But in order to understand many other procedures in sign production let me outline, at this point, a distinction between two different sorts of type/token-ratio; I shall call them *ratio facilis* and *ratio difficilis*. There is a case of *ratio facilis* when an expression-token is accorded to an expression-type, duly recorded by an expression-system and, as such, foreseen by a given code.

There is a case of *ratio difficilis* when an expression-token is directly accorded to its content, whether because the corresponding expression-type does not exist as yet or because the expression type is identical with the content-type. In other words, there is a *ratio difficilis* when *the expression-type coincides with the sememe* conveyed by the expression-token. Using a formulation that will be partly criticized in the following sections, one could say that in cases of *ratio difficilis* the nature of the expression is *motivated* by the nature of the content.

It is not difficult to isolate and to understand the cases of *ratio facilis*; they are all those described in 3.4.8.; the sign is made up of a fairly simple expression-unit corresponding to a fairly precise content-unit. It is the case of words and of various visual entities (for example road signals as well as strongly stylized pictorial entities, such as occur in handicrafts and primitive painting); in order to produce a sign-vehicle meaning so and so, one must produce an object constructed in such and such a way (according to the model provided by the expression-system).

This kind of *ratio facilis* does not govern a double but a replica, since the expression-type establishes some features as pertinent, and some others as variable and inessential for the isolation of a given unit [11].

Even many *texts* are replicable according to a *ratio facilis*; suppose that in a certain primitive civilization there exists a given ritual dance or liturgical ceremony which conveys a vast portion of social content; this civilization may have *undercoded* some basic movements (event though permitting a lot of free variations) that allow one to isolate a given behavior as the replicable sign-vehicle of a given social content. A type/token-ratio can be *facilis* even when the type is very imprecise, provided it has been socially recorded. It would seem more difficult to isolate examples of *ratio difficilis*. As a matter of fact they depend on two different situations of sign production.

First situation: the expression is a precise unit correlated to a precise content, such as occurs with kinesic pointers, and nevertheless the design of the expression in some way depends on the corresponding sememe. These signs are easily replicable and have the curious property of being submitted both to a *ratio facilis* and to a *ratio difficilis* (see 3.4.10.).

Second situation: the expression is a textual *cluster* that should convey imprecise portions of content or a *content-nebula*. Such is the case of many text-oriented cultures (see 2.14.6.) which have not elaborated a highly differentiated content-system to which a highly elaborated expression-system corresponds. But this is also the case of many undercoded sign-functions in a grammar-oriented culture. In such a situation the expression must be elaborated according to a *ratio difficilis* and frequently cannot be replicated since the content, even expressed, cannot completely be analyzed and recorded by its interpreters. In this case the instances of *ratio difficilis* concern activities of code-making (see 3.1.2.). In the following two paragraphs I shall deal with some preliminary instances of these two different situations in which *ratio difficilis* is required in order to produce expressions.

3.4.10. Topo-sensitivity

A propos of kinesic pointers (see 2.11.5.), we have seen that there is no need to have something close to a pointing finger for that finger to acquire a meaning. The pointing finger has a seme of «closeness» and this semantic marker is grasped even if one points into empty air. The presence of the actual thing is not necessary in order to understand the pointer as a sign, even though it is necessary that something be there when the pointer is used to mention. But even when indicating nothing, the pointing finger is nevertheless a physical phenomenon whose nature is different from that of the verbal pointer /that/. It is just this physical nature which must be now analyzed inasmuch as it is the effect of a complex act of sign production.

In a pointing finger the expressive continuum (or matter) is given by a part of the human body. In this continuum pertinent features have been selected according to an expression-form system. Therefore in this sense a pointing finger is subject to a *ratio facilis* and can be indefinitely replicated.

Nevertheless when it has been said that a pointing finger has four syntactic markers (latitude, apicality, movement toward and dynamic stress) which convey certain semantic markers (such as closeness, direction, distance), it has been noted that the semantic unit «direction» is not independent of the syntactic feature /movement toward/; the force or the weakness of the stress directly conveys markers of distance or closeness. This does not occur with verbal pointers like /this/ whereby the content is arbitrarily correlated to the sign-vehicle.

In kinesic pointers the seme of «closeness» is independent of the presence of the indicated thing (as noted in 2.11.5.) but the movement of the finger must be *toward* that point in the space where the actual or supposed thing is or should be. It is true that the notion of «a thing in that place» is not a 'thing' but a portion of the content, yet one of the features of this supposed content is precisely a spatial situation. The pointing finger *means* a spatial situation and that spatial situation is intensionally analyzable even if extensionally null; in intensional terms it has certain semantic properties, one of them being that of having spatial co-ordinates. Now, these spatial co-ordinates of the conveyed content to some extent determine the spatial properties of the expression, i.e. the physical properties of the signal, thus introducing a *ratio difficilis* within a productive process apparently obeying a *ratio facilis*. Thus a non-verbal index has the same sign-function structure as has a verbal one, the same capacity to be analyzed into syntactic and semantic markers, but some of its syntactic markers seem to be *motivated* by its content.

Thus the attempt to subsume every kind of sign within the same semiotic categories gives rise to a new category which is *not* common to every kind of sign. One might over-hastily conclude from this that, even if not dependent upon its proximity to the referent, a pointing finger is nonetheless 'similar' to its possible referent and is therefore 'iconic'.

One of the aims of the following pages will be that of demonstrating that one cannot so easily equate motivation and similarity. But the problem does nonetheless exist, and the theory of codes outlined in chapter 2 cannot eliminate it.

But there are other reasons to render the pointing finger different from a verbal index.

Buyssens (1943) stated that a directional arrow, in itself, does not mean anything; but it may, for example, assume the meaning «turn left» if placed in a particular urban context (or external circumstance). This is not true.

Suppose we find a «turn» signal and a «stop» signal in a city's traffic department store, and thus view them without relation to any specific urban context. We are nonetheless able to recognize and to distinguish «stop» from «turn». This means that there exists a precise convention whereby those graphic sign-vehicles do have a meaning and thus do convey a precise portion of content. But, while the «stop» signal has the same meaning to everyone everywhere, the «turn to . . . » signal acquires the fullness of its meaning only when certain circumstantial features (relating to its placement in this rather than that place) add additional meanings such as «left» or «right».

It could be said that the position in which the road signal is placed is simply a circumstantial selection that awaits interpretation, or that the fact that the sign is located in that place is nothing more than a mention («this is the place where you have to turn»).

But this situation recalls another, involving verbal signs. These latter always occur *before* and *after* other signs, within the context of the phrase. Thus in the expression /John beats Mary/ it is their relative positions that make Mary a victim and John unduly violent; if /John/ were in the place of Mary and vice versa, things would run better for Mary. Contextual position (the order of words in the phrase marker) changes the meaning of an expression to such a degree that Morris (1946) proposed to list syntactical positions among a category of signs to be called "formators". The syntactical position would thus be a particular syncategorematic sign.

This being so, one can also single out certain 'formators' which are in some way *topo-sensitive* (through owing their meaning to their spatial or temporal co-ordinates, as happens with the direction of movement in the case of the pointing finger); moreover (as with the pointing finger), the nature of these co-ordinates on the expressive plane is motivated by the nature of the co-ordinates on the content plane. In other words /Mary/ is placed after /John/ because first «John» beats and then «Mary» is beaten.

All the examined examples have the feature of *vectorialization* in common, whether a real movement realizing a direction (the finger) or a virtual direction and movement realized by a feature of order (the phrase). The same happens with the road arrow situated at a given point: the entire sign («turn left») is topo-sensitive because one of its expressive features consists in pointing at the left rather than at the right of the addressee [12].

One might say that features of vectorialization make a sign 'similar' to its referent. In this case it would be no longer necessary to elaborate such a category as *ratio difficilis* and it would suffice to say that certain signs do not have an expression type but directly imitate the object for which they stand. However, the category of *ratio difficilis* has just been established in order to avoid such a naive interpretation (which will be criticized in 3.5) and a different theorization of vectorializations will be given in 3.6.5.

3.4.11. Expression-clusters and content-nebulas

Let us now consider some examples in which the motivation exercised by the content on the expression seems to be so strong as to challenge, along with the possibility of replicas, the very notion of *coded* correlation (and therefore of conventional sign-function). We shall first of all examine those cases in which one must express a large number of content-units whose aggregation has not been previously coded and therefore constitutes a *discourse*. Let us define a discourse as the equivalent of a text on the expression plane.

One may encounter two types of discourse for which no pre-established text exists.

The first is that of factual statements concerning unheard-of events, these events constituting a new combination of cultural units that the content system has already recognized and classified. To take the problem of verbally describing or visually representing a golden mountain or a new chemical compound, since these entities are the result of a *combination* of previously recorded semantic units and since the code already provides the corresponding expression-units (both 'categorematic' and 'syncategorematic'), the format of the expression will be established according to the requirements of the content — but not according to its *form*! Therefore this is not a case of *ratio difficilis*: the combination of the words /golden/ and /mountain/ has nothing to do with (it is not 'similar' to) the orographic structure of the imagined phenomenon. In other words, if an astronomer discovers that small red elephants may be observed living on the moon, every time Capricorn enters into the orbit of Saturn, then his content-system will undoubtedly be upset (and he will have to restructure his world-view) but his expression-system will not be disturbed at all, for the laws of the code allow him to 'map out' such a new state of the world (as well as to produce new words for new definable content-units, since the redundance of the expression-system allows him to articulate new lexical items).

But one encounters a quite different set of problems in the case of a new and *undefinable* content-unit (if in such circumstances one can still talk of a 'unit') or rather in that of a *content-nebula* which cannot be analyzed into recognizable and definable content units. One might speak of a new discourse which has no satisfactory interpretants. Suppose that one had to express the following situation: «Solomon meets the Queen of Sheba, each leading a procession of ladies and gentlemen dressed in Renaissance style, and bathed in a pure and still morning light that gives bodies the air of mysterious statues, etc., etc.». Everyone would recognize in this 'verbal' discourse something vaguely similar to a well-known pictorial 'text' by Piero della Francesca: but the verbal expression does not 'interpret' the pictorial one. At most, the former suggests the latter only because the latter has already been expressed and recorded by our culture. And even in this case only certain of the verbal expressions refer to recognizable content units (Solomon, to meet, Queen of Sheba, etc.), while many others by no means convey the sort of content that one might receive when looking at the painting (it goes without saying that even such an expression as /Solomon/ represents a rather imprecise interpretant of the corresponding image painted by Piero). When the painter begins work, the content (in its nebula-like structure) is neither coded nor divided into precise units. It has to be *invented*.

But the expression, too, has to be invented: as noted in 2.14.6., only when a highly differentiated content-system has evolved will a culture dispose of the corresponding expression-system. So we have a paradoxical situation, in which expression must be established according to a content model which does not yet exist as such.

The sign producer has a fairly clear idea of *what* he would like to 'say', but he does not know *how* to say it; and he cannot know *how* to do so until he has discovered *precisely what* to say. The lack of a definite content-type makes it impossible to find an expression-type, while the lack of an appropriate expression device makes the content vague and inarticulate. The difference between mapping into the expression a new but foreseeable content and mapping into the expression a content-nebula is that between a *rule-governed creativity* and a *rule-changing creativity*. Thus the painter has to invent a sign-function, and since every sign-function is based on a code, he has to propose a new way of coding.

To propose a code is to propose a correlation. Usually correlations are fixed by convention. But in this case the convention does not exist and the correlation must therefore be founded on something else. In order to make it acceptable, the producer must base his correlation on some evident motivation, for instance a stimulus. If the expression as stimulus is able to direct attention toward certain items of the suggested content, the correlation is then posited (and *après coup* could even by recognized as a new convention).

Thus, given a content-type that is in some way cognizable, its pertinent features must be 'projected' into a given expression continuum by means of certain transformational rules. This does not mean that the expression must 'imitate' the form of the object; a critique of this naive approach to the problem will be proposed in 3.5. If the content-type is complex, then the transformational rules will be equally complex, and will sometimes escape detection, being rooted in the signal's microscopic texture. In this way the sign (or text) becomes *dense*.

The more the content-type is new and uncoded or is the result of unfamiliar acts of mentioning, the more the producer must elicit in the addressee perceptual reactions that are to some extent equivalent to the ones he might have in the presence of the actual event. It is this extreme mode of stimulation that has permitted the formation of the notion of an 'iconic' sign as the *naturally motivated* and *analogical* result of an 'imprint' of the object itself on a given material continuum.

3.4.12. Three oppositions

When examining kinesic pointers we have discovered that signs can exist that are at once replicable and motivated. As a matter of fact, phenomena like replicability or motivation are not features by which one sign may be distinguished from another; they are modes of production that play differing parts in the constitution of various sorts of sign-functions. This is also the case with an opposition such as 'arbitrary vs. motivated'. Yet for many centuries this opposition seemed to be so evidently a matter of experience that the whole history of philosophy of language has been dominated by this question, beginning with Plato's *Cratylus*, which opposed *Nomos* (law, convention, arbitrariness) to *Physis* (nature, motivation, iconic relationship between sign and things).

One should not undervalue these positions, but the problem that they express must be re-thought in a more rigorous way — if only because in recent times the opposition 'arbitrary vs. motivated' (already associated with 'conventional vs. natural') has finally been coupled with a third opposition, 'digital vs. analogical'. Insofar as the term 'analogical' is understood in a double sense (see 3.5.4.) — as something concerning rules of proportionality

and as something connected with an immediate 'unspeakable' similarity — and insofar as, in the first sense, analogical is opposed to digital,
arbitrary signs are roughly equated with digitally analyzable ones. The same
happens in the case of the third opposition and the whole system usually
takes the following (apparently logical) form:

digital	vs.	analogical
arbitrary	vs.	motivated
conventional	vs.	natural

in which the vertical columns are supposed to list *synonymous* categories.

Even a superficial glance at many sign phenomena tells us that the
equation is not true and that therefore the oppositions are not synonymous; a
photograph is perhaps 'motivated' (the traces on the paper are produced by
the disposition of the matter in the supposed referent) but it is digitally
analyzable, as happens when it is printed through a raster; the smoke
revealing the presence of a fire is motivated by the fire but is not analogous to
it; a painting representing the Virgin Mary is 'analogous' to a woman, but it is
recognized as the Virgin Mary because of a conventional rule; a certain type
of fever is naturally motivated by TBC but it is due to a convention that it is
recognized as a reliable medical symptom. The movement of the pointing
finger toward the supposed object is maybe motivated by the spatial
co-ordinates of the object but the choice of the pointing finger as index is
highly arbitrary; in fact the Cuna Indians use an entirely different device, the
'pointing lips gesture' (Sherzer, 1972). A cat's paw print is motivated by the
form of a given cat's paw but it is by convention that a hunter assigns to that
expressive shape the content (the abstract notion of) «cat».

One must, at this point, face the problem of the so-called iconic signs,
in order to discover how many semiotic phenomena are commonly covered
by this all-embracing term. So-called iconism in fact covers many semiotic
procedures, many ways of producing signals ordered to a sign-function, and
we will see that, even though there is something different between the word
/dog/ and the image of a dog, this difference is not the trivial one between
iconic and arbitrary (or "symbolic") signs. It is rather a matter of a complex
and continuously gradated array of different modes of producing signs and
texts, every sign-function (sign-unit or text) being in turn the result of many
of these modes of production.

3.5. Critique of iconism

3.5.1. Six naive notions

It was said in 2.1. that a sign-function is the correlation between an expression and a content based on a conventionally established code (a system of correlational rules), and that codes provide the rules that generate sign-functions. If there exist signs that are to some degree motivated by, similar to, analogous to, naturally linked with their object, then the definition given in 2.1. should no longer be tenable.

The only way to maintain it is to demonstrate that even in these types of signs a correlational convention is in operation. The core of the problem is obviously the notion of convention, which is not co-extensive with that of arbitrary link, but which is co-extensive with that of *cultural* link. If one examines the mode of production of signs one must not only analyze the mode of production of the signal in itself but also its mode of correlation to its content, the correlating operation being part of the production. To produce a signal such that it may be correlated to a content is to produce a sign-function; the modes whereby either a word or an image are correlated with their respective contents are not the same. The problem is to find out whether the former is a cultural correlation (and therefore a conventional one) and the latter is not; or whether, on the contrary, both involve some sort of cultural correlation even though these correlations are operationally different (*ratio facilis* vs. *ratio difficilis*). In order to prove that the image of a dog also signifies a dog by means of a cultural mode of correlation, one must first of all challenge some naive notions. These notions are:

(i) that the so-called iconic sign has the *same properties* as its object;
(ii) that the so-called iconic sign is *similar* to its object;
(iii) that the so-called iconic sign is *analogous* to its object;
(iv) that the so-called iconic sign is *motivated* by its object.
Permeating the critique of these assumptions is a contrasting one, which risks attaining an equal dogmatism, i.e.:
(v) That the so-called iconic signs are *arbitrarily* coded.

We shall see that it is possible to assert that they are culturally coded without saying that they are totally arbitrary, thereby restoring to the category of conventionality a more flexible sense. But when one has solved these problems one is faced with a last possible assumption:

(vi) that the so-called iconic signs, whether arbitrary or not, are analyzable into pertinent coded units and may be subject to a multiple *articulation*, as are verbal signs.

We shall see that, if one accepts (v) without reservations, one is also forced to accept (vi), which could lead to a lot of difficulties. But if one views (v) in the flexible and prudent way outlined above, (vi) is no longer strictly and directly dependent upon (v). One could thus assume that so-called iconic signs are culturally coded *without* necessarily implying that they are arbitrarily correlated to their content and that their expression is discretely analyzable.

3.5.2. Iconism and sharing 'properties'

According to Morris (1946) a sign is iconic "to the extent to which it itself has the properties of its denotata". At first glance common sense might mislead one into agreeing with this definition. But a more thorough examination in the light of that same common sense forces one to realize that the definition is more or less tautological and in any case rather naive.

What does it mean to say that the portrait of Queen Elizabeth, painted by Annigoni, has the same properties as Queen Elizabeth? Morris (1946:1.7.) knows very well that "the portrait of a person is to a considerable extent iconic, but is not completely so since the painted canvas does not have the texture of the skin, or the capacities for speech and motion, which the person portrayed has. The motion picture is more iconic but again not completely so".

Such an approach, when pushed to its limit, would persuade both Morris and common sense to destroy the notion of iconism; "a completely iconic sign would always denote since it would be itself a denotatum", which is the same as saying that the true and complete iconic sign of Queen Elizabeth is not Annigoni's portrait but the Queen herself (or a possible science fiction *doppelgänger*). Morris himself, in the following pages, corrects the rigidity of the notion and states: "An iconic sign, it will be recalled, is any sign which is similar in some respects to what it denotes. Iconicity is thus a matter of degree" (1946: 7.2.). And since, going on to deal with non-visual iconic signs, he even speaks of onomatopoeia, clearly the question of degree appears to be extremely elastic, since the iconic relationship between a /cock-a-doodle-doo/ and the crowing of a cock is very weak; so much so that the French onomatopoeic sign is /cocquerico/, and the Italian one /chicchi-

ricchi/: the problem lies first of all in the meaning given to the expression "in some respects": if an iconic sign is similar to the thing denoted *in some respects*, then we arrive at a definition which satisfies common sense, but not semiotics.

Secondly there are certain perplexities surrounding the notion of 'similarity to objects'. Is one really sure that iconic signs are 'similar' to the objects they stand for? Indeed, is one sure that they stand for objects at all? Let us examine an advertisement. An outstretched hand offers me a glass foaming over with freshly poured beer, while over the outside of the glass extends a thin layer of vapor which immediately conveys a sensation of coldness. It would be interesting to see which of the properties of the object this picture contains. There is neither beer nor glass on the page, nor is there a damp and icy film. I feel certain visual stimuli, colors, spacial relationships, incidences of light and I coordinate them into a given perceptual structure. The same thing happens when I look at an actual glass of beer; I connect together some stimuli coming from an as yet unstructured field and I produce a *perceptum* based on a previously acquired experience.

Thus I can only assume that in the iconic experience certain perceptual mechanisms function which are of the same type as the one involved in the perception of an actual object, but the stimuli that I am concerned with in the first case are not the same as those that I am concerned with in the second. At most, a theory of perception will tell me that there are previous expectations, or models, or codes, that rule both perceptual coordinations. The solution would then be to propose that iconic signs do not possess the 'same' physical properties as do their objects but they rely on the 'same' perceptual 'structure', or on the same system of relations (one could say that they possess the same perceptual sense but not the same perceptual physical support). Thus when looking at the actual glass of beer I perceive on a given surface the presence of a uniform layer of transparent material which, when struck by light, gives off silver reflections, thereby producing that *perceptum* which I call " icy film on the glass"; on the other hand in the drawing I perceive on a given paper surface a film of non-transparent material composed of two or more different shades of color that, by their mutual contrast, create the impression of incident luminosity. What kind of structural relationship remains unchanged between film and light, on the one hand, and two different colors on the other? And does the result of the two procedures produce the 'same' perceptual effect? Is it not better to assume that, on the basis of *previous learning*, I view as one and the same perceptual result what are in fact two different perceptual results? Suppose now that I draw the outline of a horse on a sheet of paper by one continuous and elementary line. The sole property that my horse possesses (one continuous black line) is precisely the property that a real horse *does not* possess. My drawing has defined by that line the space inside the horse separating it from the space outside the horse, whereas the actual horse is in fact a body within or against a space.

Admittedly, if I see the profile of a horse against the background of the sky, the contrast between the boundaries of that body and the background can appear under some circumstances as a continuous line at whose limits the light is absorbed into the dark body. But the process is more complex, the boundaries are not so clear and therefore the black line iconically rendering this perceptual experience is decidedly a simplifying and selective one. Thus a *graphic convention* allows one to transform, on paper, the elements of a *schematic conceptual or perceptual convention* which has motivated the sign.

Maltese (1970:VIII) suggests that the continuous line produced by the imprint of a body upon a malleable substance is matter not of visual but of tactile experience. The visual stimulus, which is in itself very poor from an informational point of view, suggests (by means of synesthesia) a tactile experience. That kind of stimulus is not a sign at all. It is only one among the various features of an expressive device that contributes to establishing the correspondence between that expression and a given content(«human hand», or better «a human hand pressed on that point there»). Thus the profile or the global imprint of the hand are not iconic signs which possess some of the properties of the hand; they are *surrogate stimuli* that, within the framework of a given representational convention, contribute to the signification; they are sheer material configurations that simulate perceptive conditions or components of iconic signs (Kalkofen, 1973, commenting on previous statements of mine — see Eco, 1968).

A certain type of naive theorizing will quickly identify the production of surrogate stimuli with iconism, therefore speaking of iconism *à propos* of phenomena that can only metaphorically be defined as such.

Let's take an example. Everyday experience tells us that saccharine 'resembles' or has some properties of sugar. Chemical analysis demonstrates that no common objective property exists between the two compounds, even if we examine the structural formulae as well as the chemical components. Sugar (saccharose) is a disaccharid with the basic formula $C_{12}H_{22}O_{11}$, while saccharine is a derivative of o-sulphamidebenzoic acid. Nor do we consider the relationship of visual resemblance, because in that case sugar would be much more similar to salt. So we can say that what we define as equal properties, shared by the two compounds, concerns not their form but their *effect*. Saccharine simulates perceptive conditions similar to those of sugar (even though in many respects it produces a different taste experience). Both are 'sweet'. 'Sweetness' is not a property of the two compounds, but the result of their interaction with our taste buds. But this result is *emically* pertinent within a culinary culture that has opposed all that is sweet to all that is bitter on the one hand, and all that is salt on the other — isolating emergent features within the two phenomena that are not common to the two compounds alone, but to their interactive relation with the subjects' palates. It goes without saying that for a refined cook 'sweetness' as such does not exist, but various types of sweetness do, so that saccharine moves into a relationship of diversity (rather than resemblance) with sugar.

So one can see how many problems have come to take the place of the presumed resemblance between the two compounds. Let us simply attempt to list them: a) formal (chemical) structure of the compounds, depending upon the point of view selected as pertinent by the analysis; b) structure of the perceptive process (interaction between compound and taste buds), which may be defined as equal or unequal according to the point of view selected as pertinent (according to the parameter 'sweet vs. bitter' it is "equal", but according to others, for example 'granular vs. soft' it is "unequal"); c) structure of the culinary-semantic field, which determines the paradigmatic choice of pertinent elements in the recognition of equality and inequality. Within these three types of phenomena the presumed 'naturalness' of resemblances dissolves itself into a network of cultural stipulations that determine and direct ingenuous experience.

3.5.3. Iconism and similarity: similitude

There is another and far subtler definition: that proposed by Peirce. According to him a sign is a icon when it "may represent its object mainly by its similarity" (2.276).

To say that a sign is *similar* to its object is not the same as saying that it possesses some of its properties. In any case this definition relies on the notion of 'similitude', which has a scientific status and is less imprecise than that of 'sharing properties'.

Popular handbooks on geometry define *similitude*, roughly speaking, as the property shared by two figures that are alike in all respects except in size. Granted that difference in size is not a negligible feature (the difference in size between a lizard and a crocodile could matter quite a lot in everyday life) to decide to disregard it does not sound quite 'natural' and seems on the contrary to be culturally or conventionally founded; one decides to recognize as similar two things because one chooses certain elements as pertinent and disregards certain others. This kind of decision asks for a certain training; if I ask a child to compare a miniaturized school model of a pyramid and the Cheops Pyramid, asking if they are the same or 'similar', the most obvious answer would be "no"; only after a certain amount of training would my naive interlocutor be able to realize that I am looking for a 'geometric' similarity. The only unchallengeable impression of resemblance is due rather to phenomena of *congruence*, where two figures of equal size can be made to coincide or to fit on top of one another. But they must be two geometrical figures; a death-mask is congruent with the real face of a dead man by making abstraction from matter, color and differences in texture; and it is doubtful whether a non-trained informant would be able to recognize the former as the congruent reproduction of the latter.

But similitude can be even more exactly defined as the property shared by two figures that have equal angles and sides that are proportionally equivalent. Once again the criterion for similitude is based on precise rules that select some parameters as pertinent and disregard some others as irrelevant. Since the rule is proposed and accepted, there is undoubtedly a 'motivation' that links two equivalent sides (they are not related one to another by means of a mere convention); but in order to make the motivation detectable a conventional rule is needed. Optical illusions teach us that in many cases there are 'motivated' reasons for judging two figures as equivalent — and the motivation is rooted on psychological factors — but only when the geometrical rule is recognized, the parameters applied and the proportions checked, can the correct judgment of similitude be pronounced.

Geometrical similitude is based on spatial parameters chosen as pertinent elements; but in the theory of graphs one finds other forms of so-called similarity that are not based on spatial parameters; thus certain topological relationships, or relations of order, are chosen that cannot be translated into spatial relations if not by means of another cultural decision. According to the theory of graphs the three representations in Table 36 express the same relationships even if they are not spatially (and therefore geometrically) 'similar'.

The three graphs convey the same information (for example about types of interdisciplinary correlation between six departments of the same university) but they do not realize the same geometrical properties. This happens because a convention has isolated not the spatial disposition of the buildings of the six departments, but the type of scientific collaboration that

Table 36

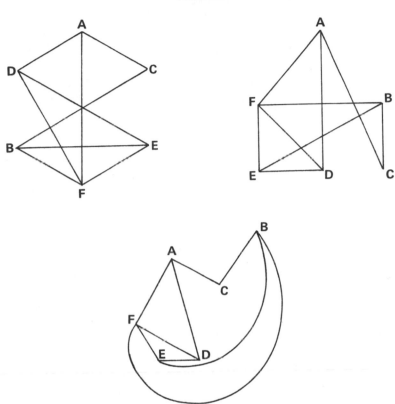

may take place between them. Suppose that F is a Physics Department, A a Philosophy Department, D a Mathematics Department and C a Theology Department: one can easily see that mathematics and physics have many topics in common and so have physics, mathematics and philosophy, while theology has topics in common with philosophy, but could hardly have much to do with mathematics and physics. From the point of view of 'common scientific services' the three graphs are said to be 'isomorph'.

This kind of *isomorphism* may be called a form of similarity but it would be very difficult to assert that it is a geometric similitude. To call such a relationship 'iconic' is a mere metaphor.

Unfortunately this is exactly the kind of metaphor used by Peirce in his otherwise masterful little treatise on *Existential Graphs* (4.347-573), in which he studied the properties of logical diagrams. An existential graph is one in which the relations entailed by a syllogism like

All men are passionate
All saints are men
Therefore all saints are passionate

are expressed by the geometrical form

Table 37

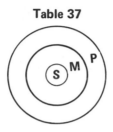

while the syllogism

No man is perfect
But any saint is a man
Hence, no saint is perfect

is expressed by the geometrical form:

Table 38

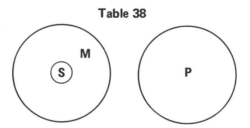

Á propos of a diagram of this sort Peirce says that its beauty springs "from its being veridically iconic, naturally analogous to the thing represented, and not a creation of conventions" (4.368). This assumption sounds rather whimsical if one is accustomed to associate the idea of iconism with a visual relationship between similar spatial properties. It is true that the diagrams show spatial relationships but these spatial properties do not stand for other spatial relationships! To be or not to be passionate is not a matter of spatial distribution. In terms of classical logic it is a matter of possessing or not possessing a given property. The inherence of a property to a subject (the relationship *subjectum-praedictum*) is, however, a naively realistic concept; to have passions is not an accident that belongs to a *subjectum*, except in Aristotelian and medieval metaphysics, and even if it were so, the representation furnished by the first graph would have to be reversed. If it is not so, this is because the graph does not translate the classical notion of inherence of a predicate to a subject, but the modern notion of class appartenance. Anyway to make up part of a class is not a spatial property (except if one belongs to the class of all the men meeting in a given place); it is a purely abstract relation. How, in the graphic representation, does the appartenance to a class become appartenance to a given space? By a mere *convention* (even if based on certain mental mechanisms, used to thinking or to imagining either by temporal succession or by spatial proximity) that *establishes* that certain abstract relations can be *expressed* by spatial situations. Naturally the convention follows a proportional criterion of the type 'space a : space b = entity a_1 : entity b_2' just as in a geometrical similitude there is a criterion of proportionality between sides of apparently different size. Therefore there is a convention establishing the way in which a proportion (a particular kind of non-arbitrary motivation) has to be posited and interpreted. To call this complex kind of isomorphism 'iconism' is a mere metaphorical license.

Peirce takes a lot of similar licences *à propos* of iconism, and in some way does so *pour cause*; he is in fact trying to define that particular kind of relation between an expression and its content-type that we have called *ratio difficilis*. But Peirce does not abandon the reference to objects, and 'iconism' thus remains for him an umbrella-term that covers many different phenomena such as a mental image, a graph, a painting. A graph does in fact exhibit a certain proportionality between a given expression and a given content, that content not being an object but a logical relation. It represents an example of correlation between an expressive item and a content-schema taken as its type without passing through a process of verification with the object. It reinforces the opinion I have expressed in 3.4.9. that in cases of *ratio difficilis* what matters is not the relationship between an image and its object but rather that between an image and its content. The content, in this case, is the result of a convention, as is the proportional correlation. The elements of motivation exist, but they can only work when they have been conventionally accepted and coded.

Both geometrical similitude and topological isomorphism are a sort of *transformation* by which a point in the effective space of the expression is made to correspond to a point in the virtual space of a content model. What marks the difference between different sorts of transformation is both the mode of correspondence and the class of elements made pertinent by the conventionalizing procedure, so that only these must be retained as invariant while the others are varied. Thus some procedures aim to preserve metric properties, others topological properties, and so on. In any case there is a transformation, in the technical sense of the term. Every biunivocal correspondence of points in space (and let us consider as space even the virtual one of abstract relational content-models, as in the case of translation into spatial terms of the relations of appartenance to different class) is a *transformation*. A transformation does not suggest the idea of natural correspondence; it is rather the consequence of rules and artifice. Thus even the continuous line tracing the profile of the horse (see 3.5.2.) may be considered as the institution of a relation of similitude by a transformed correspondence point to a point between the abstract visual content model of a horse and an image drawn on a given surface. The image is motivated by the abstract representation of the horse, but it is nevertheless the effect of a cultural decision and as such requires a trained eye in order to be detected as a horse's profile. Similitude is *produced* and must be *learned* (Gibson 1966).

3.5.4. Iconism and analogy

In the light of what has been said up to now, is it possible to call so-called iconic signs analogous?

If analogy is a sort of native and mysterious parenthood between things or between images and portrayed things, one is obliged to reject so unverifiable a category. But if analogy is understood in the only sense that permits verification, then the notion can be accepted. Except that in this sense analogy and similarity appear to be purely synonymous terms.

Let us see whether one can explain what analogy is by observing the functioning of a so-called 'analogical' computer. This for example establishes that a certain intensity of current x denotes a physical size y, and that the denotative relation is based on a proportional one. Proportion may be correctly defined as a type of analogy, but not all definitions of analogy reduce themselves to that of proportion. [13] In any case, in order that there be a proportion there must be at least three terms. We cannot say "intensity x is to size y" if we don't complete it with "as size y is to ... ". We then realize that a computer is called analogical not because it establishes a constant relation between two entities, but because it establishes a constant proportionality between two series of entities, of which one is assumed as the sign-vehicle of the other. In other words the proportion depends upon the fact that if size 10 corresponds to intensity 1, size 20 will correspond to intensity 2, and so on. The relationship may only be defined as analogical because a correlation between a given intensity of current and a given physical size has been arbitrarily established from the outset, but the computer could make equally exact calculations if it had been established that the intensity 3 corresponded to size 9, intensity 6 to size 18, and so forth. As may be seen, it is not the analogy that institutes the relationship but the proportional relationship that renders legitimate the analogy. But why was it established that size y corresponds to intensity x? If one replies "arbitrarily" or "for economic reasons" then the problem no longer exists. But let us suppose that the reply is that it was done because there was an analogy between intensity x and size y. This analogy will not be a proportion, and other terms are lacking; so that it can be no better defined than as a "resemblance". But to say of two entities that they resemble each other means that they have a reciprocal iconic relation. So this is why in order to define a form of analogy that is not a geometric proportion one resorts to the notion of iconism. We are thus faced with the absurdity of having semiotics resort to analogy to explain iconism, while invoking iconism to explain analogy. We have a *petitio principii*.

Thus even analogy, like similarity, does not exclude cultural convention; on the contrary it requires it as an operational starting-point. When on the other hand 'analogous' is used as a synonym for 'unspeakable' the term is being taken in its most vague and imprecise metaphysical sense. Once this halo of inappropriate connotations is eliminated, analogy proves to be what operationally it is: a procedure instituting the basic conditions for a transformation.

3.5.5. Reflections, replicas, empathic stimuli

Since transformation seems to be, as yet, the best operational explanation of the impression of iconism, let us eliminate some embarrassing phenomena that might otherwise be supposed to come under the heading of 'similarity'. I refer to (a) specular reflections; (b) doubles and replicas depending on the *ratio facilis*; (c) so-called 'expressive' signs.

Specular reflection could be called a sort of congruence, insofar as congruences are a type of equality, thus establishing a bi-univocal relation founded on the properties of being reflexive, symmetrical and transitive. In this sense specular reflection is equality and not similitude.

But the first thing to make clear is that a specular reflection cannot be taken as a sign if one follows the definition given in this book. Not only can it not be properly called an image (since it is a virtual image, and therefore not a material expression $(^{14})$) but even granted the existence of the image it must be admitted that it does not stand *for* something else; on the contrary it stands *in front* of something else, it exists not instead of but because of the presence of that something; when that something disappears the pseudo-image in the mirror disappears too $(^{15})$). Even admitting that what happens in a *camera obscura* is something 'similar' to the phenomenon of specular reflection (which is not questionable), what changes is the fact that an image remains traced somewhere, and any successive discussion about its iconic properties deals with the imprinted image and not with the process of projection itself.

The singularity of specular reflections is demonstrated by the fact that if one tries to apply to them the schema of a communicational process many puzzling conclusions arise: source and addressee coincide (at least in cases where a human being looks at him or herself in the mirror); receiver and transmitter coincide; expression and content coincide since the content of the reflected image is just the image of a body, not the body itself; as a matter of fact the referent of a mirror image is pure visual matter.

The image in a mirror is not a sign for it and cannot be used in order to lie (if not by producing a false object to be reflected, but in this case what stands for the supposed object is the false body, not its reflection).

The second phenomenon that we shall not consider as a case of iconism is the existence of doubles (see 3.4.7.). A double is not the icon of its model-object except in a very specific case: i.e. when an object is chosen as an ostensive sign in order to visually describe the character of every object of the same class (see 3.6.3.). $(^{16})$

The third exclusion concerns replicas ruled by a *ratio facilis*. When governed by a *ratio facilis*, replicas are such insofar as they reproduce certain pertinent features established by their type; and particularly when dealing with signs whose expression is based on spatial parameters, it would seem that such features ought to be reproduced by means of a certain degree of similarity. A road signal is the same as its type just as an uttered phoneme is the same as its emic model, because in both cases a relation of similarity is established. Why would we not assume that the actual recognition of token signs is governed by a principle of similarity and is therefore an example of iconism?

First of all, the type of a phoneme or of a replicable visual item also prescribes the material continuum in which the token should be realized. This does not happen in the case of so-called iconic signs (governed by the principles of *ratio difficilis*), and it is precisely because of this that transformational rules are needed; two similar triangles remain so even if one is drawn on a sheet of paper and the other is cut from linen.

Secondly the presumed 'iconism' that should govern the correspondence of a token to its type is not a *theorem* that semiotics could demonstrate; it is one of its *postulates*. The very notion of a sign and of its replicability (and thus of its social nature) depends on postulating that such a recognition is possible. The rules of this recognition are deeply rooted in the mechanisms of human perception and must be assumed as already given in any semiotic enquiry. Thus a token is not the sign of its type (even if under some circumstances it can be assumed as such, thus becoming an ostensive sign; see 3.6.3.).

The partial replica (like the absolute one) does not concern the expression as a functive of a sign-function; it concerns the expression as a signal, and the conditions for a good partial replica are a matter for information engineering (or phonetics, or some other science).

The problem changes when the conditions of replicability concern the expression as a functive, i.e. when the signal's production procedures affect not only its recognizability as a signal, but also the recognizability of the expressed content. These are cases of *ratio difficilis* in which the model for the replica is a content-type.

Finally I propose not to consider as 'iconic' the so-called 'expressive' properties of certain signals, by which they are supposed to 'induce' a feeling of similarity between the signal and a given emotion.

Many artists (see for instance Kandinskij) have theorized extensively around the fact that a certain line can suggest (or 'express') a feeling of force, another a feeling of weakness, another a feeling of stability, another a feeling of imbalance, and so on. The psychology of *empathy* (*Einfühlung*) has studied such phenomena, which do undoubtedly take place in our perception of many so-called 'signs' traced by human hands or found in the natural environment.

We may consider all these cases of empathy as mere *stimulations* that should be studied by the physiology of the nervous system. In a semiotic framework it does not make sense to assert or to deny that these 'expressive' properties of signals are based on the 'universal' structure of the human mind or that they can vary according to many biological or cultural variables.

Nevertheless such phenomena could be taken into account by semiotics

in two cases: (i) when the precise effect usually elicited by a stimulus is
culturally recorded so that the stimulus acts as a *conventional* sign for the
sender, though not for the addressee, as the former possesses a sort of code of
stimuli (see 3.6.6.); (ii) when a given effect is clearly due to a cultural
association and a certain signal does not suggest, let us say, feelings of 'grace'
because of a 'natural' and 'universal' structure of the mind but because of a
conventional and coded link between that signal and that feeling; in this
second case we are dealing with a sign-process, but it is not an iconic one.

In these two cases one can speak of *programmed stimulation*. Insofar as
the expression relies on more or less coded units and the reaction of the
addressee cannot be completely foreseen, one must consider programmed stimulation as the invention of a complex text; as such it will be examined in 3.6.7.

3.5.6. Iconism and convention

With these potential mistakes eliminated, we must now give a clearer
definition of real similarity. In this paragraph I shall stress that to say that a
certain image is similar to something else does not eliminate the fact that
similarity is also a matter of cultural convention; in the following one I shall
try to demonstrate that similarity does not concern the relationship between
the image and its object but that between the image and a previously
culturalized content. Both points are strictly related to each other. As regards
the first point, there are many proofs to support this assumption.

Ernest Gombrich has emphasized the conventionality of imitative codes
in his *Art and Illusion* (1956), where for example he explains what happened
to Constable when he elaborated a new technique for portraying the presence
of light in a landscape. Constable's painting *Wivenhoe Park* was inspired by a
poetics of the scientific rendering of reality and to us seems decidedly
'photographic', with its detailed portrayal of trees, animals, water and the
luminosity of a patch of field caught by the sun. And yet we know that when
his works appeared for the first time no one felt that his technique of
contrasting tones was some sort of imitation of the 'actual' effects of light,
but rather that he was taking a strange liberty. Constable therefore had
invented a new way of coding our perception of light, and of transcribing it
onto canvas [17].

Naturally we succeed in understanding a given technical solution as the
representation of a natural experience because there has been formed in us a
codified *system of expectations*, which allows us to enter into the semantic
world of the artist. Maybe an 'iconic' solution is not conventional when it is
proposed, but it becomes so step by step, the more its addressee becomes

acquainted with it. At a certain point the iconic representation, however stylized it may be, appears to be more true than the real experience, and people begin to look at things through the glasses of iconic convention. Gombrich gives many astounding examples of this sort of perceptual cramp caused by overwhelming cultural habits.

Villard de Honnecourt, the architect and artist of the thirteenth century, claimed to be copying a real lion, and yet reproduced it according to the most obvious heraldic conventions of the time. His perception of the lion was conditioned by current iconic codes; or else his codes of iconic transformation prevented him from transcribing his perception in any other way; and probably he was so used to his own codes that he thought he was transcribing his perceptions in the most suitable possible way. Dürer portrayed a rhinoceros covered with scales and imbricated plates; as a result this image of the rhinoceros remained constant for at least two centuries and reappeared in the books of explorers and zoologists; and although these latter had seen actual rhinos and knew that they do not have imbricated plates, they were unable to portray the roughness of their skin except by imbricated plates, because they knew that only these conventionalized graphic signs could denote «rhinoceros» to the person interpreting the iconic sign.

But it is also true that Dürer and his imitators had tried to reproduce via these means certain perceptual conditions that photographic reproduction does not convey. In Gombrich's book Dürer's drawing certainly appears ridiculous in comparison with the photo of an actual rhinoceros, which seems to have an almost smooth and uniform skin; but if we were to examine the skin of a rhinoceros close to, we would notice such roughness that, from a certain point of view (in the case, for example, of a parallel between human skin and that of the rhinoceros), Dürer's graphic exaggeration, which pays excessive and stylized attention to that roughness, would be rather more realistic than the image in the photograph which by convention portrays only the great masses of color and makes the opaque surfaces uniform, distinguishing them by differences of tone. Thus one could say that Dürer's rhinoceros is more successful in portraying, if not actual rhinoceroses, at best our cultural conception of a rhinoceros. Maybe it does not portray our visual experience, but it certainly does portray our semantic knowledge or at any rate that shared by its addressees.

This goes to show that signs ruled by a *ratio difficilis* are motivated, but r tainly by a content-form. If one considers the most common procedures in visual representation with some degree of phenomenological detachment, the above assumption can be made more acceptable.

3.5.7. Expression and content in similarity

Suppose that, after having drawn the horse quoted in 3.5.2., one wants to transform it into a zebra. Provided that image is a very schematic one, one need only draw some black sinusoidal stripes on the back of the horse and the transformation will be complete. It may not even be necessary to draw sinusoidal stripes; the mere presence of stripes may be quite sufficient.

This means that we have selected the fundamental aspects of the percept on the basis of 'recognition codes'; if at the zoo we see a zebra in the distance, the elements which we recognize immediately (and remember) are its stripes, and not its profile, which vaguely resembles that of an ass or mule. And so when drawing a zebra we try to make its stripes recognizable even though the outline of the animal is very similar to that of a horse, and without the stripes would probably be interchangeable. But let us suppose that there exists an African community where the only known quadrupeds are the zebra and the hyena, and where horses, asses and mules are unknown. It is no longer necessary to see stripes in order to recognize the zebra (it could even be identified in the dark, without being able to distinguish the skin) and when drawing a zebra, it would be more important to emphasize the shape of its muzzle and the length of its legs in order to distinguish it from the hyena (which also has stripes, so that the stripes no longer constitute a differentiating factor). Presuming that they exist, recognition codes (like any others) make provision for conveying *pertinent* features of the content. The recognizability of the iconic sign depends on the selection of these features. But the pertinent features must be *expressed*. Therefore there must exist an *iconic code* which establishes the equivalence between a certain graphic device and a pertinent feature of the recognition code.

Here I might introduce an experience that I had with my own son when he was four years old. I once found him lying on his stomach on top of a table, and pivoting on it he began to spin round like the needle of a compass, with his arms and legs stretched out. He said: "I'm a helicopter". On the basis of *his own* recognition codes he was extracting from the complex structure of the helicopter the fundamental feature by which it is distinguished from other machines — its rotary blades; of the three rotary blades he had retained only the image of two blades opposite each other — the elementary structure through whose transformation one arrives at various groupings of blades; he had retained the basic geometric relation between the two blades, a straight line pivoting upon its center and rotating through 360 degrees. And having grasped the basis of this relationship, he was reproducing it *in* and *with* his own body. At this point I asked him to draw a helicopter, thinking that, since he had grasped its elementary structure, he would have been able to reproduce it in his drawing. Instead he drew a clumsy central structure around which he stuck in any order an indefinite number of parallelepipedal forms, as if the object were a porcupine, explaining: "And here there are lots and lots of wings". When he used his own body, he reduced the experience to an extremely simple structure, but when he used a pencil he made the object into a fairly complex one.

Now clearly with his body he was also imitating the movement of the blades, while in his drawing he had to suggest this movement through the addition of more wings; but he could have portrayed the movement as an adult would have, for example by numerous straight lines intersecting at the center, so as to form a star. The fact is that he was not yet capable of putting into graphic code the type of structure which he had so well succeeded in portraying with his body. He had perceived the helicopter, and worked out models of recognition, but he was not able to fix the equivalence between a conventional graphic device and a pertinent feature of the recognition code. The definition of an iconic sign as possessing certain properties of the denoted object becomes even more problematic at this point.

Are the properties which it has in common with the object *seen* or *known*? During the same period my child drew the outline of an automobile with all four wheels in sight; he identified and reproduced the properties which he knew. Later he learned to code his graphic procedures and portray the automobile with two wheels (the other two, he explained, were behind); now he was reproducing only the properties which he saw. The Renaissance artist reproduces the properties which he sees, the cubist painter those which he knows (but the general public is on the whole used to recognizing only those which it sees and does not recognize on canvas those which it knows). Thus the iconic sign may possess: (a) optic (visible), (b) ontological (supposed), and (c) conventionalized properties of the object. By conventionalized properties I mean those depending on an iconographic convention which has catachresized the previous creative rendering of an actual perceptual experience. A typical example is provided by the iconographic representation of the sun as a circle from which many short lines radiate. The original experience of the sun was gained by looking at it through partly closed eyes. In this case it looked like a shining point from· which emanated uneven rays. If we accept a certain graphic convention these rays can be represented by so many straight black lines and the shining point by a white circle. Consequently the iconographic convention (which codifies the original experience) also seems adapted to our sophisticated and scientific experience of the sun, which is understood to be an incandescent sphere from which emanate 'rays' of light. But the scientific notion of a luminous ray is an abstraction which has been influenced by precisely the classical iconography referred to above and by the Euclidean geometry which went with it. Whether light is understood as *quanta* or *waves*, it has nothing to do with the conventional feature which denotes a ray. Yet this schematic representation of the sun seems to *imitate* the scientific idea of the sun rather well.

The fact is that relationships do indeed exist but not between the image and the sun as object, but between the image and the abstract model of the sun as a scientific entity. Thus a schematic representation reproduces some of the properties of another schematic representation.

The 'iconic' code thus established either a correlation between a graphic sign-vehicle and an already coded perceptual unit, or one between a pertinent unit of the graphic system and a pertinent unit of a semantic system depending on a previous codification of perceptual experience.

3.5.8. Pseudo-iconic phenomena

We have seen that the umbrella-term 'iconism' covers many different phenomena: some of them having nothing to do with signification (specular reflection, duplicative replicas, mere stimulation), others being strung out along a sort of gradated continuum from minimal convention (congruences, such as the death mask) to maximal convention as in stylization or characterization (the heraldic-like representation of the sun as circle).

In section 3.6.7. we shall have to return to this gradated continuum of possibilities. But let us first consider certain other phenomena that are commonly considered iconic and that might be classified in a different way, since they involve different sign production procedures and only give an *impression* of similarity, as opposed to realizing the type of similitude defined in 3.5.3. People usually say that icons are similar to their object because they embody some of its features. They know that such signs do not imitate (or reproduce) all the features of the object, but assert that, provided certain emergent features are present, these will suffice to establish the impression of similarity. The most prudent attitude in this case is to propose that the iconic device may possess certain elementary iconic markers and that sometimes a minimal resemblance is due to the fact that the iconic sign, even though different in shape from its object (the above-mentioned elementary markers apart), performs the *same function*.

What I shall try to demonstrate is that both the elementary markers and the acknowledged identity in function are not the result of, but the *constitutional operation* which gives rise to, the impression of iconism. Gombrich (1951) in his essay on the hobby horse (which, in its most elementary form, is simply a broom handle that the child uses as if it were a horse), notes that the relation of presumed iconism is not based on any formal similitude, other than in the rather vague sense that the horse possesses as a pertinent feature a linear dimension that is also to be found in a stick.

In fact the only aspect that the stick has in common with a real horse is that it can be straddled; hence the child has rendered emergent or pertinent — on the basis of his own physical and psychological motiva- tions — one of the *functions* permitted by the horse. He has found an object that functions as *Ersatz* of a horse not because it 'resembles' it, but because it serves an analogous function.

The example of the stick given by Gombrich is revealing. It can become the icon of a horse, a sceptre, or a sword. The element that recurs in all these objects (and that the stick seems to reproduce) is the feature of *linearity* (vertical or horizontal). But it cannot be said that the stick's vertical quality 'imitates' that of the spade; insofar as this vertical quality is a feature of both objects it is the *same* verticality. We are thus confronted by a classic *intrinsically coded act,* or rather by signification through the use of a part of the referent.

The most recent studies of kinesics (cf. for example Ekman and Friesen, 1969) bring into evidence gestural signs which are not entirely arbitrary (as are the conventional signs for yes and no) but are based on a certain similarity to the object represented, thus constituting kinesic *iconic signs.*

One example could be that of a child who points the finger of his right hand and pretends it is a pistol and that his thumb is the hammer (accompanying the gesture with an onomatopoeic sign which represents shooting). But there are other signs which are not directly iconic, and which Ekman and Friesen call *intrinsically coded acts.* Let us use the example of the pistol again; the boy may realize the same fantasy by moving his bent finger as if it were actually pressing on the trigger, while the other fingers are closed in a fist as if they were clutching the butt. In this case the gun is not being imitated. Nor is the act of shooting being imitated. The act of shooting is being denoted by means of a gestural sign-vehicle which is otherwise only physically present as part of the supposed referent (there is no pistol but there is a hand gripping it; and the significant gesture is precisely that of a "hand grasping a pistol").

So that here we have *a part of the referent* used as a sign-vehicle, or a part of the object, metonymically used for the whole (see for a further analysis Verón, 1970; 1973; Farassino, 1973; a different theory of these gestures will be proposed in 3.6.3.).

Signs of this kind are common enough in daily use. If a barber can display a cylinder with red, white and blue stripes to denote his presence we have a *symbol* in Peirce's sense, an arbitrary sign; if he displays a placard on which is drawn a razor we have an *icon*; but if, as some barbers used to do, he displays a bowl used to soap the customer (Mambrino's helmet in *Don Quixote*), part of the complex of objects denoted by the sign-vehicle becomes − by metonymy − the sign-vehicle itself. A part of the referent is *semioticized* and arbitrarily taken as symbolic of the whole complex to which it refers. In this way many so-called iconic signs become reclassified as examples of intrinsically coded acts. The red that appears in the drawing of a red flag is not 'similar' to the red of the real flag: it is *the same* red. If this is true, one could again accept Morris's definition, according to which the iconic sign possesses some of the properties of its denotata, or Peirce's, according to which it "refers to the object . . . by virtue of characters of its own". However, to arrive at the icon of a red flag a red-colored blob is not enough; the red must be contained within a square, or a rectangle, or a parallelogram with undulating sides, etc. This geometrical feature is not something that *belongs* to the object flag in the same way that the color red belongs to it: the square in the drawing is only 'similar' to that of the piece of cloth from which the flag is made. The difficulty in defining the characteristics of an iconic sign is not only caused by this multiplicity of relationships (in the case of the flag we have on the one hand the presence of the referent itself, and on the other a 'similar reproduction' of a characteristic of the referent); it is also caused by the fact that certain relationships that seem to belong to the same category in fact belong to different ones. For example, it has been stated that the pertinent property 'verticality' is the same in the stick and the horse; so why is the 'squared' nature of the flag not the same as that of the drawing of the flag? We are here confronted by two differing levels of abstraction: linearity (verticality or horizontality) is a *spatial dimension*, it represents a mode of perceiving and choosing space, while a square is already a *figure constructed in space*.

A reference to 'old' philosophical questions would not be out of place in order to clarify this difference; in Kant's first *Kritik* space, like time, is a pure intuition, the elementary form that we confer upon experiential data in order to be able to perceive them and place them within the categories.

Notions such as verticality and horizontality are not therefore intellectual abstractions, but the intuitive mode within which we frame our perceptions. According to Kant, they are to be studied by Transcendental Aesthetics, whereas geometrical figures ought to come under the aegis of Transcendental Logic, and more precisely that of the Analytics of the Pure Principles of the Intellect (being based upon the Axioms of Intuition), and thus *a priori* constructions that make possible the application of formal categories to sensory data. Cassirer (1906:20) observes that "space and time are nearer to empirical material than are the categories", and this would explain why a spatial determination such as verticality can give rise to an intrinsically coded act (can, that is, be a sort of concrete experience capable of being used as the sign of itself); whereas the notion of a square — an intellectual construct, and thus an abstraction that never exists *de facto* — cannot constitute a referent used as the sign of itself, and must thus give rise to a reproduction of itself.

It is merely the limitations of linguistic usage that make us understand "vertical properties" and "squared properties" as abstractions on the same level. In reality, we are here concerned with differing levels. The spatial dimensions are not an intellectual construction, but the *constructive conditions* for a possible object, and as conditions they may be reproduced, equal to themselves, in varied circumstances. On the other hand the idea of a square is already an *object* constructed within the framework of such conditions, and it cannot be reproduced as equal to itself, but only as an abstraction similar to previous constructions.

This doesn't stop the stick, which reproduces within itself the condition 'verticality', from standing for the horse, nor the square, which reproduces a geometrical construct that is 'isomorphic' to the form of the flag, from being a sign that stands for that flag. On a primary semiotic level both are signs. It is simply that the first does not pose problems of iconicity, and the second does. Iconism is not a homogenous phenomenon, but a label that covers differing phenomena that have yet to be completely classified and analyzed.

That the linearity of the stick is not a construct but a condition of every other possible construction (and thus an intuitive artifice able to determine a space) is also demonstrated by another fact. What constitutes the reliability of the substitution stick-horse and stick-sword is not the mere presence of a vertical object, but also the presence (in the case of the horse) of a body astride it and (in the case of the sword) of a hand grasped round the presumed hilt. So much is this the case that we even have the imitation of a horse when the child caracoles without anything between his legs, and the imitation of a sword when he moves his closed fist (with nothing in it) and pretends to fence. Verticality plus the presence of the gesture (which is not an 'imitation' of the gesture but the real gesture that would be made if the real object were present) constitute the imitation not of a single object but of an entire mode of behavior. Throughout this process, within which use is made of intrinsically coded acts or *contiguous* signs, iconism (in the classic sense of the term) makes no appearance, and to have talked about it in this way constitutes a curious example of optical illusion.

The only object that appeared to have an iconic function, instead, serves to impose the necessary spatial conditions for the realization of an intrinsically coded act.

If in the gesture of the child caracoling on the hobby horse there is something that can be called iconic, this is so because: (a) a linear dimension has been used as an expressive feature in order to substitute for the linear dimension that equally, but to a very limited degree, characterizes a horse as such; (b) one part of an entire behavioral pattern, functioning as an intrinsically coded act, has been used as an expressive device in order to convey the idea that the stick is a horse. But at this point one would do well to isolate features of expression from those of content; if the same feature appears to be both conveying and conveyed, how does one set about analyzing this sign? Since one can hardly deny that the hobby horse is a sign, the only solution is to better distinguish the *imitans* from the *imitatum*, that which stands for something from that for which something else stands.

A final ambiguity linked to the idea of resemblance is caused by the fact that — on the level of very elementary formal phenomena such as high-low, right-left, or long-wide — everything resembles everything else. Which means that there exist certain formal characteristics that are so generic as to belong to almost all phenomena, and that they may be considered iconic in relation to all phenomena. Jakobson (1970a) points out some differing cultural conventions in which, for instance: a) yes is expressed with a downward movement of the head and no with a movement from right to left; b) yes is expressed with a downward movement and no with an upward movement; c) yes is expressed with a lateral movement and no with an upward movement. One is obliged to conclude that signs of consent and dissent are arbitrary, but Jakobson finds iconic motivations for some of them: bending the head forward to say yes recalls movements of submission; moving it laterally to say no expresses the desire to turn the face away from the interlocutor; lifting the head up to say no expresses a desire to separate oneself from the interlocutor and place him at a distance. However, this does not explain why someone who says no by throwing back his head will then say yes by turning it sideways; in the absence of an iconic explanation Jakobson resorts to a systematic one, and points out that (given a previously established iconic form) its antonym arises by purely formal opposition. It is in fact possible to explain the yes expressed by moving the head sideways iconically as well: it could signify the desire to offer one's face to the interlocutor repeatedly, rather than the desire to turn it away a number of times (as occurs when the same gesture is used to express no). The truth of the matter is that right and left or forward and backward are such universal features that they are able to become iconic reproductions of every phenomenon. So that if it is legitimate to trace back a number of arbitrary gestures to underlying iconicity it is equally legitimate to trace apparently iconic relationships back to arbitrary underlying codifications.

3.5.9. Iconic articulation

In the case examined above people had mistaken for an icon what was in fact a *constitutive condition* for the impression of iconism. In the cases examined in 3.5.6., we discovered elements of conventionality at the heart of 'iconic' procedures. One might thus be inclined to an opposite and equally dogmatic conclusion, i.e. that iconic signs are *entirely* a matter of convention (just as verbal signs are) and that they ought to be susceptible to *multiple articulation* and *complete digitalization*. So – in opposition to the usual equation 'iconic=analogical=motivated=natural' – one might reverse the situation identifying conventional (and cultural) with arbitrary, and arbitrary with digital (though this was demonstrated as incorrect in 3.5.1.).

But since the possibility of some degree of articulation in visual signs has featured notably in recent research, I should like to return to this problem once more. Particularly so because the denial of such forced identifications and the assumption that, beyond a certain limit, so-called iconic signs are not articulable into smaller units may give rise to the possibility of a new classification, based on the difference between grammar-oriented and text-oriented procedures (see 2.14.6).

The most naive way of formulating the problem is: are there iconic sentences and phonemes? Such a formulation undoubtedly stems from a sort of verbocentric dogmatism, but in its ingenuousness it conceals a serious problem.

Everyone accepts that images convey a certain content. If one tries to verbalize that content one finds some easily recognizable semantic units; for instance, a meadow with a house, two horses, a dog, a tree, a girl. Are there within the image expression-units corresponding to these content units? If the answer is yes, the next question is: are these units coded, and if they are not, how can they be recognized? Supposing that such units exist, are they open to analytical subdivision into smaller and meaningless units (by combining a limited number of which, infinite major units can be generated)?

We have seen that in order to realize iconic equivalents for perception only certain pertinent aspects are selected. Children under four do not acknowledge the human torso as a pertinent feature and portray man with only head and limbs. But if on the level of large-scale units of recognition it would be possible to isolate pertinent features, on the 'microscopic' levels the problem is more confused. The presence of discrete units in verbal language is found on all levels: from lexical units to phonemes, and from phonemes to distinctive features, everything would seem open to analysis. On the level of the supposed iconic codes, however, we are confronted with a more confused panorama. The universe of visual communications reminds us that we communicate both on the basis of *strong* codes (such as language) and indeed *very strong* ones (such as the Morse code) and on the basis of *weak* codes, which are barely defined and continuously changing, and in which the free variants prevail over the pertinent features.

In the English language there are various ways of pronouncing the syntagm [gud] with different intonations and accents; but nevertheless certain distinctive features remain which are not redundant and which thus define the limits within which a given 'etic' emission may be recognized either as /good/ or as /god/.

The borderline between [u] and [o] is strongly coded. But in the realm of graphic representation, I can make use of an infinite number of ways of portraying a horse. I can evoke it with a play of light and shadow, I can symbolize it with painstaking brushwork or define it with extreme realism (at the same time I can show a horse standing, galloping, three-quarters, rampant, with his head bent to eat or drink, etc.). Admittedly I can also say /horse/ verbally in a hundred different languages and dialects; but as long as I use languages and dialects, no matter how many, they can be codified and listed, whereas the *thousand different ways* of drawing a horse are not foreseeable. On the other hand, verbal expressions are only comprehensible to those who know the languages concerned, whereas the hundreds of different ways of drawing a horse can be understood even by whose who are not acquainted with visual conventions (except in cases of a high degree of schematization). Therefore we find ourselves faced with the fact that there exist *large-scale* blocks (texts) whose articulatory elements are hard to discern.

One can make use of a series of commutations in order to find out — given, for example, the outline of a horse — what features would it be necessary to change in order to affect its recognizability; but this operation only allows for the coding of an infinitesimal sector of the process. In other words, although one gets the impression of understanding a *text*, one does not know how to decode it. In an iconic text such complex contextual relations are involved that it seems difficult to separate pertinent units from free variants.

One can isolate pertinent discrete units within iconic continuum, but as soon as they are detected, they seem to dissolve again. Sometimes they are large conventionally recognizable configurations, sometimes merely small segments of line, dots, black areas (as in a drawing of the human face, where a dot represents the eye and a semicircle the lips; yet we know that in a different context the same type of dot and the same semicircle would instead represent, say, a banana and a grape pip). Thus iconic *figurae* do not correspond to linguistic phonemes because they do not have positional and oppositional value.

These pseudo-features can sometimes assume contextual meanings (dot=eye, when placed in an almond-shaped form) but they are not organized into a system of rigid differences so that the value of a dot is determined by presence or the absence of a straight line or of a circle. Their positional value varies according to the convention instituted by the context. Thus we find *a mass of idiolects*, some of which are recognized by many, some by a select few; free variants far outweigh pertinent features, or rather free variants become pertinent features and vice versa according to the context. So iconic codes — if they exist — seem to last *l'espace d'un matin*, and as such look very similar to the aesthetic idiolects defined in 3.7.6 [18].

This also helps us to understand why a person who speaks does not seem to be born with any special ability, but if someone can draw, he already seems 'different' from others, because we recognize in him the ability to articulate elements of a code which does not belong to the whole group; and we recognize in him an autonomy in relation to normal systems which we do not recognize in any speaker except a poet (see Metz, 1964:84).

So that, at this juncture, anything taken as an iconic sign must be viewed as: (a) *a visual text* which is (b) *not further analyzable* either into signs or into *figurae*.

An iconic sign is indeed a text, for its verbal equivalent (except in rare cases of considerable schematization) is not a word but a phrase or indeed a whole story; the iconic representation of a horse does not correspond to the word /horse/ but rather to a description (a black horse, standing up, or jumping, etc.), to a mention (this horse is galloping) or to some other different speech act (look, what a beautiful horse!). If inserted in a scientific text, an iconic sign can correspond to a statement of the type /all horses have four legs and such visual properties . . . /.

The units composing an iconic text are established − if at all − by the context. Out of context these so-called 'signs' are not signs at all, because they are neither coded nor possess any resemblance to anything. Thus insofar as it establishes the coded value of a sign, the iconic text is an act of *code-making*.

3.5.10. Getting rid of 'iconic signs'

Thus iconic signs are partially ruled by convention but are at the same time motivated; some of them refer to an established stylistic rule, while others appear to propose a new rule. In certain texts only large-scale coding is permitted, i.e. a prudent *undercoding*. In other cases the constitution of similitude, although ruled by operational conventions, seems to be more firmly linked to the basic mechanisms of perception than to explicit cultural habits. Some phenomena commonly called iconic turn out not to be so. At the furthest boundary of our enquiry we have encountered texts that seem to be innovatory rules 'promising' future semiotic possibilities, rather than signs.

One and only one conclusion seems possible at this point: *iconism is not a single phenomenon*, nor indeed a uniquely semiotic one. It is a collection of phenomena bundled together under an all-purpose label (just as in the Dark Ages the word "plague" probably covered a lot of different diseases). As we have seen, some of these hidden phenomena can in no sense be viewed as semiotic, and indeed others are not iconic at all. But granted this conclusion, a methodological principle is brought sharply into focus: *it is the very notion of sign which is untenable* and which makes the derived notion of 'iconic sign' so puzzling.

The notion of sign is untenable when confused with those of significant elementary *units* and *fixed* correlations; there are on the contrary 'signs' that result from the correlation of an imprecise expressive texture and convey a vast and unanalyzable portion of content; and there are expressive devices that convey different content according to different contexts, thus demonstrating what had already been assumed in 2.1., i.e. that sign-functions are the frequently transitory result of processual and circumstantially based stipulations. But it is not only iconic signs that are *circumstantially sensitive*. They cannot be classified as a *unique* category since, as we have seen, some of the procedures that rule so-called iconic signs can circumscribe other kinds of signs, while many of the procedures that govern other kinds of signs enter into the definition of the so-called iconic ones.

What we have succeeded in isolating up to now have been *modes of producing sign-functions*, not types of signs. There is a radical fallacy in the project of drawing up a typology of signs. But if instead one classifies modes of sign production, one can include both grammatically isolated sign-functions and more global textual units which assume the role of large-scale (undercoded) sign functions, such as the so-called 'iconic signs' considered in this section: macro-units which undoubtedly have a significant function but in which it is impossible to isolate signs as grammatical units [19].

A problem naturally arises: when dealing with these macro-units can one speak of codes? Are there non-coded macro-significant units (which would bring us back to the difference between analogy and arbitrariness)? All these problems will have to be discussed in the next section, where I shall deal with a typology (not of *modi significandi* but) of *modi faciendi signa*.

3.6. A typology of modes of production

3.6.1. A four-dimensional classification

The classification of modes of production outlined in Table 39 takes into account four parameters:

(i)   the *physical labor* needed to produce expressions (ranging from the simple recognition of a pre-existent object or event as a sign to the invention of previously non-existent and un-coded expressions);

(ii)   the *type/token-ratio*, whether *facilis* or *difficilis* (see 3.4.9.);

(iii) the type of *continuum* to be shaped; this continuum can be either *homomaterial* or *heteromaterial*; a continuum being homomaterial when the expression is shaped within and by the same material stuff as that with which the possible referent of the sign-function could be made (in cases where signs are used to mention things). All other cases imply a heteromaterial continuum which is arbitrarily selected (except in a few cases in which the matter of the expression is imposed by the direct action of the referent; for instance imprints are impressed upon a given material by the imprinter);

(iv)   the mode and complexity of *articulation*, ranging from systems in which there are precise combinational units that are duly coded or overcoded to those in which there are texts whose possible compositional units have not yet been further analyzed.

TABLE 39
A Typology of Modes of Sign Production

PHYSICAL LABOR required to produce expressions	RECOGNITION	OSTENSION	REPLICA	INVENTION
TYPE/TOKEN RATIO — Ratio difficilis	IMPRINTS		VECTORS	CONGRUENCES / PROJECTIONS
TYPE/TOKEN RATIO — Ratio facilis	SYMPTOMS / CLUES	EXAMPLES / SAMPLES / FICTIVE SAMPLES	STYLIZATIONS — COMBINATIONAL UNITS / PSEUDO-COMBINATIONAL UNITS	PROGRAMMED GRAPHS / STIMULI (TRANSFORMATIONS)
CONTINUUM to be shaped	HETEROMATERIAL (MOTIVATED)	HOMOMATERIAL	HETEROMATERIAL (ARBITRARILY SELECTED)	HETEROMATERIAL (ARBITRARILY SELECTED)
Mode and rate of ARTICULATION	Pre-established (coded and overcoded) GRAMMATICAL UNITS (according to different modes of pertinence)			Proposed undercoded TEXTS

The table records the way in which expressions are physically *produced* and not the way in which they are semiotically *correlated* to their content; the latter is implied by two decisions that must be made either before or after the production of the expression.

For instance, in the case of recognition of symptoms, there is undoubtedly a pre-established motivation due to a preceding experience which has demonstrated that there is a constant physical relationship between a given agent and a given result; it has therefore been decided, *by convention*, that these resultant objects must be correlated with the notion of that agent under any circumstances, even when one cannot be sure that an existing agent has really produced the result. In the case of words (which may be classed among 'systematically combinable units') the correlation is posited after the production of the physical unit and is in any case independent of its form (this assumption being valid even if by unverifiable historical chance the origin of words had some sort of imitative motivation).

For this reason such non-homogeneous objects as a symptom and a word are posited in the same row; every object listed there can be produced according to its pre-existing expression-type (*ratio facilis*) and this happens irrespective of the reasons for which these objects were selected as the expression of a given content. All of them could be produced by a suitably instructed machine which only 'knows' expressions, while another machine could assign to each expression a given content, provided it was instructed to correlate functives (in other words, two expressions can be differently motivated but can function in equally conventional fashion).

On the other hand, all objects ruled by a *ratio difficilis* are so motivated by the semantic format of their content (see 3.4.9.) that it is irrelevant whether they have been correlated with it on the basis of previous experience (as in the case of footprints, where the semantic analysis of the content has already been performed) or whether the content is the result of the experience of 'inventing' the expression (as in the case of paintings). Therefore the motivated way in which they have been chosen (see the further analysis of imprints and projections below) does not affect their mode of production according to a ratio *difficilis*; they are correlated to certain aspects of their sememes — thereby becoming expressions whose features are also content-features, and thus *projected semantic markers* [20].

In this sense a machine instructed to produce these objects should be considered to have also received semantic instructions. One might say that since it is instructed to produce expressions, it is being fed with schematic semantic representations [21].

The items recorded in the row corresponding to the parameter 'type/ token-ratio' may look like 'signs', since to some degree they recall pre-existing sign typologies. But they are not; they are short-hand formulas that should be re-translated so as 'to produce imprints', 'to impose a vectorial movement' or 'to replicate combinable units' and so on.

'Imprints' or 'examples' must, at most, be understood as physical objects which, because of certain of their characteristics (not only the way in which they are made, but also the way in which they are singled out) become open to a significant correlation, i.e. ready to be invested with dignity of functive. In other words they are potential expression features or bundles of features. According to the system into which they are inserted, they may or may not be able to convey by themselves a portion of content. So that although they can also act as signs, they will not necessarily do so. It must be clear that the whole of Table 39 speaks of physical procedures and entities that are *ordered* to the sign-function but that could subsist even if there were no code to correlate them to a content. On the other hand, they are produced in order to signify and the way in which they are produced renders them able to signify in a given way.

A ready-made expression like /cherry brandy/ is the result of two procedures depending on a double type/token-ratio; it is constructed from two combinational units ordered by a vectorial succession; likewise a pointing finger is both a vector and a combinational unit, while a road arrow is both a stylization and a vector. Therefore items like 'vectors' or 'projections' are not types of signs and cannot be equated with typological categories such as 'indices' or 'icons'. For instance both 'projections' and 'imprints' could appear to be icons but the former would imply an arbitrarily selected expression-continuum and the latter a motivatedly established one, while both of them (equally governed by a *ratio difficilis*) would be motivated by a content-type (though imprints are 'recognized', while projections are 'invented').

Imprints and vectors look like indices, but are in fact dependent on two different type/token-ratios. Moreover, certain categories (e.g. 'fictive samples') come under two headings: they are the result of a double labor, since something must be replicated in order to be shown (ostension).

All these problems will be dealt with further in the following paragraphs. I have only anticipated some examples in order to stress the fact that one must not look at Table 39 in order to find types of signs. This table only lists types of productive activity that can give rise, by reciprocal and complex interrelations, to different sign-functions, whether they are *coded* units or *coding* texts.

3.6.2. Recognition

Recognition occurs when a given object or event, produced by nature or human action (intentionally or unintentionally), and existing in a world of facts as a fact among facts, comes to be viewed by an addressee as the expression of a given content, either through a pre-existing and coded correlation or through the positing of a possible correlation by its addressee.

In order to be considered as the functive of a sign-function the object or event must be considered *as if* it had been produced by ostension, replica or invention and correlated by a given kind of type/token-ratio. Thus the act of recognition may re-constitute the object or event as an imprint, a symptom or a clue. To interpret these objects or events means to correlate them to a possible physical causality functioning as their content, it having being conventionally established that the physical cause acts as an unconscious producer of signs. As we will see, the inferred cause, proposed by means of abduction, is pure content. The object can be a fake or can be erroneously interpreted as an imprint, a symptom or a clue, when in fact it is the chance product of other physical agents: in such a case the 'recognized' object expresses a content although the referent does not exist.

In the *recognition of imprints*, the expression is ready-made. The content is the class of all possible imprinters. The type/token-ratio is *difficilis*. The form of the expression is motivated by the form of the supposed content and has the same visual and tactile markers as the corresponding sememe, even though the marks of the sememe can be 'represented' by the imprint in various ways. For example the size of the imprinter determines (or motivates) the size of the imprint, but there is a similitude rule establishing that the size of the latter is always larger than the size of the former (even if infinitesimally). The weight of the imprinter determines the depth of the imprint, but this process is governed by a proportional rule (that is, an analogy in the strict sense outlined in 3.5.4.). With fingerprints, size is not a pertinent parameter since they can be correlated to their content even if enormously magnified.

These observations may help to clarify in what sense one could say that an imprint represents both a metaphorical and a metonymical operation. In fact imprints appear to be 'similar' to the imprinting agent and substitute for or represent it; and they can be taken as a proof of past 'contiguity' with the agent.

This explanation may work (and may indeed be used to distinguish imprints from clues and symptoms, see below) provided one accepts that the

A THEORY OF SEMIOTICS

similarity of imprints to their possible cause is not immediately detectable, since certain transformational operations must be understood to have taken place, and that past contiguity with the referent is the result of a labor of presupposition performed when the sign is viewed as *focusing on the world* and interpreted as a *mention* (see Table 31).

All this means that, first of all, one must *learn* to recognize imprints (or to fake them). Imprints are usually coded; a hunter learns how to recognize the imprint of a hare without mistaking it for a rabbit's. Insofar as they are coded, they rely on oppositional expressive systems; roughly speaking, one is dealing with oppositions such as 'hare vs. rabbit', though in fact these oppositions should be the product of a more finely analyzable system of pertinent spatial features. Semiotics has not yet done sufficient work on such expressive systems, but one of its provisional boundaries would be that of 'imprints' being not signs but rather objects to be inserted into a sign-function; in fact the trace of an animal, viewed as a sign-function, does not only imply spatial or tactile parameters (size or weight) but also *vectorial* cues (see 3.6.5.).

A trace is also interpreted in terms of its direction. This direction is another productive cue that can be falsified; one can shoe a horse backward so as to give the impression that the horse was going in the opposite direction. When interpreted as an imprint and as a vector, a given trace is correlated not so much with a coded unit (cat, horse, hare, SS soldier and so on) as with a discourse (a horse passed by three days ago going in that direction). Therefore the expression is no longer a sign but rather a text [22].

The correlational dynamics of imprints could be better explained when speaking of projections (3.6.9.) and in fact they are recognized as if they were projected on purpose. As projections, imprints can also be complex texts, in the sense that they can be imprints of very complex events; and in this way they cannot longer be considered as coded units.

But in the present section I am considering *coded* imprints, corresponding to a coded content; in this sense they are pertinent macro-units in some way analyzable into pertinent elementary features.

Anyway imprints are doubly motivated: once by the form of their content, and once by the presupposed relationship to their cause; therefore an imprint is a heteromaterial object (a cat's paw mark in the mud is not materially the same as its possible cause) but its matter is strictly motivated by its cause.

Imprints (like any other recognition procedure) are *conventionally* coded, but the code is not established by an arbitrary social decision but is instead motivated by *previous experiences*; the correlation between a given form and a given content has been mediated by a series of mentions, inferences based upon uncoded circumstances, meta-semiotic statements [23]. Since the experience of an event was constantly associated with a given imprinted form, the correlation, first *proposed* as the result of an inference, was then *posited*.

In the *recognition of symptoms*, the expression is ready-made. The content is the class of all possible causes (organic alterations). The type/token-ratio is *facilis*, for red spots do not have the same semantic markers as measles, nor does smoke have the same as fire. Nevertheless within the sememic representation of their content there is, among the markers, both the description and the representation of the symptoms.

This explains the way in which a symptom is correlated to the notion of its cause; the notion of the symptom constitutes part of the sememe of the cause and it is thus possible to establish a metonymical correlation between the functives (by a *pars toto* procedure). The process is notion-to-notion (or unit-to-unit) and the effective presence of the referent is not required. There can be smoke even if there is no fire at all, which means that symptoms can be falsified without losing their significant power. The ratio being *facilis*, it would be incorrect to speak of a certain 'iconicity' of symptoms; they have nothing to do with their content (or referents) in terms of similarity. When symptoms are not previously coded, their interpretation is a matter of complex inference and leads to the possibility of code-making.

Symptoms can be used for mentioning (smoke means «there is fire», red spots on the face mean «this child has measles»). In this case the mentioning procedure works as follows: by a coded and proved causality (contiguity) of the type 'effect to cause', an effective presence of the causing whole is *deduced*.

In the *recognition of clues*, one isolates certain objects (or any other kinds of trace which are not imprints) left by someone on the spot where he did something, so that by their actual presence the past presence of the agent can be inferred. It is evident that, when used for mentioning, clues work in exactly the opposite way from symptoms; by a coded and proved contiguity (of the type 'owned to owner') a possible presence of the causing agent is *abduced*. In order that the abduction be performed, the object must be conventionally recognized as belonging to (or being owned by) a precise class of agents. Thus if at the scene of a murder I find a dental plate I may presume that, if not the murderer, at any rate someone who has no more natural teeth has been there. If on the floor of a political party's office, recently broken into, I find the badge of the rival organization, I may presume that the burglars were the 'bad guys' (obviously clues can also be falsified, and in cases like this they usually are).

As a matter of fact clues are seldom coded, and their interpretation is frequently a matter of complex inference rather than of sign-function recognition, which makes criminal novels more interesting than the detection of pneumonia.

One could say that imprints and clues, even though coded, are 'proper names', for they refer back to a *given* agent. The objection does not affect the fact that they refer, in any case, to a content, for there is nothing to stop the class to which the expression refers from being a one-member class (see 2.9.2.).

But in fact very seldom can imprints and clues be interpreted as the traces of an individual agent (indeed maybe never). When looking at the footprint on the island, Robinson Crusoe was not able to think about an individual. He detected «human being». When discovering Friday he was undoubtedly able to express the index-sensitive proposition «this is the man who probably left the footprint». But even if he had previously known that there was one and only one man on the island he would not, when looking at the footprint, have been able to refer it to a precise individual; the primary denotation of the expression would have been «human being» and the rest would have had to be a matter of inference. It is very difficult to imagine an imprint that mentions a referent without the mediation of a content [24]. The only case would be that in which one sees a given individual in the act of producing a footprint; but in this case the footprint would not be 'recognized' as a sign, for it would not be 'instead of' something else, but 'along with' it (see the case of mirrors in 3.5.5.) [25]. The same happens with clues. Even if I know that only one particular man, among the murdered person's circle of friends, has a dental plate, I cannot regard the object left at the scene of the crime as a sign referring back to a «person x». The object simply means «person without teeth», and the rest is once again a matter of inference.

On the contrary many clues are overcoded objects. Suppose that I find a pipe in the same place. What makes me sure that a man was there? A social rule establishing that gentlemen smoke pipes and ladies don't (the opposite would happen if I found a bottle of Chanel No. 5).

3.6.3. Ostension

Ostension occurs when a given object or event produced by nature or human action (intentionally or unintentionally and existing in a world of facts as a fact among facts) is 'picked up' by someone and *shown* as the expression of the class of which it is a member.

Ostension represents the most elementary act of *active* signification and it is the one used in the first instance by two people who do not share the same language; sometimes the object is connected to a pointer, at others it is regularly picked up and shown; in both cases the object is disregarded as a token and becomes, instead of the immediate possible referent of a mention, the expression of a more general content.

Many things have been said about signification by ostension (see for instance Wittgenstein, 1945:29-30) and a purely ostensive language has been invented by Swift. Let me only remark here that in ostension there is always an implicit or explicit *stipulation of pertinence*. For example, if I show a packet of brand *X* cigarettes to a friend who is going shopping, this ostension can mean two different things: either «please buy some cigarettes» or «please buy this brand of cigarettes». Maybe in this latter case I would have to add certain indexical devices, such as tapping with the finger on the part of the packet which bears the name of the brand, and so on. Likewise, in other circumstances only a previous stipulation of pertinence makes clear whether, when showing a packet of cigarettes, I mean «packet of cigarettes» or simply «cigarettes».

At other times ostension may suggest an entire discourse, as when I show my shoes to someone not in order to say «shoes», but rather «my shoes are dirty» or «please shine my shoes». In these latter cases the object is not only taken as a sign but also as a referent and the indication constitutes an act of mentioning. As a matter of fact it is as if I were saying «shoes (ostension) + these (mention) + shoes (referent)».

This theory solves the problem of 'intrinsically coded acts or object' (see 3.5.8.) without implying that a part or all of the referent will constitute a part of the definition of the sign-function; the shoes are first of all viewed as an expression which is made with same stuff as its possible referent. Therefore ostensive signs (depending on choice) are *homomaterial*.

In principle ostensive production should be considered as governed by a *ratio difficilis*, for the shape of the expression is determined by the shape prescribed by the sememic composition of the content; yet in fact they constitute expressions whose form is already established by a sort of repertoire, and therefore they should be considered as governed by *ratio facilis*. For this reason I have classified them half way between both ratios. In practice they are already produced (as functional objects) and the problem of their type/token-ratio vanishes; but theoretically speaking (and considering them as if they had to be produced) they constitute a particular category of sign-functions in which both the ratios coincide.

Another characteristic of expressions produced by ostension is that they can be taken in two ways: as the conventional expression of a cultural unit (a cigarette means «cigarettes») or as the intensional description of the properties recorded by the corresponding sememe. So I can show a cigarette in order to describe the properties of a cigarette (it is a cylindrical body, several inches long, white etc.). This is the only case in which *doubles* can be used as signs.

So, as with doubles, in ostension the type/token-ratio becomes a token/token-ratio. Theoretically speaking, type and token coincide, which explains why *ratio facilis* and *ratio difficilis* also coincide.

All these observations might well lead to the conclusion that — in expressions produced by ostension — to distinguish expression from referent is a rather Byzantine exercise, which is by no means the case. Suppose that a crowd of men, each of whom has received a piece of bread, hold up these pieces (different in shape and size) shouting /more!/. The differences between referents disappear and only major pertinent features are virtually retained; the crowd is saying «we want more bread» (irrespective of its shape and maybe of its exact quantity). Inasmuch as it is shown, the bread works as a sign, and it is 'made' more elementary than it really is, becoming conventionally and virtually deprived of many of its physically detectable properties.

When an object is selected as a whole to express its class, this constitutes a choice of *example*. The mechanism governing the choice and the signifying correlation are based on a synecdoche of the kind 'member for its class'. When only part of an object is selected to express the entire object (and thereby its class) this constitutes a choice of *sample*. The mechanism governing the choice and the signifying correlation is based on a synecdoche of the kind 'part for the whole (of a member of a class)'. Instances of this case are those in which a tailor shows a small portion of a fabric in order to refer to the entire cut or indeed directly to the jacket (or shirt) made with this fabric, or a musical quotation referring to a whole work (/play me 'ta-ta-ta-taaa'/ may mean «play me Beethoven's *Fifth*»). On the other hand, an instance of 'metonymical' sample may be given by a lancet's meaning «surgeon».

As Goodman (1968) remarks in an interesting discussion on samples, a sample can be taken as the sample of "samples". Goodman also remarks that a polysyllabic word can be taken as the example of the general class of polysyllabic words. Since it is the case of *a double*, chosen or produced in order to exemplify not the physical properties of that token but the semantic properties of a metalinguistic sememe (see note 25), a preceding or presupposed discourse is always needed in order to stipulate the pertinence level. Without this previous convention, the ostension of the word /polysyllabic/ would be taken as the description of the properties of the expression /polysyllabic/ and not of every polysyllabic word, such as for instance /monosyllabic/.

Looking at Table 39, one may note that there is one sort of sample that is listed both under the heading of ostension and under that of replica. These are *fictive samples*, i.e., the sign-functions that Ekman and Friesen (1969) have called 'intrinsically coded acts' (see 3.5.8.).

If I pretend to hit someone with a fist, the meaning of the whole act is «I punch you». One could say that this was a regular ostension for I have chosen a token gesture in order to represent its class. As a matter of fact I have not so much 'picked up' an existing gesture as 're-made' it, and in remaking it I have disregarded certain properties of the gesture (for instance, I do not really punch my interlocutor, and I therefore stop the trajectory of the gesture a little before its fullfilment). Thus I have replicated part of a gesture as a sample of the entire gesture. Thus so-called intrinsically coded acts are at once both ostension and replicas. Mimicry belongs to this category, as do 'full' onomatopoeias (that is, 'realistic' reproductions of a given sound by a human voice or other instrument, as opposed to onomatopoeic stylizations, such as /thunder/) [26].

Fictive samples are also homomaterial, because the replica is performed using the same stuff as that of the partially reproduced model. Therefore to call these full onomatopoeias 'iconic', in the same way that one calls the image of an object iconic, is to categorize them imprecisely, since images must be classified among projections (see 3.6.7.) where the expression-continuum is different from the stuff of the possible referent and the correspondence is fixed by transformational rules. A fictive sample does not need transformational rules since it is a *homomaterial replica* (a partial double) and as such has the advantage of being governed by a *ratio facilis*, while images are governed by a *ratio difficilis*. That a so-called intrinsically coded act is a matter of convention can be demonstrated by the fact that, in order to work as a sign-function, it required a previous stipulation [27].

3.6.4. Replica: combinational units

This mode of production governs the most usual elements of

expression, so that, when defining the notion of sign, one takes into account only replicable objects intentionally produced in order to signify. Thus the best known kinds of replicas are phonemes and morphemes; expression-units constructed according to a *ratio facilis*, using a continuum completely alien to their possible referents, and arbitrarily correlated to one or more content-units.

But this unit-to-unit correlation is not typical of replicas alone. Recognition and ostension likewise isolate units and symptoms, imprints, clues, examples, samples and fictive samples are coded by a unit-to-unit correlation. There are conventions by which a certain trace means «hare», a certain medical symptom means a given sickness, and an object taken as an example means a precise category. It is true that a footprint can 'say' more than «man», as we have seen, and that a packet of cigarettes may also mean «buy me some cigarettes», but then it is equally true that the word /cigarette/ may, under certain circumstances, stand for an entire discourse. This means that all the sign-functions depending on replica, ostension and recognition articulate given units in order to produce more complex texts.

Granted that this is so, one may go on to list under the heading of replicas not only verbal devices, but also ideograms, emblems (like flags), alphabetic letters, various coded kinesic features (for instance gestures meaning «come here», «yes», «no» and so on), musical notes, various traffic signals («stop», «walk», «no turn»), elementary graphic features, symbols in formal logic and mathematics, proxemic features and so on.

It is true that a word can be analyzed into more elementary, non-significant units (phonemes) and phonemes into more elementary, non-articulatory features, while an ideogram or an emblem must be taken as an unanalyzable unit. But this only means that replicable expressions work on different *pertinence levels* and may be subject to two, one, or no articulation.

During the sixties, semiotics was dominated by a dangerous verbo-centric dogmatism whereby the dignity of 'language' was only conferred on systems ruled by a double articulation. A typical example of this fallacy is Lévi-Strauss's discussion on the 'linguistic' properties of paintings, tonal music and post-Webernian music.

In verbal language there exist elements of first articulation, endowed with meaning (morphemes), which combine to form broader syntagmatic strings; these elements can subsequently be analyzed into elements of second articulation (phonemes). There is no doubt that meaning in language arises through the interplay of these two types of elements; but this does not mean that every semiotic process must come about in the same way. Instead

Lévi-Strauss maintains that language cannot exist unless these conditions are fulfilled.

In his *Entretiens* (1961) with a radio interviewer, he had already developed a theory of visual works of art which outlined this viewpoint and he developed it more fully in the "Ouverture" to *The Raw and the Cooked*. In the former case he referred to a theory of art as iconic sign which he had elaborated in *The Savage Mind*, where he spoke of art as "a reduced model" of reality. Art is considered as the capture of nature by culture; it raises the brute object to the level of sign, and reveals in it a previously latent structure. But art signifies by means of a certain relationship between its sign and the object which inspired it; thus if it were not an arbitrary and a conventional phenomenon of a linguistic order it would no longer have the character of sign. If in art an appreciable relationship between signs and objects subsists, this is certainly due to the fact that, in one way or another, it presents the same types of articulation as verbal language.

Like verbal language, painting is supposed to articulate units which are endowed with meaning and which can be considered equivalent to morphemes (and here Lévi-Strauss clearly refers to identifiable images, and therefore to iconic signs); these units can be analyzed into minor articulatory elements (forms and colors) which only have oppositional value and are devoid of any autonomous meaning. According to Lévi-Strauss the 'non-figurative' schools forgo the primary level "and claim that the secondary level is sufficient". They fall into the same trap as atonal music, they lose all ability to communicate and slip into "the heresy of the century", the claim of "wanting to build a sign system on a single level of articulation".

Lévi-Strauss's text, which elaborates perceptive observations on the problems of tonal music (in which he recognizes, for example, elements of second articulation) is in point of fact based on a series of unfortunately dogmatic assumptions, namely that: 1) there is no language without double articulation; 2) double articulation is not mobile, the levels cannot be substituted or interchanged, their structure is based on deep natural structures of the human mind. But if one instead examines the functioning of various sign systems, one realizes that: (a) there are systems with various types of articulation or none at all; (b) there are systems whose level of articulation is changeable.

Obviously one may suppose that there probably does exist a profound articulatory matrix which governs every sign-system and all its possible articulatory transformations, but this matrix must not be identified with one of its surface manifestations. This is precisely what Lévi-Strauss does when, for instance, he attributes a privileged status to the tonal system in music, forgetting that tonal system was born at a given historical moment and that the Western ear has grown accustomed to it. Lévi-Strauss rejects the atonal system (as well as the whole of non-figurative painting) for not being governed by a detectable double articulation, thus proposing the tonal system in music and figurative procedures in painting as basic and natural metalanguages, exclusively entitled to define (or reject) every other musical or visual 'language'.

To confuse the laws of tonal music with the laws of music *tout court* is rather like believing that if one has a pack of French playing cards (52 plus one or two jokers), the only possible combinations among them are those established by bridge. Whereas on the contrary, bridge is a sub-system which makes possible an endless number of different games, but which could be replaced, still using the same cards, by poker, another sub-system which restructures the articulatory elements constituted by individual cards, enabling them to assume different combinational values and to form other significant arrangements (pair, three of a kind, flush, etc.). Clearly a given game (be it poker, rummy or bridge) isolates only some possible combinations among those permitted by the cards, but it would be a mistake to believe that any one of these combinations is the basic one.

It is true that the 52 (or 54) cards provide a choice which operates within the continuum of possible positional values — as do the notes of the tempered scale — but clearly various sub-systems can be constructed within this system; equally, there are card games which choose different numbers of cards — the 40 cards of the Neapolitan pack, the 32 cards of German skat. The real system which presides over card games is a combinational matrix which can be studied by games theory; and it would be useful if musical science were to study the combinational matrices which permit the existence of diverse systems of attraction; but Lévi-Strauss identifies cards with bridge, confuses an event with the structure which makes multiple events possible.

Playing cards bring us face to face with a problem which is very important for our investigation. Does the system of playing cards have two articulations? If poker vocabulary is made possible by the attribution of meanings to a particular articulation of several cards (three aces of different suits, equal to «three of a kind»; four aces equal to «four of a kind») we should consider the combinations of cards as significant strings of first articulation while the cards which form the combinations are elements of second articulation.

Nevertheless the cards are not distinguished merely by the position they assume in the system, but by a twofold position. They are opposed as different values within a hierarchic sequence of the same suit (ace, two, three . . . ten, jack, queen, king) and they are opposed as hierarchic values belonging to four sequences of different suits. Therefore two tens combine to form a «pair»; a ten, a jack, a queen, a king and an ace combine to form a «sequence»; but only the cards of the same suit can combine to form a «suit» or a «royal flush».

Therefore some values are pertinent features as far as certain significant combinations are concerned, and others are so as far as certain others are concerned. But is the single card the ultimate term of any possible state of articulation, thus resisting further analysis? If the seven of hearts constitutes a positional value in respect to the six (of any suit) and in respect to the seven of clubs, what is the single heart if not the element of an ulterior and more analytic articulation?

The first possible answer is that the player (who 'speaks' the language of the cards) is not in fact called upon to articulate the unit of suit, because he finds it already articulated in values (ace, two . . . nine, ten); but this point of view, though it may appear logical to the poker player, is already questionable to a player of other games (like the Italian 'scopa') in which the points (the units) are added up, and in which therefore the pertinent unit is that of suit (even if the additions have preformed addendae).

All these considerations force one to recognize that it is wrong to believe: 1) that every sign system act is based on a 'language' similar to the verbal one; 2) that every 'language' should have two fixed articulations. One should on the contrary assume that: (i) semiotic systems do not necessarily have two articulations; (ii) the articulations are not necessarily fixed.

Let us here list a series of different articulatory possibilities, following the proposal set out by Prieto (1966). It will be seen that there exist systems with two articulations, systems with only the first articulation, systems with only the second articulation and systems without articulation. Let us recall that (i) the elements of second articulation (called *figurae* by Hjelmslev) are purely differential units which do not represent a portion of the meaning conveyed by the elements of first articulation; (ii) the elements of first articulation, commonly called 'signs', are strings composed by elements of second articulation and convey a meaning of which the elements of second articulation are not a portion; (iii) there are signs whose content is not a content-unit but an entire proposition; this phenomenon does not occur in verbal language but it does occur in many other semiotic systems; granted that they have the same function as verbal sentences, we shall call these non-verbal sentences '*super-signs*'. In many semiotic systems these super-signs must be considered as strictly coded expression-units susceptible of further combination in order to produce more complex texts (Prieto, following Buyssens, calls these super-signs /*sèmes*/, but I prefer to avoid such a term, which may be confused with the term /seme/ or /*sème*/ employed in compositional analysis and standing for «semantic marker», therefore possessing a quite different meaning).

A typical example of super-sign is an 'iconic' statement such as a man's photograph which not only means «person x» but «so and so, smiling, wearing glasses, etc.» (which could be a mere description) or «so and so is walking», which clearly corresponds to a verbal sentence.

Thus following Prieto's suggestion, let us try to list various types of semiotic systems with various types of articulation:

A. *systems without articulation*: provide for super-signs which cannot be further analyzed in compositional elements:
  1) *systems with a single super-sign* (for example the blind man's white cane; its presence indicates «I am blind»; whereas its absence does not necessarily mean the opposite, as might be the case, however, for *systems with zero sign-vehicle*);
  2) *systems with zero sign-vehicle* (the admiral's flag on a ship; its presence indicates «admiral on board» and its absence «admiral off board»; the directional signals of an automobile, whose absence means «I am proceeding straight ahead»);
  3) *traffic lights* (each unit indicates an operation to carry out; the units cannot be articulated among themselves to form a text, nor can they be further analyzed into underlying articulatory units);
  4) *bus lines labelled by single numbers or letters of the alphabet.*
B. *Codes with second articulation only*: the units are super-signs. These cannot be analyzed into signs but only into *figurae* (which do not represent portions of the content of the main units):
  1) *bus lines with two numbers*: for example line /63/ indicates that it «runs from place X to place Y»; the unit can be segmented in the *figurae* /6/ and /3/, which do not have any meaning;
  2) *naval 'arm' signals*: various *figurae* are allowed for, represented by various inclinations of the right and left arm; two *figurae* combine to form a letter of the alphabet; this letter is not usually a sign because it is without meaning. It acquires the latter only if it is considered as an articulatory element of verbal language and is articulated according to its laws; however, it can acquire a conventional value within the naval code, indicating for instance «we need a doctor» and must then be considered as a super-sign.
C. *Codes with first articulation only*: the main units can be analyzed into signs but not thereafter into *figurae*:
  1) *the numeration of hotel rooms*: the unit /20/ usually indicates «first room, second floor»; it can be subdivided into the sign /2/, which means «second floor» and into the sign /0/, which means «first room»;
  2) *street signals with units analyzable into signs*: a white circle with a red border which contains the black outline of a bicycle means «cyclists not allowed» and can be broken down into the expression //red border//, which means «not allowed» and the image of the bicycle, which means «cyclists».
D. *Codes with two articulations: super-signs can be analyzed into signs and figurae*:

1) *verbal languages*: phonemes are articulated into morphemes and these in turn into broader syntagms;

2) *telephone numbers with six digits*: some can be broken down into groups of two digits, each of which indicates (according to position) a section of the city, a street, an individual; whereas each sign of two digits can be broken down into two *figurae* which have no meaning.

E. *Codes with mobile articulation*: in some codes there can be both signs and *figurae* but not always with the same function; the signs can become *figurae* or vice versa, the *figurae* super-signs, other phenomena can assume the value of *figurae*, etc.:

1) *tonal music*: the notes of the scale are *figurae* which are articulated into signs (partially significant configurations) such as intervals and chords; these are further articulated into musical syntagms. A given melodic succession is recognizable no matter what instrument (and therefore what timbre) it is played on; but if one changes the timbre for every note of the melody in a conspicuous fashion, one no longer hears the melody but merely a succession of timbres; and so the note is no longer a pertinent feature and becomes a free variant while the timbre becomes pertinent. In other circumstances the timbre, instead of being a *figura*, can become a sign bearing cultural connotations (such as a rustic bagpipe-pastoral) (cf. Schaeffer, 1966);

2) *playing cards*: here we have elements of second articulation (the units of the suits, such as hearts or clubs) which combine to form signs endowed with meaning in relation to the game (the seven of hearts, the ace of spades). These may combine into 'card-sentences' such as «full» or «royal flush». Within these limits a card game would be a code relying upon an expression-system with two articulations; but it must be noted that there exist in this system (a) some signs without second articulation, e.g. 'iconological' super-signs such as "King" or "Queen"; (b) iconological super-signs which cannot be combined into sentences together with other signs, such as the joker or, in certain games the Jack of Spades. Moreover the *figurae* can, in turn, be distinguished by both shape and color, and can be selected according to various pertinent criteria from game to game; thus in a game in which hearts are of greater value than spades, the *figurae* are no longer without meaning, but can be understood as signs. And so on: within the card system it is possible to introduce the most varied conventions of play (even those of fortune-telling) through which the hierarchy of articulations can change.

F. *Codes with three articulations*: according to Prieto it is difficult to imagine such a type of code for, in order to have a third articulation unit, one needs a sort of *hyper-unit* (the etymology is the same of 'hyperspace') composed of 'signs' of the more analytical articulation so that its analytical components are not parts of the content that the hyper-unit conveys (in the same way in which *figurae* are analytical components of signs but the former are not conveying a part of the meaning of the latter). It seems to me that the only instance of third articulation can be found in cinematographic language. Suppose (even if it is not that simple) that in a cinematographic frame there are visual non-significant light phenomena (*figurae*) whose combination produces visual significant phenomena (let us call them 'images' or 'icons' or 'super-signs'). And suppose that this mutual relationship relies on a double articulation mechanism.

But in passing from the frame to the shot, characters perform gestures and images give rise, through a temporal movement, to kinesic signs that can be broken into discrete kinesic *figurae*, which are not portions of their content (in the sense that small units of movement, deprived of any meaning, can make up diverse meaningful gestures). In everyday life it is rather difficult to isolate such discrete moments of a gestural continuum: but this does not hold true for the camera.

Let me stress the fact that kinesic *figurae* are indeed significant from the point of view of an 'iconic' language (i.e. they are significant when considered as photographs) but are not significant at all from the point of view of a kinesic language! Suppose that I subdivide two typical head gestures (the sign for /yes/ and the sign for /no/) into a large number of frames: I would find a large number of diverse positions which I would not be able to identify as components of one particular gesture. The position //head tilted toward the right// might be either the *figura* of the sign //yes// coupled with the pointer //indication of the person on the right// or the figura of a sign //no// coupled with //lowered head// (a gesture that may convey various connotations). Thus the camera offers kinesic *figurae* devoid of content, which can be isolated within the spatial limits of the frame (see Eco, 1968, B.3.I.).

All these alternatives are suggested simply to indicate how difficult it is to fix, in the abstract, the level of articulation of some systems The important thing is avoid trying to identify a fixed number of articulations in fixed interrelationship. According to the point of view from which it is considered, an element of first articulation can become an element of second articulation and vice versa.

After establishing that systems have various types of articulation and that therefore there is no reason to bow to the linguistic model, we must also remember that a system is often articulated by setting up as pertinent features those elements which are the syntagms of a more analytic system; or that, on the contrary, a system considers as syntagms (the ultimate limit of its combinational possibilities) those elements which are the pertinent features of a more synthetic system. A similar possibility was observed in the example of sailors' arm signals.

Language considers phonemes to be its ultimate articulatory elements, but the code of naval flags involves *figurae* that, in relation to phonemes, are more analytic (position of the right arm and position of the left arm), these combining to provide syntagmatic configurations (ultimate in relation to that code) which correspond, practically speaking (even though they transcribe letters of the alphabet and not phonemes) to the *figurae* of the verbal language.

However, a system of narrative functions contemplates large-scale syntagmatic chains (or the kind /*hero leaves his house and meets an enemy*/) which, for the purposes of the narrative system, are pertinent features, while for the purposes of the linguistic one they are syntagms. Thus a code decides on what level of complexity it will single out its own pertinent features, entrusting the eventual internal (analytic) codification of these features to another code. If one takes the narrative unit /*hero leaves home and meets an enemy*/ the narrative code isolates it as a complex content-unit and does not concern itself about the language in which it can be expressed and the stylistic and rhetorical devices which contribute to its construction.

All these are examples of successive overcoding. Usually in overcoding the minimal combinational units are the maximal combined chains of a preceding basic code. But sometimes there also is overcoding when the minimal combinable units or the minimal analyzable clusters of a given code are submitted to a further analytical pertinentization.

See for instance the various experiments in which a scanner is used to decompose and analyze an image into distinctive features, convey them to the computer by means of binary signals, and reproduce them in output through a plotter that draws very complex rasters capable of defining any type of image (their complexity is merely a matter of the complexity of the technical apparatus, but in theory it is by no means impossible to reproduce by means of a very refined raster Leonardo's *Mona Lisa*, once it has been programmed in input by means of a very complex sequence of binary signals).

For example, Huff (1967) has produced and analyzed a number of images showing how they could be composed of: (a) elementary units formed by four dots of two sizes, allowing five combinational possibilities; (b) an infinite array of dot sizes, allowing continuous gradations; (c) elementary units formed by a grouping of three dots with two variations in size, so that their combinational possibilities support four types of elements (three small, none large; two small, one large; one small, two large; none small, three large); (d) arrays of dots of two sizes; (e) etc. In every case a question is raised: are we still confronted with a series of analogical sizes? Or are we faced with a series of discrete units such as phonemes, which are distinguished from each other by a series of distinctive features? In this case the distinctive features of the minimal graphic units, described by Huff, are: color, density, form, position of the elements, not to speak of the configurations of the lattice.

In any case Huff himself poses the problem of a binary reduction of the graphic code: "Perhaps (the designer) will even explore the minimal situation by working with elements of only two sizes, ergo, a binary system. In so doing he does meet a most formidable problem: for, in order to maintain a continuous surface, he must solve between two textural gradients in a manner other than the photomechanical process does. Perhaps these operative economies, practised by students of hand-produced rasters, constitute a finesse of little consequence for the computer graphic technique which hypothetically has the capability to formulate the light and shade characteristics of any conceivable surface, thereby matching the photomechanical process. It does seem, however, that the gradation of one size elements in tones of brightness rather than the gradation of one-color elements in varying sizes, though resourcefully adventurous, is ill directed effort — somehow contrary to the fundamental simplicity of digital or binary computers".

Clearly Huff's discussion concerns the practical possibilities of graphic realization and not the theoretical possibilities of an absolute binary reduction of the code. In this last sense the examples given by Moles (1968) seem more decisive. He shows for example lattices composed of a single right-angle triangle placed in the upper or lower corner of a square compartment, so as to be able to function in the opposition 'empty place vs. full place'.

In any case discussion of the binary possibilities of rasters in photomechanical reproduction (which is governed by criteria of practicality) is outweighed by discussion of the possibility of a realizing any 'iconic' image by giving digital instructions to a computer which then transmits them to an analogical plotter [28].

Obviously the computer digitally commands a plotter which restores the image by 'analogical' means (Soulis and Ellis, 1967:150-151). Cralle and Michael (1967:157) further explain that "When we wish to plot something, we also have to say where to plot it. The addressing scheme normally chosen is obtained by imagining a two-dimensional Cartesian coordinate system, superimposed on the screen of the CRT. In both the horizontal (x) and the vertical (y) directions we can assign integers for each point to which the electron beam may be digitally deflected". Experiments of 'iconic' reproduction by means of computers, such as those carried out in the Bell Telephone laboratories by Knowlton and Harmon, by the Japanese Computer Technique Group, show that the digital programming of 'iconic' signs can by now achieve in future high degrees of sophistication and that a greater sophistication and complexity is merely a question of time and economic means. Unfortunately this digital reduction concerns the possibility of *replicating the expression* using another continuum by a procedure which is not the one used by the artist. It *does not* concern the articulatory nature of the *original* expressive functive.

Computer experience tells us that it is possible (in principle) to analyze the original signal in *figurae*, but not that the signal was *actually* articulated by combination of pre-existent discrete entities. And in fact such entities are hardly identifiable, since the original signal was composed through a 'continuous' disposition of a 'dense' stuff. Thus replicability through computers or other mechanisms does not directly concern the code governing the replicated sign. It is rather a matter of *technical codes* governing the transmission of information (a signal-to-signal process), to be considered within the framework of communication engineering (see 1.4.4.). One could suspect that such procedures are rather connected with the production of doubles (see 3.4.7.) or partial replicas (see 3.4.8.). And this is so when a computer transfers an original 'linear' drawing into a plotted copy. But things go differently when an 'absolutely dense' oil painting is 'translated' into a 'quasi-dense' raster; in such a case it is very difficult to decide if one is dealing with a partial replica, an 'icon' or a pseudo-double.

Let us speak of *transformation from expression to expression* that offers a satisfactory laboratory model of the procedures required in cases of projection by *ratio difficilis* (see the models of projections in 3.6.7.).

These examples also demonstrate that, even in cases of non-replicable super-signs, there is the possibility of rendering them replicable using mechanical procedures that institute a 'grammar' there where was only a 'text'. In this sense these experiments provide us with certain challenging theoretical suggestions about the nature of *inventions*.

Every assumption about the analogical nature of 'iconic' signs was always based upon (or aiming to support) the notion of the ineffability and the 'unspeakability' of those devices that signify through being mysteriously related to the objects. To demonstrate that at least the signals ordered to those sign-functions are open to analytical decomposition does not solve the problem but does eliminate a sort of magic. One could therefore say that the digital approach constitutes a sort of psychological support for the student who wants to further understand the mystery of iconism. When deciphering a secret message one must first be sure that it is indeed a message and therefore that there is an underlying code, to be 'abduced' from it; in the same way the knowledge that iconic signals *also* are digitally analyzable can help to promote a further enquiry as to their semiotic nature.

3.6.5. Replica: stylizations and vectors

To return to the problem of replicas, one can replicate:

(i)   features of a given system that must be combined with features of the
        same system in order to compose a recognizable functive;

(ii)   features from a weakly structured repertoire, recognizable on the basis
        of perceptual mechanisms and correlated to their content by a large-
        scale overcoding, that must not necessarily be combined with other
        features;

(iii)   features of a given system that must be added to a bundle or to a string
        of features from one or more other systems in order to compose a
        recognizable functive.

Features of type (i) have been considered in the preceding paragraph.
Verbal language, for instance, combines elements of second articulation to
construct elements of first articulation and therefore phrases. Features of
type (ii) are *stylizations*; features of type (iii) are *vectors*.

I mean by stylizations certain apparently 'iconic' expressions that are in
fact the result of a convention establishing that they will not be recognized
because of their similarity to a content-model but because of their similarity
to an expression-type which is not strictly compulsory and permits many free
variants.

A typical example of this sort of replica is the King or the Queen in a
pack of cards. We do not 'iconically' recognize a «man» and then a «King»;
we immediately grasp the denotation «King» provided that certain pertinent
elements are respected. It is also on this basis that 'iconograms' are coded, i.e.
recognizable categories in painting such as the Virgin Mary, Saint Lucy,
Victory, Athena, the Devil. In these cases the immediate denotation is a
matter of 'invention' (they are productions governed by a *ratio difficilis* that
establishes certain similarities with a male or female body and so on) while
their full signification (this «man» is «Jupiter») is due to the presence of
overcoded replicable features (stylizations).

So a painted image of the Devil is a super-sign which will be further
analyzed when speaking of 'inventions'. But, among other procedures, the
replica of large-scale *overcoded* properties contributes to the structuring of
such a sign-function. Insofar as it is an iconogram, the image of the Devil is a
replica of a previously coded type, irrespective of a lot of free variants.

In fact when looking at the King of Spades or an image of the Virgin
Mary we do not really have to grasp the representative meaning of the image,
we do not interrogate the expression in order to guess, through a sort of
backward projection at the format of the content-type. We immediately
recognize this large-scale configuration as if it were an elementary feature.
Some general properties having been respected, the expression is recognized

as being conventionally linked to a certain content; the content can also be conceptually grasped without having recourse to its spatial and figural markers. The iconogram is a *label*.

In this sense even vaster configurations can be taken as stylizations; even if a more analytical glance will show them to be composed by more subtle operations. But if this analysis is not performed, they are received as if governed by a *ratio facilis*, even if they display the same markers as the corresponding sememe (*ratio difficilis*).

Let us list some of these large-scale stylizations, each category constituting a repertoire of conventional expression, therefore a sub-code:

(i)   *heraldic features* such as the unicorn that supports the arms of the British royal family;

(ii)   *schematic onomatopoeias*, such as /to sigh/ or /to bark/ (these could be analyzed as degenerate full onomatopoeias, and therefore as fictive samples (see 3.6.3.) but in fact they are currently accepted as arbitrary expressions;

(iii)   *coded macro-ambiental features*, such as, in architecture, a house, a temple, a square, a street;

(iv)   *complex objects* and their *customary images* (like the cars portrayed in advertising);

(v)   *musical types* (a march, 'thrilling' music);

(vi)   literary or artistic *genres* (Western, slapstick comedy);

(vii)   all the elements of the so-called *recognition codes* (see 3.5.) by which a leopard is characterized by spots and a tiger by stripes (granted that an elementary 'feline' outline has been recognized on the basis of certain similarity procedures);

(viii) *iconograms*, as studied by iconology: the Nativity, the Last Judgment, the Four Horsemen of the Apocalypse and so on.

(ix)   *pre-established* evaluative and appreciative *connotations* conveyed by iconological means, and mainly used in Kitsch-art: a Greek temple conventionally connoting «classical beauty», a given feminine image historically connoting «grace» or «sex»;

(x)   other characterizations, such as one perfume immediately connoting «seduction» or «lust» while another connotes «cleanliness», the incense smell connoting «church», and so on.

Beyond a certain limit it is very difficult to distinguish a stylization from an invention, and frequently the decision is taken not by the sender but by the addressee, who in effect performs a labor of stylization on a given expression. Everyone has experienced how a given musical composition that has for many years been enjoyed as a complex text, with all its features subjected to intensive scrutiny, is at a certain point (as one's taste becomes accustomed to the musical object in question) simply received as an unanalyzed form that means approximately «Fifth Symphony» or quite simply «Romanticism» or «Music».

Thus stylizations are *catachreses* of previous inventions, super-signs that could and should convey a complex discourse (being a text) and indeed almost take on the function of proper names. Their replica, however imprecise it may be, is taken as a sufficient token, and as such faithful to its expression-type. They are the proof that a *ratio difficilis* may, by force of continuous exposure to communication and successive conventions, become a *ratio facilis*.

Stylization may also combine with other devices to make up a discourse; for instance, by putting together certain stylizations with combinational visual replicas, a road signal could 'say': «this road is closed to trucks, cars must run at no more than 30 miles and U-turning is forbidden; please make no noise since there is a hospital in the vicinity».

Let us now examine those features that are not combinable with features of the same system but which exclusively collaborate with features of other systems so as to make up an expression. I have called them *vectors*.

The classic example is the one (already given in 2.11.4., 2.11.5. and 3.5.7.) of the pointing finger: dimensional features realized by a part of a human body, such as «linearity» and «apicality» are the same as those realized by a graphic arrow; in this sense the pointing finger should be considered as an expression produced by an aggregation of combinational units, like a verbal expression, and so should the arrow. But the finger *moves toward* something; there is a feature of *direction* (which naturally characterizes a lot of other kinesic features, though here these features of movement can be articulated with other features of the same type). This directional feature orientates the attention of the addressee according to parameters such as 'left', 'right' or 'up' and 'down' and so on. But these are not simple spatial parameters of the type 'left vs. right', to be used as combinational units in other kinesic configurations; they should instead be viewed as 'left-to-right vs. right-to-left'.

The addressee does not have to physically follow that direction (nor indeed does there have to be anything in the indicated direction for the pointers to be significant, see 2.11.5.). As a matter of fact there are two 'directions': one is actually and physically perceptible and is an expressive feature; the other is the 'signified' direction and is mere content. The directional feature is produced according to a *ratio difficilis* because the *produced* direction is the same as that of which one is 'speaking'.

In order to understand vectors, one must also think of other kinds of directional feature, and one must free the term 'direction' from spatial connotations (this perhaps being better realized by the word 'vector' or 'vectorialization'). One may thus regard as vectorial devices the increasing or decreasing of vocal pitch and dynamics in paralinguistic features: for instance when uttered, a 'question intonation' is a vectorialization; the nature of a musical melody is grasped not only because of the articulation of combinational units but because of their precise temporal succession. Thus even syntactic-phrase markers must be considered as vectors [29].

In /John beats Mary/ it is the direction of the phrase (a spatial direction in the written phrase and a temporal one in the uttered one) that makes the content understandable; by changing round the proper names the entire content is reversed. Again, a vectorialization is neither a sign nor a complete expression in itself (except taken as an expression signifying a pure vectorial correlation as in /a⊃b/), but rather a productive feature that, in conjunction with others, contributes to the composition of the expression [30]. One could say that in some cases a vector by itself can give rise to a sign-function; suppose that I hum an upward pitch-curve; I can succeed in signifying «question» (or «I am questioning» or «what?») by imposing a direction on a sound-continuum without resorting to any other device. But this is a case of coded stylization.

Many vectors are governed by a very schematic *ratio difficilis* so easily recognizable that, as happens with stylizations, a sort of catachresizing process takes place and the *ratio difficilis* practically becomes a *ratio facilis*. The case of the interrogative humming cited above is a typical example of this process.

3.6.6. Programmed stimuli and pseudo-combinational units

Half way between replica and invention there are two kinds of productive operation that are not usually considered as semiotically definable. The first one concerns the disposition of non-semiotic elements intended to elicit an immediate response in the receiver. A flash of light during a theatrical performance, an unbearable sound, a subliminal excitation, and so on, are to be listed among stimuli rather than signs, as was stressed in 3.5.5. But in the same paragraph we noted that, when the sender knows the possible effect of the displayed stimulus, one is obliged to consider his knowledge as a sort of *semiotic competence*, for *to him* a given stimulus corresponds to a given foreseeable reaction that he expressly aims to elicit. In other words, there is a sign-function by which the stimulus is the expression plane of a supposed effect functioning as its content plane.

Nevertheless the effect of a stimulus is never completely predictable, especially when inserted among other more specifically semiotic elements within a text as a pseudo-sign. Suppose that a speaker is elaborating a persuasive discourse according to the rules of judiciary rhetoric and trying to arouse in his addressees feelings of pity and compassion. He can utter his phrases in a throbbing voice, or with barely detectable vibrations that *could* suggest that he is tempted to cry. These supra-segmental features could obviously be either paralinguistic devices or mere symptoms indicating his emotional state; but they might also be stimuli he inserts into the discourse in order to provoke some degree of identification in his listeners and to pull them toward the same emotional state. He is using these devices as *programmed stimulations* but does not know exactly how they will be received, detected, interpreted. The speaker is thus half way between the execution of certain rules of stimulation and the displaying of new unconventionalized elements that might (or might not) become recognized as semiotic devices. Sometimes the speaker is not sure of the relation between a given stimulus and a given presupposed response, and he is more *making* than performing a tentative coding of programmed stimuli. Therefore these devices stand between replica and invention; and may or may not be semiotic devices, thus constituting a sort of ambiguous threshold. So that even though the expressive string of programmed stimuli can be analyzed into detectable units, the corresponding content remains a nebula-like conceptual or behavioral 'discourse'. The expression, made of analyzable and replicable units (governed by a *ratio facilis*) may then generate a vague discourse on the content plane. Among such programmed stimuli one might list: (i) all the programmed synesthesiae in poetry, music, painting, etc.; (ii) all so-called 'expressive' signs, such as those theorized by artists like Kandinskij, i.e. visual configurations that are conventionally supposed to 'convey' a given feeling directly (force, grace, instability, movement and so on) and that have also been studied by the theorists of *Einfühlung* or empathy; insofar as these devices hold a motivated relationship with psychic forces or 'reproduce' physical experiences, they should be dealt with in the paragraph concerning projections (3.6.7.); insofar as they are displayed by a sender who knows their emphatic effect, they are programmed stimulation (and therefore precoded devices) of which, however, the result (on the content plane) is only partially foreseeable; (iii) all production of substitutive stimuli described in 3.5.8.; (iv) many projections, about which more will be said in 3.6.7.

Anyway one should carefully distinguish between this sort of programmed stimulus and the more explicitly coded devices used to express emotions, such as body movements, facial expressions, and so on, now so precisely recorded by the latest researches in kinesics (Ekman 1969) and in paralinguistics.

Another kind of spurious semiotic operation is *pseudo-combination*. The most typical example is an abstract painting or an atonal musical composition. Apparently a Mondrian painting or a Schoenberg composition is perfectly replicable and therefore appears to be composed by systematically combinable units. These units are not apparently endowed with meaning but they do follow combinational rules.

Nobody can deny that there is an expression system even though the content plane remains, as it were, open to all comers. These examples are thus more *open signal textures* than sign-functions; for this very reason they appear to invite the attribution of a content, thus issuing a sort of interpretive challenge to their addressee (Eco, 1962). Let us call them visual or musical *propositional functions* that can only 'wait' to be correlated to a content, each being susceptible of many different correlations.

Thus when hearing a post-Webernian sound cluster one detects the presence of replicable musical units combined in a certain fashion and sometimes one also knows the rule governing this kind of aggregation of material events.

However, the problem seems to change when one is dealing with abstract expressionist paintings, random music, John Cage's happenings and so on. In these cases one can speak of textural clouds which lack any predictable rule. Can one then continue to speak of a pseudo-combinational operation? It is exactly this kind of artistic operation which prompted Lévi-Strauss (1964) to deny any linguistic nature to these phenomena, in view of their lack of discrete units or of oppositions based on an underlying system.

One could respond that in these cases the entire material texture, through its very absence of rules, opposed itself to the entire system of rules governing 'linguistic' art, thus creating a sort of macrosystem in which manifestations of pure noise are opposed to manifestations of informational order. This solution has the advantage of elegance and does in fact explain many of the intentions behind the work of '*informel*' artists, but it is equivalent to maintaining that even in non-semiotic phenomena there is a semiotic purport insofar as they are displayed in order to make absent semiotic phenomena relevant. In this sense the creation of '*art informel*' would be the same as silence in order to 'express' refusal to speak.

As a matter of fact there is another reason why many examples of this kind of art have at least the nature of pseudo-combinations. The clue is given by artists themselves when they tell us that they examine the very veining of material, the texture of the wood, canvas, iron or sounds and noises, trying to find in them relationships, forms, new visual or auditory paths. The artist discovers at the deeper level of the expression-continuum a new system of relations that the preceding segmentation of that continuum, giving rise to an expression form, had never made pertinent. These new pertinent features, along with their mode of organization, are so detectable and recognizable, that one becomes able to isolate the work of a given artist, and thus to distinguish, for instance, Fautrier from Pollock or Boulez from Berio.

In this case the establishing of pseudo-combinational units does not precede the making of the work itself; on the contrary, the growth of the work coincides with the birth of the systems. And, provided that these forms convey a content (which is sometimes identical with a metalinguistic account of the nature of the work and its ideological purport), an entire code is proposed as the work is established.

Let me stress that we are here dealing with three problems: (i) the segmentation performed below the level of the recognized expression form, that is, a further segmentation of the expression-continuum; this aspect will become very important in section 3.7. when speaking of the aesthetic text; (ii) the complexity of this segmentation at various levels, which sometimes makes it impossible to detect distinguishable units, thereby making it impossible to establish replicable expression types; when this happens pseudo-combinational units cannot be replicated (in post-Webernian music some sound-clusters can be replicated − indeed there is a score prescribing their way of performance − while others can only be 'suggested' by the composer and require an inventive participation on the part of the performer; a Dubuffet painting can hardly be replicated); (iii) the invention of new expression levels along with their possible segmentation and systematization; in such cases pseudo-combinational procedure turns into purely *inventive* procedure, thus bringing us to the last item in the present classification of *modi faciendi signa*.

In Table 39 pseudo-combinational units are nevertheless listed among the modes of production governed by a *ratio facilis* because, as long as they are replicable, they have to reproduce an expression type, though it seems doubtful that they represent a definite case of sign-function so much as one of an 'open' signal. But if their constitutive units are not detectable, they are not replicable, and they thus remain half way between sign production and the proposal of new possibilities for manipulating continua.

It is not by chance that programmed stimuli have on the contrary been listed in the same row as examples and samples, in a middle position between *ratio facilis* and *ratio difficilis*. Sometimes, as the empathy theorists assume, there is a sort of 'motivated' link between a certain line and a certain feeling, and thus cases of stimulation rely on procedures of projection or stylization.

3.6.7. Invention

We may define as invention a mode of production whereby the producer of the sign-function chooses a new material continuum not yet segmented for that purpose and proposes a new way of organizing (of giving form to) it in order *to map* within it the formal pertinent element of a content-type. Thus in invention we have a case of *ratio difficilis* realized within a heteromaterial expression; but since no previous convention exists to correlate the elements of the expression with the selected content, the sign producer must in some way *posit* this correlation so as to make it acceptable. In this sense inventions are radically different from recognition, choice, and replica.

Everybody recognizes an expression produced by *recognition* because a previous experience has linked a given expression-unit with a given content-unit. Everybody recognizes an expression produced by a *choice* made on the basis of a common mechanism of abstraction, such as the acknowledging of a given item as representative of the class to which it belongs. Everybody recognizes an expression produced by *replica*, because the replica replicates an expression-type which has already been conventionally correlated with a given content. In all these cases, whether the *ratio* is *facilis* or *difficilis*, everybody recognizes the correspondence between a token and its type because the type already exists as a cultural product. Whether the token expression reproduces a content type, as in the case of imprints, or an expression type, as in the case of phonemes and words, the procedure follows certain basic requirements.

If one views a type (whether of content or of expression) as a set of properties that have been singled out as pertinent, the token is obtained by mapping out the elements of the original set in terms of those of the token set. This procedure can be represented by Table 40, where the *x*s represent the pertinent properties of the type and the *y*s non-pertinent and variable elements [31].

In cases of *ratio facilis* mapping presents no problem; it simply involves the reproduction of a property using the same sort of material as that prescribed by the type. In the case of a phoneme the type may, for instance, prescribe 'labial+voiced' (thereby implying: by means of human phonation), thus establishing how to produce a [b].

Table 40

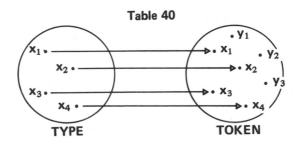

TYPE   TOKEN

The notion of mapping is somewhat more problematic in cases of *ratio difficilis*, because the type of a *ratio difficilis* is a content unit, a sememe, and its properties are semantic markers, and are not in principle linked to any particular expression continuum.

So what does one mean by mapping the pertinent properties of a glass of wine within another material so as to produce the recognizable wet imprint of a glass of wine upon a table? Formulating the question in this way might make for a puzzling answer, but this is because of one's 'referential' bias. As a matter of fact the imprint of a glass of wine does not have to possess the properties of the object «glass of wine» but it does have to possess those of the cultural unit «imprint of a glass of wine». And in this case the semantic representation of the entity in question entails no more than four semantic markers, i.e. «circle», «red», «length of the inradius (or diameter)» and «wet». To map these markers within another material simply means to realize the geometrical and chemical *interpretants* of the sememes «circle», «red», «diameter X» and «wet». This done, the mapping process is complete, and the realization of a token of the content type a comparatively easy matter. In this sense one *cannot* maintain that the imprint of a hare's paw is an iconic feature in the same way as is the image of a hare. In the former case the content type is culturally established, whereas in the latter one it is not (except in cases of stylization).

The only problem would appear to be: in what sense does a circle of a given diameter realized upon a table map the semantic markers «circle» and «diameter X»?

But on second thoughts, that question is not so different from asking in what sense a labial and voiced consonant maps the abstact phonological type 'labial+voiced' in sound. In the latter case the answer seems easy enough:

there are certain sound parameters which permit the realization and recognition of the replica (as to how the realization of a parameter is recognizable, this sends us back to basic perceptive requirements that, as was noted in 3.4.7. and 3.4.8., are postulates rather than theorems for a semiotic theory).

Thus one need only repeat that (as was underlined in 3.4.2.) various expressions may be realized whether in accordance with spatial parameters or phonic parameters in order to justify listing the replica of a circle in the same theoretical row as the replica of a phoneme. The only difference is that the sound features governing the reproduction of a phoneme are not content markers, while the spatial features governing the reproduction (even if virtual, as in the recognition of imprints) of a geometrical figure are. This — as we have seen — is exactly the difference between *ratio facilis* and *ratio difficilis*.

Now if one considers Table 39, one notices that all the cases of *ratio difficilis* concern content types in which the most important semantic markers are *toposensitive*, i.e. figural or vectorial properties. This brings us back to the problem outlined in 2.7.2.: not every semantic marker can be verbalized. When semantic markers can be verbalized they have undoubtedly acquired a maximum of abstraction; previously culturalized and frequently expressed through verbal devices, they can even be arbitrarily correlated with other non-verbal devices (for example a geometrical form in a road signal meaning «stop»), and through the mediation of verbal habits they can easily be detected. In these cases it is true that, as Barthes and other theorists say, non-verbal semiotic systems rely on the verbal one. But there are markers that cannot be verbalized, at least not completely, so that they cannot be conveyed by a metalinguistic definition verbally expressed.

The spatial disposition of the imprint of a hare's paw cannot be verbally meta-described. It is, however, hard to assert that is has no cultural 'existence', and the proof is not in the fact that it can be 'thought' (which would be an extra-semiotic and somewhat mentalistic argument) but in the fact that it can be *interpreted* in many ways. For instance one can conceive of an algorythm which, when fed into a plotting machine as input, would produce as its output a drawing of a hare's paw. The fact that this drawing is more schematical than a real imprint is a further proof of the present thesis: the cultural notion of such an imprint (a sememe) is neither the same as its perceptual model nor as the corresponding object.

The process from perceptual model to semantic model and from semantic model to an expressive model governed by a *ratio difficilis*, may be represented as in Table 41.

Table 41

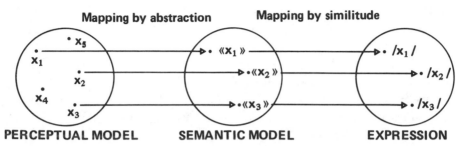

In other words, given a *perceptual* model as a 'dense' representation of a given experience, assigning to the perceived object x the properties x_1, x_2, x_3, $x_4 \ldots x_n$, that perceptual model gives rise to a *semantic* model which preserves only, let us say, three of the properties of the dense representation. It is not said that all those selected semantic markers are necessarily verbalizable items; many of them may be toposensitive relationships.

At this point it would be possible to *express* this semantic model (a sememe) by means of an expressive device. If the markers of the sememe were non-toposensitive, the correlation content-expression could be an arbitrary one. Since, however, in this case some markers are toposensitive, the correlation is *motivated*, and must follow in principle the rules governing every type/token-ratio, i.e. rules of transformation.

Let us now add something about the double mapping outlined in Table 41. The first kind of mapping (from percept to sememe) does not need to be semiotically explained: it follows the rules governing every phenomenon of abstraction — both in conceptual and 'visual' thinking — and is therefore a procedure depending on the mechanisms of human intelligence (which is not to say that even this procedure could not be seen as a semiotic one, but rather that the definition of this problem constitutes one of the 'political' boundaries of semiotics — see *Introduction*).

The second kind of mapping should be identical to that which governs the production of a triangle that is *similar* to another, given certain spatial parameters and conventions (such as that size is irrelevant, but sides must be proportional and angles 'equal'). Let us call this procedure a *transformation*: "every biunivocal correspondence of points in space is a transformation. What concerns us is the existence of particular transformations that leave certain prominent properties of the geometrical entities to which they are applied unchanged" [32]. This concept of transformation fits cases of token-to-token reproduction as well as those of type/token-ratio perfectly (this being one of the postulates of semiotics). But it also explains cases such as the production (even if virtual) of an imprint, which is why in 3.6.2. even imprints were said to be cases of transformation.

But in cases of type/token-ratio, mapping by similitude takes place between an expression type (and thus the model of an object) and an expression token (and thus another physical object). In the case of the imprint, on the other hand, we are considering *similitudes established between a semantic model and its physical expression.* We are once again concerned with the difference between *ratio facilis* and *ratio difficilis.*

At this point two problems arise:

(i)   how to 'map' from a content-model into an expressive one, i.e. from a non-physical reality into a physical continuum;

(ii)   how various kinds of mapping may be listed according to a degree of conventionality reached by the content-type and its toposensitive complexity.

If, in Table 39, imprints (even if accidentally replicated rather than recognized) were not classified as straightforward transformations under the heading of *inventions*, this was for a good reason. In the case of an imprint the content-model already *exists.* It has, in one way or another, been culturally established. When replicating an imprint one is mapping from something *known.* And there exist similitude rules establishing how to ombody in a material continuum certain semantic toposensitive properties of a sememe (as in the case of the glass of wine). So the mapping procedure by *ratio difficilis* in Table 41 is not so different from that performed in cases of *ratio facilis* (Table 40). This mapping is undoubtedly *motivated* by the sememic representation of the supposed object but is at the same time ruled by *mapping conventions.* The main problem arises when trying to determine how it is possible to map onto an expression continuum the properties of something which (because of its cultural oddity or formal complexity) is *not yet culturally known.*

It must be stressed that one is not here concerned with the representation of a golden mountain, or a man with ten eyes and seven legs. It is very easy to infer the nature of unknown elements from the *addition* of known ones, just as language manages to express unheard-of events by articulating recognizable units. But the real puzzling problem is not so much how one may represent a man with ten eyes and seven legs as why one may *visually represent* (and *recognize* as *represented*) a given man with *two* eyes and *two* legs. How it is possible to represent a man standing and a lady sitting under a tree, a calm landscape with clouds and a corn-field behind them, a given light and a given mood — as happens in Gainsborough's *Mr. and Mrs. Andrews*?

Since this complex content is not a unit but a *discourse* (and the painting is not a sign but a *text*), and since that content was not previously known by the addressee grasping for the first time from an expression for which *no type* previously existed, how is it possible to define this phenomenon semiotically? The only solution would seem to be that painting is not a semiotic phenomenon, because there is neither pre-established expression nor pre-established content, and thus no correlation between functives to permit signification; thus a painting should appear a 'mysterious' phenomenon which *posits* functives instead of being posited by them.

Nevertheless, if such a phenomenon seems to escape the correlational definition of 'sign-function', it certainly does not escape the basic definition of a sign as something which *stands for* something else: for Gainsborough's painting is exactly this, something physically *present* which conveys something *absent* and, in certain cases, could be used in order to mention a state of the world.

3.6.8. Invention as code-making

With this example we have arrived at a critical point in the present classification of modes of sign-production. We now have to define a semiotic mode of production in which something is mapped from something else which was not defined and analyzed before the act of mapping took place. We are witnessing a case in which a significant convention is posited at the very moment in which both the functives of the correlation are *invented*.

But for the semiotician this latter definition has a rather familiar ring to it. It curiously resembles the problems (so vigorously rejected by at least three generations of linguists) surrounding the origins of language or the historical rise of semiotic conventions.

Now if such a problem can be rejected when it is proposed from an abstract and roughly archeological point of view, it cannot be escaped when approached from the viewpoint of a phenomenology of modes of sign-production. Let us therefore assume that the problem of these transformations listed as inventions and based on a *ratio difficilis* (depending on a toposensitive content model) raises the question of the activity of *code-making* (see Table 31 and paragraph 3.1.2.).

We may now revise the mapping process as proposed in Table 41 as follows (Table 42).

Table 42

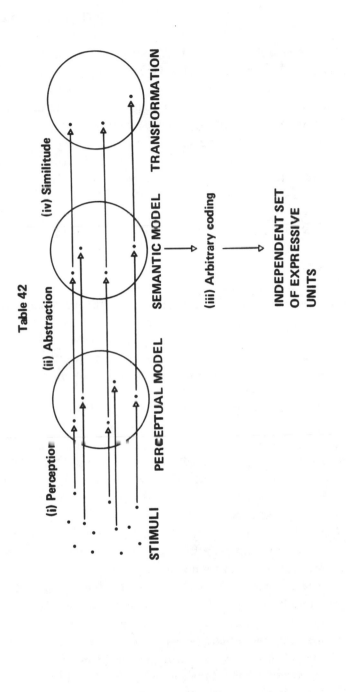

(i) Perception   (ii) Abstraction   (iv) Similitude

STIMULI   PERCEPTUAL MODEL   SEMANTIC MODEL   TRANSFORMATION

(iii) Arbitrary coding

INDEPENDENT SET
OF EXPRESSIVE
UNITS

Here (i) relevant elements are picked up from an unshaped perceptual field and organized in order to build a percept; (ii) by means of abstractive procedures very similar to the rules that govern cases of stylization (see 3.6.5.) the percept is mapped onto a semantic representation, the latter being the cultural simplification of the former; (iii) this semantic representation is either arbitrarily associated with a set of expressive devices, as in the case of systematically combinational elements and other kinds of replicas, or (iv) mapped into a transformation according to conventional rules of similitude. These procedures explain every kind of sign production listed in Table 39, *except inventions*.

An invention can take place in two ways, one moderate and the other radical:

(a) *Moderate inventions* occur when one projects directly from a perceptual representation into an expression-continuum, thereby realizing an expression-form which dictates the rules producing the equivalent content-unit (Table 43).

This is the case, for instance, in Gainsborough's painting, as indeed in all so-called 'classical' paintings. The same thing happens in the *first* reproduction (or recognition) of an imprint.

From the *sender's* point of view, a perceptual structure is considered as a coded semantic model (even though nobody else would yet view it in this way), and its perceptual markers are mapped into an as yet unshaped continuum according to the more commonly accepted rules of similitude. The sender therefore proposes rules of correlation even though the functive-content does not as yet exist. But from the *addressee's* point of view the result is simply an expressive structure.

Using the painting as an imprint, he makes his way *backward* inferring and extrapolating similitude rules, and finally re-constitutes the original percept. However, the process is not an easy one; sometimes addressees refuse to collaborate, and consequently the convention fails to establish itself. The addressee must be helped by the sender and consequently a painting can never afford to be entirely the fruit of an inventive transformation. It must offer various clues: stylizations, perhaps some pre-coded combinational units, a number of fictive samples and of programmed stimuli. Thus, by dint of a series of complex adjustments, the convention is established.

When this process is successful a new content-plane, lying between the percept (which is only remembered by the painter) and the physically testable expression is brought into being. This is not so much a unit as a

Table 43

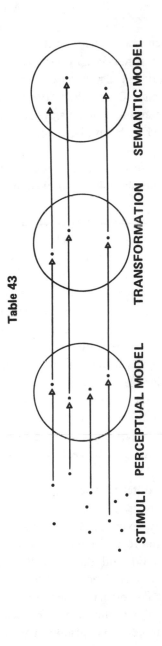

STIMULI PERCEPTUAL MODEL TRANSFORMATION SEMANTIC MODEL

discourse. What had been raw content-continuum perceptually organized by the painter in the first instance now gradually becomes a new cultural arrangement of the world. A sign-function emerges from the exploratory labor of code-making, and so establishes itself that the painting generates habits, acquired expectations, and mannerisms. Expressive visual units become sufficiently fixed to be available for further combinations. Stylizations come into being.

The painting now offers manipulable units that may be used for further sign-production. The semiosic spiral, enriched by new sign functions and interpretants, is now ready to start all over again.

(b) The case of *radical inventions* is rather different, in that the sender more or less bypasses the perceptual model, and delves directly into the as yet unshaped perceptual continuum, mapping his perception as he organizes it (Table 44).

In this case the transformation, the realized expression, is a shorthand device whereby the sender fixes the results of his perceptual labor. Only after carrying out this expressive labor can he arrive at a perceptual model and then subsequently a sememic representation. This process has been present at all the great innovative moments in the history of painting. Take the case of the Impressionists, whose addressees absolutely refused to 'recognize' the subjects represented and said that they 'did not understand', that the painting 'did not mean anything', that real life was not like that, etc. This refusal was due to the addressees' lack not only of a semantic model to which the mapped items might be referred, but also of a percept to guess at, since they had never perceived in this way.

In such cases what takes place is a radical code-making, a violent proposal of new conventions. The sign-function does not as yet exist, and indeed sometimes fails to establish itself at all. The sender gambles on the possibility of semiosis, and loses. In one or two cases it is only centuries later that the gamble comes off and the convention is established. All these procedures will be further examined in the section devoted to the aesthetic text, thereby implying that code-making and invention are aesthetic activities.

Curiously enough, this assumption carries speculation about languages back to the position adopted by Giambattista Vico, who proposed that languages rise as poetic inventions and are only accepted by convention afterward. This is not to say that the conclusion of this chapter should be interpreted as a verification of idealistic theses that, when carried to extremes, result in the rejection of any semiotic science (or at least of any recognition of the social import of codes). In fact, *no one ever really*

Table 44

witnesses cases of total radical invention, nor indeed of total moderate invention, since texts are maze-like structures combining inventions, replicas, stylizations, ostentions and so on. Semiosis never rises *ex novo* and *ex nihilo*. No new culture can ever come into being except against the background of an old one.

As was said in 2.1. and 2.4. there are no signs as such, and many so-called signs are texts; signs and texts being the result of a labor of correlation in which many variously intertwined modes of sign production take part. If 'invention' were a category within a typology of signs, then it would be possible to isolate absolute and radical inventions, which would constitute real examples of the birth of language, demonstrating the continuous recurrence of the 'auroral' moment through which, every day in everyone's life, language comes into the world — just as Croce's linguistics maintained, overestimating the creative power of the speaking subject.

But since invention is, on the contrary, one among various modes of sign production, collaborating with others to correlate functives and to establish various sign-functions, the idealistic fallacy is avoided.

Man is continuously making and re-making codes, but only insofar as other codes already exist. In the semiotic universe there are neither single protagonists nor charismatic prophets. Even prophets have to be socially *accepted* in order to be right; if not, they are wrong.

3.6.9. A continuum of transformations

The products of semiotic invention, even if viewed as potential super-signs, are 'fuzzy' signs. They do not establish straightforward oppositions as much as possible *gradations* and they are more subject to undercoding than to coding. It would be wrong to assert that a painting is a complex of recognizable signs like a poem. But it would be equally wrong to maintain that a painting is not a semiotic phenomenon; it represents the moment in which a semiotic phenomenon comes into being, the proposal of a possible code by making use of remnants of previous ones. This being the case, it must be stressed that there are different kinds of transformations, some of them closer to the making of a double for the purposes of pure perception or use, others more akin to a semiotic procedure. Let us list, at any rate, three grades within this continuum.

First of all there are *congruences or casts* [33]: a point in the physical space of the expression corresponds to *each* point in the space of a *real object*. One example of this is a death mask. But death masks can be 'understood' even if one does not know the model-object (and as a matter of fact they are frequently displayed in order to allow one to detect the physical properties of a person one has never known). Death masks are not absolute congruences (in the full geometrical sense of the term); they discard as irrelevant skin texture, color and many other properties; in fact they can also be reproduced on a smaller scale without losing their representative power. So they, too, must be governed by conventions of similitude. When looking at a death mask one 'maps backward'. But at the end of the projection stands not an object, but a content-type; therefore they are sign-functions.

Furthermore, it is clear enough that death masks can be faked. So that, however you look at it, these heteromaterial casts must be signs. Only homomaterial congruences are not signs, and these are in fact absolute replicas or doubles! Secondly there are *projections* [34]: points on the space of the expressive token correspond to *selected* points on the space of *toposensitive perceptive or semantic models*. Strong similitude rules are at work; one must in fact learn to recognize this kind of 'image'. There are different styles of projection, and they are easily falsifiable.

Any naive interpreter of a projection 'reads' it as an imprint, that is, as the direct mapping from the actual aspects of a thing!

On the contrary, the projection is always the result of a mapping convention by means of which given traces on a surface are stimuli compelling one *to map backward* and to postulate a content-type where one only sees an expression-token. So it is always possible to *project from nothing* or from contents to which no referent corresponds (as in a classical painting representing mythological heroes). The existence of social conventions in projections (so that is is possible to map from a perceptual or a semantic model) make easy the reverse procedure, that is, to map from the projection to an unexisting and supposedly projected entity. What reinforces our criticism of naive iconism is that since it is possible to draw false iconic signs, iconism is a matter of a highly sophisticated semiotic convention [35]. When considered as mentions, projections are frequently false; they try to assert that something exists, which actually *looks like* the expression item, when this is not the case at all; they can thus display images of Julius Caesar as well as of Mr. Pickwick, irrespective of the differing ontological status of the two. It is in cases of projections that the so-called 'scales of iconism' can be accepted as heuristically useful.

Thirdly, there are *graphs* or *topological transformations* [36], in which spatial points in the expression correspond to points of non-toposensitive relation; such is the case in Peirce's existential graphs (see 3.5.3.): a spatial expression displays information about a correlation which is not spatial at all but which instead concerns, for instance, economic relationships, as when one uses the graph of Table 45

Table 45

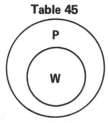

to express the following relationship: "every dependent worker belongs to the class of exploited and alienated proletarians".

In any case this whole range of inventive representations, from congruences or casts to graphs, displays not signs but texts; when these texts first appear there is as yet no distinction between *pertinent* and *irrelevant* features. It is only in the course of decoding them that pertinent features emerge, and they begin to produce signs (and thus their own mannerisms). Because of the difficulty of isolating the content-type to which they refer (by a procedure of *ratio difficilis*), these texts are not easily replicable.

To successfully copy a painting is no mean feat, and to farce a Rembrandt may well be considered a para-artistic achievement, for it is very difficult to detect the pertinent properties on which the significant power of the expression relies, and only remarkably skilled counterfeiters have a capacity for isolating and reproducing them. When only one person in the world is able to falsify a *mode of invention* (i.e. not to copy a given painting, but to paint according to the same type of inventive procedure) the code proposed by that painting has not yet been accepted by a culture; when it becomes possible to paint *à la manière de*, then the invention (as a code-making proposal) has succeeded semiotically; a new convention exists. But it is clear that the present discussion is continuously shifting from the problem of code-making and of the acquisition of new conventions, to the problem of the aesthetic use of a language. Any discussion of invention inevitably opens up the problem of the ambiguous, self-focusing and idiolectal use of a code, and compels us to return, once more, to the discussion on aesthetic texts.

3.6.10. Productive features, signs, texts

The typology of modes of production of the signal, outlined in this section, has definitely clarified the fact that what one usually calls 'signs' are the result of many intertwined modes of production. For instance, a perfume of incense, if smelled in a church, is only a case of *recognition*, that is, a symptom by which one recognizes that a liturgical ceremony is taking place. When produced, it is at the same time the *replica* of a *stylization* and a *programmed stimulus*. When used during a play in order to suggest a mystical situation, it is both a *programmed stimulus* and a *fictive sample* (the incense for the whole ceremony).

A smile can be a *symptom* or the *replica* of a *stylization*, and sometimes even a *vectorialization*. A musical melody, when quoted in order to recall the entire symphony from which it has been extrapolated, is a *sample*; but it can be the *replica* of a text composed by *combinational units* and, sometimes, even a complex of *programmed stimuli* mixed with *pseudo-combinational units*. And it is usually all these things together. A geographical map is the result of a previous *transformation* (half way between a *projection* and a *graph*) which has definitely become a *stylization*, and as such is the result of a *replica*. Clothes in general are replicable *stylizations* with intertwined *pseudo-combinational units and programmed stimuli*.

The problem becomes more difficult when one must define a painting. In any case, a painting is certainly not 'a sign': it is a complex text resulting from the network of many modes of production.

One might suppose that a portrait of a given man represents a perfect case of 'proper name' necessarily sending back to a physical referent (while the verbal proper names have been demonstrated in 2.9.2. to have a content). One could better say that such a portrait is neither a sign nor a complex super-sign but rather a *mention* (/this is a man and he possesses these properties . . . /). On the other hand it might be said that the same portrait is equivalent to a *description*. Goodman (1968:1.5.) remarks that there is a difference between the *picture of a man* (the portrait of Napoleon) and a *man-picture* (the portrait of Mr. Pickwick). In fact such a portrait embodies different types of activities, practically covering the entire range of types of semiotic labor outlined in Tables 31 and 39. It is a *mention* because, through *programmed stimuli*, it displays the surrogate of a percept and by means of some graphic devices attributes to it the markers of a possible corresponding sememe; it is an *invention* insofar as the perceptual model does not yet exist; it is a *factual judgment* (/there exists a man so and so/) and a *description* (/a man so and so/). Being still uncoded it is at the same time relying on a lot of already coded features, and the invention is made acceptable by the intervention of coded *imprints, stylizations, samples, pseudo-combinational units, vectorializations*, and so on. Therefore such a portrait is a complex text whose content ranges from a coded detectable unit («Mr. So and So») to an infinite discourse or a content-nebula. But as far as the portrait is accepted and recognized by a culture, it creates a 'type' (in the sense of a 'literary type', intended as the representation of some 'universal' properties: the Hero, the Gentleman, the Beautiful Lady, *la belle dame sans merci*, and so on). At this point it becomes the model for further stylizations. So what in a given historical period may be viewed as an inventive projection, in another period becomes a stylization.

The same happens with the so-called 'architectural signs'. Even if many researches in semiotics of architecture have tried to isolate the existence of 'architectural signs' [37], it is absolutely clear that even the most elementary architectural configuration is always a *text*. Let us consider for instance a staircase. It is undoubtedly a semiotic device which signifies certain functions: but to compose such a device productive labor is requested to display the following features: (i) articulation of *pseudo-combinational units*; (ii) *vectorializations* (the staircase indicates a direction making recourse to toposensitive parameters); (iii) *programmed stimulations* (the staircase in a certain way obliges one to move one's feet for climbing up); (iv) *stylizations* (the staircase corresponds to a precise typology); and so on.

It is not without sense to try to isolate precise expression-units in architecture, but it is indispensable to take into account the lot of productive features that these units bring into play.

All this reminds us that, the more a text become complex, the more complex is the relationship between expression and content. There may be simple expression units that convey content-nebulae (see for instance many cases of programmed stimulation); expression-clusters that convey a precise content unit (a triumphal arch can be a very elaborate architectural text and nevertheless convey a strictly conventional abstraction such as «victory»); precise grammatical expressions, composed of replicable combinational units, such as the phrase /I love you/, that in certain circumstances convey dramatically a content-nebula; and so on.

This must not allow one to neglect to isolate precise sign-functions when they are detectable, but serves to remind one that in the semiosic process we are usually facing undercoded or overcoded texts.

When more analytical units are not detectable, it is not a case of denying the existence of a semiotic correlation; the presence of the cultural convention is not only witnessed by the emergence of so-called elementary signs. It is first of all revealed by the detectable existence of modes of semiotic production (recognition, ostension, replica and invention) that the present section has outlined and whose presence demonstrates that — even when there are not precise unit-to-unit correlations — there is, however, a posited sign-function.

3.7. The aesthetic text as invention

3.7.1. The semiotic purport of the aesthetic text

The aesthetic use of a language deserves attention on a number of different levels: (i) an aesthetic text involves a very peculiar labor, i.e. a particular *manipulation of the expression* (see 3.7.2.); (ii) this manipulation of the expression releases (and is released by) a *reassessment of the content* (see 3.7.3.); (iii) this double operation, producing an idiosyncratic and highly original instance of sign-function (see 3.7.4.), is to some degree reflected in precisely those codes on which the aesthetic sign-function is based, thus releasing a process of *code changing* (see 3.7.5.); (iv) the entire operation, even though focused on codes, frequently produces a new type of *awareness about the world* (see 3.7.6.); (v) insofar as the aesthetic labor aims to be detected and scrutinized repeatedly by the addressee, who thereby engages in a complex labor of interpretation, the aesthetic sender must also focus his attention on the addressees' possible reactions, so that the aesthetic text represents a network of diverse *communicational acts* eliciting highly original responses (see 3.7.7.).

In all these senses the aesthetic text represents a sort of summary and laboratory model of all the aspects of sign-function: it can perform any or all productive functions (being composed of various types of judgment and acting as a meta-semiotic statement) and it can require any kind of productive labor.

At the same time Table 31 can be viewed as the simplified representation of what happens when an aesthetic text is produced and interpreted.

All of which shows clearly enough why the semiotician may be interested in examining the aesthetic experience. But there are other reasons for attempting a semiotic approach to aesthetic texts, since one may also hope to thereby clarify many problems that traditional philosophical aesthetics has left unsolved.

Typical of many philosophical aesthetic theories is that, rather than define the poetic message, they list the effects that any reader of poetry (or viewer of a visual work of art) may feel. What differentiates the response of philosophical aesthetics from that of the layman is the sophisticated architecture of rhetorical devices which, by means of an imaginative interplay of metaphors, translate a sum of truisms.

Some so-called aesthetic definitions of art can be translated by the statement "art is art" or "art is what produces an aesthetic effect".

One example is Croce's theory of the cosmic quality of art: the whole life of the cosmos breathes within the artistic representation, the individual pulsates with the life of the Whole, and the Whole is revealed in the life of the individual. "Every genuine artistic representation is in itself the universe . . . . In every word the poet writes and in every creature of his imagination there lies the whole of human destiny, all human hopes, illusions, griefs, joys, greatness and misery; the entire drama of Reality, which develops and grows up upon itself for ever, suffering and rejoicing . . . . " [38]. This definition of poetic effect seems to correspond to certain impressions that we have had in our aesthetic experience; but it is vague and unsatisfying because it says, in an elegant way, *what* we feel or have felt, but not *why*. So we must now see whether the semiotic approach gives a better explanation of this effect.

3.7.2. An ambiguous and self-focusing text

According to the well-known subdivision of the functions of language put forward by Jackobson, a message can possess either one or a combination of the following functions: a) referential; b) emotive; c) imperative; d) phatic; e) metalinguistic; f) poetic. The message assumes a poetic function (though in this context it is preferable to call it an 'aesthetic' one, granted that we are dealing with every kind of art) when it is *ambiguous* and *self-focusing*. Obviously all six functions can coexist in a single message; in the greater part of everyday language (as well as in aesthetic messages) they are constantly interrelating and overlapping, although one of the functions usually predominates, thereby characterizing the message. Semiotically speaking ambiguity must be defined as a mode of violating the rules of the code. There are totally ambiguous messages (such as /wbstddd grf mu/, which violates both phonetic and lexical rules), syntactically ambiguous messages (such as /John has a when/, which violates subcategorization rules) and semantically ambiguous messages (such as the well-known /green colorless ideas sleep furiously/) but not all these types of ambiguity necessarily produce an aesthetic effect (even though, when inserted in an appropriate context, they could).

Another form of ambiguity is the *stylistic* one. Coseriu (1952), distinguishing between *system* and *norm*, suggests that a *langue* may allow different performances, all considered as 'grammatical', yet some of them will acquire an appearance of 'normality', while others will be considered as stylistic (i.e.: upper-class, vulgar, literary) variations. Latin allows one to say /*Petrus amat Paulum, Petrus Paulum amat, Paulum Petrus amat*/, but the third expression looks *less normal* than the preceding two. In receiving the third one, the addressee immediately grasps a connotation of excessive elegance.

These norms depend on *stylistic subcodes* assigning an additional connotation both to isolated words and (more frequently) to *ready-made sentences*. Stylistic norms are thus an instance of *overcoding* (see 2.14.3.). When hearing /*Paulum Petrus amat*/ I am not really concerned with the fact that a man named Petrus loves a man named Paulus; I am interested in the 'poetic' (or perhaps 'Kitsch') nuances that the expression may suggest. Ready-made rhetorical sentences are also examples of overcoding.

Some stylistic approaches to criticism (Spitzer 1931) speak of the aesthetic as a *deviation from the norm*. This is not entirely satisfactory because not every deviation from the stylistic norm constitutes an aesthetic achievement: /*Amat Paulum Petrus*/ is semantically comprehensible and stylistically deviant but it sounds merely rather odd. Moreover, the theory does not make clear whether poetic deviation has to be viewed in relation to the everyday norm or to a poetically established one. In fact there can be deviations of both types.

However, ambiguity is a very important device because it functions as a sort of introduction to the aesthetic experience; when, instead of producing pure disorder, it focuses my attention and urges me to an interpretive effort (while at the same time suggesting how to set about decoding) it incites me toward the discovery of an unexpected flexibility in the language with which I am dealing.

A first step toward an aesthetic definition of ambiguity might be represented by the postulate according to which in aesthetic texts an ambiguity on the expression plane *must* involve a corresponding ambiguity on the content plane. /*Paulum Petrus amat*/ or /*Amat Paulum Petrus*/ undoubtedly deviate from certain expressive norms but do not affect the conveyed content, which remains unchanged. /Colorless green ideas sleep furiously/ is more akin to an aesthetic achievement because the shock received by the breaking of certain rules forces the hearer to reconsider the entire organization of the content.

A characteristic of aesthetic texts singled out by the Russian formalists is the *'priëm ostrannenja'* (Šklovskij, 1917), the so-called "device of making it strange" (Erlich, 1954): in order to describe something which the addressee may have seen and recognized many times, the author unexpectedly uses words (or any other kind of sign) in a different way. One's first reaction is a sense of bewilderment, of being almost unable to recognize the object. Somehow the change in expressive device also changes the content. Thus art "increases the difficulty and the duration of perception" and describes the object "as if one were seeing it for the first time" so that "the aim of the image is not to bring closer to our understanding the meaning it conveys but to create a particular perception of the object". This explains the poetic use of archaisms, the difficulty and obscurity of artistic creations when presented for the first time to an audience as yet unprepared for them; or those rhythmic violations which art brings into play at the very moment when one expects obedience to the customary 'golden rules': "in art there is 'order' and yet there is not a single column of a Greek temple that follows this order exactly, and aesthetic rhythm consists of a prosaic rhythm that has been violated . . . . it is a question not of complex rhythm but of violation of that rhythm and of a violation such that it cannot be predicted; if violation becomes the rule, it loses the force that it had as an operational obstacle". Thus Šklovskij (1917) anticipates by some thirty years the analogous conclusions of so-called 'informational aesthetics' (Moles, 1958; Bense, 1965; Meyer, 1967; Zareckij, 1963).

A violation of norms on both the expression and the content plane obliges one to reconsider their correlation, which can no longer be the same as that foreseen by the usual code. In this way the text becomes self-focusing: it directs the attention of the addressee primarily to *its own shape*. There are self-focusing messages in which the ambiguity ratio is at its most elementary level and yet these messages are more akin to an aesthetic achievement than are merely ambiguous ones. Jakobson's study of a political slogan such as /I like Ike/ (1960) has become famous [39].

3.7.3. The manipulation of the continuum

Ambiguity and a self-focusing quality are by no means entirely concentrated upon the planes of expression and content as considered up to now. In the aesthetic text both the labor of the sender and the attention of the addressee are focused on the *lower levels* of the expression plane.

So let us consider, by examining a few examples of aesthetic experience, some of the qualities of an aesthetic sign-vehicle. These qualities are obviously already familiar to any aesthetic enquiry, but they deserve a semiotic explanation. That someone likes Ike (meaning) is immediately understood whether the sender says /I like Ike/ or /It is Ike that I like/ (sign-vehicles); and in both cases certain formal rules of the expression system are observed. But these rules do not necessarily emerge in everyday linguistic usage; language is used, frequently without a complete consciousness of the underlying competence, in order to communicate contents. Nevertheless, as Jakobson has demonstrated, in the case of /I like Ike/ the addressee's attention is focused on the phonic matter of the message. There is something in this sentence which goes beyond the usual correlation between expression and content; something that, as it were, falls very easily *upon the tongue*. That something seems to be so ungraspable that the first aesthetic reaction consists in asserting that art, above and beyond its own 'linguistic' form, also conveys a *'je ne sais pas quoi'*. In this way aesthetics becomes the philosophy of the unspeakable.

Suppose we are looking at an Italian Renaissance palace with an ashlar-work facade. If the palace were drawn or photographed one could understand the architect's 'idea', the so-called, 'form' of the artifact and other drawings could provide one with the plan and the entire set of geometrical rules which directed the builder. But when the palace is *directly viewed* something else happens.

Not only does it *take time* to comprehend, imposing a shifting angle of vision, and thus introducing *time* as one of the indispensable components of the architectural experience. But also the material itself, with its unevenness and its tactile stimulation, adds something to our conceptual understanding. The architectural system has given rise to a certain number of units, i.e. stones of a certain size; each is clearly a pertinent element of a segmented masonry-continuum. But what about the *inner texture* of the individual stones, since undoubtedly much of the appeal of ashlar work derives from this factor? Modern aesthetics would say that aesthetic enjoyment brings into play even the *microstructures* of the material from which is made [40]. Which is true enough, except that a semiotic definition of these microstructures must go on to say that they represent the pertinent elements of a further segmentation of the material in question, thus suggesting the possibility of a *more basic* form of the expression. Aesthetics is not only concerned with *hypersystems* such as the various connotations that the work of art conveys above and beyond its immediate communicative appearance; it is also concerned with a whole series of *hypostructures*.

Let us return to the comparison between the semiotic levels of a code and those of a sign-function, as outlined in 2.2 (Table 6). The theory of codes considers an expression level in which, on the basis of an as yet unshaped continuum, a syntactic system gives rise to a structured set of signal-units; the code assigns the units of this plane to units of a content plane in which an as yet unshaped continuum has been structured into a set of cultural units by a semantic system.

When on the contrary one considers a sign-function in itself one has to take into account a sign-vehicle conveying a given meaning. The sign-vehicle is realized by moulding a particular channel; in other words, the stuff of which the sign-vehicle is made is the continuum from which the expression form has cut out its expression units; these units, if not inserted into a sign-function, are mere *signals*. A signal is a material fact and can consequently be studied and qualified by information theory. The signal is the token aspect of a unit of the expression-substance. Let us call this physical aspect of the signal the *matter of the sign-vehicle*.

The examples of aesthetic enjoyment examined above prove that in the aesthetic sign-vehicle matter plays an important part, and does so because it has been rendered semiotically interesting. In other words not only can the sign-vehicle (as an expression-unit) be detected as a pertinent element of the expressions system; even the material consistency of the sign-vehicle becomes a field for *further segmentation*. Using the everyday rules of a language I can utter a word in many ways, changing the pronunciation, stressing certain syllables differently, or altering intonation patterns; yet the word remains the same. But in aesthetic discourse every free variation introduced in 'uttering' the sign-vehicle has a 'formal' value. This means that even those features that usually pertain to the continuum and that a semiotic approach does not need to consider (instead leaving them to some physical or physiological discipline) here become semiotically relevant. In the aesthetic text the matter of *the sign-vehicle becomes an aspect of the expression-form*.

A red flag on a highway or at a political meeting can be based on various differently manipulated matters in order to be grasped as an expression: but the quality of cloth and the shade of red are in no way relevant. What is important is that the addressee detects /red flag/. Yet a red flag inserted in a pictorial work of art depends, among other things, upon its chromatic quality, in order to be appreciated (and to convey its signification).

In order to produce the conventional sign /cross/ one need only to cross two sticks. In order to produce a cross for the treasury of a medieval king, it was necessary to use gold and precious stones; each gem contributed to the aesthetic effect of the work because of its size, its weight, its transparency, its brilliancy, etc. Gold and jewels were appreciated because they could be manipulated and insofar as they actually were manipulated in a certain way. But even when viewed as an occurrence of a specific material, they were worthy of particular attention: *that material was already charged with cultural signification*. So that, wrought with equal care, a cross out of iron and glass would not have had the same aesthetic relevance; gold and jewels were *significant stuff* before the craftsman began to work on them.

In practice there is an *empirical limit* beyond which this material consistency, even though segmented to its utmost, can only be viewed both by the artist and the addressee as a *cluster* of unpredictable hypoforms. Beyond this limit there may still be perceptive and emotional effects but there are no more significations. Once it has moved beyond this threshold the work of art seems to *stimulate reactions* but *not to communicate contents*. Which might seem to confirm the opinion of those who assert that in art there is something more than 'language', a sort of irreducible 'aesthetic information' radically different from 'semantic information' (Moles, 1958; or Brandi's distinction between 'semiosis' and *'astanza'* or 'presence', 1968) [41].

But if these microstructures are not considered formally, then it is easy enough to assert that in aesthetic experience there exists a *'je ne sais pas quoi'* that escapes 'rational' consideration. I can recognize a phrase, an image, a melody but something remains that I cannot grasp by means of the commonly accepted semiotic categories. Thus the impression of 'unspeakability'. Fortunately a lot of pre- and para-semiotic disciplines are nowadays able to tell us something more precise about these phenomena.

For instance during the last century many techniques for measuring microstructures have been developed. From Birkhoff's formula to the various proposals put forward by Bense, and certain techniques arising from the application of information theory (Moles and others), the distribution and order of textural items is becoming increasingly open to quantitative measurement: electronic computers, along with their scanning and plotting devices, are able to analyze lines, points and spatial intervals in their structural interrelationships, while sound-recordings and oscillographs are revealing the spectral formants of sounds, there defining structures where frequencies, durations and stresses were previously conceived of as the ultimate terms of musical science. Tonal nuances, intensity of colors, consistency and rarefaction of materials, tactile sensations, synaesthetic associations, all so-called 'emotive' performances, such as supra-segmental features and 'musical' gestures, vocal inflexions, *portamenti* and *vibrato* in singing, plus many other features that until a few decades ago were considered as uncoded, are now being investigated by semiotic disciplines that deal with the so-called *lower levels* of communication (Stankiewicz, 1964). Supra-segmental features and free variants that linguistics was not able to recognize as proper objects for study are now being tackled by *paralinguistics* — as well as, in other semiotic codes, whistling and drum languages or gestures, mimicry, facial expressions.

Recent Soviet studies on the levels in poetry (Toporov, 1965; Kolmogorov, 1962) remind us that, as Hjelmslev (1928) said, it is dangerous to establish a theoretical distinction between grammatical and extra-grammatical elements, or between the intellectual and the emotional use of a language. Both so-called extra-grammatical elements and emotional effects obey rules which have not yet been isolated. Trubeckoj (1939:IV.4.) described as 'emphatic' and therefore as 'expressive' (although conventional) certain phonological features that have since been coded into oppositional systems, or at any rate into gradated sequences.

3.7.4. Aesthetic overcoding: expression

It is no chance that, having started out from the material consistency of the aesthetic sign-vehicle, we have arrived at contemporary disciplines which do not study aesthetic phenomena at all (or at least not in particular) but are rather branches of a theory of codes. The reason for this is that there is a strong relation between the further segmentation of the token matter of a given sign-vehicle and the *further segmentation of the expression plane* of an entire semiotic system. In other words, the aesthetic experience, by revealing that within its basic matter there is a further space in which sub-forms and sub-systems can be isolated, suggests that the codes on which the aesthetic sign relies can likewise be systematically submitted to such further segmentation. The pertinentization of the token matter of the token sign-vehicle demands the pertinentization of those aspects of the expression-continuum that have up to now been considered as 'hyposemiotic stuff'.

The aesthetic experience thus advocates the 'semiotic civil rights' of the 'segregated' continuum. A work of art performs a semiotic redemption of its basic matter (thus succeeding in a task that the Plotinian God never managed to accomplish, in spite of his emanational power).

After having experienced the pertinentization of matter achieved by the aesthetic sign-vehicle, one is forced to reconsider the expression system as a whole, in order to see whether it, or *any* of the sign productions permitted by it, can be subjected to the same *mise en forme*. Thus the diagram à la Hjelmslev outlined in 2.2.3. must be rewritten as in Table 46.

Hjelmslev (1943:52) asserted that "purport remains, each time, substance for a new form", only qualifying his statement with the remark that this further segmentation of the continuum is a matter for other approaches than the linguistic one. We have now seen that this further segmentation is neither extraneous to the linguistic approach nor to the various semiotic ones.

Table 46

Content	continuum			
	units			
	system			
Expression	system			
	units			
	continuum	system		
		continuum	system	
			continuum	...etc...

As long as semiotics continues to develop, the continuum will be further segmented and therefore better *understood*: the aesthetic experience provides a special opportunity for increasing this understanding.

As the first of its results, this further 'culturalization' of matter produces a further conventionalization of sign production (which is in some ways another sort of *overcoding*). One immediate consequence for aesthetics and art criticism is that this kind of new knowledge removes many phenomena from the realm of individual 'creativity' and 'inspiration' and restores them to that of social convention [42]. But a study of this kind also becomes indispensable for the reverse process; since it is only when all that can be coded has been coded that actual innovation and real insight into the expressive possibilities of a given communicative medium can occur.

The study of all the systems that enrich the expression-continuum of each code (which may already be known, but are never exhaustively *exploited* as far as the flexibility of the expression plane is concerned) represents one of the main tasks undertaken by the discipline that the Prague School called *poetics* [43].

3.7.5. Aesthetic overcoding: content

Thus an increased degree of organization within an expression-continuum will inevitably involve a parallel increase within the content-continuum. Looking at a work of art, the addressee is in fact forced to question the text under the pressure of a twofold impression: on one hand he 'guesses' that there is a *surplus of expression* that he cannot completely analyze (though maybe he could). On the other hand he vaguely senses a *surplus of content*. This second feeling is clearly aroused by the surplus of expression but it occurs even when this surplus of expression is not consciously grasped.

Suppose we are reading the well known verse by Gertrude Stein: *A rose is a rose is a rose is a rose*. At first glance nothing would seem to be more 'normal' than this sentence. From the point of view of the expression all the elementary rules of the English code are fully respected. As for the content, it seems to offer the most elementary kind of information, the tautology for truism. In order to convey a tautological content the expression seems to rely upon an *excess of redundancy* (the same redundancy being realized on the content plane; tautology is in fact mere semantic redundancy).

Nevertheless the message gives the impression of saying something that is semantically rich and therefore highly ambiguous. The feeling of ambiguity is suggested, first of all, by the excess of expressive redundancy, which violates a stylistical norm. Rather as, when white is perceived, the physicist recognizes an excessive simultaneous overlapping of colors, so this stubborn repetition of a banal statement makes one suspect that each time the same expressive items return they mean something different. Neither botany nor logic has ever accustomed one to accept as normal such an uninformative statement, which constitutes a sort of deviation from definitional norms. These two excesses of redundancy (on expression and content planes respectively) produce an *increase of informational possibilities*: the message has in effect become a source of further and unpredictable information, so that it is now semantically ambiguous.

From this point on, the addressee is entitled to suppose that /rose/, in every one of its occurrences, might be connected with different connotative subcodes, e.g. the allegorical, the iconological, the iconic. The work is thus 'open' to multiple interpretations (44). The contextual interaction brings to life more and more meanings and, as soon as they come to light, they seem fraught with yet other possible semantic choices. It is indeed difficult to avoid the conclusion that a work of art *communicates too much* and therefore *does not communicate at all*, simply existing as a magic spell that is radically impermeable to all semiotic approach.

3.7.6. Aesthetic idiolect

However, this 'magic spell' is not as radically impermeable as might seem to be the case. First of all, it is open to a semiotic commutation test; if one changes one contextual element, all the others lose their primitive function and are usually unable to acquire another; they remain unbalanced, as on a chessboard where a bishop has been replaced by a third castle. If there is such *contextual solidarity*, then there must be a *systematic rule*.

This means that a work of art has the same structural characteristics as does a *langue*. So that it cannot be a mere 'presence'; there must be an underlying system of mutual correlations, and thus a semiotic design which cunningly gives the impression of non-semiosis.

The aesthetic text is like a multiple match played by different teams at a time, each of whom follows (or breaks) the rules of their own game. Is it possible that in such a situation the way in which the baseball players deviate from their norm has something to do with the way in which the soccer players deviate from their own? This is rather the impression given by a work of art, so that a foul committed by a baseball player reveals itself not only as a witty solution that the rules of baseball must henceforth admit, but also as a device that should put into a different strategical perspective the 'hands!' committed by a distant soccer player.

Thus art seems to be a way of interconnecting messages in order to produce a text in which: (a) *many* messages, on different levels and planes of the discourse, are *ambiguously* organized; (b) these ambiguities are not realized at random but follow a *precise design*; (c) both the normal and the ambiguous devices within a given message exert a *contextual pressure* on both the normal and ambiguous devices within all the others; (d) the way in which the norms of a given system are offended by one message *is the same* as that in which the norms of other systems are offended by the various messages that they permit.

At every level (for every message) the solutions are articulated according to a homologous system of solutions, and every deviation springs from a *general deviational matrix*. Therefore, in a work of art *a super-system of homologous structural relationships* is established rather as if all levels were definable on the basis of a single *structural model* which determined all of them. But every system ruled by that deviational matrix is not only homologous to the others so ruled. Where this is the case, a work of art might be an admirable complex of interconnecting structures, but it would not necessarily have any particular semiotic status. However, on the basis of this structural arrangement of mutual homologies, the work of art seems to acquire a new status as a *super sign-function*.

Insofar as the aesthetic text has a self-focusing quality, so that its structural arrangement becomes one of the contents that it conveys (and maybe even the most important one), the way in which the rules are rearranged on one level will represent the way in which they are rearranged on another. Furthermore, it is the ambiguous arrangement of one level that provokes a reassessment on another: in /a rose is a rose is a rose is a rose/ the puzzling redundancy of the lexical level stands for a semantic complication on the definitional one. Thus the deviational matrix not only represents a structural rearrangement: it entails a rearrangement of the codes themselves. It thus represents the proposal of a *new coding possibility*.

This new code is apparently spoken by only one speaker, and understood by a very restricted audience; it is a semiotic *enclave* which society cannot recognize as a social rule acceptable by everyone. Such a type of private code is usually called an 'idiolect'. The rule governing all deviations at work at every level of a work of art, the unique diagram which makes all deviations mutually functional, is the *aesthetic idiolect*. Insofar as it can be applied by the same author to many of his own works (although with slight variations), the idiolect becomes a general one governing the entire *corpus* of an author's work, i.e. his *personal style*. Insofar as it is accepted by an artistic community and produces imitations, mannerisms, stylistic habits, etc., it becomes a *movement-idiolect*, or a *period-idiolect*, studied by criticism or the history of ideas as the main artistic feature of a given historical group of period. Insofar as it produces new norms accepted by an entire society, the artistic idiolect may act as *a meta-semiotic judgment changing common codes* [45].

The work-idiolect, the *corpus*-idiolect, the movement-idiolect and the period-idiolect form a hierarchy of increasingly abstract models each of which constitutes the individual performance of an underlying competence, granted that not only do competences allow performances but that performances also establish new forms of competence. The aesthetic idiolect produces over-coding rules; for example nowadays it is impossible to perform certain lexical cross-breedings without recalling Joyce's pun-technique. If someone, whether consciously or unconsciously, follows the rule for making *mots-valise à la Joyce* he is not speaking 'ungrammatical' English so much as 'Finneganian'. What he is really saying is far less important than the underlying statement: "*I am joycing*".

To detect an aesthetic idiolect is no easy matter, and can in fact only be accomplished when the idiolect in question is highly standardized. The more the work submits to 'commercial' influence, the more connected to previous idiolectal experiences its underlying idiolect will seem; the more the work is immediately recognizable as 'true art' (i.e. Kitsch art, Midcult, philistine

Beauty, *art pompier*, pocket-*musée imaginaire*), the more the idiolectal model will recur unvaried and clearly recognizable on all levels.

But even when the critic has isolated the idiolect of a work, this does not mean that he is in possession of a formula that could engender similar works. If considered as a work-idiolect the formula could only permit the production of another work that was absolutely identical to the first. If considered as a *corpus* or period-idiolect, the structural model is no more than a general schema to be embodied in a new substance. The difference between that schema and a given work is the same as that between a code and its possible messages. But another reason for the irreproducibility of works of art is that however carefully the idiolect is isolated, it will never take into full account the form of the work's lower levels. As a matter of fact although each further act of criticism will bring to light more precise idiolectal definitions of the work, the greater the stature of the latter, the more the critical process will constitute continuous and unfinished approximations. In other cases the formula can produce satisfactory new works; but here the more exactly the imitator understands the idiolect, the more eager he will be to emphasize the model that he has isolated; thus *pastiches* are more acceptable than mere imitations. When successful, a *pastiche* (such as Proust's re-making of Balzac or Flaubert) represents a witty piece of criticism; it clarifies the characteristics of its models, ironically stressing some of their nodal or peripheral devices. The ruling presence of the aesthetic idiolect can be either detected by a critical analysis or confusedly 'felt' by an intelligent though non-technical reading.

The addressee 'senses' the surpluses of both expression and content, along with their correlating rule. This rule must exist, but to recognize it requires a complex process of abduction: hypotheses, confrontations, rejected and accepted correlations, judgments of appurtenance and extraneity. This process produces three of the results mentioned in 3.7.1.: existing codes are focused and submitted to change or partial revision; the relation between accepted content-systems and states of the world is frequently challenged; and a new type of 'conversational' interaction is established between the sender and his addressee.

Let us examine these three results in the following paragraphs.

3.7.7. Aesthetic code-changing

The semiotic notion of an aesthetic idiolect explains the vague impression of 'cosmicity' that the addressee feels when contemplating a work of art. Insofar as every one of its levels is semiosically interconnected, the aesthetic text continuously transforms its denotations into new connotations; none of its items stop at their first interpretant, contents are never received for their own sake but rather as the sign-vehicle for something else. If the idiolect were rendered metalinguistically explicit, the reading of the work would be nothing more than a correct decoding.

Peirce recognized that a moment of hypothetical tension arouses a feeling similar to that engendered by a piece of music. One can thus understand why and how the interpretive effort demanded by a work of art releases this kind of strong and complex feeling that aestheticians have named in various ways (pleasure, enjoyment, excitement, fulfillment and so on), always believing that it was a form of 'intuition'. There is some degree of philosophical laziness in merely labelling as 'intuition' every experience that demands an excessively subtle analysis in order to be described. But common artistic experience also teaches us that art not only elicits feelings but also *produces further knowledge*. The moment that the game of intertwined interpretations gets under way, the text compels one to reconsider the usual codes and their possibilities. Every text threatens the codes but at the same time gives them strength; it reveals unsuspected possibilities in them, and thus changes the attitude of the user toward them.

Through the close dialectical interrelationship maintained between message and code, whereby each nourishes the other, the addressee becomes aware of new semiosic possibilities and is thereby compelled to rethink the whole language, the entire inheritance of what has been said, can be said, and could or should be said. By increasing one's knowledge of codes, the aesthetic message changes one's view of their history and thereby *trains* semiosis. While doing this, the aesthetic experience challenges the accepted organization of the content and suggests that the semantic system could be differently ordered, had the existing organization been sufficiently frequently and persuasively challenged by some aspect of the text.

But to change semantic systems means *to change the way in which culture 'sees' the world*. Thus a text of the aesthetic type which was so frequently supposed to be absolutely extraneous to any truth conditions (and to exist at a level on which disbelief is totally 'suspended') arouses the suspicion that the correspondence between the present organization of the content and 'actual' states of the world is neither the best nor the ultimate. The world could be defined and organized (and therefore perceived and known) through other semantic (that is: conceptual) models.

This epistemological principle might seem to be mere metaphorical license. It is certainly a common enough experience to 'feel' (while reading a poem, watching a play, looking at a painting, etc.) that maybe 'things' are not quite as they usually seem. However, to simply suggest that a work of art 'tells the Truth' would be of little semiotic value and would not greatly differ from certain poetic statements (like "Beauty is truth, truth beauty"), which, when assumed as philosophical principles, are really astoundingly silly.

So that, in order to be verified, this semiotic principle requires a thoroughgoing analysis of the semantic shiftings engendered by an aesthetic text (see for instance, Eco, 1973 f : although not aiming at an exhaustive demonstration, that essay at least tries to furnish general directions for a further and more concrete examination of the problem). If aesthetic texts can modify our concrete approach to states of the world then they are of great importance to that branch of a theory of sign production that is concerned with the labor of connecting signs with the states of the world.

3.7.8. Aesthetic text as a communicational act

Finally, aesthetic texts possess one quality that makes them a peculiar example of sign production labor intended to establish pragmatic relations between communicators, through a complex network of presuppositional acts. Inasmuch as the idiolect constitutes a sort of final (though never completely achieved) definition of the work, to read an artistic product means at once: (i) to *induce*, that is to infer a general rule from individual cases, (ii) to *abduce*, that is to test both old and new codes by way of a hypothesis; (iii) to *deduce*, that is to check whether what has been grasped on one level can determine artistic events on another, and so on. Thus all the modes of inference are at work. Like a large labyrinthine garden, a work of art permits one to take many different routes, whose number is increased by the criss-cross of its paths.

First of all the comprehension of an aesthetic text is based on a dialectic between acceptance and repudiation of the sender's codes — on the one hand — and introduction and rejection of personal codes on the other. If the more usual form of abduction consists in proposing tentative codes in order to disambiguate an uncoded situation, then aesthetic abduction consists in proposing certain tentative codes in order to make the author's message understandable. The addressee does not know what the sender's rule was; he tries to extrapolate it from the disconnected data of his aesthetic experience. He may believe that he is correctly interpreting what the author meant, or he may decide to test new interpretive possibilities upon the text the author has set out before him. But in so doing, he never wants to completely betray the author's intentions. So that in the interpretive reading a dialectic between *fidelity* and inventive *freedom* is established. On the one hand the addressee seeks to draw excitement from the ambiguity of the message and to fill out an ambiguous text with suitable codes; on the other, he is induced by contextual relationships to see the message exactly as it was intended, in an act of fidelity to the author and to the historical environment in which the message was emitted.

In this dialectic between fidelity and initiative two kinds of knowledge are generated: (a) a combinational knowledge about the entire range of possibilities available within the given codes; (b) a historical knowledge about the circumstances and the codes (indeed all the norms) of a given artistic period. Thus the semiotic definition of the work of art explains why, (i) in the course of aesthetic communication an experience takes place which can neither be reduced to a definite formula nor foreseen in all of its possible outcomes; (ii) yet at the same time this 'open' experience is made possible by something which should have (and indeed has) a structure at all levels. Thus the semiotic definition of an aesthetic text gives the *structured model* for an *unstructured process of communicative interplay*.

A responsible collaboration is demanded of the addressee. He must intervene to fill up semantic gaps, to reduce or to further complicate the multiple readings proposed, to choose his own preferred paths of interpretation, to consider several of them at once (even if they are mutually incompatible), to re-read the same text many times, each time testing out different and contradictory presuppositions.

Thus the aesthetic text becomes a multiple source of *unpredictable 'speech acts'* whose real author remains undetermined, sometimes being the sender of the message, at others the addressee who collaborates in its development [46].

3.8. The rhetorical labor

3.8.1. Rhetoric's legacy

A theory of sign production must take into account the labor performed in order to overcode and to switch codes. As was said in 3.1.1., this activity is commonly registered under the heading of rhetoric. In this section I shall try to show: (i) in what sense traditional rhetorical categories can be inserted into a semiotic framework; (ii) in what sense some of the problems connected with overcoding and code-switching go beyond the usual rhetorical framework and ask for either a new and semiotically oriented rhetoric or for new and autonomous branches of semiotics; (iii) in what sense many of the discussions about 'ideology' and 'ideological discourse' come within the scope of a semiotically oriented rhetoric and how the entire problem of ideology can be studied from a semiotic point of view (Genette, 1966; Todorov, 1967; Groupe μ, 1970; Barthes, 1970). In order to achieve these aims, let us try to summarize and schematize the objects of classical rhetoric, adding certain items that ancient rhetoric did not consider, but that modern rhetoric, whether semiotically oriented or not, either does or should.

Table 47

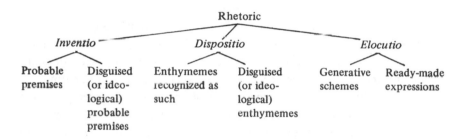

Classical rhetoricians viewed their discipline as the art of persuasion. Persuasion was not necessarily an underhand device but rather a socially oriented form of reasoning that did not deal with 'first principles' (such as those of formal logic, i.e. identity, non-contradiction and the excluded middle principle) and could not therefore use apodictic syllogisms. Thus rhetoric, like dialectics, was only dealing with *probable* premises (and therefore ones that were open to discussion); while dialectics aimed to derive an acceptable conclusion from these premises on reasonably logical grounds, rhetoric overtly dealt with *enthymemes*, i.e. syllogisms that also moved from probable premises, but to *emotionally* and *pragmatically* influence the listener. In recent times the so-called 'new rhetoric' (Perelman, 1958) has definitely reduced apodictic discourses to axiomatical systems alone, and has listed all other types of discourse (from philosophy to politics or theology) under the rhetorical heading. Thus almost all human reasoning about facts, decisions, opinions, beliefs and values is no longer considered to be based on the authority of Absolute Reason but instead intertwined with emotional elements, historical evaluations, and pragmatic motivations. In this sense the new rhetoric considers the persuasive discourse not as a subtle fraudulent procedure but as a technique of 'reasonable' human interaction, controlled by doubt and explicitly subject to many extra-logical conditions.

If rhetoric is considered in this way, it represents one of the more complex manifestations of sign production, involving the choice of given probable premises, the disposition of rhetorical syllogisms (or other forms of many-valued logic) and the necessary 'clothing' of expressions with rhetorical figures. This activity has its own rules (Perelman has listed many of them) and in the last analysis it constitutes the object of a *semiotics of conversational interaction*. The main requirement of this activity is that the rules be respected; and one of the most important of these rules is an explicit recognition of the one-sidedness of the premises and an acceptance of the principle that, under different circumstances, the issues might also differ.

But there is also 'aberrant' performance of the same type of sign production which results in an 'ideological' discourse (and under that heading I would list all forms of fraudulent propaganda and mass persuasion, as well as many so-called 'philosophical' statements); I mean by ideological discourse a mode of argument that, while using probable premises and considering only a partial section of a given semantic field, pretends to develop a 'true' argument, thus covering up the contradictory nature of the Global Semantic System and presenting its own point of view as the only possible conclusion (whether this attitude is deliberately and cynically adopted by a sender in order to deceive a naive addressee, or whether the sender is simply the victim of his own one-sidedness). The problem of the ideological discourse, which may help to throw a new light on the structure of the Global Semantic System, will be examined in 3.9. It too concerns a triple manipulation at all rhetorical levels (*inventio*, *dispositio* and *elocutio*).

3.8.2. *Elocutio* as overcoding

In order to better understand these points something has to be said about what is commonly and restrictively believed to be 'rhetoric' in its entirety, that is, the various techniques of *elocutio*. In order to force the listener to pay attention to the premises and arguments one must stimulate his attention; it is here that *rhetorical figures* (or the various figures of thought, figures of speech and tropes) come in, these being the embellishments by means of which the discourse acquires an unusual and novel appearance, thus offering an unexpectedly high rate of information.

Unfortunately, in the last two centuries rhetoric has suffered from a rather bad reputation because of the two ways in which the notion of 'figure of speech' can be viewed. According to the ancient theorists a figure of speech was a *schema of unexpectedness* that provided the rules for replacing a word (along with corresponding concept), by means of other words and concepts. In this sense they are *generative rules* of *overcoding*: and this is how figures of speech will be considered in the following paragraph.

But rhetorical usage, throughout the centuries, has generated a lot of *ostablished* rhetorical expressions. Starting as the theory of a particular type of manipulation of language, rhetoric has become, step by step, a store of pre-established instances of manipulation. Thus rhetoric frequently meant a repertoire of *ready-made sentences* offered as models of 'good writing' or 'good speaking'. This repertoire included either pre-tested stylistic devices with an overcoded connotation of "artistry" (one outlet for these ready-made syntagms is Kitsch — see Eco, 1964), a mode of sign production which cajoles its audience by the use of formulas which have already been tried out and have acquired a certain prestige, or pre-established connotations with a fixed emotional value (figures such as /fatherland/, /free world/, the image of the mother and child connoting 'pure' feelings, etc.), and so on.

In this sense rhetoric is the result of a millenary overcoding that has in some cases produced catachreses, that is, figures of speech so strictly coded that the entity for which they stood has definitely lost its proper sign-vehicle, as in the case of the /table's legs/.

These and other results of rhetorical overcoding cannot be the object of a theory of sign production and should rather be that of a theory of codes that deals with overcoded ready-made expressions. When used in sign production, they have a merely ornamental role and when employed to cover up a cruder content (as in the case of an expression like /peace with honor/ used instead of «peace but not immediately») they fall under the heading of *elocutio* as used in ideological discourses (see 3.9.).

3.8.3. Metaphor and metonymy

But rhetorical figures are not merely 'embellishments'. When originally and creatively used they do in fact change the way in which the content is taken into consideration. A semiotic explanation of rhetorical figures can be attempted by developing the theory of the sememe (as outlined in 2.11.) along with that of Model Q (see 2.12.).

In this paragraph I shall limit myself to a further consideration of two typical rhetorical figures, *metaphor and metonymy*. According to Jakobson (1956) these depend respectively on the axe of paradigm and syntagm; they thus represent two different procedures: one of substitution by similarity and the other of substitution by contiguity.

If one considers two sememes some of whose 'readings' have semantic markers in common, one can easily understand what is meant by 'similarity'. Granted that both the sememe «dog» and the sememe «friar» possess the same connotative marker of «fidelity» (to their master) and «defense» (dogs defend their masters and friars defend the principles of the religion) it was easy during the twelfth century to invent for an order of mendicant friars (the Dominicans) the metaphor "dogs of God" (*domini canes*) [47]. In this way the notion of 'similarity' no longer involves a suspected resemblance based on the thing itself (even though it often helps to make people believe so); a 'similarity' between semantic markers is simply a *semic identity*. On the other hand metonymy often seems to be a simple matter of overcoding; substitution by syntagmatic contiguity is based on the fact that, given a ready-made syntagm, established habits will permit one of its elements to be substituted for another. Thus given the accepted semiotic judgment /the President of the United States officially lives in the White House/ it is easy to use /the White House/ as a metonymy for /the President of the United States/.

However, a further consideration of such mechanisms shows that the fact of living in the White House is conventionally accepted as a semantic property of the cultural unit «President of the U.S.» – granted that a semantic system is more like an encyclopedia than a dictionary (see 2.11.3.).

Thus, in order that there be a conventionally accepted contiguity between two items of a ready-made syntagm it is necessary that such a syntagm be a semiotic statement. Since a semiotic statement attributes to a sememe some of its coded markers, metonymy also relies on the sememic spectrum of a given cultural item. Instead of being a case of semic identity it is a case of *semic interdependence*.

This semic interdependence can be of at least two types: (i) a marker standing for the sememe to which it belongs (/the sails of Columbus/ for «the ships of Columbus»); (ii) a sememe standing for one of its markers (/Harry is a regular fish/ for «Harry swims very well»).

However, the notion of semic interdependence does not take into account the difference between *synecdoche* and *metonymy* posited by classical tradition: the former being 'a substitution within the framework of the conceptual content', and the latter a substitution 'with other aspects of reality with which a given thing is customarily connected' (see for instance Lausberg, 1949).

It is true that such a distinction is based on a confusion between intensional and extensional approaches and does not take note of the nature of the sememe as encyclopedia. In this latter perspective one cannot accept that the relationship between 'grapes and bunch' is a synecdoche while the one between 'grapes and Bacchus' is a metonymy, since even the fact that grapes (and wine) are in some way connected to Bacchus should be registered by the semantic representation of «grapes».

But it cannot be denied that the dichotomy we have proposed is poorer than the traditional classification. Distinctions such as *pars pro toto, totum pro parte, genus pro specie, species pro genere* etc. (concerning synecdoche) and *causa pro effecto, effectus pro causa, a possessore quod possidetur, inventas ab inventore, ab eo quod continet quod continetur*, etc. (concerning metonymy) seem to be rather important from a semantic point of view [48].

One could object that the addressee usually 'understands' a metonymy or a synecdoche disregarding these distinctions and only grasping general relationships of interdependence. But it is also true that these distinctions directly concern the 'good' organization of the sememe and the problem (discussed in 2.11.1.) of *semiotic entailment* or "meaning inclusion". As a matter of fact, if a sememe were a non-hierarchical aggregation of disconnected markers, one should say that the sememe «male» has the denotative marker «human» and the sememe «human» can have a connotative marker of «male». But the system of semiotic inclusions asks for a precise hierarchization; therefore every marker denotes (by semiotic entailment) the class in which it is included and connotes the members of which it is the class (see also Greimas' opposition between 'axes and semes' in 2.9.5.). Thus a sememe denotes the *genus* of which it is a *species* by *hyperonymy*, and connotes the *species* of which it is a *genus* by *hyponymy* («scarlet» denotes «red» and «red» connotes «scarlet»). This explains all the rhetorical distinctions linked to the phenomenon of synecdoche. As for metonymy, a satisfactory solution can be reached by inserting within the semantic representation n-places predicates according to a typology of *roles* or 'cases' (cf. 2.11.1.). In this way one can record relations such as *causa pro effecto* and vice versa, *a possessore quod possidetur, ab eo quod continet quod continetur* etc.

Let us examine the *Aeneid*, 10,140:

vulnera dirigere et calamos armare veneno

where /vulnera dirigere/ means «to inflict a blow (in order to cause wounds)» and stands for /dirigere tela/, /dirigere ictus/, /dirigere plagas/ or /vulnerare/. Let us suppose that it stands for /dirigere tela/ (with /dirigere ictus/ the result would be the same). A tentative representation of /telum/, excluding many other possible selections and referring to *a standard* Latin, appears as follows (where R is the Result of the action exercised):

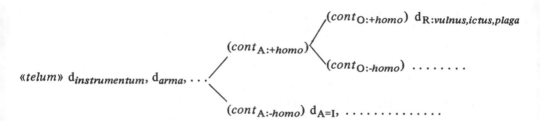

Then /vulnera dirigere/ is a metonymy of the type (i) — marker for sememe — and represents a case of substitution of the instrumental cause by the effect. If the same expression stands for /vulnerare/ the rhetoric mechanism would not change, except that it would be a little more complex:

$$\textit{vulnerare} \quad d_{actio} \quad\quad d_{ferire} \quad\quad, d_{A:homo}, d_{O:homo}, d_{P:vulnus}, d_{I:telum} \cdots c_{directio}$$
$$\textit{factum} \quad\quad \textit{percutere}$$
$$\textit{motus} \quad\quad \textit{icere}$$

In fact «vulnus» instead of «vulnerare» would be a substitution of the efficient cause by the effect, but there is also a partial substitution of the connotation of «direction» for the directional act of wounding: a very risky synecdoche indeed (that can work only when supported by the 'stronger' metonymy).

Let us now suppose that, in order to indicate a friend of mine who is a bachelor, I say /that unlucky seal!/. Provided that my audience has read Katz, Fodor and Postal (and in the circle that I move in everybody has), the substitution is easily understood. The problem that arises here is whether this rhetorical figure is a metaphor or a metonymy. Since /bachelor/ as human male being and /bachelor/ as seal are both readings of the same sememe, one should speak of replacing a sememe with one of its markers and therefore of a type (i) metonymy. Nevertheless it is clear that the substitution was based on the 'identity' of the marker «unmated» (which is more general than «never-married» and which in any case springs from «never-married» because of the redundancy rules). At this point only two solutions are possible: either the two «bachelors» are simply different but synonymous sememes, or one must speak of metaphor even when dealing with a semic identity between two different readings of the same sememe. In any case, insofar as metaphor is no longer considered as a similarity between things, and metonymy is no longer considered as a contiguity between things, the categories of both semic identity and semic interdependence are a matter of *infra-* or *inter-sememic connections*. In this perspective even semic identity is permitted by the underlying texture of the semantic system, so that a sort of *structural contiguity* supports and governs all these rhetorical interactions. Metaphors and metonymies are made possible by the existence of a semantic global universe whose format is that of Model Q. [49].

3.8.4. Rhetorical code-changing

At this point it becomes necessary to establish by what rule 'good' metaphors or metonymies are distinguished from 'bad' or 'trivial' ones. A tentative solution might be as follows: a good metaphor occurs when the 'identical' markers are comparatively peripheral and particularly characteristic of the two sememes in question. To call a group of warriors /men!/ is clearly an embryonic metonymy because all soldiers are men, but «man» is a marker shared by many other sememes and consequently this kind of substitution does not particularly characterize a warrior. But if one says /I have two thousand swords at my disposal/ in order to convey that one has two thousand warriors at one's command, then we have a more successful metonymy since warriors are the only type of men to have swords.

A better example of successful metonymy is offered by the interdependence established by the Romans between «gladiator» and «ready to die» or «death-seekers» (*Ave Caesar, morituri te salutant!*). In this latter case not only does the metonymy seem more 'inventive' but it increases one's awareness of the semantic entity «gladiator».

Suppose now that one substitutes «warrior» by «gladiator», and «gladiator» by «*moriturus*». Not only are warriors seen in a less customary light but they are also characterized by a peripheral marker that is shared by other sememes that might up to this point have been considered far removed from the one under examination. For instance it now becomes possible to associate a warrior metaphorically with a «scapegoat» (as a «*moriturus*» by definition), so that an army of warriors may be defined as /the scapegoats of the King's ambitions/. Insofar as «scapegoat» has a marker of «innocence» the way to a more complex network of substitutions is open; the warriors can become /two thousand innocent swords/. And so on. At the extreme point of this substitutional shifting the way in which warriors are usually viewed has enormously changed; the connotations of «fierceness», «courage», «pride», and «victory» do not disappear, but merge with *antonymous* connotations such as «fear», «sorrow», «shame» and «defeat».

The rhetorical tracing of underlying connections in the semantic fields has revealed fertile contradictions. Since it has to take place between branches of the sememes, and since any node within these branches is the patriarch of a new sememe (see Model Q), rhetorical substitution, by establishing further connections, runs the whole gamut of the Global Semantic Field, revealing its 'topological' structure. In this activity contextual and circumstantial selections are frequently switched and overlapped, and short circuits of all sorts create sudden and unpredictable connections. When this process is rapid and unexpected and joins up very distant points, it appears as a 'jump' and the addressee, though confusedly sensing its legitimacy, does not detect the series of steps within the underlying semantic chain that join the apparently disconnected points together. As a result he believes that the rhetorical invention was the product of an intuitive perception, a sort of 'illumination', or a sudden revelation, whereas in fact the *sender* has simply caught a glimpse of the paths that the semantic organization entitled him to cross. What was for him a rapid but distinct look at the possibilities of the system becomes for the *addressee* something vague and indistinct. The latter attributes to the former a superior intuitive capacity, whereas the former knows that he had a more immediate and articulated view of the underlying structure of the semantic system. Both have, however, discovered a new way of connecting semantic units, so that the rhetorical process (which can, in some cases, equal the aesthetic one) thus proves itself to be a form of knowledge, or at least *a way of upsetting acquired knowledge* [50].

Suppose, reformulating Table 15 in 2.9.6. in order to get an *ad hoc* example, that there is an axis containing two semantic units (u_1 and u_2), that are usually considered mutually incompatible, because their first respective denotative markers are units derived from an oppositional axis (α_2 vs. α_1), but that, through α_1, have a connotation γ_1 in common (Table 48).

Let us now suppose that, through a series of rhetorical substitutions, a sememe can be named (and therefore rendered rhetorically equivalent: ≒) either (i) by one of its markers (a case of metonymical substitution, represented by *mtn*, followed where necessary by the marker via which the connection is made), or (ii) by another sememe with which it shares a given marker (a case of metaphorical substitution represented by *mtf*, followed by the marker upon which the substitution relies), as shown in Table 49.

Table 48

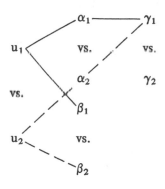

Table 49

$$((u_1 \, (mtn \, \alpha_1) \equiv \gamma_1) \cdot (\gamma_1 \, (mtn \, \alpha_2) \equiv u_2)) \rightarrow (u_1 \, (mtf \gamma_1) \equiv u_2)$$

Provided that the rules not of formal logic but of rhetoric are in play, then u_1 (because of its equivalence to u_2) acquires both markers α_1 and α_2, which were previously seen to be antonymically incompatible (Table 50).

Table 50

Sometimes the incompatibility thus challenged reveals itself in some form of 'wit' (a baroque device, as in *oxymorons*: /a strong weakness/). Sometimes the oppositional axis is really upset and the addressee must ask himself whether it needs to be reorganized. At other times the incompatibility remains unaccepted by the codes, despite which the rhetorical figure continues to operate, thus creating a feeling of unbalance and allowing logicians to assert that natural languages have no logic.

It is in fact frequently the case that sign production procedures in natural language are without logic but do involve rhetoric, this latter being nothing more than a *fuzzy logic*. When only words and elementary figures of thought are involved, these incompatibilities are commonly accepted as legitimate rhetorical games.

It would seem therefore that only *elocutio* is involved, while both the premises (the concern of *inventio*) and the arguments (the concern of *dispositio*) remain unchallenged.

But suppose, for instance, that the semantic tree of «bachelor» proposed in the KF Model could be rewritten as in Table 51, in accordance with the Revised Model:

Table 51

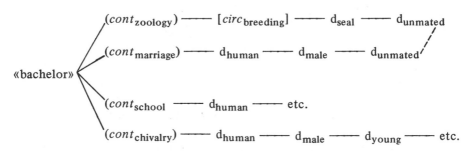

It is thus possible to metaphorically substitute the bachelor-seal for the bachelor-man because both possess the very specific marker «unmated» and to elaborate the rhetorical definition /that unlucky seal/ for a friend who has never married. Through a further metonymical series of substitutions it would then be possible to substitute «animal» for «human» and to call him a /poor beast/. Everybody would accept this series of substitutions as a pleasantly ironical joke without denying its legitimacy on the grounds of a two-valued logic or of an excessively rigorous semantic theory.

Nevertheless the joke may conceal a 'poetic truth' which is simply a form of inferred knowledge: what if being a bachelor really were a sad condition, in spite of the many peripheral connotations which suggest that bachelors are free, happy, ready for all sorts of erotic adventures? These suspicions entail a revision of many customary premises; a jocular figure of speech may thus release a discussion about whole areas of accepted values.

3.8.5. Rhetorical code-switching

However, the discussion of accepted values becomes explicit when it assumes an enthymematic aspect. When enthymematic reasoning explicitly assumes that the premises from which it starts are probable (i.e. matters of opinion), the rules of the game are observed and straightforwardly persuasive intercourse results. But very little is needed to turn a straightforwardly persuasive argument into an 'ideological' one. The threshold between these two types of reasoning will be demonstrated by a concrete example.

In 1969, and for many years before, dietetic foods were largely advertised in the American market. Since sugar was supposed to produce fatness, and fatness was linked with several illnesses, including heart attacks, dietetic foods eliminated sugar and replaced it with cyclamates. In November 1969 a medical research program discovered that cyclamates could produce cancer. Thus all dietetic foods that advertised the presence of cyclamates among their main ingredients had to be removed from the market. Because this decision was causing an economic crisis among many industrial corporations, new packaged dietetic foods were sold advertising the absence of cyclamates, and further stressing their elimination by adding the label: "with sugar added".

At first sight the solution might sound rather paradoxical, for it is clearly idiotic to advertise a dietetic food by stating that it contains sugar — a substance widely recognized as a fattening element. Nevertheless this new approach to advertising was accepted by the consumers.

In order to explain this phenomenon one might well assume that until November 1969 American society accepted some sort of implicit coding which established the series of mutually exclusive oppositions and connotatively established implications recorded in Table 52.

Table 52

sugar	=	fat	=	heart attack	=	death	=	(-)
vs.		vs.		vs.		vs.		
cyclamates	=	thin	=	(no heart attack)	=	life	=	(+)

A sort of hyperconnotation marked the second column as positive (+) and the first as negative (-). On the grounds of this coded series of correspondences and opposition, a series of semiotic statements could maintain that sugar produced fatness (and therefore heart attacks) while cyclamates produced slimness (and therefore guaranteed a longer life).

The factual statement associating cyclamates with cancer acted (through the authority of the scientists that pronounced it) as a meta-semiotic statement which gave rise to new semiotic statements associating cyclamates with cancer and death. Thus within the space of a few days the social competence accepted a new series of correspondences and oppositions (see Table 53).

Table 53

$$\begin{array}{ccccccc}
\text{sugar} & = & \text{(no cancer)} & = & \text{life} & = & (+) \\
\text{vs.} & & \text{vs.} & & \text{vs.} & & \\
\text{cyclamates} & = & \text{cancer} & = & \text{death} & = & (-)
\end{array}$$

The fact that sugar was fattening fell into the background. Many newspaper interviews showed that people were of the firm belief that it was better to get fat than to get cancer. And it was easy to accept the idea that a more arduous slimming process achieved through eating lightly sugared products was preferable to a predictable neoplasm.

One must remember that the sememic spectrum of «sugar» *did not change*: it continued to be coded as fattening and therefore (by a normal redundancy rule connecting obesity with circulatory diseases) as somewhat dangerous to health. All that happened was that the sememic representation of «cyclamate», although not losing the marker «slimming», acquired that of «cancer». Thus in order to explain the reversal of the oppositional series, one must postulate the existence of a rhetorical premise which was in fact accepted by everybody and recorded in the interviews: "Better fat than dead". Insofar as this premise was a typical rhetorical *'endoxon'*, a matter of common opinion, the rules of enthymematic reasoning permitted its use for persuasive discourse. By doing so, in November 1969 one would have been performing an acceptable persuasive argument.

Suppose that my doctor had said: "Well, clearly you'll have to lose weight, but cyclamates are far too dangerous; you'd do better to give up those dietetic foods for a while. You know what I mean: better fat than dead". The argument would have been acceptable, since the doctor was not claiming to demonstrate an absolute truth, but merely trying to persuade me about a choice between two sets of values.

What made the advertiser's argument into a typical example of propaganda and 'ideological' discourse was the fact that the positive status acquired by sugar when compared to cyclamates (the axis placing them in opposition being roughly 'ways of dying') was applied to an argument concerning dietetic foods (the axis in question being: 'ways of slimming'). Thus sugar appeared to have a positive effect on slimming, when in fact it had nothing of the sort. It thus was surreptitiously given a «slimming» marker to which it had never had any right, socially recognized or otherwise.

This 'ideological' operation was performed by *code-switching* and thereby displacing an emotional connotation. A recognized but forgotten (or concealed) premise ("better fat than dead") charged sugar with a positive marker (but only according to the uncoded contextual selection «vs. cyclamates»). The ad-men then retained this marker as if it could be conventionally associated with the sememe «sugar» in every context.

This example demonstrates two things: (i) the way in which code-shifting is brought about; (ii) the fact that semantic sub-systems acquire a given status in accordance with a given contextual selection and that this status does not or ought not to remain the same when viewed from a different contextual point of view. The discussion about cyclamates was an example of 'ideological' code switching, because it pretended that the structure of a given semantic sub-system remained the same under any circumstances.

In any case the problem of ideological code-switching deserves a more thorough examination. In order to do so let us summarize all the preceding points and then establish a more abstract laboratory model.

3.9. Ideological code switching

3.9.1. Ideology as a semiotic category

In 2.14.1. when dealing with the interpretation of the expression /he follows Marx/ I said that it involved a degree of ideological connotation (is following Marx good or bad?) that determined the interpretation but did not depend on any previous coding. In this sense the ideological background on which the interpreter relied in order to disambiguate the sentence was reached through a complex inference, involving a series of presuppositions about the sender or the object of the sentence. Detection of the speaker's world vision depends on a process of interpretation rather than on previous codes. Thus ideology would appear to be an extra-semiotic residue which is able to determine semiotic events, acting as a catalyst in many abductive processes, but which escapes cultural coding (see also Table 30).

But what has to be presupposed (since it is not assured by any previously established code) is that the sender subscribes to a given ideology, whereas the ideology itself, the object of the presupposition, is an organized world-vision which must be subjected to a semiotic analysis.

A semantic system or sub-system is one possible way of giving form to the world. As such it constitutes a *partial interpretation* of the world and can theoretically be revised every time new messages which semantically restructure the code introduce new positional values. A message which states that /Martians eat babies/ not only charges the sememe «Martians» with a connotation of «cannibalism» but carries a whole chain of connotations resulting from the global axiological attribution of «negativity». Clearly a series of messages which explain that Martians do eat babies, but babies of a different species, just as we eat 'baby' animals, could change the global axiological connotation. But such a revision of the code implies a series of meta-semiotic statements which question the connotative subcodes — this being the critical function of science.

But in general any addressee will turn to his own cultural inheritance, his own partial world vision, in order to choose the subcodes that he wishes to apply to the message. To define this partial world vision, this prospective segmentation of reality entails a Marxist notion of ideology as 'false conscience'. Naturally, from the Marxist point of view this false conscience is born as a theoretical disguise (with pretensions to scientific objectivity) for concrete social relationships and given material conditions of life.

Ideology is therefore a message which starts with a factual description, and then tries to justify it theoretically, gradually being accepted by society through a process of overcoding. For a semiotics of codes there is no need to establish how the message comes into existence nor for what political or economic reasons; instead, it is concerned to establish in what sense this new coding can be called 'ideological'.

3.9.2. A laboratory model

Let us imagine a container divided into two parts, Alpha and Beta, by a partition in which there is a small hole. At both sides gas molecules move at different speeds. To guard the hole there is what the kinetic theory of gases calls 'Maxwell's demon'. The demon is an intelligent being who confounds the second principle of thermodynamics by allowing slower molecules to pass from Beta to Alpha, while only letting the faster ones through from Alpha to Beta. He thus causes an increase of gas temperature in Beta. We might also imagine that our demon (who is more intelligent than Maxwell's) assigns the same speed to all fast molecules. Knowing both the number of molecules and the standard velocity, we should be able to ascertain both pressure and heat with the same unit of measure.

Let us image that the demon, for every *n* molecules passing into Beta, emits a signal: each signal-unit communicates only the number of molecules judged *pertinent* for our purpose (for instance a given calculation of the pressure and heat tolerable in a given situation). So that it is the purpose that determines *the criteria of pertinence*. If the demon — as an emitter — has a very simple code such as "yes vs. no" one needs no more than an electric signal to indicate the unit of measure. Repetitions of the signal indicate the sum of the units of measure. Let us suppose that /Z/ denotes «minimum» (heat and pressure) and /ZZZZ/ denotes «maximum».

Table 54

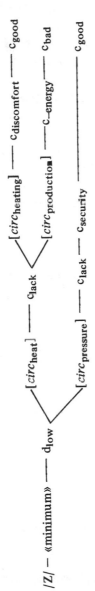

$|Z| - \langle\!\langle \text{minimum} \rangle\!\rangle \longrightarrow d_{low}$

$[cir c_{heat.}] \longrightarrow c_{lack}$

$[cir c_{heating}] \longrightarrow c_{discomfort} \longrightarrow c_{good}$

$[cir c_{production}] \longrightarrow c_{-energy} \longrightarrow c_{bad}$

$[cir c_{pressure}] \longrightarrow c_{lack} \longrightarrow c_{security} \longrightarrow c_{good}$

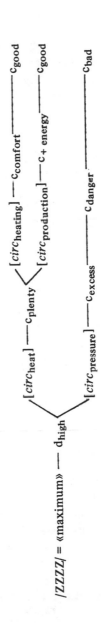

$|ZZZZ| = \langle\!\langle \text{maximum} \rangle\!\rangle \longrightarrow d_{high}$

$[cir c_{heat.}] \longrightarrow c_{plenty}$

$[cir c_{heating}] \longrightarrow c_{comfort} \longrightarrow c_{good}$

$[cir c_{production}] \longrightarrow c_{+ energy} \longrightarrow c_{good}$

$[cir c_{pressure}] \longrightarrow c_{excess} \longrightarrow c_{danger} \longrightarrow c_{bad}$

If the receiver of the message is a machine, it registers «minimum» or «maximum» values and reacts according to instructions received. The signal, in this case, is not a 'sign', nor does the machine 'understand' its 'meaning'. If on the contrary the receiver is a human being, his reaction transforms the signal into a *sign* that is the correlation between an expression and a content. But at the same time the human addressee will add certain connotative markers to the denotative ones.

For instance, the expression /ZZZZ/ when referring to the 'calculus for heat' connotes certain positive values that cannot be taken into account when the 'calculus for pressure' is considered. Moreover, if a given quantity of heat is required in order to make the room more comfortable, it will connote certain markers that obviously change when the heat is needed as a form of energy for producing something. The same goes for the expression /Z/ («minimum») so that one can establish a sememic representation for both expressions, according to different circumstantial selections (Table 54).

Both sememes, if they are to be established, require that culture subdivide the semantic space into a series of oppositional sub-systems of which only a limited number are taken into account by the various readings of the sememe.

Thus every circumstantial selection isolates oppositions that are sometimes semantically identical, sometimes not entirely homogeneous, and at others straightforwardly contradictory (Table 55).

Table 55

(1) PRESSURE	(2) HEATING	(3) PRODUCING
min vs. max	min vs. max	min vs. max
low vs. high	low vs. high	low vs. high
lack vs. excess	lack vs. plenty	lack vs. plenty
security vs. danger	discomfort vs. comfort	-energy vs. +energy
good vs. bad	bad vs. good	bad vs. good

If we represent the composition of a given sememe as the successive branching into different positions of diverse semantic axes (see 2.9.6.) then the representation of the sememe «maximum» should have at least two incompatible readings represented respectively by a continuous and a dotted line (Table 56).

3.9.3. Ideological manipulation

I shall define as an 'ideological' *inventio* a series of semiotic statements based on a previous bias (either explicit or otherwise), i.e. the choice of a given circumstantial selection that attributes a certain property to a sememe, while concealing or ignoring other contradictory properties that are equally predicable to that sememe, granted the non-linear and contradictory format of its semantic space. Thus semiotic statements represented by either continuous or dotted lines will be viewed as ideological ones.

A non-ideological statement would be a meta-semiotic one that showed the contradictory nature of its semantic space. This kind of meta-semiotic statement is represented in Table 57.

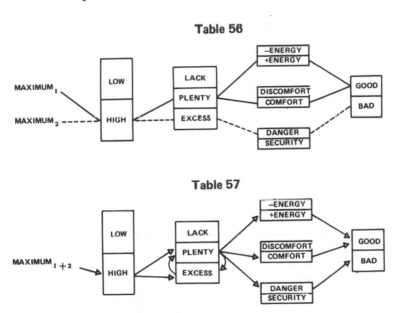

Table 56

Table 57

I shall define as an 'ideological' *dispositio* an argument which, while explicitly choosing one possible circumstantial selection as its main premise, does not make clear that there exists a contradictory premise or an apparently complementary premise which leads to contradictory conclusions – thus concealing the contradictory nature of its semantic space.

I shall also define as an 'ideological' *dispositio* an argument which although undertaking the comparison of two different premises, chooses ones that do not possess mutually contradictory markers, thus consciously or unconsciously concealing those that could upset the 'linearity' of the argument.

Suppose that there is someone who believes (or wants to make people believe) that maximum heat in the Alpha-Beta system can give both optimal heating and an optimal state of productivity. This person can set out his argument so as to show that such aims are mutually compatible and that they jointly produce a "desirable" situation (which we might call «welfare»). The argument can thus arrange the two sub-systems on which both circumstantial selections rely in the symmetrical fashion outlined in Table 58.

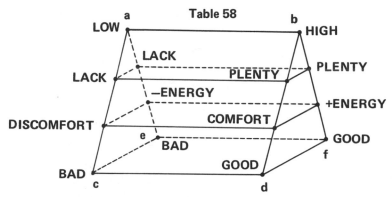

Table 58

HEATING≡PRODUCTIVITY (heating='abcd', productivity='abef')

This enthymematic model shows that there is no contradiction between the pursuit of optimal heating and that of optimal productivity.

The oppositions and the successive connotations of the square 'abcd' (representing the premise "high heat makes for good heating") are so complementary to these of the square 'abef' (representing the premise "high heat makes for good production") that if one considers the lateral triangles 'ace' and 'bdf' one will see that «discomfort» can be considered as a metonymy for «-energy» and «comfort» as a metonymy for «+energy». According to the rhetorical rules outlined in 3.8.3. these substitutions are in fact permitted by the sememic representation outlined in Table 54. It is in fact obvious enough that loss of energy can cause a less comfortable heating situation (while comfort can in turn be caused by a good supply of energy): the substitution of effect for cause or vice versa providing an excellent example of metonymy.

3.9.4. A semiotic critique of ideology

The above example of *dispositio* is 'ideological' because it does not take into account the potential contradiction between, on the one hand, «production and pressure» and on the other «heating and pressure».

Let us set out in Table 59 the symmetrical correspondences between these two sub-systems, in order to demonstrate the contradiction which clearly arises.

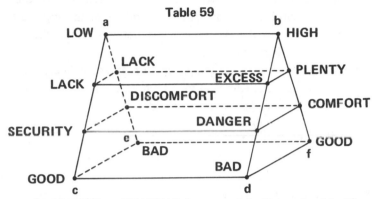

Table 59

PRESSURE vs. HEATING (pressure='abcd', heating='abef')

It will be seen that the lateral triangles present pairs of antonymous markers: «excess vs. plenty», «security vs. discomfort», «danger vs. comfort» are not mutual interpretants, nor can they be mutually substituted (except in cases of ironical oxymoron). The second level of this prismatic structure shows the incompatibilities that arise when the two points of view are compared; the base diagrammatically demonstrates the whole network of mutual incompatibility, each link producing an opposition 'good vs. bad'. The same happens when setting out 'pressure vs. production' diagrammatically.

Table 60 needs no further commentary.

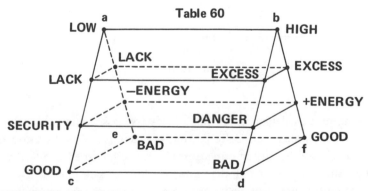

Table 60

PRESSURE vs. PRODUCTIVITY (pressure='abcd', productivity='abef')

When the connections showed by Tables 58, 59 and 60 are disregarded, two ideological discourses may potentially occur, one asserting that heating and producing are primary values to be pursued at any cost for the sake of general happiness, while concealing that they are not compatible with general security, since they produce danger; the other asserting that the most important thing is absolute security for all members of the social group in question, while concealing the fact that, if completely attained, this excludes any increase in productivity and welfare.

I am not trying to argue that the production of a good heating system is a 'bad' goal; nor indeed that aiming at maximum safety is a 'bad' idea. On the contrary, any honestly persuasive discourse about the aims of a social group must take into account all of these goals; but it must at the same time acknowledge on what grounds (i.e. according to which premises) the values are preferred and to what extent they are mutually exclusive.

In fact a critical survey of the values in question will show that they are mutually exclusive *only if* taken as absolute (i.e. logically formalized). Whereas in fact they are all *fuzzy concepts*. A critical survey of the semantic composition of these concepts would show that they were open to gradation; there is a series of intermediate states between «-energy» and «+energy» and likewise between «security» and «danger» (danger being a very low state of security and vice versa). It would thus be possible to isolate a middle portion of the energy scale which coincided with that of the security scale (provided that their 'gradients' were inversely proportional).

Table 61

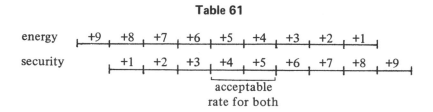

But in making such a calculation one has already trespassed upon the realm of 'ideology' by performing a critically persuasive discourse. This discourse can obviously be rejected by any interlocutor who has established a radical scale of priorities, such as "better rich than safe" (or "better safe than rich") [51]. A critical semiotic survey of ideological discourses does not eliminate the speaker's pragmatic and material motivations and therefore does not change the world (or the material bases of life). It can only contribute to making them more explicit [52].

The ideological discourse endeavors to conceal these various options, and must therefore involve a rhetorical labor of code shifting and overcoding. Thus anyone who accepts the harmonious and symmetrical correspondence between production and heating (Table 59) may well forget that the semantic unit «maximum» on which he bases his view represents not only a maximum of heat and energy but also a maximum of pressure. The only connotations connected to this unit are those of «plenty», «comfort» and «energy», which rapidly become *names* for it [53]; consequently, when someone maintains that maximum heat also means «danger», the statement is received as semantically anomalous, and believed to be referentially false. It is thus 'ideologically' interpreted as a malignant effort to disrupt the 'law and order' which governs one's uncontradicted semantic universe (i.e. one's culture, world vision, religion, 'way of life', etc.).

To recall that /maximum heat/ is not only an expression suggesting «wealth» and «comfort», but also a sign originally produced in order to mention a state of the world, and to realize that, physically, this state of the world was and *is* a growth in pressure — all this would mean putting *on its feet* a 'philosophy' that was used to standing *on its head*. But ideology is a partial and disconnected world vision; by disregarding the multiple interconnections of the semantic universe, it also conceals the pragmatic reasons for which certain signs (with all their various interpretations) were produced. This oblivion produces a false conscience [54]. Thus a theory of codes (which looks so independent from the *actual* world, naming its states through signs), demonstrates its heuristic and practical power, for it reveals, by showing the hidden interconnections of a given cultural system, the ways in which the labor of sign production can respect or betray the complexity of such a cultural network, thereby adapting it to (or separating it from) the human labor of transforming states of the world [55].

3.9.5. The ultimate threshold

This transformation cannot be performed without organizing such states of the world into semantic systems. In order to be transformed, the states of the world must be *named* and structurally arranged. As soon as they are named, that system of sign systems which is called 'culture' (which also organizes the way in which the material forces are thought of and discussed) may assume a degree of extra-referential independence that a theory of codes must respect and analyze in all its autonomy. Only in that way is it possible to outline a theory of sign production that (even when approaching the relationship between signs and things in terms of Truth and Falsehood) will profit from a purely semiotic approach.

When the Alpha-Beta system gives rise to an ideological imbalance, and semantic sub-systems stand 'on their heads', there are only two possible ways of stopping the process:(i) to make the Alpha-Beta container *explode*, so that the existence of pressure comes to light and destroys the oblivion of false conscience; this act, sometimes called 'revolution', represents another semiotic threshold that our discipline must recognize and cannot afford to trespass upon; when the Alpha-Beta container explodes, the whole system of semiotic units will go up with it, and will need to be re-built (even though there may be no semioticians around to record the new phenomenon).

(ii) to demonstrate (through a survey of the contradictory format of the semantic universe, getting back toward its sources as far as is possible by moving along the branches of the content systems and across the various code shiftings and concretions of different sign-functions) how much broader than most ideologies have recognized is the format of the semantic universe.

Granted that it is daring, but by no means absurd, to maintain that issues (i) and (ii) are mutually compatible, the semiotician may not have much *to say* on this matter, but he will have something *to do*. The labor of sign production releases social forces and itself represents a social force. It can produce both ideologies and criticism of ideologies. Thus semiotics (in its double guise as a theory of codes and a theory of sign production) is also a form of *social criticism*, and therefore one among the many forms of *social practice*.

NOTES

1. In fact any of the judgments listed in (viii) can be translated as a non-'locutory' act. For instance semiotic judgments can produce speech acts like "Are all bachelors males?", "If only all bachelors were males!", "I assure you that all bachelors are males!"; "Is this object a pencil?", "Look, a pencil!", "What a horrible pencil!"; etc. Factual judgments are susceptible to the same type of translations: "Is moon really walked on by human beings?", "Is that pencil really black?", "I define this pencil as black", "Gosh! Human beings on the moon!", "Eco-freaks, beware! Man has arrived on the moon!". Even if logically speaking all these speech acts can be reduced to assertive sentences, and even if transformationally speaking their underlying phrase markers can be reduced to that of a declarative sentence (Katz, 1972:201 ff; *sed contra*, Lakoff, 1971 a), they pose a lot of semiotic problems. I shall not be particularly dealing with them in this book but I am inclined to view the disciplines investigating such problems from language analysis to sociolinguis-

tics, from researches in interactional behavior to ethnomethodology as constituting an essential chapter of general semiotics (Austin, 1962; Searle, 1969; Cohen, 1973; Gumperz and Hymes, 1972; Cicourel, 1973).

2. When a factual judgment is emitted, the most natural attitude is to test it. Testing factual judgments is the first duty of the scientist, the historian, the newsman as well as the prudent man. It would be wrong to say that semiotics is not concerned with this activity of testing; except in the case of testing mentions, factual judgments do not send immediately back to an actual *perceptum* and demand for more mediating operations, each of them implying the recourse to a new level of semiotic conventions (for example an historian must check a factual judgment by controlling written records, archeological witnesses, and so on). This kind of labor, recorded in Table 3 under the head of 'focusing on world' should be further approached by a general semiotics. Up to now this labor has been studied by logical semantics (as well as by the methodologies of the various sciences). That until now semiotics and logic seem to have marched quite independent of each other (in spite of the methodological and philosophical chance offered by Peirce) is due to the fact that (except in the case of Morris) semiotics was more linked with linguistics and cultural anthropology. But this threshold between logic and semiotics becomes more and more imprecise and it comes to be widely trespassed by the latest researches in generative semantics and transformational grammar.

3. The way in which both factual and semiotic judgments can change the code (a way that will be further analyzed by the various sections of the present chapter) could solve a widely discussed epistemological problem, i.e. the possible relationship between a structural and a dialectic logic. If semiotic systems are structures and if the first property of a structural arrangement is the mutual solidarity of its elements (therefore implying an homeostatic permanence of the structural whole), how then can structures transform themselves into other structures (i.e., how then can codes change)? There are many positions held by different authors in some way concerned with a dialectical interpretation of structural approach; Sève (1967) maintains that structures are only transitory configurations of the 'material process' and that a structural logic is only the science of the "internodal segments of the dialectical contradiction"; thus structural logic is only an 'analytical reason' which, even though useful and necessary, does not grasp in its totality the dialectical process. Godelier (1966) maintains that there are two types of contradictions, the one *within* the structure and the one *between* the structures; the former practically corresponds to the self-contradictoriness of each code as outlined in 2.12-13.; the latter depends on the appearance of new material phenomena and could be equated with the necessity for factual judgments outlined in the present chapter (see for instance the example of cyclamates given in 3.8.5.). This double aspect of code changing is also considered by Lotman (1970) in his typology of culture, and he too accepts the idea of continuously intertwined action of both principles (changing *from outside* and changing *from inside*). The cybernetical and mathematical background of this question is dealt with by Apostel (1960) and especially by Piaget (1968). I think that the dialectic between semiotic judgments and factual judgments, along with the dialectic between codes and sign production, can constitute the basis for a dialectical theory of structural evolution in semiotics.

4. After having elaborated his criticism of Russell's dichotomy between meaning and denotation (and after having reduced it to the more suitable complementarity of signifying and mentioning) Strawson advances a conclusion which perfectly fits its philosophical purposes but does not help us in developing a semiotic theory. He says: "Neither Aristotelian nor Russellian rules give the exact logic for any expression of ordinary language, for ordinary language has not exact logic." The purpose of a theory of codes was to see if ordinary languages have, if not an *exact* one, at least *one logic*. Maybe the problem is not of finding a logic, if logic is only the theory of a formalized language. The *problem is to find a semiotic theory* which is surely different from a formal logic, but which is nevertheless able to dissolve the shade of skepticism suggested by Strawson's quotation, which may lead to the suspicion that natural languages cannot have a theory, which has to be refused if a semiotics is to subsist.

5. Once this is asserted, one may easily admit that there is a lot of difference between the semiotic function performed by a photograph and the one performed by an actual object. But in the present context identities are more important than differences. Another objection might be that the above theory of mention does not hold as far as individuals are concerned. What does it mean to say /this man is John/? According to what has been said in 2.9.2. *à propos* of denotation of proper names, it means that the semantic properties commonly correlated by a group-code to the lexeme /John/ coincide with the semantic properties that the same group-code might correlate to a given *perceptum*. It means that one must associate to the token perceptum the same notion that presumably associates to the lexeme /John/: a man who is the brother of Mary, the assistant manager of the local bank, the one that I have frequently described as the best of my friends and so on.

6. A difference exists between two ways of intending the use of /is/ and of the pointer in mentioning. If — indicating a penguin — I say /This is a cat/ and I mean «this object has the property of being a cat», then I pronounced a semiotic index-sensitive judgment which simply represents a *wrong* use of the code; from the point of view of a theory of mentioning it leads to a *false* statement. If on the contrary I mean «the name of this animal is 'cat'», then I have pronounced an exageratedly arbitrary meta-semiotic judgment that can be erroneously accepted only by a naive anthropologist who has chosen me as an untrustworthy informant.

7. Since the above analysis is performed according to the Revised Model proposed in 2.11. and since the above page represents an effort to approach the classical problems of philosophical semantics from the point of view of a semiotically oriented semantic theory (a 'merging' that has been foreboded in note 1 of this chapter) it would have been more challenging to test the power of this approach on the sentence /the present king of France is a bachelor/. May I propose from now on the use of this sentence as a symbolic guarantee of a possible merging of different approaches to the same set of problems?

8. Anyway, even though accepting the idea that Proust can translate Elstir, it would be hardly believable that Mondrian can translate Spinoza's *Etica more geometrico demonstrata* . . . .

9. See in Goodman (1968:99 ff.) an interesting discussion on artistic fakes and on the 'autographic' and 'allographic' arts; the former are not susceptible of notation and do not support free performance, the latter can be translated into conventional notation and the resulting score can be

performed through variations of a certain extent (like music). The difference between autographic and allographic is linked to the distinction between *dense* and *discrete* signals (see later, 3.4.6.).

10. Given a scale of replicability, as far as one steps down from its top (n/n of fidelity) to the inferior degrees, after a certain ratio, one seems to have trespassed on a threshold; one passes from the universe of replicas to one of similarities (see 3.5.3.). As a matter of fact such a scale is not an homologous one because the very notion of property changes beyond the threshold; in cases of replicas it is a matter of real 'same' properties, in cases of similarities it is a case of transformed and somewhat projected properties (see 3.6.7.).

11. Let us assume that in every case of *ratio facilis* there is the possibility not only of customary replicas but even of absolute duplication; it is possible to print a double of a previous word, to print a double of a king of spades and obviously to produce a double of a road signal (every replica, in this last case, being at the same time a double). The signs ruled by a *ratio facilis* can be translated by some other notation (see note 9). I can translate phonemes by means of Morse dashes and points, musical sounds from the temperate scale into written notes, and so on.

12. One should thus reformulate Morris's position by saying that these formators are just features and not signs, in the same way as a phoneme is not a sign but a combinational feature whose presence or absence changes the nature of the word. But this assumption, although it tightens up the analysis, does not change the problem. There are certain expressive features that seem to be motivated by the toposensitive markers of their content. (That is, features which directly convey a given portion of the content expressed by the expression of which they are a syntactic component).

13. On the manifold senses of the word 'analogy' during the whole history of philosophical, theological and mathematical thought, see *La linea e il circolo* by Enzo Melandri (1968). However fascinating this concept may have been and may be, I prefer to retain here only its most concretely operational sense. Even because, when speaking of iconic signs, analogy is frequently used as a synonym of unspeakability, ineffability, native resemblance: that is, simply in order not to recognize iconic devices as signs and to avoid any semiotic enquiry on them.

14. See Gibson, 1966, p. 227: "Physical optics makes a distinction between 'real' and 'virtual' images. In optics, what I have called a screen image (the picture made by projecting shadows on a surface, the structuring of an array by artificial variation of illuminations) is called a 'real' image, and so it is. What I call an optic array (the structured stimulus for an eye, chambered or compound) when it comes from a mirror or a lens is said to produce a 'virtual' image. The apparent face in the mirror and the apparently near thing in the field of a telescope, are objects in effect, not in fact, but they are not pictures or sculptures or screen images".

15. One could say that mirrored image is used as a sign in some cases, such as when I see in the mirror a person coming behind me or when I use two mirrors in order to check the cut of my hair on the nape of my neck. But these are mere cases of artificial extension of my sight, not so different from the fact of using a magnifying glass in order to see what usually I cannot.

16. The problem of ill-counterfeit doubles remains open half way

between a real double, a tentative replica and an iconic representation of the original. What is a bad imitation of a wooden cube? the Xerox of a drawing? a photomechanical reproduction of a painting, perfect in any particular, except the texture of the canvas substituted by a sheet of appropriate paper? Some of these phenomena could be listed among imprints (see 3.6.2.), some others seem to escape a precise definition. I think that, even though they are produced as doubles, they may become signs when chosen as such; in this case their semiotic nature depends on the context in which they will be inserted, and on the kind of explanation that accompanies them.

17. To prove the conventionality of the transcriptional systems, Gombrich also refers to two photographs of the same corner of Wivenhoe Park, which clearly indicate how little Constable's park has in common with that of the photograph; but he does not then go on to suggest that the photograph constitutes the parameter for judging the iconicity of the painting. No square inch in the photograph is identical with a mirror image; the black-and-white photograph only reproduces gradations of tone between a very narrow range of greys. Not one of these tones corresponds to what we call "reality". The scale depends largely on the photographer's choice in the darkroom; given two photographs (reproduced by Gombrich), the one printed within a narrow scale of greys produces an effect of misty light while the other, where stronger contrasts were used, gives a different effect.

18. If every complex iconic representation is a code in itself, then there is not one iconic code, but *many*, maybe thousands and thousands of them. Take as an hypothesis that the known languages are not the only languages in the verbal universe, but that there are a million other possible, and actually existing, languages as well; this does not spare us the task of studying semiotically how these languages are structured. It is the same in the iconic universe. The assumption that there exist as many 'languages' as messages is then a drastic assumption. It can be translated as follows: 1) there exist as many iconic languages as personal styles of an author; 2) there exist as many iconic languages as there are styles and manners typical of a school or period; 3) if the various iconic works of art treat the existing codes ambiguously, as also happens with verbal works of art (which is the *"langue"* of Joyce?), the iconic styles reserved for non-aesthetic uses follow instead more predictable systems of rules; therefore there are recognizable iconic codes in mass communication, photography, comic strips and movies.

19. To the extent that Peirce established part of his program of a typology of signs (only 10 types on the programmed 66) every sign appears as a bundle of different categories of signs. There is not an iconic sign as such, but at most an Iconic Sinsign which at the same time is a Rheme and a Qualisign, or an Iconic Rhematic Legisign (2.254). Nevertheless the classification was still possible for, according to Peirce, the different trichotomies characterized the signs from different points of view and signs were not only precise grammatical units but also phrases, entire texts, books. Thus the partial success of the Peircian endeavor (along with his almost complete failure) tells us that if one wants to draw a typology of signs one must, first of all, renounce the straight identification of a sign with a 'grammatical' unit, therefore extending the definition of sign to every kind of sign-function.

20. All this once again requires that the concept of semantic

component be freed from a verbo-centric fallacy. The semantic representation of a given expression also contains non-verbalizable markers, such as directions, spatial dispositions, relations of order and so on. Thus the content of the word /dog/ must have among its markers images of dogs, while the content of the image of a dog must have among its markers also the concept of «dog» (along with its intensional description) and the corresponding word in all possible languages. As has been said in 2.11.3. such a semantic encyclopedia is more a regulative hypothesis than a matter of individual knowledge; it is the virtual social semantic representation of a given sememe, which must be postulated in order to permit a theory of codes, able to explain every concrete act of communication.

21. However, one ought not to believe that this makes the difference between an analogical and a digital machine, for even an analogical one can produce tokens according to a *ratio facilis* (see TV scanning and broadcasting).

22. When Robinson Crusoe discovered the footprint of Friday on the seashore, the footprint conventionally denoted «man» but also connoted «barefooted». Being imprinted on the sand with a feature of direction, the context *//footprint+position+direction//* also was a text meaning: «a man has passed here».

23. Since Robinson believed himself to be the only human being on the island, a labor of inference and presupposition had thus to be performed by him so as to arrive at the conclusion: «I am not the only man here» or «there is another man on the island». This could have involved some meta-semiotic statements about the definition of the island.

24. When a trace is not previously coded, one is obliged to think that every point in the trace must have corresponded to a point on the imprinting referent. One could say that the imprint in this case is really an index, in Peirce's sense. As a matter of fact, in this case the imprint is not a sign but an act of mention. An act of mention has to be verified. But to verify a mention (see 3.3.5.) means that − given the expression /this object is six meters long/ − one has to decide if the referent, taken as an ostensive sign (3.6.3.) can be called an object and if its dimensional properties can be defined as /six meters long/. In other words, in order to check a mention, one must already know the properties of the mentioned object. Suppose now that an explorer discovers the tracks of an unknown animal. One usually believes that it is enough to reconstruct by the traces the imprinting objects by a sort of *backward projection*. But in order to abduce the animal as the cause of the imprint, one must already possess some general content-schema. It is only by interpreting the traces as those of one or more *known* animals that one can extrapolate the form of the paw of the *unknown* one. The explorer is not merely tracing a sort of direct line between the elements of the track and the elements of its cause; a series of content units works as *mediating cues*. In other words, the explorer is abducing an unknown code using excerpts of the existing ones. Only in science fiction is there the case of imprints of 'I-don't-know-what'; and in these cases it is absolutely impossible to go backward from the trace to the referent, which is called, *faute de mieux*, 'The Thing'.

25. Suppose that one finds a huge footmark. The first naive inference could be: here has passed a giant. There is a content unit (duly coded) that

has made the inference possible. But this unit is usually marked with the connotation «legendary». Thus one is interpreting a mention and discovering that this mention is mentioning something unexisting and therefore not mentionable. In such a case it is possible to assert that the mention is false; therefore the expression is a lie. If the lie had been expressed through words it would have been a mere lie; since it is expressed by a drawing, it is usually enjoyed as a *joke*. For it is easy to produce words, but it is less easy to produce images, especially if they are customarily produced by unintentional agents; moreover, the perfection of the image requires more skill than the perfection of a phrase. Thus the fake is amusing for two reasons: (1) it is an elementary case of artistic skill; (2) it falsifies something that was commonly believed to be non-falsifiable, that is, the product of a non-intentional agent. Men are supposed to lie, things aren't; thus to make things lie seems to be a rather curious achievement. So we laugh.

26. When, in a Western movie, Indians emit a coyote's cry, this full onomatopoeia plays a double role. Indian to Indian it is a purely arbitrary device, duly coded so as to transmit certain information; Indian to Whites it is a fictive sample produced in order to mean «coyote» (instead of «Indians»); therefore it is a lie.

27. Jocular gestures of menace, if not previously coded, may be taken as effective ones. If one looks at Marcel Marceau without knowing mimicry conventions one believes that he is a fool.

28. The science of music offers us an excellent model for research. Music, insofar as it has a tonal 'grammar' and has elaborated a system of notation, analyzes the continuum of sounds into pertinent features (for pitch-tones and semitones; for rhythm — metronomical beats, crochets, semibreves, etc.). Any musical discourse can be accomplished by articulating these features. The immediate objection is that, even though the notation prescribes how 'to speak' musically on the basis of a digital code, still the single message (execution) is enriched with non-coded free variants. Thus a *glissando*, a trill, a *rubato*, the length of a pause are considered (both in common and in critical language) as 'expressive' devices. But, although it recognizes these expressive facts, the science of musical notation does everything possible to codify and make replicable even the variants. It codifies the *tremolo*, the *glissato*, adds notations such as "allegro ma non troppo", etc. As will be noted, these codifications are not digital, but 'analogical', and proceed by degrees (more or less) summarily defined. But though they are not digital they can be digitalized; to demonstrate this, however, one goes not to the level of notation for an interpreter, but to that of *technical codes* of sound transcription and reproduction. Every minimal expressive variation in the grooves followed by a phonograph needle on a record corresponds to a precise feature. It will be said that these features cannot be considered as discrete either, since they proceed as a continuum of curves, of more or less accentuated oscillation. But when one considers the physical process by which we pass from this continuum of gradated curves, through a sequence of resultant electric signals and a sequence of acoustic vibrations, to the reception and retransmission of the sound through the amplifier, one is concerned with digital phenomena. From the groove to the needle, before the input into the electronic blocks of the amplifier, sound is reproduced through a continuous model; but from the input into the

electronic blocks to the output of sound from the amplifier, the process becomes discrete. The communications engineer is always trying, even in computers, to transfer analogical models into digital codes, a process which is always possible. The discrete nature of the signal is confirmed by the existence of noise. Noise can exist in the channel precisely because the emission of electrons, which is what the signal is, is a discrete phenomenon. If the passage of information were continuous for the whole process, there would be no noise.

29. The whole of generative grammar is practically concerned with the problem of vectorialization in the 'deep' phrase marker. The notions of "government", "command" and "embedding" are vectorial notions (concerning hierarchical dispositions, 'up and down' or 'before and afterward' relations). In this sense, vectorializations should be considered as contextual features, which however does not contradict the assumption made in 2.9.3., according to which the representation of the sememe involves even combinational rules. In principle, since a vectorial device is a position within a spatial or temporal arrangement, given the representation of items in the form of n-places predicates, one could assume that any representation of argument displays, as a contextual selection, the representation of its role within a given context. For instance

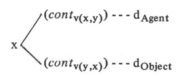

But such a solution gives rise to a first problem: is the vectorial position to be represented the one realized by surface structure or the one realized by deep structure? Lakoff (1971 a) shows that the expression /Sam claimed that John had dated few girls/ is open to both readings /Sam claimed that the girls whom John had dated were few/ and /The girls whom Sam claimed that John had dated were few/. Vectorial devices in surface structure are misleading and only a correct 'vectorialization' of the quantifier in a deeper semantic structure can disambiguate the expression. Nevertheless the labor of producing signs (and in particular 'code observing') consists in mapping the deep semantic representation in the surface structure by several rules or "constraints". These rules establish how vectorial devices may be realized and interpreted in surface structure. At this point the semantic representation (in terms of generative semantics) is an interpretant, or a compound of vectorial devices, which acts as a *metalinguistic* device able to explain the labor of choosing and producing signs. Thus vectorializations are present (i) in the metalinguistic representation of a semantic theory, (ii) in the semantic representation of the combinational possibilities of a given sememe, (iii) in the very labor of inference and presuppositions displayed in interpreting a context. Since all these problems are not sufficiently clear either for a transformational grammar or for an interpretive or for a generative semantics (and they are rather a matter of a discussion in progress) let us assume that, for the time being, the problem of vectorial devices in verbal languages is a very puzzling one and demands further research. This demonstrates that even the

most peculiar problems of a linguistically oriented semantics *cannot* be solved
without solving general semiotic problems concerning vectors at large.

30. In different languages the position of the lexeme within the surface
structure does not represent the vectorial feature which permits the correct
disambiguation of the sentence. For instance, in Italian one commonly says
/Giovanni ama Maria/ (John loves Mary) — where the Agent comes before
the Object — but it is also possible to say (even if with a shade of 'poetry')
/ama Maria Giovanni/. In this second case the position does not permit us to
recognize who is the Agent. Nevertheless, when speaking, the 'positional'
feature is easily substituted by a paralinguistic one (as Lakoff shows, 1971 b):
if I say /ama Maria, *Giovanni*!/ stressing on the second name, I have
explicitly 'vectorialized' (and paralinguistic devices are substituted, in the
written expression, by comma and exclamation mark). Sanders (1974)
reminds us that in Spanish it is possible to say both /Manuel me presentó a ti/
(Manuel presented me to you) and /Manuel te me presentó/. But in the
second case we are entitled to speak of overcoding, since the expression can
be considered as a ready-made syntagm, or an idiom.

31. For all the problems dealt with in this paragraph I am indebted to
Krampen (1973) and Volli (1972). The whole discussion on iconic signs
which has developed in *VS* magazine (1972, 1973) through the interventions
of Farassino, Casetti, Bettetini, Volli, Verón, Metz, Osmond-Smith and others
has been useful in order to clarify many points of the present discourse,
which is presented as a critical summary of the above contributions. I am also
indebted to Tomás Maldonado (personal communications), Thomas A.
Sebeok (personal communications), Roman Jakobson (personal communications) and many others.

32. Volli (1972:25), referring to the conceptions of geometry expressed
by Klein in his Erlangen Program, 1872, according to which "every geometry
is the study of the properties that remain unchanged in relation to a
determined transformation group".

33. "Let us first of all consider *congruences*, which is to say the
transformations which make each segment *correspond to a segment of equal
length*. They leave the metrical properties of the geometrical entities
unchanged, and therefore obviously do the same for the affinitive, projective
and topological ones, etc. We are concerned with what we would intuitively
call the 'equality' of geometrical figures. Two objects 'with the same form'
even if made of different substances, within the limits of the approximation
mentioned above, are evidently the simplest possible iconic signs of each
other; their iconic relation can be rigorously defined in terms of congruence between the respective forms of expression. It may be noted that
mirror reflections are also congruences" (Volli, 1972:25).

34. Let me range under the name of 'projections' all the phenomena as
homotetiae and projective transformations: "Another interesting type of
transformation is provided by the *homotetiae*, which in elementary geometry
are called similarities and do not preserve all the metrical properties of the
figures, while the affinitive, projective and topological properties remain
unchanged. A plastic model of a building is the most typical example of an
iconic sign based on *homotetiae*. We then have *projective transformations*,
which are those that give rise, among other things, to correspondences of
perspective, and in addition to the topological properties maintain unchanged

all the projective properties, such as that of 'being a straight line', 'being a second degree curve', the two-way relationship between the four points of a straight line, etc. Photographs and most graphic reproductions constitute examples of iconic signs based on projective transformations of the form of expression of the object. But in this type of sign both the perceptual principles of approximation, and the fact that the form of expression of the iconic sign is the transformation of only one part of that of the object, play an important part" (Volli, 1972:25).

35. Even the projections that seem to work as 'indexical' imprints of a given set of objects are in themselves the result of a highly simplified mapping from a few pertinent traits of a perceptual model. See Gibson (1966:190 ff.) for the way the representation of a room is realized from a given station point. The most customary mode of projection consists in considering only edges and borders. While the scientific (even though abstract) representation of the scatter-reflection of lights from surfaces gives "a dense space-filling network of reverberating rays from everywhere, every normally recognizable image of the object in the room maps only the rays from the *faces* of the surfaces and objects . . . not those from the *facets* of things . . . . It can be observed that each face, as defined by edges or corners of the surfaces, corresponds to a perspective projection"; moreover, all is mapped from a monocular point of view. It is the addressee that, in interpreting the image, fills up the empty spaces and maps backward from the 'iconic' abstraction to the perceptual model. The representation of a perceptual field is based on projective conventions, and as such has to be learned. For this reason the representation of unknown objects becomes difficult and cannot be solved by means of projective conventions, so it needs both programmed stimuli and a combination of stylizations of various types.

36. "Finally we have *topological transformations*, which only conserve certain very elementary properties, such as the continuity of lines and the arrangement of potential systems. The most typical and important example of iconic signs that derive from topological transformations is that of *diagrams*. The diagram of the underground or of a railway system, or that of the structure of an electric or electronic apparatus only have certain fundamental properties of arrangement in common with the object to which they refer, yet they conserve a great capacity for explanation, clarity and information. Topological transformations can also take into account orientation, as in a map of a city that reproduces one-way streets" (Volli, 1972:25-26).

37. In Eco (1968) — English translation as Eco (1973 *e*) — I tried to define architectural signs as manufactured objects and circumscribed spaces that signify possible functions (going up and down, coming in or out, sheltering, gathering together, sleeping, eating, celebrating events, etc.) on the basis of previous codes. In this sense I distinguished between processes of stimulation (a step that I stumble over in the dark, forcing me to raise my legs) and processes of signification: a //staircase// consists of the articulation of morphological elements which express the function for ascending; the staircase can be used only if recognized as such, and can be recognized without being used (it can even signify its function without in fact allowing it, as in cases of *trompe-l'oeil*). Thus the content of an architectural expression is a class of possible functions. In Eco (1968) I had also

distinguished between two types of signified function: *primary functions*, i.e. the first and immediate denotative content of the expression (such as going upstairs, standing at the window, living together, etc.), and *secondary functions*, i.e. the mediate connotative content (such as various 'symbolic' meanings, «mystic atmosphere», «deference», «triumph», and so on). In the article listed as Eco (1972 *c*) I have also tried to propose a model for the compositional analysis of architectural objects, such as for instance a column, taking into account many contextual and circumstantial selections, such as for instance the presence of the column among ruins, which adds to the object many 'archeological' and 'historical' connotations, duly recorded by the critical literature on architectural aesthetics. Both Eco (1968) and Eco (1972 *c*) were still linked to the notion of signs criticized in the present book. One should now read them by substituting for the notion of 'architectural sign' that of 'architectural text' in which many modes of sign production are simultaneously at work.

38. *Breviario di estetica*, Bari: Laterza, 1913, 9th ed. 1947, pp. 134-35.

39. "The political slogan 'I like Ike' [*ay layk ayk*], succinctly structured, consists of three monosyllables and counts three diphthongs [*ay*], each of them symmetrically followed by one consonantal phoneme, [..*l*..*k*..*k*]. The make-up of the three words presents a variation: no consonantal phonemes in the first word, two around the diphthong in the second, and one final consonant in the third. A similar dominant nucleus [*ay*] was noticed by Hymes in some of the sonnets of Keats. Both cola of the trisyllabic formula 'I like/ Ike' rhyme with each other, and the second of the two rhyming words is fully included in the first one (echo rhyme), [*layk*] − [*ayk*], a paronomastic image of a feeling which totally envelops its object. Both cola alliterate with each other, and the first of the two alliterating words is included in the second: [*ay*] − [*ayk*], a paronomastic image of the loving subject enveloped by the beloved object. The secondary, poetic function of this electional catch phrase reinforces its impressiveness and efficacy". In fact this message acquires part of its 'charm' because it brings into play phonic elements, and thus a sort of 'musical' quality which is linked neither to syntactic devices nor to semantic ones. It obviously shows that if one changes the expression the content is also affected (one cannot obtain the same effect by saying /It is Ike that I like/ or /Ike is liked by me/). But it also shows that a particular pronunciation of the slogan (perhaps one with slang overtones), reinforces its 'aesthetic' effect.

40. By integrating and articulating differently a classification suggested by Bense (1965) we may say that in an aesthetic message there are many levels of information: (a) *physical supports*: in the verbal languages they are tones, inflexions, phonetic emissions; in visual languages they are colors, stuffs; in music they are timbres, pitches, dynamic stresses, temporal durations; they are expression-purport or elements of the material continuum which the signal is made of; (b) *differential elements of the expression plane*: phonemes, rhythms, metrical lengths, positional relations, geometric and topological forms, etc.; (c) *syntactic rules*: grammar rules, proportional relationships in architecture, perspectives in painting, musical scales and intervals; (d) *denotative contents*; (e) *connotative contents*; (f) *overcoded ready-made strings*: stylistic subcodes, rhetorical systems, iconographical models, and so on; (g) *others*. Bense, however, speaks of a global 'aesthetic

information' which is not achieved on any of these levels in particular, but rather on the level that he calls '*Mitrealität* (which is signified by all the correlated levels). Bense's '*Mitrealität*' seems like the general contextual situation of improbability that the work exhibits, but the term (because of the Hegelian mold of the author) is slightly colored with idealistic connotations. *Mitrealität* seems then to denote a certain 'essence' — maybe the Beauty — which can be intuitively grasped but not semiotically singled out. On the contrary one of the tasks of a semiotic approach to aesthetics must be its capability to analyze and describe in systematic terms why the impression of *Mitrealität* arises. In the following paragraphs the notion of aesthetic idiolect will satisfy this need.

41. Nevertheless, even though one admits that the author is molding something that elicits responses without really 'communicating' contents, one has to assume that either the author or the art analyst *knows* that these clusters of unpredictable and undetected microstructures ought to produce a predictable response. There is at least a moment in which the relationship between clusters and responses is *coded* (or abduced) as a semiotic correlation. These are cases of *programmed stimuli* (see 3.6.6.). Imagine that a critic knows that a given artistic procedure (recognized as 'the secret of that great master') appears in many works of that master and *inflexibly* produces an 'unspeakable' feeling and a specific kind of enjoyment; this kind of knowledge would constitute the last (and at any rate the more satisfactory) form of 'rationalization' that semiotics can exert about a work of art.

42. The complexity of the inferior levels, which seems to escape any definition, has induced some aestheticians to consider these levels as extraneous to the poetic form. Galvano della Volpe (1960), who was fighting against the various idealistic theories of the 'ineffability' of art, in order to avoid everything which could escape a rationalistic approach to art, has excluded all the 'musical' values that cannot be coded. These values were relegated to the range of 'hedonistic' elements, stimulators of an extra-aesthetic enjoyment. Hence the repudiation of many phonetic phenomena that, according to many critics, constitute the principal appeal of poetry; hence the rhythm looked suspiciously at; hence the statement that the aesthetic value is what remains when a work is translated into another material support, where musical devices can change in impact but there remains a kind of logical and conceptual pattern capable of keeping the really significant relationships. It is curious that this effort toward a 'rationalistic' theory of art happens to leave to the 'irrational' elements much more than they deserve. To renounce extension of the rationalistic analysis to the lower levels of the expression form leads to equating 'rational' with 'seman-tic' — which is a very poor way to refute the idealistic approach to the 'unspeakability' of art. The correct trend, even from the point of view of Della Volpe, should be, on the contrary, the one outlined in the present chapter, that is, to overcode the expression substance.

43. "Poetics deals primarily with the question, *What makes a verbal message a work of art?* Because the main object of poetics is the *differentia specifica* of verbal art in relation to other arts and in relation to other kinds of verbal behavior, poetics is entitled to the leading place in literary studies. Poetics deals with the problem of verbal structure, just as the analysis of painting is concerned with pictorial structure. Since linguistics is the global

science of verbal structure, poetics may be regarded as an integral part of linguistics . . . . Many poetic features belong not only to the science of language but to the whole theory of signs, that is, to general semiotics. This statement, however, is valid not only for verbal art but also for all varieties of language since language shares many properties with some other systems of signs or even with all of them (pansemiotic features)" (Jakobson, 1960:351).

44. See Eco, 1962, where the theory of the 'open work' is approached from a pre-semiotic point of view.

45. The aesthetic idiolectic has not to be considered a code ruling one and only one message (which, however, should not be viewed as a theoretical contradiction); it is rather a code ruling the various different messages which compose that complex network of messages called 'aesthetic text'. Nevertheless it is (or it may in principle be) a code ruling one and only one text, a code destined to produce a unique discourse. This (and nothing else) explains the creative and individual character of a work of art. Ruled by the idiolectal aesthetic code and connecting various messages which are to be taken as radical instances of a rearranged underlying system, the work of art is a *system of systems* (see Jakobson and Tynianov, 1927; Wellek and Warren, 1942).

46. Roland Barthes (1963c.) once said that the work of art *"est une forme que l'histoire passe son temps à remplir"*. I agree with this statement but I would prefer to re-translate it into the categories of the present semiotic approach: the work of art is a text that is adapted by its concrete addressees so as to fulfill many different communicative purposes in diverse historical or psychological circumstances, without ever completely disregarding the underlying rule that has constituted it.

47. The above example is perhaps a too perfect one, for there is also, along with the semantic substitution, a witty phonetic echoing: thus the metaphor is reinforced by the *pun*, that is, the substitution on the content plane is reinforced by the co-presence on the expression plane. On this aspect of the 'metaphor+pun' see Eco, 1973b, on Joyce's technique; the pun is a figure of speech that, instead of substituting a 'tenor' by a 'vehicle' (according to Richard's definition) makes the word corresponding to the vehicle embody the word corresponding to the tenor. In such cases the 'necessity' of the substitution is reinforced, such as happens with the rhyme according to Jakobson, where a parallelism on the expression plane co-involves a parallelism on the content plane. Thus, and the remark is particularly valid for medieval culture, one is further convinced that *nomina sunt numina* or that *nomina sunt consequentia rerum*.

48. These distinctions are also recorded by the medieval definitions of *loci*: *"Quis, quid, ubi, quibus auxiliis, cur, quomodo, quando"*. But these questions only partially concern the format of the sememe. Some of them concern contexts and circumstances, therefore a series of uncoded presuppositions. Let us then assume that there exist cases of empirical contiguity that cannot be recorded by a semantic theory. For instance, when dreaming, one frequently relies on connections based only on one's personal and idiosyncratic experience. More open to coding appear some metaphors such as the substitution of penis by vertical objects (already discussed in semiotic terms by Morris, 1938). Thus it would be risky to call metonymies all the substitutions by 'contiguity' occurring during the dreams or the psycho-

analytic verbal interaction – and interpreted as such by the analyst. Psychoanalysis seems to be rather a matter of interpretation of as yet uncoded texts, producing further overcoding, and the discourse of the patient has many points in common with an aesthetic text whose idiolect has to be discovered by the critic. Many of the 'contiguities' discovered in this text are contextual presuppositions, called "referentials" by Hiz (cf. 2.11.1.).

49. The functioning of metaphors and metonymies explains the mechanism of every other trope, that is, all the substitutions by *immutatio*. *Periphrasis* is the substitution of a lexeme with the whole (or a great part) of the markers of the corresponding sememe. *Antonomasia* is both a sub-case of synecdoche (*species pro individuo*) and periphrasis. Since the sememic representation analytically (or semiotically) includes the negation of the antonym, *litotes* are a common case of substitution of the sememe by a marker, and *ironies* are the direct use of the antonym (but, being in fact figures of speech and of thought, they involve more complex contextual substitutions). *Emphases* are types of synecdoche, and *hyperboles* are types of metaphor. A different discourse should be made for the figures of speech and of thought (which proceed by *adjectio*, *detractio* and *transmutatio*) and which rely on phonological, syntactical and inferential mechanisms. Groupe μ in *Rhétorique générale* carefully distinguish between figures of expression (*metaplasms* and *metataxes*) and figures of content (*metasemenes* and *metalogisms*); it must be stressed that the suggestions offered by the present book work only for a study of metasemenes.

50. Katz (1972:8.4.) proposes to add a rhetorical representation to the canonical theory of grammatical components, saying that "the theory of grammar requires a next subtheory, namely, a theory of rhetorical form, and, further, that grammars require a new component to express the rhetorical interpretation of superficial phrase markers". Katz thus assumes that rhetorical manipulation may only alter surface structures without interfering with their semantic interpretation. It should be clear that the theory outlined in this book is exactly the opposite, even if one might admit that in exceptional cases some rhetorical manipulation may only determine very peripheral connotations. But also, in these cases, rhetoric is concerned with semantics and I think that it is impossible to consider the rhetorical component independent of the semantic one; they are rather to be viewed as two sides of the same semiotic problem.

51. For example: "Our society has to improve and to increase production; many sacrifices will be required of every member of the community in order to achieve our goal. Individuals do not count in respect to the collective welfare". The same kind of coding is implicitly established by another statement of the type: "Productivity produces money, money produces welfare; obviously in this struggle for life – or in this free competition – somebody must be overcome; this is the price to pay for an affluent economy". All these statements constitute implicit meta-semiotic judgments imposing some *semantic rules for connecting values*. On the other hand different premises may be stated: "Better poor than slaves of our own affluence"; "A society in which somebody dies in order to produce wealth for somebody else is an insane society"; "Burn grass not oil"; "Social security must be the first care of this government". All of these statements (easily recognizable as belonging to different ideologies) are nevertheless as many

examples of rhetorical persuasive efforts to make people think in another way; therefore they constitute meta-semiotic judgments aiming to assign new connotations to old semantic items.

52. There are no objective rules for transformation of an ideology into another one; the disconnection of the semantic space allows one to demonstrate that different biases produce different semantic organizations. There is no theory of the ideologies that would be able to test and to improve them. There is a semiotic technique of analysis that allows one to destroy an ideology by opposing to it another ideology, the latter showing the falsity of the former (and vice versa). The choice of the right or of the correct bias is not a semiotic matter. Semiotics helps us to analyze different ideological choices; it does not help us to choose.

53. At this point we can take up and develop a problem already aired by Barthes (1964 b), that of the relationship between rhetorical formulae and ideological positions. It is not likely that a Communist would indicate the necessity of the Third World's struggle against the Western powers by the phrase /the defense of the free world/ even if he considered the autonomy of colonial people to be the only form of freedom for which it was worth fighting. The rhetorical formula /defense of the free world/ is henceforward strictly associated with political positions which are identified with the United States, their allies and their ideological vision. Naturally the same operation could be accomplished on a formula such as /brotherly help to the socialist allies/. Thus a certain way of using a language is identified with a certain way of viewing society.

54. The whole of the above discussion verifies the most current definitions of ideology. The sense given to this term by the French 'idéologues' of the eighteenth century is practically equivalent to our conception of semiotics as a 'genetic' criticism of ideologies. Ideology as conscious code-switching is what Engels called "a process that the so-called thinker accomplishes consciously but with false conscience. The true moving forces that determine him remain unknown (otherwise it will not be an ideological process," (*Letter to Mehring*). Ideology as unconscious code-switching is described by Jaspers as "the complex of thoughts and representations appearing as an Absolute Truth to the thinking subject for the interpretation of the world . . . producing a self-deception, a concealment, an escape (from reality)" *Die geistische Situation der Zeit*). On the other hand the Marxist 'positive' sense of 'ideology' as an intellectual and political 'weapon' serving the social purpose of active modification of the world does not contradict the preceding negative definition; in this sense an ideology is taken without denying its one-sidedness and without concealing what it refuses; except that a previous system of premises has clarified what one wants to get and what one prefers (see note 50), on the basis of a given theory of society and of material needs.

55. The ideological labor can assume even more complex forms. Through metaphorical substitution it is possible to equate «energy=comfort» and to oppose them to «danger». It is possible to translate «danger» into «less security» and therefore demonstrate that more energy implies less security, which is a price that might be paid to have high comfort. It is possible to introduce surreptitious fuzzy concepts without establishing their exact gradation; suppose that the productivity theorist, having asserted as an

acceptable premise that All Comfort for All is incompatible with All Security for All, proposes a pseudo-logical square of the type

All Comfort for All − All Security for All
Some Security for Some − Some Comfort for Some

in which appearently the first antonymous tuple opposes two contraries, the second one two converses, while a general comfort which implies some security seems to be a fair issue. It suffices to recognize «All» and «Some» as *fuzzy operators* that change their own semantic nature depending on their positions, and the pretended logical exactness of the square is challenged: does All Comfort for All mean «equally distributed to everybody» (socialism) or «potentially at the disposal of everybody» (free competition)? *How much is* the first «Some» quantifying «Security»? And for *how many* is the second one? The 'game' could continue indefinitely. Only when each term is sent back to its position within the codes and semantically analyzed, can the ideological labor can be unmasked and be taken back to a persuasive discourse based upon a *logic of preference*.

4: THE SUBJECT OF SEMIOTICS

Since it has been said that the labor of sign production also represents a form of social criticism and of social practice, a sort of ghostly presence, until now somewhat removed from the present discourse, finally makes an unavoidable appearance. What is, in the semiotic framework, the place of the *acting subject* of every semiosic act?

If one of the topics of a theory of sign production is the relationship between sender and addressee, which constitutes the basis for a consideration of the various kinds of 'speech acts', one could remark that very little attention has been devoted, in the preceding chapters, to the 'transcendental' or 'empirical' protagonist of these processes.

A theory of the relationship sender-addressee should also take into account the role of the 'speaking' subject not only as a communicational figment but as a concrete historical, biological, psychic subject, as it is approached by psychoanalysis and related disciplines. Anyway the approach followed in this book requires that the following assumptions be made:

(i) The subject of an act of *utterance* (which is not necessarily the same as the 'grammatical' subject of the *statement* because there is a difference between *sujet de l'énonciation* and *sujet de l'énoncé*) [1] must be considered one among the possible *referents* of the message or text, however

314

explicit or implicit it may be. It is thus one of the objects of the possible mentions the message performs, and as such it has to be studied by the disciplines concerned with the various physical or psychic objects *of which* languages speak.

(ii) Insofar as the subject, along with some of its properties and attitudes, is presupposed by the statements, then it has to be 'read' as an element of the conveyed content. Any other attempt to introduce a consideration of the subject into the semiotic discourse would make semiotics trespass on one of its 'natural' boundaries.

I am aware of the fact that some semiotic approaches do trespass on this threshold, making semiotics the study of this creative activity of a semiosis-making subject, and intending this subject not as a phenomenological transcendental Ego but a 'deep', profound subject [2].

Let me then assume that maybe semiotics is destined to overcome one of its natural boundaries and to become not only the theory of codes and of sign production but also of the 'deep' individual origins of any 'wish to produce signs'. In this perspective some of the topics of my theory of sign production (such as for instance the activity of code-making and of code-changing) can be taken into account by a theory of text-creativity and of *'textualité'*.

But let me also assume that, from the point of view of the present book, the most reliable grasp that semiotics can have on such a subjective activity is the one provided by a theory of codes: *the subject of any semiotic enquiry being no more than the semiotic subject of semiosis, that is, the historical and social result of the segmentation of the world that a survey on Semantic Space makes available.* This subject is a way of looking at the world and can only be known as a way of segmenting the universe and of coupling semantic units with expression-units: by this labor it becomes entitled to continuously destroy and restructure its social and historical systematic concretions.

Semiotics can define the subject of every act of semiosis only by semiotic categories; thus the subject of signification is nothing more than the continuously unaccomplished system of systems of signification that reflects back on itself.

I would like to eliminate any shade of idealism from such an assertion. I am not denying the existence and the importance of individual material subjects which, when communicating, obey, enrich, change and criticize signification systems (see 3.9.4.).

I am only assuming that semiotics cannot define these subjects except within its own theoretical framework, in the same way in which, examining referents as contents, it does not deny the existence of physical things and states of the world, but assigns their verification (and their analysis in terms of concrete properties, change, truth and falsity) to other types of approach.

In this book semiotics has been provided with a paramount subject matter, *semiosis*. Semiosis is the process by which empirical subjects communicate, communication processes being made possible by the organization of signification systems. Empirical subjects, from a semiotic point of view, can only be defined and isolated as manifestations of this double (systematic and processual) aspect of semiosis. This is not a metaphysical statement, but a methodological one; physics knows Caesar and Brutus as spatio-temporal events defined by an interrelationship of elementary particles and must not be concerned with the motivation of their acts, nor with ethical evaluation of the result of these acts. Semiotics treats subjects of semiosic acts in the same way: either they can be defined in terms of semiotic structures or — from this point of view — they do not exist at all.

As Peirce said: "Since man can think only by means of words or other external symbols, these might turn round and say: 'You mean nothing which we have not taught you, and then only so far as you address some word as the interpretant of your thought'. In fact, therefore, men and words reciprocally educate each other; each increase of a man's information involves, and is involved by, a corresponding increase of a word's information . . . . It is that the word or sign which man uses IS the man itself. For, as the fact that every thought is a sign, taken in conjunction that life is a train of thought, proves that man is a sign; so that every thought is an *external* sign, proves that man is an external sign. That is to say, the man and the external signs are identical, in the same sense in which the words *homo* and *man* are identical. Thus my language is the sum total of myself: for the man is the thought" (Peirce, 5.313-314).

Obviously when empirical subjects are able to criticize the ideological adjustment of a signification system, one is witnessing a concrete act of social practice; but this act is made possible by the fact that a code can criticize itself because of the contradictory format of the Global Semantic Space, as outlined in 2.13.

When one asserts that there is no metalanguage at all, one confuses the theory of codes with the theory of sign production; empirical subjects can metalinguistically *use* the codes just because *there is no* metalanguage; for everything in a self-contradictory code is metalanguage. If the format of a Global Semantic Space is the one outlined by Model Q (see 2.12.) then the

deep subject of any concrete semiotic critical practice is its very contradictory format.

There is sign production because there are empirical subjects which
display labor in order to physically produce expressions, to correlate them to
content, to segment content, and so on. But semiotics is entitled to recognize
these subjects only insofar as they manifest themselves through sign-
functions, producing sign-functions, criticizing other sign-functions and
restructuring the pre-existing sign-functions. By accepting this limit, semiotics
fully avoids any risk of idealism.

On the contrary semiotics recognizes as the only testable subject matter
of its discourse the social existence of the universe of signification, as it is
revealed by the physical testability of interpretants — which are, to rein-
force this point for the last time, *material expressions*.

What is behind, before or after, outside or *too much* inside the methodological "subject" outlined by this book might be tremendously important. Unfortunately it seems to me — at this stage — beyond the semiotic threshold.

NOTES

1. On the opposition *'énonciation* vs. *énoncé'*, see the vast discussion
which has taken place especially in France in the last decade: Benveniste,
1966; Lacan, 1966; Todorov, 1970; Kristeva, 1968; Ducrot, 1972; Chabrol,
1973.

2. "One phase of semiology is now over: that which runs from Saussure
and Peirce to the Prague School and structuralism, and has made possible the
systematic description of the social and/or symbolic constraints within each
significant practice . . . . A critique of this 'semiology of systems' and of its
phenomenological foundations is possible only if it starts from a theory of
meaning which must necessarily be a theory of the speaking subject . . . . The
theory of meaning now stands at a cross-roads: either it will remain an
attempt at formalizing meaning systems by increasing sophistication of the
logico-mathematical tools which enable it to formulate models on the basis of
a conception (already rather dated) of meaning as the act of a *transcendental
ego*, cut off from its body, its unconscious, and also its history; or else it will
attune itself to the theory of the speaking subject as a divided subject
(conscious/unconscious) and go on to attempt to specify the types of
operations characteristic of the two sides of this split: thereby exposing them,
that is to say, on the one hand, to bio-physiological processes (themselves
already an inescapable part of signifying processes: what Freud labelled
'drives'), and, on the other hand, to social constraints (family structures,
modes of production, etc.)" (Kristeva, 1973; see for a broader development
of these theses, Kristeva, 1969). It may be said that, when these subjective
determinants of a text are expressed as contents of the text itself, they

become undoubtedly a semiotic matter; see the case of the ideological and economical motivation of an ideological discourse, in 3.9., which were made explicit by the same form assumed by a series of judgments about the Alpha-Beta System, or by previous rhetorical premises, stated or presupposed in the course of a persuasive discourse. When these extra-textual 'drives' are not displayed by the text as an activity of *'écriture'*, then I cannot see a way to assume them into a semiotic framework.

In this sense a threshold-trespassing semiotics could be conceived, which the present book does not dare to take into account, and it is not by chance that Kristeva found it necessary to call such a research not 'semiotics' but *'sémanalyse'*.

REFERENCES

Theses and Collections

1929   *Thèses presentées au Premier Congrès des philologues slaves* (Travaux du Cercle Linguistique de Prague 1) (now in Vachek, ed., 1964).
1961   *Poetics* (Polska Akademia Nauk, Proceedings of the International Conference of Work-in-Progress, Warsaw, August 1960) (The Hague: Mouton).
1966   "Problèmes du langage", *Diogène* 51.
1970   *I linguaggi nella società e nella tecnica* (Convegno promosso dalla Ing., C. Olivetti and C. Milano, ottobre 1968) (Milano: Comunità).
1970   *Sign—Language—Culture* (The Hague: Mouton).
1973   *Recherches sur les systèmes signifiants* (Symposium de Varsovie, 1968) (The Hague: Mouton).

ALEXANDER, CHRISTOPHER
    1964   *Notes on the Synthesis of Form* (Cambridge: Harvard College).
ALLARD, M., ELZIÈRE, M., GARDIN, J.C., AND HOURS, F.
    1963   *Analyse conceptuelle du Coran sur cartes perforées* (The Hague: Mouton).
AMBROGIO, IGNAZIO
    1968   *Formalismo e avanguardia in Russia* (Roma: Editori Riuniti).
ANTAL, LÁSZLÓ
    1964   *Content, Meaning and Understanding* (The Hague: Mouton).
APOSTEL, LÉO
    1960   "Matérialisme dialectique et méthode scientifique", *Le Socialisme* 7-4.

319

APRESJIAN, J.
   1962   "Analyse distributionelle des significations et champs sémantiques structurés", *Langages* 1, 1966.

ARGYLE, MICHAEL
   1972   "Non-Verbal Communication in Human Social Interaction", in Hinde, R.A., ed., *Non-Verbal Communication* (Cambridge: Cambridge University Press).

ARGYLE, M., and DEAN, J.
   1965   "Eye-contact, distance and affiliation", *Sociometry* 28.

ARGYLE, M., and INGHAM, R.
   1972   "Gaze, Mutual Gaze and Proximity", *Semiotica* VI/2.

ARNHEIM, RUDOLF
   1969   *Visual Thinking* (Los Angeles: University of California Press).

ASHBY ROSS, W.
   1960   *Design for a Brain*, 2d ed. (London: Chapman and Hall).

ATTNEAVE, FRED
   1959   "Stochastic Cognitive Processes", *Journal of Aesthetics and Art Criticism*, XVII 4.

AUSTIN, J.L.
   1961   "The Meaning of a Word", *Philosophical Papers* (Oxford: Clarendon Press).

   1962   *How to Do Things with Words* (Oxford: Oxford University Press).

AVALLE, D'ARCO SILVIO
   1965a   *"Gli Orecchini" di Montale* (Milano: Saggiatore).
   1965b   Intervento in *Strutturalismo e critica* (in Segre, ed., 1965).
   1970   *Tre saggi su montale* (Torino: Einaudi).
   1972   *Corso di semiologia dei testi letterari* (Torino: Giappichelli).

BACH, EMMON
   1966   "Linguistique structurale et philosophie des sciences", *Diogène* 51.

BACH, EMMON, AND HARMS, ROBERT, EDS.
   1968   *Universals in Linguistic Theory* (New York: Holt).

BALDINGER, KURT
   1966   "Sémantique et structure conceptuelle", *Cahiers de lexicologie* VIII 1.

BALLY, CHARLES
   1932   *Linguistique générale et linguistique française* (Bern: Franke).

BARBUT, MARC
   1966   "Le sens du mot 'structure' en mathématique", *Les Temps Modernes* 264.

BARISON, F.
   1961a   "Considerazioni sul 'Praecoxgefühl' ", *Rivista Neurologica* 31 305.
   1961b   "Art et schizophrénie", *Evolution Psychiatrique* I 69.

BARTHES, ROLAND
   1953   *Le degré zéro de l'écriture* (Paris: Seuil).

1957   *Mythologies* (Paris: Seuil).

1963a   *Sur Racine* (Paris: Seuil).

1963b   "L'activité structuraliste", *Lettres Nouvelles* (now in Barthes, 1964c).

1963c   "Littérature et signification", *Tel Quel* (now in Barthes, 1964c).

1964a   "Eléments de sémiologie", *Communications* 4.

1964b   "Rhétorique de l'image", *Communications* 4.

1964c   *Essais critiques* (Paris: Seuil).

1966a   "Introduction à l'analyse structurale des récits", *Communications* 8.

1966b   *Critique et verité* (Paris: Seuil).

1967a   *Système de la mode* (Paris: Seuil).

1967b   "L'arbre du crime", *Tel Quel* 28.

1968   "L'effet de réel", *Communications* 11.

1970a   *S/Z* (Paris: Seuil).

1970b   "L'ancienne rhétorique", *Communications* 16.

1971   *Sade, Loyola, Fourier* (Paris: Seuil).

1973   *Le plaisir du texte* (Paris: Seuil).

BASTIDE, ROGER, ED.

1962   *Sens et usages du mot "structure"* (The Hague: Mouton).

BAUDRILLARD, JEAN

1968   *Système des objets* (Paris: Gallimard).

BEAUJOUR, MICHEL

1968   "The Game of Poetics", *Yale French Studies* 41.

BENSE, MAX

1965   *Aesthetica* (Baden-Baden: Agis).

BENSE, M., AND WALTHER, E.

1973   *Wörterbuch der Semiotik* (Köln: Kiepenheuer & Witsch).

BENVENISTE, EMILE

1966   *Problèmes de linguistique générale* (Paris: Gallimard).

1969   "Sémiologie de la langue", *Semiotica* I/1 and I/2.

BERTIN, JACQUES

1967   *Sémiologie graphique* (Paris: Mouton and Gauthier Villars).

1970   "La graphique", *Communications* 15.

BETTETINI, GIANFRANCO

1968   *Cinema: lingua e scrittura* (Milano: Bompiani).

1971   *L'indice del realismo* (Milano: Bompiani).

1973   *The Language and Technique of the Film* (The Hague: Mouton).

BIERWISCH, MANFRED

1970   "Semantics", in Lyons, J., ed., *New Horizons in Linguistics* (London: Penguin).

1971   "On Classifying Semantic Features", in Steinberg and Jakobovits, eds., 1971.

BIRDWHISTELL, RAY L.

1952   *Introduction to Kinesics* (Washington: Department of State, Foreign Service Institute).

1960   "Kinesics and Communication", in Carpenter, E., and McLuhan, M., eds., *Explorations in Communications* (Boston: Beacon Press).
1963   "Some Relations between American Kinesics and Spoken American English", American Association for the Advancement of Science (in Smith, ed., 1966).
1965   "Communication as a Multichannel System", *International Encyclopedia of Social Sciences* (New York).
1970   *Kinesics and Context* (Philadelphia: University of Pennsylvania).

BLOOMFIELD, LEONARD
1933   *Language* (New York: Holt).

BOLINGER, DWIGHT L.
1961   *Generality, Gradience and the All-None* (The Hague: Mouton).

BONOMI, A., AND USBERTI, G.
1971   *Sintassi e semantica nella grammatica trasformazionale* (Milano: Saggiatore).

BONSIEPE, GUY
1965   "Visual/Verbal Rhetoric", *Ulm* 14-16.
1968   "Semantic Analysis", *Ulm* 21.

BOSCO, NYNFA
1959   *La filosofia pragmatica di C.S. Peirce* (Torino: Ed. di "Filosofia").

BOULEZ, PIERRE
1966   *Relevés d'apprenti* (Paris: Seuil).

BRANDI, CESARE
1966   *Le due vie* (Bari: Laterza).
1968   *Struttura e architettura* (Torino: Einaudi).

BREMOND, CLAUDE
1964   "Le message narratif", *Communications* 4.
1966a   "L'analyse conceptuelle du Coran", *Communications* 7.
1966b   "La logique des possibles narratifs", *Communications* 8.
1968a   "Postérité américaine de Propp", *Communications* 11.
1968b   "Pour un gestuaire des bandes dessinées", *Langages* 10.
1973   *Logique du récit* (Paris: Seuil).

BURKE, KENNETH
1931   *Counter-Statements* (Chicago: University of Chicago Press).

BURSILL-HALL, G.L.
1971   *Speculative Grammars of the Middle Ages* (The Hague: Mouton).

BUYSSENS, ERIC
1943   *Les langages et le discours* (Bruxelles: Office de Publicité).
1967   *La communication et l'articulation linguistique* (Paris-Bruxelles: P.U.F.).

CARNAP, RUDOLF
1942   *Introduction to Semantics* (Cambridge: Harvard University Press).
1947   *Meaning and Necessity* (Chicago: University of Chicago Press).
1955   "Meaning and Synonymy in Natural Languages", *Philosophical Studies* 7.

CARPENTER, E., AND MCLUHAN, M., EDS.
  1960   *Explorations in Communications* (Boston: Beacon Press).
CASSIRER, ERNST
  1906   *Das Erkentnisproblem in der Philosophie und Wissenschaft der neuren Zeit* (Berlin: Bruno Cassirer).
  1923   "Philosophie der simbolischen Formen'— *I. Die Sprache* (Leipzig).
  1945   "Structuralism in Modern Linguistics", *Word* 1-2.
CHABROL, CLAUDE, ET AL., EDS.
  1973   *Sémiotique narrative et textuelle* (Paris: Larousse).
CHARBONNIER, GEORGES
  1961   *Entretiens avec C. Lévi-Strauss* (Paris: Plon-Juilliard).
CHATMAN, SEYMOUR
  1966   "On the Theory of Literary Style", *Linguistics* 27.
  1974   "Rhetoric and Semiotics", report to the First Congress of the IASS (mimeographed).
CHERRY, COLIN
  1961   *On Human Communication* (New York: Wiley).
CHOMSKY, NOAM
  1957   *Syntactic Structures* (The Hague: Mouton).
  1962   *Current Issues in Linguistic Theory* (Ninth International Congress of Linguistics) (now in Katz and Fodor, eds., 1964).
  1965a *Aspects of the Theory of Syntax* (Cambridge: M.I.T.).
  1965b "De quelques constantes de la théorie linguistique", *Diogène* 51.
  1966   *Cartesian Linguistics* (New York: Harper and Row).
  1967   "The Formal Nature of Language", in Lenneberg, E.H., ed., *Biological Foundations of Language* (New York: Wiley).
  1968   *Language and Mind* (New York: Harcourt, Brace).
  1969   "Deep Structure, Surface Structure and Semantic Interpretation", in Steinberg and Jakobovits, eds., 1971.
CHURCH, ALONZO
  1943   "Carnap's *Introduction to Semantics*", *Philosophical Review* 52.
  1951   "The Need for Abstract Entities in Semantic Analysis", *Proceedings of the American Academy of Arts and Sciences* 80, 1.
CICOUREL, AARON V.
  1973   *Cognitive Sociology* (London: Penguin).
CIV'JAN, T.V., NIKOLAEVA, T.M., SEGAL, D.M., AND VOLOCKAJA, Z.M.
  1962   "Žestovaja kommunicacija i ee mesto sredi drugich sistem čelovečeskogo obščenija", in *Simpozium po strukturnomu izučeniju znakovich sistem* (Moskva) (Italian transl. in Faccani and Eco, eds., 1969).
COHEN, JONATHAN
  1962   *The Diversity of Meaning* (London: Methuen).
  1973   "Spoken and Unspoken Meanings", *TLS* October 5.
CONKLIN, H.C.
  1955   'Hanunoo Color Categories'", *Southwestern Journal of Anthropology* 11 (now in Hymes, ed., 1964).

COONS, E., AND KRAEHENBUEHL, D.
1958   "Information as Measure of Structure in Music", *Journal of Music Theory* 11, 2.
CORTI, MARIA
1965   "Intervento", in Segre, G., ed., *Strutturalismo e critica* (Milano: Saggiatore).
1969   *Metodi e fantasmi* (Milano: Feltrinelli).
COSERIU, EUGENIO
1952   "Sistema, norma y habla", *Revista de la Faculdad de Humanidades y Ciencias* 9 (now in *Teoria del lenguaje y linguistica generál*, Madrid, 1962).
CRALLE, R.K., AND MICHAEL, G.A.
1967   "A Survey on Graphic Data Processing Equipment for Computers", in Krampen and Seitz, eds., 1967.
CRESSWELL, R.
1968   "Le geste manuel associé au langage", *Langages* 10.
CRESTI, EMANUELA
1972   "Oppositions iconiques dans une image de bande dessinée reproduite par Lichtenstein", *VS* 2.

DAMISCH, HUBERT
1972   *Théorie du nuage* (Paris: Seuil).
DE CAMPOS, HAROLDO
1967   *Metalinguagem* (Petropolis: Vozes).
1969   *A arte no horizonte do provável* (São Paulo: Perspectiva).
1973   *Morfologia do Macunaima* (São Paulo: Perspectiva).
DE FUSCO, RENATO
1967   *L'arte come mass-medium* (Bari: Dedalo).
1973   *Segni, storia e progetto dell'architettura* (Bari: Laterza).
DE JORIO, A.
1832   *La mimica degli antichi investigata nel gestire* (Napoli).
DELEUZE, GILLES
1968   *Différence et répétition* (Paris: P.U.F.).
DELLA VOLPE, GALVANO
1960   *Critica del gusto* (Milano: Feltrinelli).
DE MAURO, TULLIO
1965   *Introduzione alla semantica* (Bari: Laterza).
1966   "Modelli semiologici: l'arbitrarietà semantica", *Lingua e stile* 1.
1968   "Some Proposals Concerning a Formalized Theory of Lexical Noeme and the Historical and Social Character of Linguistic Phenomena", in *I linguaggi nella società e nella tecnica* (Milano: Comunità, 1970).
1971   *Senso e significato* (Bari: Adriatica).
DERRIDA, JACQUES
1967a   *L'écriture et la différence* (Paris: Seuil).
1967b   *De la grammatologie* (Paris: Minuit).

DINNEEN, FRANCIS P.
 1967 *An Introduction to General Linguistics* (New York: Holt).
DOLEZEL, LUBOMIR
 1966 "Vers la stylistique structurale", *Travaux Linguistiques de Prague* 1.
DORFLES, GILLO
 1962 *Simbolo, comunicazione, consumo* (Torino: Einaudi).
 1966 *Nuovi riti, nuovi miti* (Torino: Einaudi).
 1968 *Artificio e natura* (Torino: Einaudi).
DUCROT, OSWALD
 1972 *Dire et ne pas dire* (Paris: Hermann).
DUNDES, ALAN
 1958 *The Morphology of North American Indian Folktales* (The Hague: Mouton).
 1962 "From Etic to Emic Units in the Structural Study of Folktales", *Journal of American Folklore* 75 (296).
 1964 "On Game Morphology: A Study of the Structure of Non-Verbal Folklore", *New York Folklore Quarterly* 20 (4).

ECO, UMBERTO
 1956 *Il problema estetico in Tommaso d'Aquino*, 2d ed. (Milano: Bompiani, 1970).
 1962 *Opera aperta* (Milano: Bompiani).
 1963 "The Analysis of Structure", in *The Critical Moment* (London: Faber).
 1964 *Apocalittici e integrati* (Milano: Bompiani).
 1966 "James Bond: une combinatoire narrative", *Communications* 8.
 1967 "Rhetoric and Ideology in Sue's 'Les Mystères de Paris' ", *International Social Sciences Journal* XIX 4.
 1968a *La definizione dell'arte* (Milano: Mursia).
 1968b "Lignes d'une recherche sémiologique sur le message télévisuel", in *Recherches sur les systèmes signifiants* (The Hague: Mouton, 1973).
 1968c *La struttura assente* (Milano: Bompiani).
 1971 *Le forme del contenuto* (Milano: Bompiani).
 1972a "A Semiotic Approach to Semantics", *VS* 1.
 1972b "Introduction to a Semiotics of Iconic Signs", *VS* 2.
 1972c "A Componential Analysis of the Architectural Sign /Column/", *Semiotica* V/2.
 1973a "Social Life as a Sign-System", in Robey, D., ed., *Structuralism* (Oxford: Clarendon Press).
 1973b "Looking for a Logic of Culture", *TLS*, October 5 (now in Sebeok, ed., 1975).
 1973c *Il segno* (Milano: Isedi).
 1973d "Sémantique de la métaphore", *Tel Quel* 55.
 1973e "Function and Sign: Semiotics of Architecture", in Bryan, J., and

Sauer, R., eds., *Structures Implicit and Explicit*, in *VIA* – Publications of the Graduate School of Fine Arts, vol. 2 (Philadelphia: University of Pennsylvania).

1973f   "On the Possibility of Generating Aesthetic Messages in an Edenic Language", in Bann, S., and Bowlt, J.E., eds., *Russian Formalism* (Edinburgh: Scottish Academic Press).

EFRON, DAVID

1941   *Gesture, Race and Culture* (The Hague: Mouton, 1972).

EGOROV, B.F.

1965   "Prostejšie semiotičeskie sistemy i tipologija siužetov", in *Trudy po znakovim sistemam* II (Tartu) (Italian transl. in Faccani and Eco, eds., 1969).

EKMAN, P., AND FRIESEN, W.

1969   "The Repertoire of Non-Verbal Behavior Categories, Origins, Usage and Coding", *Semiotica* I/1.

EKMAN, P., FRIESEN, W., AND TOMKINS, S.

1971   "Facial Affect Scoring Technique: A First Validity Study", *Semiotica* III/1.

ERLICH, VICTOR

1954   *Russian Formalism* (The Hague: Mouton).

FABBRI, PAOLO

1968   "Considérations sur la proxémique", *Langages* 10.

1973   "Le comunicazioni di massa in Italia: sguardo semiotico e malocchio della sociologia", *VS* 5.

FACCANI, R., AND ECO, U., EDS.

1969   *I sistemi di segni e lo strutturalismo sovietico* (Milano: Bompiani).

FANO, GIORGIO

1962   *Saggio sulle origini del linguaggio* (Torino: Einaudi).

FARASSINO, ALBERTO

1969   "Ipotesi per una retorica della comunicazione fotografica", *Annali della scuola superiore di comunicazioni di massa* 4.

1972   "Richiamo al significante", *VS* 3.

FAYE, JEAN-PIERRE, ED.

1969   "Le cercle de Prague", *Change* 3.

1972   *Langages totalitaires* (Paris: Hermann).

FILLMORE, CHARLES J.

1968   "The Case for Case", in Bach and Harms, eds., 1968.

1971a   "Types of Lexical Information", in Steinberg and Jakobovits, eds., 1971.

1971b   "Verbs of Judging: An Exercise in Semantic Description", in Fillmore and Langendoen, eds., 1971.

FILLMORE, CH. J., AND LANGENDOEN, D.T., EDS.

1971   *Studies in Linguistic Semantics* (New York: Holt).

FONAGY, IVAN

1964   "L'information du style verbal", *Linguistics* 4.

1971 "Le signe conventionnel motivé", *La linguistique* 7.
1972 "Motivation et remotivation", *Poétique* 11.
FONTANIER, PIERRE
1827 *Traité général des figures du discours autres que les tropes* (now in Fontanier, 1968).
1830 *Manuel classique pour l'étude des tropes* (now in Fontanier, 1968).
1968 *Les figures du discours* (Paris: Flammarion).
FORMIGARI, LIA
1970 *Linguistica ed empirismo nel 600 inglese* (Bari: Laterza).
FOUCAULT, MICHEL
1966 *Les mots et les choses* (Paris: Gallimard).
FRANK, LAWRENCE K.
1957 "Tactile Communication", *Genetic Psychology Monographs* 56.
FREGE, GOTTLOB
1892 "Über Sinn und Bedeutung", *Zeitschrift für Philosophie und philosophische Kritik* 100.
FREUDENTHAL, HANS
1960 *Lincos: Design for a Language for a Cosmic Intercourse* (Amsterdam).

GALLIOT, M.
1955 *Essai sur la langue de la réclame contemporaine* (Toulouse: Privat).
GAMBERINI, ITALO
1953 *Per una analisi degli elementi dell'architettura* (Firenze: Casa Ed. Univers.).
1959 *Gli elementi dell'architettura come parole del linguaggio architettonico* (Firenze: Coppini).
1961 *Analisi degli elementi costitutivi dell'architettura* (Firenze: Coppini).
GARRONI, EMILIO
1964a "Estetica antispeculativa ed estetica semantica", *Nuova Corrente* 34.
1964b *La crisi semantica delle arti* (Roma: Officina).
1968 *Semiotica ed estetica* (Bari: Laterza).
1973 *Progetto di semiotica* (Bari: Laterza).
GELB, I.J.
1952 *A Study of Writing* (Chicago: University of Chicago Press).
GENETTE, GÉRARD
1964 "Frontières du récit", *Communications* 8 (now in Genette, 1969).
1966 *Figures* (Paris: Seuil).
1968 "Vraisemblable et motivation", *Communications* 11.
1969 *Figures II* (Paris: Seuil).
1972 *Figures III* (Paris: Seuil).

GIBSON, JAMES J.
1968   *The Senses Considered as Perceptual Systems* (London: Allen and Unwin).

GODELIER, MAURICE
1966   "Système, structure et contradiction dans 'Le Capital' ", *Les Temps Modernes* 55.

GOFFMAN, ERVING
1959   *The Presentation of Self in Everyday Life* (New York: Doubleday).
1963   *Behavior in Public Places* (Glencoe: Free Press).
1967   *Interactional Ritual* (New York: Doubleday).
1969   *Strategic Interaction* (Philadelphia: University of Pennsylvania).
1971   *Relations in Public* (New York: Basic Books).

GOMBRICH, ERNST
1951   "Meditations on a Hobby Horse", in Whyte, L. L., ed., *Aspects of Form* (London) (now in Gombrich, E., *Meditations on a Hobby Horse and Other Essays on the Theory of Art*, London, Phaidon, 1963).
1956   *Art and Illusion* (New York: Bollingen Series, 1961).

GOODENOUGH, W.
1956   "Componential Analysis and the Study of Language", *Language* 32.
1957   "Cultural Anthropology and Linguistics", in Garvin, P., *Report on the Seventh Annual Round Table Meeting on Linguistics and Language Study* (Washington, Georgetown University) (now in Hymes, ed., 1964).

GOODMAN, NELSON
1947   "The Problem of Contrafactual Conditionals", *Journal of Philosophy* XLIV.
1949   "On Likeness of Meaning", *Analysis* 10.
1968   *Languages of Art* (New York: Bobbs-Merrill).

GRASSI, LETIZIA
1972   "Il codice linguistico e altri codici: il codice genetico", *VS* 3.

GREENBERG, JOSEPH H., ED.
1963   *Universals of Language* (Cambridge: M.I.T.).

GREIMAS, ALGIRDAS JULIEN
1966a   *Sémantique structurale* (Paris: Larousse).
1966b   "Eléments pour une théorie de l'interpretation du récit mythique", *Communications* 8 (now in Greimas, 1970).
1968   "Conditions d'une sémiotique du monde naturel", *Langages* 10 (now in Greimas, 1970).
1970   *Du sens* (Paris: Seuil).

GREIMAS, A.J., AND RASTIER, F.
1968   "The Interaction of Semiotic Constraints", *Yale French Studies* 41 (now in Greimas, 1970).

GRICE, H.P.
1957   "Meaning", *Philosophical Review*, 66.

1968   "Utterer's Meaning, Sentence-Meaning and Word-Meaning", *Foundations of Language* 4.
GRITTI, JULES
1966   "Un récit de presse", *Communications* 8.
1968   "Deux arts du vraisemblable: la casuistique, le courrier du coeur", *Communications* 11.
GROSS, M., AND LENTIN, A.
1967   *Notions sur les grammaires formelles* (Paris: Gauthier-Villars).
GROUPE μ
1970   *Rhétorique générale* (Paris: Larousse).
GUILBAUD, G.-T.
1954   *La cybernétique* (Paris: P.U.F.).
GUILHOT, JEAN
1962   *La dynamique de l'expression et de la communication* (The Hague: Mouton).
GUIRAUD, PIERRE
1955   *La sémantique* (Paris: P.U.F.).
GUMPERZ, J.J., AND HYMES, D., EDS.
1972   *Directions in Sociolinguistics* (New York: Holt).

HALL, EDWARD T.
1959   *The Silent Language* (New York: Doubleday).
1963   "A System for the Notation of Proxemic Behavior", *American Anthropologist* 65.
1966   *The Hidden Dimension* (New York: Doubleday).
1968   "Proxemics" (with comments by R. Birdwhistell, R. Diebold, Dell Hymes, Weston La Barre, G.L. Trager, and others), *Current Anthropology* 9, 2/3.
HARTLEY, R.V.L.
1928   "Transmission of Information", *Bell System Technical Journal* 7.
HAYES, ALFRED S.
1964   "Paralinguistics and Kinesics: Pedagogical Perspectives" (in Sebeok, Hayes, and Bateson, eds., 1964).
HAYES, F.
1957   "Gesture: A Working Bibliography", *Southern Folklore Quarterly* 21.
HEGER, KLAUS
1965   "Les bases méthodologiques de l'onomasiologie et du classement par concepts", *Travaux de Linguistique et de Littérature* III, 1.
HEWES, GORDON
1974   "Implications of the Gestural Model of Language Origin for Human Semiotic Behavior", Communication to the First Congress of the I.A.S.S. (manuscript). ·
HIZ, HENRY
1969   "Referentials", *Semiotica* I, 2.

HJELMSLEV, LOUIS
    1928   *Principes de grammaire générale* (Copenhagen).
    1943   *Prolegomena to a Theory of Language* (Madison: University of Wisconsin, 1961).
    1957   "Pour une sémantique structurale" (in Hjelmslev, 1959).
    1959   *Essais linguistiques* (Travaux du Cercle Linguistique de Copenhague) (Copenhagen: Nordisk Sprog-og Kulturforlag).
HOCKETT, C.F.
    1967   *Language, Mathematics and Linguistics* (The Hague: Mouton).
    1968   *The State of the Art* (The Hague: Mouton).
HUFF, WILLIAM S.
    1967   "The Computer and Programmed Design: A Potential Tool for Teaching", (in Krampen and Seitz, eds., 1967).
HUSSERL, EDMUND
    1922   *Logische Untersuchungen*   (Halle: Niemayer).
HUTT, CLELIA
    1968   "Dictionnaire du langage gestuel chez les trappistes", *Langages* 10.
HYMES, DELL, ED.
    1964   *Language in Culture and Society* (New York: Harper).

ITTEN, JOHANNES
    1961   *Kunst der Farbe* (Ravensburg: Otto Mair).
IVANOV, V.V.
    1965   "Rol' semiotiki v kibernetičeskom issledovani čeloveka i kollektiva", *Logičeskaja struktura naučnogo znanija* (Moskva) (Italian transl. in Faccani and Eco, eds., 1969).
IVANOV, V.V., TOPOROV, V.N., AND ZALIZNIAK, A.
    1962   "O vozmožnosti strukturno-tipologičeskogo izučenija nekotorych modelirujuščich semiotičeskich sistem", *Strukturno tipologičeskie issledovanija* (Moskva) (Italian transl. in Faccani and Eco, eds., 1969).
    1965   *Slavianskie jazykovye modelirujuščie semiotičeskie sistemy* (Moskva) (French transl. in Todorov, 1966a).

JAKOBSON, ROMAN
    1958   "Les études typologiques et leur contribution à la linguistique historique" (Rapport au VIIIme Congrès Internationale des Linguistes à Oslo, 1957) (now in Jakobson, 1963a).
    1959   "Boas' View of Grammatical Meaning", *The Anthropology of Franz Boas*, ed. by W. Goldschmidt, *American Anthropologist* 61, 5, 2.
    1960   "Closing Statements: Linguistics and Poetics" (in Sebeok, ed., 1960).
    1961a   "Lingistique et théorie de la communication", *Proceedings of Symposia in Applied Mathematics* XII (American Mathematical Society).

1961b "The Phonemic Concept of Distinctive Features", *Proceedings of the Fourth International Congress of Phonetic Sciences*, Helsinki (The Hague: Mouton, 1962).

1963a *Essais de linguistique générale* (Paris: Minuit).

1963b "Implications of Language Universals for Linguistics", in Greenberg, ed., 1963.

1964 "On Visual and Auditory Signs", *Phonetica* II.

1966 "À la recherche de l'essence du langage", *Problèmes du langage* (Paris: Gallimard).

1967 "About the Relation between Visual and Auditory Signs", in *Models for the Perception of Speech and Visual Form* (Cambridge: M.I.T. Press).

1968 "Language in Relation to Other Communication Systems", Convegno promosso della Ing. C. Olivetti and Co., S.p.A. per il centenario nascita di Camillo Olivetti (now in *Linguaggi nella società e nella tecnica*, Milano: Comunità, 1970).

1970a "Da i net v mimike", *Jazyk i čelovek*, in memory of P.S. Kuznecov, Moskva (now translated as "Motor Signs for 'Yes' and 'No' ", *Language in Society* 1, 1971).

1970b "Linguistics", *in Main Trends of Research in the Social and Human Sciences* 1 (The Hague: Mouton).

1973 *Questions de poétique* (Paris: Seuil).

1974 "Coup d'oeil sur le développement de la sémiotique", Introductory Report to the First Congress of the I.A.S.S. (manuscript).

JAKOBSON, R., AND HALLE, M.

1956 *Fundamentals of Language* (The Hague: Mouton).

JAKOBSON, R., AND LÉVI-STRAUSS, C.

1962 " 'Les Chats' de Charles Baudelaire", *L'Homme*, Janvier.

JAKOBSON, R., AND TYNJANOV, J.

1927 "Voprosy izučenija literatury i jazyka" (in Todorov, ed., 1965).

KALKOFEN, HERMANN

1972 *'Pictorial' Stimuli Considered as 'Iconic' Signs* (Ulm: mimeographed).

KARPINSKAJA, O.G., AND REVZIN, I.I.

1966 "Semiotičeskij analiz rannich p'es Ionesko", *Tezisy dokladov vo vtoroi letnej škole po vtoričnym modelirujuščim sistemam* (Tartu) (Italian transl. in Faccani and Eco, eds., 1969).

KATZ, JERROLD J.

1972 *Semantic Theory* (New York: Harper and Row).

KATZ, JERROLD J., AND FODOR, JERRY A.

1963 "The Structure of a Semantic Theory", *Language* 39 (now in Katz and Fodor, eds., 1964).

KATZ, J.J., AND FODOR, J.A., EDS.

1964 *The Structure of Language* (Englewood Cliffs: Prentice-Hall).

KATZ, J.J., AND POSTAL, P.M.
1964   *An Integrated Theory of Linguistic Descriptions* (Research Monograph 26) (Cambridge: M.I.T. Press).
KLAUS, GEORG
1973   *Semiotik and Erkenntnistheorie* (München-Salzburg: VEB).
KLEINPAUL, RUDOLF
1888   *Sprache ohne Worte* (Leipzig: Friedrich) (now The Hague: Mouton, 1972).
KOCH, WALTHER A.
1969   *Vom Morphem zum Textem – From Morpheme to Texteme* (Hildesheim: Olms).
KOECHLIN, B.
1968   "Techniques corporelles et leur notation symbolique", *Langages* 10.
KOENIG, GIOVANNI KLAUS
1964   *Analisi del linguaggio architettonico* (Firenze: Fiorentina).
1970   *Architettura e comunicazione* (Firenze: Fiorentina).
KOLMOGOROV, A.N., AND KONDRATOV, A.A.
1962   "Ritmika poèm Mayakovskogo", *Voprosy Jazykoznanija* 3 (Italian transl. in Faccani and Eco, eds., 1969).
KRAMPEN, MARTIN
1973   "Iconic Signs, Supersigns and Models", *VS* 4.
KRAMPEN, MARTIN, AND SEITZ, PETER, EDS.
1967   *Design and Planning 2 – Computers in Design and Communication* (New York: Hastings House).
KRISTEVA, JULIA
1967a   "L'expansion de la sémiotique", *Informations sur les sciences sociales* VI, 5 (now in Kristeva, 1969).
1967b   "Bakhtine, le mot, le dialogue et le roman", *Critique*, Avril.
1967c   "Pour une sémiologie des paragrammes", *Tel Quel* 29 (now in Kristeva, 1969).
1968a   "Distance et anti-réprésentation", *Tel Quel* 32.
1968b   "La productivité dite texte", *Communications* 11 (now in Kristeva, 1969).
1968c   "Le geste; pratique ou communication?", *Langages* 10 (now in Kristeva, 1969).
1968d   "La sémiologie aujourd'hui en URSS", *Tel Quel* 35.
1969   Σημειωτικὴ – *Recherches pour une sémanalyse* (Paris: Seuil).
1970   *Le texte du roman* (The Hague: Mouton).
1974a   *La révolution du langage poétique* (Paris: Seuil).
1974b   "The System and the Speaking Subject", *TLS*, 12, October 1973.
KRISTEVA, J., REY-DEBOVE, J., AND UMIKER, D.J., EDS.
1971   *Essays in Semiotics/Essais de sémiotique* (The Hague: Mouton).
KRZYZANOWSKI, JULIAN
1961   "La poétique de l'enigme", in *Poetics* (The Hague: Mouton).

LA BARRE, WESTON
  1964   "Paralinguistics, Kinesics and Cultural Anthropology", in Sebeok, Hayes, and Bateson, eds., 1964.
LACAN, JACQUES
  1966   *Ecrits* (Paris: Seuil).
LAKOFF, GEORGE
  1971a   "On Generative Semantics", in Steinberg and Jakobovits, eds., 1971.
  1971b   "Presuppositions and Relative Well-formedness", in Steinberg and Jakobovits, eds., 1971.
  1972   *Hedges: A Study in Meaning Criteria and the Logic of Fuzzy Concepts* (mimeographed).
LAMB, SIDNEY M.
  1964   "The Sememic Approach to General Semantics", in Romney, A.K., and D'Andrade, R.G., eds., *Transcultural Studies in Cognition* (*American Anthropologist* 66, 3/2).
LANGENDOEN, TERENCE D.
  1971   "The Projection Problem for Presuppositions", in Fillmore and Langendoen, eds., 1971.
LANGER, SUZANNE K.
  1953   *Feeling and Form* (New York and London: Scribner's).
LANGLEBEN, M. M.
  1965   "K opisaniju sistemy notnoj zapisi", *Trudy po znakovym sistemam* II (Tartu) (Italian transl. in Faccani and Eco, eds., 1969).
LANHAM, RICHARD A.
  1968   *A Handlist of Rhetorical Terms* (Berkeley: University of California Press).
LAUSBERG, H.
  1949   *Elemente der literarischen Rhetorik* (München: Hueber).
  1960   *Handbuch der literarischen Rhetorik* (München: Hueber).
LEECH, GEOFFREY
  1969   *Towards a Semantic Description of English* (Bloomington: Indiana University Press).
LEKOMCEVA, M.I., AND USPENSKIJ, B.A.
  1962   "Gadanie na igral'nych kartach kak semiotičeskaja sistema", *Simpozium strukturnomu izučeniju znakovych sistem* (Moskva) (Italian transl. in Faccani and Eco, eds., 1969).
LEPSCHY, GIULIO
  1966   *La linguistica strutturale* (Torino: Einaudi).
LEVIN, SAMUEL
  1962   *Linguistic Structures in Poetry* (The Hague: Mouton).
LÉVI-STRAUSS, CLAUDE
  1947   *Les structures élémentaires de la parenté* (Paris: P.U.F.).
  1950   Introduction à *Sociologie et anthropologie* by M. Mauss (Paris: P.U.F.).

1958a "Le geste d'Asdiwal", *Annuaire de l'EPHE* V (now in *Les Temps Modernes* 179, 1961).

1958b *Anthropologie structurale* (Paris: Plon).

1960a "L'analyse morphologique des contes russes", *International Journal of Slavic Linguistics and Poetics* III.

1960b Discours au Collège de France 5.1.1960 (now as *The Scope of Anthropology*, London, Cape, 1967).

1961 *Entretiens* (in Charbonnier, 1961).

1962 *La pensée sauvage* (Paris: Plon).

1964 *Le cru et le cuit* (Paris: Plon).

LEWIS, DAVID K.

1969 *Convention—A Philosophical Study* (Cambridge: Harvard University Press).

LINDEKENS, RENÉ

1968 "Essai de théorie pour une sémiolinguistique de l'image photographique" (Communication au Symposium Internationale de Sémiotique, Varsovie, 1968).

1971 *Eléments pour une sémiotique de la photographie* (Paris: Didier; Bruxelles/AIMAV).

LINSKY, LEONARD, ED.

1952 *Semantics and the Philosophy of Language* (Urbana: University of Illinois).

LOTMAN, JU. M.

1964 "Sur la délimitation linguistique et littéraire de la notion de structure", *Linguistics* 6.

1967a "K probleme tipologii kul'tury", *Trudy po znakovym sistemam* III (Tartu) (French transl. in *Informations sur les sciences sociales* VI, 2/3) (Italian transl. in Faccani and Eco, eds., 1969).

1967b "Metodi esatti nella scienza letteraria sovietica", *Strumenti Critici* 2.

1969 "O metajazyke tipologičeskick opisanij kul'tury", *Trudy po znakovym sistemam* IV.

1971 "Problema 'obučenija kul'ture' kak ee tipologičeskaia charakteristika", *Trudy po znakovym sistemam* V.

LOTMAN, JU. M., AND USPENSKIJ, B.A.

1971 "O semiotičeskom mechanizm kul'tury", *Trudy po znakovym sistemam* V.

LOUNSBURY, F.G.

1964 "The Structural Analysis of Kinship Semantics", *Proceedings of the 9th International Congress of Linguists* (The Hague: Mouton).

LYONS, JOHN

1963 *Structural Semantics—An Analysis of Part of the Vocabulary of Plato* (Oxford: Blackwell).

1968 *Introduction to Theoretical Linguistics* (Cambridge: Cambridge University Press).

1970 *New Horizons in Linguistics* (London: Penguin).

MACCAGNANI G., ED.
1966   *Psicopatologia dell'espressione* (Imola: Galeati).
MAHL, GEORGE, AND SCHULZE, GENE
1964   "Psychological Research in the Extralinguistic Area" (in Sebeok, Hayes, and Bateson, eds., 1964).
MALDONÁDO, TOMAS
1954   *Problemas actuales de la comunicacción* (Buenos Aires: Nueva Visión).
1959   "Kommunication und Semiotik—Communication and Semiotics", *Ulm* 5.
1961   *Beitrag zur Terminologie der Semiotik* (Ulm: Korrelat).
1970   *La speranza progettuale* (Torino: Einaudi).
MÄLL, LINNART
1968   "Un approche possible du Sunyavada", *Tel Quel* 32.
MALLERY, GARRICK
1881   *Sign Language among North American Indians* (Smithsonian Institution) (now The Hague: Mouton, 1972).
MALTESE, CORRADO
1970   *Semiologia del messaggio oggettuale* (Milano: Mursia).
MARANDA, ELLI-KAIJA KÖNGÄS AND PIERRE
1962   "Structural Models in Folklore", *Midwest Folklore* 12-13.
MARANDA, PIERRE
1968   "Recherches structurales sur la mythologie aux États-Unis", *Informations sur les sciences sociales* VI-5.
MARIN, LOUIS
1969   "Notes sur une médaille et une gravure", *Revue d'esthétique* 22 (2).
1970   "La description de l'image", *Communications* 15.
MARTINET, ANDRÉ
1960   *Eléments de linguistique générale* (Paris: Colin).
1962   *A Functional View of Language* (Oxford: Clarendon Press).
MAUSS, MARCEL
1950   *Sociologie et anthropologie* (Paris: P.U.F.).
MAYENOWA, M. RENATA
1965   *Poetijka i matematica* (Warszawa).
MCCAWLEY, JAMES
1971   "Where Do Noun Phrases Come From", in Steinberg and Jakobovits, eds., 1971.
MCLUHAN, MARSHALL
1962   *The Gutenberg Galaxy* (Toronto: University of Toronto Press).
1964   *Understanding Media* (New York: McGraw-Hill).
MELANDRI, ENZO
1968   *La linea e il circolo* (Bologna: Mulino).
MERLEAU-PONTY, MAURICE
1960   *Signes* (Paris: Gallimard).

METZ, CHRISTIAN
    1964   "Le cinéma: langue ou langage?", *Communications* 4 (now in Metz, 1968a).
    1966a   "La grande syntagmatique du film narratif", *Communications* 8 (now in Metz, 1968a).
    1966b   "Les sémiotiques ou sémies", *Communications* 7.
    1968a   *Essais sur la signification au cinéma* (Paris: Klincksieck).
    1968b   "Le dire et le dit au cinéma", *Communications* 11.
    1969   "Specificité des codes et specificité des langages", *Semiotica* I/4.
    1970a   "Au delà de l'analogie, l'image", *Communications* 15.
    1970b   "Images et pédagogie", *Communications* 15.
    1970c   *Langage et cinéma* (Paris: Larousse).
    1974   *Film Language* (New York: Oxford University Press).
MEYER, LEONARD
    1967   *Music, the Arts and Ideas* (Chicago: University of Chicago Press).
MILLER, GEORGE
    1951   *Language and Communication* (New York: McGraw-Hill).
    1967   *Psychology and Communication* (New York: Basic Books).
MINSKY, MARVIN
    1970   "The Limitation of Using Languages for Descriptions", *Linguaggi nella società e nella tecnica* (Milano: Comunità).
MINSKY, MARVIN, ED.
    1968   *Semantic Information Processing* (Cambridge: M.I.T. Press).
MOLES, A BRAHAM A.
    1958   *Théorie de l'information et perception esthétique* (Paris: Flammarion).
    1967   *Sociodynamique de la culture* (The Hague: Mouton).
    1968   "Théorie informationnelle du schéma", *Schéma et schématisation* I, 1.
MORIN, EDGAR
    1962   *L'esprit du temps* (Paris: Grasset).
MORIN, VIOLETTE
    1966   "L'histoire drôle", *Communications* 8.
    1968   "Du larcin au hold-up", *Communications* 11.
    1970   "Le dessin humoristique", *Communications* 15.
MORRIS, CHARLES
    1938   *Foundations of the Theory of Signs* (International Encyclopaedia of Unified Science 1-2, University of Chicago Press).
    1946   *Signs, Language and Behavior* (New York: Prentice-Hall).
    1971   *Writings on the General Theory of Signs* (The Hague: Mouton).
MOUNIN, GEORGES
    1964   *La machine à traduire* (The Hague: Mouton).
    1970   *Introduction à la sémiologie* (Paris: Minuit).
MUKAŘOVSKÝ, JAN
    1934   "L'art comme fait sémiologique", in *Actes du 8me congrès international de philosophie*, Prague, 1934.

1936 *Estericka funkce, norma a hodnota jako socialni facty* (Praha).
1966 *Studie z estetiky* (Praha).

NATTIEZ, JEAN JACQUES
1971 "Situation de la sémiologie musicale", *Musique en jeu* 5.
1972 "Is a Descriptive Semiotics of Music Possible?" *Language Sciences* 23.
1973 "Trois modèles linguistiques pour l'analyse musicale", *Musique en jeu* 10.
NAUTA, DOEDE, JR.
1972 *The Meaning of Information* (The Hague: Mouton).

OGDEN, C.K.
1923 See Richards, 1923.
OSGOOD, CHARLES
1963 "Language Universals and Psycholinguistics" (in Greenberg, ed., 1963).
OSGOOD, CH., AND SEBEOK, T.A., EDS.
1965 See Sebeok and Osgood, eds., 1965.
OSGOOD, CH., SUCI, G.J., AND TANNENBAUM, P.H.
1957 *The Measurement of Meaning* (Urbana: University of Illinois Press).
OSMOND-SMITH, DAVID
1972 "The Iconic Process in Musical Communication", *VS* 3.
1973 "Formal Iconism in Music", *VS* 5.
OSOLSOBĚ, IVO
1967 "Ostenze jako mezní případ lidského sdělováni", *Estetika* 4.
OSTWALD, PETER
1964 "How the Patient Communicates about Diseases with the Doctor", in Sebeok, Hayes, and Bateson, eds., 1964).

PAGNINI, MARCELLO
1967 *Struttura letteraria e metodo critico* (Messina: D'Anna).
1970 *Critica della funzionalità* (Torino: Einaudi).
1974 *Lingua e musica* (Bologna: Mulino).
PANOFSKY, ERWIN
1920 "Der Begriff des Kunstwollens", *Zeitschrift für Ästhetik und allgemeine Kunstwissenschaft* XIV.
1921 "Die Entwicklung der Proportionslehre als Abbild der Stilentwicklung", *Monatshefte für Kunstwissenschaft* XIV.
1924 "Die Perspektive als 'symbolische Form' ", *Vorträge der Bibliothek Warburg* (Leipzig-Berlin: Teubner, 1927).
1932 "Zum Problem der Beschreibung und Inhaltsdeutung von Werken der bildenden Kunst", *Logos* XXI.
1955 *Meaning in the Visual Arts* (New York: Doubleday).

PASQUINELLI, ALBERTO
1961	*Linguaggio, scienza e filosofia* (Bologna: Mulino).
PAVEL, TOMA
1962	"Notes pour une description structurale de la métaphore poétique", *Cahiers de linguistique théorique et appliquée* I (Bucuresti).
PEIRCE, CHARLES SANDERS
1931-1958	*Collected Papers* (Cambridge: Harvard University Press).
PELC, JERZY
1969	"Meaning as an Instrument", *Semiotica* I/1.
1974	"Semiotics and Logic", report to the First Congress of the IASS (mimeographed).
PERELMAN, CHAIM, AND OLBRECHTS-TYTECA, LUCIE
1958	*Traité de l'argumentation—La nouvelle rhétorique* (Paris: P.U.F.).
PETÖFI, JANOS S.
1968	"Notes on the Semantic Interpretation of Linguistic Works of Art", Symposium on Semiotics, Warsaw, 1968 (now in *Recherches sur les systèmes signifiants*, The Hague: Mouton, 1973).
1972	"The Syntactico-Semantic Organization of Text-Structures", *Poetics* 3.
PIAGET, JEAN
1955	"Rapport", in *La perception* (Paris: P.U.F.).
1961	*Les mécanismes perceptifs* (Paris: P.U.F.).
1968	*Le structuralisme* (Paris: P.U.F.).
PIGNATARI, DECIO
1968	*Informacão, Linguagem, Comunicacão* (São Paulo: Perspectiva).
PIGNATARI, D., AND DE CAMPOS, A. AND H.
1965	*Teoria da poesia concreta* (São Paulo).
PIGNOTTI, LAMBERTO
1965	"Linguaggio poetico e linguaggi tecnologici", *La Battana* 5.
PIKE, KENNETH
1954-1960	*Language in Relation to a Unified Theory of the Structure of Human Behavior* (The Hague: Mouton, 1966).
PIRO, SERGIO
1967	*Il linguaggio schizofrenico* (Milano: Feltrinelli).
PITTENGER, R.E., AND SMITH, H.L., JR.
1957	"A Basis for Some Contribution of Linguistics to Psychiatry", *Psychiatry* 20 (now in Smith, ed., 1966).
POP, MILHAI
1970	"La poétique du conte populaire", *Semiotica* II/2.
POTTIER, BERNARD
1965	"La définition sémantique dans les dictionnaires", *Travaux de Linguistique et de Littérature* III, 1.
1967	"Au delà du structuralisme en linguistique", *Critique*, Fevrier.
POUSSEUR, HENRI
1965	"La question du hazard en musique nouvelle" (Conférences au Centre de Sociologie de la Musique de l'Institut de Sociologie de l'Université Libre de Bruxelles) (now in Pousseur, 1970).

1970   *Fragments théoriques I sur la musique experimentale* (Bruxelles: Institut de Sociologie).
1972   *Musique, sémantique, societé* (Paris: Casterman).
PRIETO, LUIS
1964   *Principes de noologie* (The Hague: Mouton).
1966   *Messages et signaux* (Paris: P.U.F.).
1969   "Lengua y connotacion" (in Verón, 1969).
PROPP, VLADIMIR JA.
1928   *Morfologija skazki* (Leningrad).
1958   *Morphology of the Folktale* (The Hague: Mouton).

QUILLIAN, ROSS M.
1968   "Semantic Memory" (in Minsky, ed., 1968).
QUINE, WILLARD VAN ORMAN
1953   *From a Logical Point of View* (Cambridge: Harvard University Press).
1960   *Word and Object* (Cambridge: M.I.T. Press).

RAIMONDI, EZIO
1967   *Tecniche della critica letteraria* (Torino: Einaudi).
1970   *Metafora e storia* (Torino: Einaudi).
RAPAPORT, ANATOL
1953   "What Is Information?", *Etc.* 10.
RAPHAEL, BERTRAM
1968   "SIR: A Computer Program for Semantic Information Retrieval" (in Minsky, ed., 1968).
RASTIER, FRANÇOIS
1968   "Comportement et signification", *Langages*, 10.
RICHARDS, I.A.
1923   *The Meaning of Meaning* (with C.K. Ogden) (London: Routledge and Kegan Paul).
1924   *Principles of Literary Criticism* (London: Routledge and Kegan Paul).
1936   *The Philosophy of Rhetoric* (New York: Oxford University Press).
ROSIELLO, LUIGI
1965a   Intervento in *Strutturalismo e critica* (in Segre, ed., 1965).
1965b   *Struttura, uso e funzioni della lingua* (Firenze: Vallecchi).
1967   *Linguistica illuminista* (Bologna: Mulino).
ROSSI, ALDO
1966   "Semiologia a Kazimierz sulla Vistola", *Paragone* 202.
1967   "Le nuove frontiere della semiologia", *Paragone* 212.
ROSSI, PAOLO
1960   *Clavis Universalis—Arti mnemoniche e combinatoria da Lullo a Leibniz* (Milano: Ricciardi).
ROSSI-LANDI, FERRUCCIO
1953   *Charles Morris* (Milano: Bocca).

1961 *Significato, comunicazione e parlare comune* (Padova: Marsilio).
1968 *Il linguaggio come lavoro e come mercato* (Milano: Bompiani).
1973 *Semiotica e ideologia* (Milano: Bompiani).

RUSSELL, BERTRAND
1905 "On Denoting", *Mind* 14.

RUWET, NICOLAS
1959 "Contradictions du langage sériel", *Revue Belge de Musicologie* 13.
1963a "L'analyse structurale de la poésie", *Linguistics* 2.
1963b "Linguistique et sciences de l'homme", *Esprit*, Novembre.
1966 *Introduction* (special issue on *La grammaire générative*), *Langages* 4.
1967a *Introduction à la grammaire générative* (Paris: Plon).
1967b "Musicology and Linguistics", *International Social Science Journal* 19.
1972 *Langage, musique, poésie* (Paris: Seuil).

SALANITRO, NICCOLO'
1969 *Peirce e i problemi dell'interpretazione* (Roma: Silva).
SANDERS, G.A.
1974 "Precedence Relations in Language", *Foundations of Language*, 11, 3.
SANDRI, GIORGIO
1967 "Note sui concetti di 'struttura' e 'funzione' in linguistica", *Rendiconti* 15-16.
SAPIR, EDWARD
1921 *Language* (New York: Harcourt Brace).
ŠAUMJAN, SEBASTIAN K.
1966 "La cybernétique et la langue", *Problèmes du langage* (Paris: Gallimard).
SAUSSURE, FERDINAND DE
1916 *Cours de linguistique générale* (Paris: Payot).
SCALVINI, MARIA LUISA
1972 *Para una teoria de la arquitectura* (Barcelona: Colegio Oficial de Arquitectos).
ŠČEGLOV, JU.
1962a "L postroeniju strukturnoj modeli novel o Šerloke Cholmse", in *Simpozium po strukturnomu izučeniju znakovych sistem* (Moskva) (Italian transl. in Faccani and Eco, eds., 1969).
1962b "Nekotorye čerty struktury 'Metamorfoz' Ovidjia", in *Strukturno-tipologičeskie issledovanija* (Moskva) (Italian transl. in Faccani and Eco, eds., 1969).
SCHAEFFER, PIERRE
1966 *Traité des objets musicaux* (Paris: Seuil).
SCHAFF, ADAM
1962 *Introduction to Semantics* (London: Pergamon Press).

SCHANE, SANFORD A., ED.
  1967   "La phonologie générative", *Langages* 8.
SCHAPIRO, MEYER
  1969   "On Some Problems of the Semiotics of Visual Arts: Field and Image-Signs", *Semiotica* I/3.
SCHEFER, JEAN-LOUIS
  1968   *Scénographie d'un tableau* (Paris: Seuil).
  1970   "L'image: le sens 'investi' ", *Communications* 15.
SCHLICK, MORITZ
  1936   "Meaning and Verification", *Philosophical Review* 45.
SCHNEIDER, DAVID M.
  1968   *American Kinship: A Cultural Account* (New York: Prentice-Hall).
SEARLE, J.R.
  1969   *Speech Acts* (London, New York: Cambridge University Press).
SEBEOK, THOMAS A.
  1962   "Coding in Evolution of Signalling Behavior", *Behavioral Sciences* 7, 4.
  1967a "La communication chez les animaux", *Revue Internationale des Sciences Sociales* 19.
  1967b "On Chemical Signs", in *To Honor Roman Jakobson* (The Hague: Mouton).
  1967c "Linguistics Here and Now", *A.C.L.S. Newsletter* 18 (1).
  1968   "Is a Comparative Semiotics Possible?" (Communication at 2d International Congress of Semiotics, Warsaw, August 1968).
  1969   "Semiotics and Ethology" (in Sebeok and Ramsay, eds., 1969).
  1972a *Perspectives in Zoosemiotics* (The Hague: Mouton).
  1972b "Problems in the Classification of Signs", in Scherabov Firchow, E., et al., eds., *Studies for Einar Haugen* (The Hague: Mouton).
SEBEOK, THOMAS A., ED.
  1960   *Style in Language* (Cambridge: M.I.T. Press).
  1968   *Animal Communication* (Bloomington: Indiana University Press).
  1975   *The Tell-Tale Sign – A Survey of Semiotics* (Lisse: DeRidder).
SEBEOK, T.A., HAYES, A.S., AND BATESON, M.C., EDS.
  1964   *Approaches to Semiotics* (The Hague: Mouton).
SEBEOK, T.A., AND OSGOOD, CH., EDS.
  1965   *Psycholinguistics* (Bloomington: Indiana University Press).
SEBEOK, T.A., AND RAMSAY, A., EDS.
  1969   *Approaches to Animal Communication* (The Hague: Mouton).
SEGRE, CESARE
  1963   Introduzione a *Linguistica Generale* di Ch. Bally (Milano: Saggiatore).
  1967   "La synthèse stylistique", *Informations sur les Sciences Sociales* VI, 5.
  1969   *I segni e la critica* (Torino: Einaudi). English translation: *Semiotics and Literary Criticism* (The Hague: Mouton), 1973.

SEGRE, CESARE, ED.
  1965   *Strutturalismo e critica* (Milano: Saggiatore).
SEILER, HANSJAKOB
  1970   "Semantic Information in Grammar: The Problem of Syntactic
          Relations", *Semiotica* II/4.
SÈVE, LUCIEN
  1967   "Méthode structurale et méthode dialectique", *La Pensée* 1.
SHANDS, HARLEY C.
  1970   *Semiotic Approaches to Psychiatry* (The Hague: Mouton).
SHANNON, C.E., AND WEAVER, W.
  1949   *The Mathematical Theory of Communication* (Urbana: University
          of Illinois Press).
SHERZER, JOEL
  1973   "The Pointed Lip Gesture among the San Blas Cuna", *Language in
          Society* 2.
ŠKLOVSKIJ, VICTOR
  1917   "Iskusstvo kak priëm", *Poetika* 1913 (French transl. in Todorov,
          ed., 1965).
  1925   *O teorii prozy* (Moskva).
SLAMA-CAZACU, TATIANA
  1966   "Essay on Psycholinguistic Methodology and Some of Its Applica-
          tions", *Linguistics* 24.
SMITH, ALFRED G., ED.
  1966   *Communication and Culture* (New York: Holt).
SØRENSEN, H.C.
  1967   "Fondements épistémologiques de la glossématique", *Langages* 6.
SOULIS, GEORGE N., AND ELLIS, JACK
  1967   "The Potential of Computers in Design Practice" (in Krampen and
          Seitz, eds., 1967).
SPITZER, LEO
  1931   *Romanische Stil- und Literaturstudien* (Marburg: Elwert).
STANKIEWICZ, EDWARD
  1960   "Linguistics and the Study of Poetic Language" (in Sebeok, ed.,
          1960).
  1961   "Poetic and Non-Poetic Language in Their Interrelations", *Poetics*
          (The Hague: Mouton).
  1964   "Problems of Emotive Language" (in Sebeok, Hayes, and Bateson,
          eds., 1964).
STAROBINSKI, JEAN
  1957   *J.J. Rousseau, la transparence et l'obstacle* (Paris: Plon).
  1965   Intervento in *Strutturalismo e critica* (Milano: Saggiatore) (in
          Segre, ed., 1965)
STEFANI, GINO
  1973   "Sémiotique en musicologie", *VS* 5.
  1974   *Musica Barocca: poetica e ideologia* (Milano: Bompiani).
STEINBERG, D. D., AND JAKOBOVITS, L.A., EDS.
  1971   *Semantics* (Cambridge: Cambridge University Press).

STEVENSON, CHARLES L.
1944   *Ethics and Language* (New Haven: Yale University Press).
STRAWSON, PETER F.
1960   "On Referring", *Mind* 59.
SZASZ, THOMAS S.
1961   *The Myth of Mental Illness* (New York: Harper and Row).

TODOROV, TZVETAN
1966a Review of *Slavianskie jazykvyex modelirujuščie semiotičeskie sistemy* by Ivanov, Toporov, and Sahzniak, *L'Homme*, Avril-Juin.
1966b "Les catégories du récit littéraire", *Communications* 8.
1966c "Perspectives sémiologiques", *Communications* 7.
1966d "Recherches sémantiques", *Langages* 1.
1967   *Littérature et signification* (Paris: Larousse).
1968a "L'analyse du récit à Urbino", *Communications* 11.
1968b "Du vraisemblable qu'on ne saurait éviter", *Communications* 11.
TODOROV, TZVETAN, ED.
1965   *Théorie de la littérature—Textes des formalistes russes* (Paris: Seuil).
TODOROV, T., AND DUCROT, O., EDS.
1972   *Dictionnaire encyclopédique des sciences du langage* (Paris: Seuil).
TOPOROV, V.N.
1965   "K opisaniju nekotorych struktur, charakterizujuščich preimuš-čestvenno nižšie urovni, v neskol'kich poetičeskich tekstach", in *Trudy po znakovym sistemam* II (Tartu) (Italian transl. in Faccani and Eco, eds., 1969).
TRAGER, GEORGE L.
1964   "Paralanguage: A First Approximation" (in Hymes, ed., 1964).
TRIER, J.
1931   *Der deutsche Wortschatz im Sinnbezirk des Verstandes* (Heidelberg).
TRUBECKOJ, N.S.
1939   *Grundzüge der Phonologie* (TCLP VII) (*Principes de phonologie*, Paris, Klincksieck, 1949).
TYNJANOV, JURY
1929   *Archaisty i novatory* (Leningrad: Priboj).

ULLMANN, STEPHEN
1951   *The Principles of Semantics*, 2d ed. (Oxford: Blackwell).
1962   *Semantics: An Introduction to the Science of Meaning* (Oxford: Blackwell).
1964   *Language and Style* (Oxford: Blackwell).

VACHEK, JOSEPH, ED.
1964   *A Prague School Reader in Linguistics* (Bloomington: Indiana University Press).

VAILATI, GIOVANNI
  1908   "La grammatica dell'algebra", *Rivista di Psicologia Applicata* (now in Vailati, 1911).
  1911   *Scritti* (Firenze-Leipzig: Seeber-Barth).
VALESIO, PAOLO
  1967a "Icone e schemi nella struttura della lingua", *Lingua e stile* 3.
  1967b *Strutture dell'allitterazione* (Bologna: Zanichelli).
VAN DIJK, TEUN A.
  1972   *Some Aspects of Text Grammars* (The Hague: Mouton).
VAN ONCK, ANDRIES
  1965   "Metadesign", *Edilizia Moderna* 85.
VERÓN, ELISEO
  1968   *Conducta, estructura y comunicación* (Buenos Aires: Jorge Alvarez).
  1969   "Ideología y comunicación de masas: la sematisación de la violencia politica" (in Verón, ed., 1969).
  1970   "L'analogique et le contigu", *Communications* 15.
  1971   "Ideology and Social Sciences", *Semiotica* III/1.
  1973a "Pour une sémiologie des operations translinguistiques", *VS* 4.
  1973b "Vers una 'logique naturelle des mondes sociaux' ", *Communications* 20.
VERÓN, ELISEO, ED.
  1969   *Lenguaje y comunicación social* (Buenos Aires: Nueva Visión).
VOLLI, UGO
  1972a "E' possibile una semiotica dell'arte?", in Volli, U., ed., *La scienza e l'arte* (Milano: Mazzotta).
  1972b "Some Possible Developments of the Concept of Iconism", *VS* 3.
  1973   "Referential Semantics and Pragmatics of Natural Languages", *VS* 4.
VYGOTSKY, L.S.
  1934   *Thought and Language* (Cambridge: M.I.T. Press, 1962).

WALLIS, MIECZYSLAW
  1966   "La notion de champ sémantique et son application à la théorie de l'art", *Sciences de l'art* 1.
  1968   "On Iconic Signs" (Communication at 2d International Congress of Semiotics, Warsaw, August 1968).
WALTHER, ELISABETH
  1974   *Allgemeine Zeichenlehre* (Stuttgart: DVA).
WATSON, O. MICHAEL
  1970   *Proxemic Behavior* (The Hague: Mouton).
WATZLAWICK, P., BEAVIN, J.H., AND JACKSON, D.D.
  1967   *Pragmatic of Human Communication* (New York: Norton).
WEAVER, WARREN
  1949   "The Mathematics of Communication", *Scientific American* 181.

WEINREICH, URIEL
1965 "Explorations in Semantic Theory", in *Current Trends in Linguistics*, ed. by T.A. Sebeok (The Hague: Mouton).
WELLEK, RENÉ, AND WARREN, AUSTIN
1949 *Theory of Literature* (New York: Harcourt Brace).
WHITE, MORTON
1950 "The Analytic and the Synthetic: An Untenable Dualism", in *John Dewey*, ed. by S. Hook (New York: Dial Press) (now in Linsky, ed., 1952).
WHORF, BENJAMIN LEE
1956 *Language, Thought and Reality*, ed. by J.R. Carroll (Cambridge: M.I.T. Press).
WIENER, NORBERT
1948 *Cybernetics or Control and Communication in the Animal and the Machine* (Cambridge: M.I.T. Press; Paris: Hermann).
1950 *The Human Use of Human Beings* (Boston: Houghton Mifflin).
WILSON, N.L.
1967 "Linguistic Butter and Philosophical Parsnips", *Journal of Philosophy* 64.
WIMSATT, W.R.
1954 *The Verbal Icon* (Lexington: University of Kentucky Press).
WINTER, MIKE
1973 "Semiotics and the Philosophy of Language", *VS* 6.
WITTGENSTEIN, LUDWIG
1922 *Tractatus Logico-Philosophicus* (London: Kegan Paul, Trech, Trubnerand).
1945-1949 *Philosophische Untersuchungen* (Oxford: Blackwell, 1953).
WOLLEN, PETER
1969 *Signs and Meaning in the Cinema* (Bloomington: Indiana University Press).
WORTH, SOL
1969 "The Development of a Semiotic of Film", *Semiotica* I/3.
WYKOFF, WILLIAM
1970 "Semiosis and Infinite Regressus", *Semiotica* II/1.

ZARECKIJ, A.
1963 "Obraz kak informacija", *Voprosy Literatury* 2.
ZEVI, BRUNO
1967 "Alla ricerca di un codice per l'architettura", *L'Architettura* 145.
ZOLKIEWSKI, STEFAN
1968 "Sociologie de la culture et sémiotique", *Informations sur les Sciences Sociales* VII, 1.
1969 *Semiotika a kultúra* (Bratislava: Nakladelstvo Epocha).
ŽOLKOVSKIJ, ALEKSANDR K.
1962 "Ob usilenii", *Strukturno-tipologičeskie issledovanija* (Moskva) (Italian transl. in Faccani and Eco, eds., 1969).

1967   "Deus ex machina", in *Trudy po znakovym sistemam* III (Tartu)
        (Italian transl. in Faccani and Eco, eds., 1969).
1970   Review of *La struttura assente* by U. Eco, *Voprosy Filosofii* 2.
ZUMTHOR, PAUL
1972   *Essai de poétique médiévale* (Paris: Seuil).

INDEX OF AUTHORS

347

INDEX OF SUBJECTS

351